Tulipmania

TULIPMANIA

Money, Honor, and Knowledge in the Dutch Golden Age

ANNE GOLDGAR

THE UNIVERSITY *of* CHICAGO PRESS
{CHICAGO AND LONDON}

The University of Chicago Press, Chicago 60637
The University of Chicago Press, Ltd., London
© 2007 by The University of Chicago
All rights reserved. Published 2007
Paperback edition 2008
Printed in the United States of America

17 16 15 14 13 12 11 10 09 08   2 3 4 5 6

ISBN-13: 978-0-226-30125-9 (cloth)
ISBN-13: 978-0-226-30126-6 (paper)
ISBN-10: 0-226-30125-7 (cloth)
ISBN-10: 0-226-30126-5 (paper)

LIBRARY OF CONGRESS CATALOGING-IN-PUBLICATION DATA

Goldgar, Anne.
     Tulipmania : money, honor, and knowledge in the Dutch golden
age / Anne Goldgar.
       p.   cm.
     Includes bibliographical references and index.
     ISBN-13: 978-0-226-30125-9 (cloth : alk. paper)
     ISBN-10: 0-226-30125-7 (cloth : alk. paper)
     1. Netherlands—Economic conditions—17th century. 2. Tulip
mania, 17th century. 3. Social values—Netherlands—History—17th
century. 4. Netherlands—Social life and customs—17th century.
5. Netherlands—Social conditions—17th century. I. Title.
II. Title: Money, honor, and knowledge in the Dutch golden age.
HC325.G64 2007
330.9492'03—dc22

                                                    2006039793

In memory of my dear friend Michael Montias

and with love to all my other friends
especially

Marina Benjamin
Kelly Boyd
Marika Keblusek
Jennifer Kilian
Mark Ledbury
Steve Maughan

who helped me through

"For pity's sake, Laura,
   don't talk about anything so deadly as the bulbs."

E. M. DELAFIELD, *The Way Things Are* (1927)

CONTENTS

ACKNOWLEDGMENTS

~~~~~~

THE MUNICIPAL ARCHIVE IN HAARLEM STAYS OPEN until 9 P.M. on Thursdays, and for a long period I was usually the last person to leave (even the man with the grey beard and glasses had usually left before 9). One summer night, as I was crossing the Nieuwe Gracht, I saw a wonderful sight. Twenty, thirty, or more swans were all congregated together in the water below the bridge. Their quiet, graceful, serene meeting at twilight has stayed with me ever since. It compounds the spirit of place so central to the making of this book and indeed to the events discussed in it. I am grateful, therefore, first of all to the people and places of the Netherlands, for the chance to spend so much time in the last years somewhere I increasingly love.

For that chance I must also thank wholeheartedly the National Endowment for the Humanities for giving me a fellowship in 1999–2000, as well as its unflappability when my topic mutated from public museums to tulips and collecting. Henk van Nierop and the Department of History and Regional Studies at the Universiteit van Amsterdam were kind enough to make me a guest researcher in the same year, not to mention protecting me against the strictures of the Dutch immigration service and Ministry of Justice, whose understanding of the notion of a sabbatical year was at best feeble.

Many people were generous with their time, advice, and material, something made all the more necessary by my comparative newness to this field. I was offered ideas and direction early on by Florike Egmond, Mark Meadow, Claudia Swan, Elizabeth Honig, Christopher Heuer, and S. A. C. Dudok van Heel. Sam Segal not only kindly talked to me about the topic, but gave me the run of his magnificent library and his notes on tulips and still life painting. I was fortunate to be able to talk to Mary Sprunger about Mennonites; Clé Lesger about tax and banking records;

Corry Azzi and Jim Dana about financial panics and bubbles; Roelof van Gelder about Paludanus and collecting; Frans de Bruyn about the South Sea Bubble; Pieter Biesboer about Haarlem burghers; and Marten Jan Bok about practically everything. I received valuable tips, ideas, and information from Annie Janowitz, Stephanie Schrader, Petra van Dam, Wantje Fritschy, Pamela Smith, Paula Findlen, Paul Hoftijzer, Peter Mancall, Elizabeth Wyckoff, Paul Taylor, Stuart Carroll, Sandra Raphael, Erica Fudge, Sue Wiseman, Ariel Salzmann, Betsy Wieseman, Malcolm Baker, Nicholas Dew, Rudolf Dekker, Machteld Löwensteyn, Peter Mason, Michèle Cohen, George Biddlecombe, Florence Koorn, Margot Finn, A. R. Braunmuller, Randall McNeill, Tim Spurgin, Kitty Kilian, Paul Dijstelberge, Henk Looijesteijn, Jelle Bosma, Bram Schuytvlot, Frouke Wieringa, Meghan Pennisi, Doug Hildebrecht, Simon Schama, Lorraine Daston, Lissa Roberts, Katy Kist, Jaap Haarskamp, Esther ten Dolle, Giles Mandelbrote, Ben Kaplan, Judith Pollmann, Bert Goldgar, Julia Adeney Thomas, Kirsty Milne, Richard Unger, and Francis Spufford.

Gabrielle Dorren, Marten Jan Bok, Irene van Thiel-Stroman, Garrelt Verhoeven, Johan Koppenol, Michael Montias, Frans de Bruyn, Arjan van Dixhoorn, Piet Boon, Clé Lesger, Christine Kooi, Beth Hyde, Willem Frijhoff, and Susanne Weide all gave me access to either written work before its publication and/or documentary material I was able to use in the course of writing the book. Daan de Clercq and Agnes Dunselman were both more than generous in their assistance with my genealogical investigations in the Mennonite community.

The staff of the many archives and libraries used when researching this topic were unfailingly helpful and interested. The British Library as always has been a paradise and a home; my thanks to everyone working there. In the Netherlands, Liesbeth Strasser of the Nationaal Archief in the Hague (and earlier also of the former Archiefdienst voor Kennemerland in Haarlem, now the Noord-Hollands Archief) was of particular assistance and was present at the epiphanic moment when I realized that transactions about tulips littered the rolls of the Haarlem Kleine Bank van Justitie. Piet Boon and his colleagues at the Archiefdienst Westfriese Gemeenten in Hoorn were kind enough to pull up great quantities of notarial volumes on carts for me and to help me with my questions about the Enkhuizen archives. In particular I was welcomed and made to feel part of the family at the Noord-Hollands Archief. Besides the brief sighting of a convention of swans, the many pleasant hours I spent reading notarial and judicial records while looking out on the little brick-paved courtyard outside the Janskerk will remain always in my heart.

Overarching discussions about the project and its direction came in particu-

ACKNOWLEDGMENTS

lar from Michael Montias, Marten Jan Bok, Natalie Zemon Davis, John Brewer, Tony Grafton, and Mark Ledbury. Their comments and ideas did much to shape the book. I am also grateful for the questions and ideas posed at seminars and talks in Haarlem, Amsterdam, Antwerp, London, Sussex, Cambridge, Manchester, York, Warwick, the Folger Library, the Huntington Library, and the Getty Art Institute.

I would also like to thank the students over the years in my course on early modern cultural history. Our discussions contributed greatly to my ideas here; I just hope they didn't get sick of hearing about tulips.

It has been a great pleasure to find myself at last in the capable and sensitive hands of the University of Chicago Press. I cannot praise enough my editor, Douglas Mitchell, and his magnificent editorial assistant, Tim McGovern; not to mention Joel Score, Levi Stahl, Maia Wright, Anita Samen, and Joyce Dunne. I would especially like to thank Sharon Bautista, who did such a wonderful job in helping to obtain the illustrations. My father, Bert Goldgar, was generous with his encouragement and time, especially in helping read the proofs. Justin Elliott also provided invaluable proofreading assistance and support in the book's final stages.

The road to publication of this book has been unusually rocky, and for that reason I must thank all the friends who supported me through hard times, and to whom the book is dedicated. Kelly Boyd was always there for a (lengthy) chat, not to mention on-tap assistance in computer emergencies. Marina Benjamin helped me puzzle out the vagaries of publishing world while doling out her usual radiant warmth and wonderful cooking. Marika Keblusek proved a delightful friend and research companion, who with generosity of spirit was permanently on call to help me unravel the rushed and stilted prose of seventeenth-century court records. Jennifer Kilian was herself: generous and kind and always willing to listen. Her cats also provided me with much-needed entertainment. Steve Maughan was a calming influence in various crazy stages of the book, not least the last, while quietly pursuing his own research and doing odd jobs around my house. Mark Ledbury could not have done more to take me through the writing of the book; he discussed every chapter with me, before and after it was written, as well as providing encouragement and good cheer via e-mail and phone virtually hourly through the whole period of writing. The late Michael Montias shaped my thinking in so many ways; I will always treasure the times we spent having dinner in Amsterdam chattering away about subjects boring to nearly everyone else in the world (who was whose brother-in-law in 1635 and whether they lived on the Brouwersgracht). Michael told me once that there was no one else he could talk to about these things but me. This was not true, but it was gracious of him to say so. The world has lost a great scholar in him, and I have lost a great friend.

Finally, I thank my parents for always having been there, and my colleagues, whom I adore.

King's College London
September 2006

ILLUSTRATIONS

Figures

1. Hubertus Quellinus, western pediment of Amsterdam town hall, 1664, after design by Artus Quellinus, in *Prima pars praecipuarum effigierum ac ornamentarum . . . Curiae Amstelrodamensis . . .* (1665–1668). Permission of British Library, shelfmark 788.i.4. {10}

2. Christoffel van den Berghe, *Flowers in a gilt-mounted porcelain vase*, c. 1616. Courtesy of Sotheby's. {27}

3. Jacob de Monte, *Portrait of Carolus Clusius*, c. 1584. Leiden, University Library, Icones 19. {35}

4. Peter Paul Rubens, *The Four Philosophers*, 1611. Galleria Palatina, Palazzo Pitti, Florence. Photo: Nicolo Orsi Battaligni/Art Resource, New York. {37}

5. Title page of Carolus Clusius, *Rariorum plantarum historia* (Antwerp: Christoffel Plantin, 1601). Leiden, University Library, shelfmark 661 A 3. {42}

6. Title page of Rembertus Dodonaeus, *Cruydt-Boeck* (Leiden: Officina Plantiniana, 1608). Leiden, University Library, shelfmark 659 A 7. {43}

7. *Tulipa serotina flava* from Clusius, *Rariorum plantarum historia* (1601), p. 144. Permission of British Library, shelfmark 441.i.8. {45}

8. Crispijn van de Passe, *Spring*, from Van de Passe, *Hortus Floridus* (Arnhem: Jan Jansz, 1614). Permission of British Library, shelfmark 445.b.29. {46}

9. North side of Haarlem. Detail of Pieter Wils map of Haarlem in Jan Blaeu, *Toonneel der Steden van de Vereenighde Nederlanden, met hare Beschrijvingen* (Amsterdam: Jan Blaeu, 1649). Permission of British Library, Maps 9.TAB.25. {48}

10. South side of Haarlem. Detail of Pieter Wils map of Haarlem in Blaeu, *Toonneel der Steden* (1649). Permission of British Library, Maps 9.TAB.25. {49}

11. Adriaen van de Venne, scholar showing an aristocrat a tulip, from *Zeeusche Nachtegael* (Middelburg: Jan Pietersz van de Venne, 1623). Permission of Koninklijke Bibliotheek, The Hague, shelfmark 10 H 23. {54}

12. Photo of Prinsengracht 483, Amsterdam, bought by Jan Hendricxsz Admirael in 1643. Permission of Rijksdienst voor de Monumentenzorg, Zeist, Netherlands. {64}

13. Cabinet of Ole Worm. Ole Worm, *Museum Wormianum* (Amsterdam: Lowijs

and Daniel Elzevier, 1655). Leiden, University Library, shelfmark Magazijn 5-656 A 8. {68}

14. Cup made of a nut. Carolus Clusius, *Exoticorum libri decem* (Leiden: Officina Plantiniana, 1605), p. 193. Permission of Koninklijke Bibliotheek, The Hague, shelfmark 177 A 3. {76}

15. Nautilus cup, 1651. Foot made by Willem Claesz Brugman; shell carved by Joan Belkien. Stedelijk Museum het Prinsenhof, inv. PDZ 6. Permission of Gemeente Musea Delft. {77}

16. *Hortus botanicus* in Leiden. Engraving by Willem Swanenburgh after Jan Cornelisz Woudanus. Permission of Atlas van Stolk, Rotterdam, no. 1271–72. {79}

17. Abraham Susenier, shell still life, c. 1659. Permission of Dordrechts Museum, Dordrecht, inv. DM/992/697. {82}

18. Emblem on the folly of shell collecting. Roemer Visscher, *Sinnepoppen* (Amsterdam: W. Jansz, 1614). Permission of Koninklijke Bibliotheek, The Hague, shelfmark 341 C 4. {84}

19. Emblem on the folly of tulip collecting. Visscher, *Sinnepoppen* (1614). Permission of Koninklijke Bibliotheek, The Hague, shelfmark 341 C 4. {85}

20. Hendrick Goltzius, *Portrait of Jan Govertsz van der Aer*, 1603. Permission of Museum Boijmans van Beuningen, Rotterdam. {91}

21. Simon van de Passe, *Memento Mori*, 1612. Permission of Museum Boijmans van Beuningen, Rotterdam. {93}

22. Jacques de Gheyn the elder, *Vanitas*, 1603. The Metropolitian Museum of Art, Charles B. Curtis, Marquand, Victor Wilbour Memorial, and the Alfred N. Punnett Endowment Funds, 1974 (inv. 1974.1). {94}

23. Adriaen van de Venne, symbol of widowhood, in Jacob Cats, *Houwelijck* (Middelburg: Jan Pietersz van de Venne, 1625), part 6, p. 53. Author's collection; kind gift of Mark Meadow. {95}

24. Joris Hoefnagel, *Allegory on the Brevity of Life*, 1591. Palais des Beaux-Arts, Lille, inv. 732. Photo: Réunion des Musées Nationaux/Art Resource, New York. {96}

25. *Gebiesd van Coornart*, tulip portrait from the tulip book of P. Cos, f. 63. Permission of Wageningen UR Library. {99}

26. Anon., pencil drawing of man looking at a tulip book. Courtesy of Haboldt and Co., Paris. {101}

27. Hans Holbein, *Portrait of Benedikt von Hertenstein*, 1517. The Metropolitan Museum of Art, Rogers Fund aided by subscribers, 1906 (06.1038). {103}

28. Alexandre-François Desportes, *Diane et Blonde*, first quarter of the eighteenth century. Photo: © Nicolas Mathéus. Musée de la Chasse et de la Nature, Paris. {105}

29. Diego Rodriguez de Silva y Velázquez, *Portait of Don Sebastián de Morra*, c. 1648. Museo del Prado, Madrid. Photo: Scala/Art Resource, New York. {106}

Plates

PLATES FOLLOW PAGE 172

and Isabella in a collector's cabinet, c. 1626. Permission of the Walters Art Museum, Baltimore, inv. 37.2010.

9. Jan Philips van Thielen, *Tulip still life*, first half of seventeenth century. Courtesy of Johnny van Haeften, London.

10. Michiel Jansz van Mierevelt. *Double portrait with tulip, bulb, and shell*, 1606. Courtesy of Galerie Sanct Lucas, Vienna.

11. Pieter Holsteyn, tulip portrait, *Semper Augustus*. Courtesy of Sotheby's.

12. Jan Brueghel II, *Satire on Tulipmania*, c. 1640. Permission of Frans Hals Museum, Haarlem, inv. os 75-699.

13. Hendrick Gerritsz Pot, *Floraes Mallewagen*, c. 1640. Permission of Frans Hals Museum, Haarlem, inv. os I-286.

INTRODUCTION

SOMETIME IN THE LATE 1630S OR EARLY 1640S—
we don't know exactly when—the Haarlem market gardener Pieter Jacobsz was talking to his brother-in-law, Abraham Louwesz. They were talking about weighty matters, matters of great import. They were talking about tulips. Louwesz recalled the conversation in 1645.

"Before the death of my brother-in-law Pieter Jacobsz," Louwesz said, "I was at his house, and he let me see a little bulb and put it in my hand, and he said to me, that is a Gouda. Upon which I said to my brother-in-law, then that must certainly have cost you a lot of money. Whereupon my brother-in-law said to me in answer, That is true, but it still isn't paid for."[1]

"That must have cost you" and "it still isn't paid for": these, in essence, are the themes of tulipmania. Although Jacobsz was in an unusual position, having actually received a bulb for which he had not paid, it was the high prices, and the breaking of contracts, that characterized this famous yet puzzling event. Long after Pieter Jacobsz had promised to buy his Gouda bulb, the seller was still in pursuit of his money, chasing Louwesz now that Jacobsz was dead. He was far from alone.

In the mid-1630s, Holland famously went wild about tulips. Nowadays the flowers seem intertwined with Dutch life; windmills, clogs, cheese, and tulips define the Netherlands in a sort of generalized repertory of national stereotypes. The Dutch flower industry today is world-renowned, with a market share of 70 percent of the international production of flowers and 90 percent of the trade; and of these flowers tulips are by far the most important. But the association was anything but obvious in the seventeenth century. Tulips then were new to Holland, and they were rare. To us the ultimate in Dutch domesticity, in the 1630s this fragile and changeable bloom represented novelty, unpredictability, excitement—a splash of the exotic east, a collector's item for the curious and the wealthy, rather than a simple and unpretentious flower in a jug on the kitchen table. "[I]t may well bee said, he is not humane, that is not allured with this object," wrote the English gardener John Parkinson in 1629 about flowers. The Dutch, if anything, were even more rapturous in their praise of tulips. The frontispiece of one album of flower watercolors from 1636, picturing a tulip garden, contains verses addressed to "O noble tulip sweet o highly prized flower"; the album itself lavishly portrays 125 different tulips with brilliant red and white, red and yellow, and purple and white stripes and flames (see plate 1).[2]

What is rare and curious is also expensive. Tulips, for a short time, were remarkably so. They had been collector's items from their first entry into Europe in the mid-sixteenth century, and we hear of high prices some decades before the 1630s, but it was in the period starting around the summer of 1636 that prices for some bulbs rose to enormous heights. The stories have been passed down through the years: tulips the price of houses; tulips worth fortunes; tulips, briefly, the mad and improbable focus of existence for the Dutch. Tulips, we are told, were the center of life for the *bloemisten*, as those who grew and traded in tulips were sometimes known. One disdainful commentator wrote in January 1637 that among these people "no one speaks asks about or talks of anything but Flora, so that they have their heads so full of it, that they can neither think nor dream of anything else." Because for most of the year the bulbs were in the ground, sales came to take the form of contracts for future payment and delivery. After the fact, these came to seem like empty promises, and the trade a *windhandel*, a business dealing in the empty wind. For almost inevitably—and the legends of tulipmania emphasize this inevitability—such a trade could not last. In early February 1637, the bottom fell out of the market. Buyers for the most part would not pay, and sellers were left holding the bulbs. An obvious folly—for who, subsequent accounts have stressed, would be so foolish as to pay a fortune for a tulip bulb?—came to its apparently deserved end.[3]

Even as the tulip craze was in full swing, it incited amazement among contemporaries. William Crowne, passing through Europe in 1636 on a diplomatic mission to the Holy Roman Emperor, took note of a variety of wonders for the benefit of the readers of his travel account. Among these were a Moravian baron of eighty-two whose seventy-five-year-old wife had twins, not to mention the bishop of Mainz who, "being much troubled with Mice," built a tower to get away from them, "but even thither they pursued him also, and eate him up." Tulipmania evidently fell into a similar category, a bizarre event worth reporting to a public hungry for prodigies. For Crowne, the comparable wonder to be noted about the small town of Vianen, south of Utrecht, was that "the rarest thinges in it, are Flowers, for there was a *Tulip-roote* sold lately for 340. pounds. . . ."

In the same way, Laurens van Zanten, author of a contemporary book of wonders, which divided world history into categories such as earthquakes, storms, fires, comets, plagues, wars, famines, enormous heat and cold, and incredible ways to die, felt tulipmania a prodigy equally worthy of mention. But the tulip craze was not only amazing; it was also stupid. The Haarlem priest Jodocus Cats wrote his nephew, a fellow priest, on February 5, 1637, that, like the plague that had been raging since 1635, now "another sickness has arisen . . . It is the sickness of the *blommisten* or *floristen*." For Cats, this sickness was a sickness in the head. Never, he said, had the world seen such craziness being committed. One bulb, already a fantastic ƒ600, had tripled in price in the space of as many weeks.[4] The Amsterdam poet Gerrit Jansz Kooch included a poem about "het Wonderlijck Jaer der bloemisten Anno 1637" ("the Wonderful Year of the bloemisten Anno 1637"), probably written in the 1670s, in a manuscript collection of verses which, when they dealt with events, were mainly about floods or unusual weather.[5]

Nor was it only in the 1630s that tulipmania was a byword for idiocy. "I fear that what I am going to say will command no belief," the historian of Haarlem Theodorus Schrevelius wrote eleven years later, in 1648. He thought the tulip craze was appalling—"I don't know what kind of angry spirit was called up from Hell" to poison the world, he said—but despite the seriousness of the crisis, he feared the ridicule of posterity. "Our Descendants doubtless will laugh at the human insanity of our Age, that in our times the Tulip-flowers have been so revered." And so it has proven. Accounts such as Schrevelius' have been woven into a tale of stupidity, greed, and madness that has been told again and again. The outlines of the tale have become legendary, to be invoked almost ritually whenever either the Netherlands or financial speculation is in question. Novels, plays, even operas have been written about the craze. Wild stories are told of huge fortunes won and lost, and all focused on the most improbable of objects: the tulip bulb. It is no wonder that tulipmania is one of the best-known incidents in Dutch history.[6]

IN 1913 ERNST HEINRICH KRELAGE, A LEADING BULB-GROWER and vice-president of the Dutch Gardening Council, was already pleading that "there is more than enough written about [tulipmania]." This did not stop him from spending much of his own adult life on the subject, publishing both a history of the trade and an edition of the satirical pamphlets it engendered in 1942, and, in 1946, an enormous history of three centuries of bulb export with a sizeable section on the tulip. His initial feeling that the subject of tulipmania should be put to rest was, admittedly, founded on his own interest as the head of a major bulb company and one of the leaders of the trade; in 1913 a gladiolimania threatened, and Krelage could only reflect on the damage this taint of insanity might do to his business. But his short-lived opinion that we need no more books on tulipmania lives on. The newspaper columnist Miles Kington, for example, who will probably not be writing a book about tulips in thirty years' time, commented on the spate of such books several years ago that "frankly, one book about tulips is about as much as people can take."[7]

Why, then, another one? A look at the history of the history of tulipmania provides food for thought. As we survey the literature through its 360 or so years, certain themes, certain stories, become old friends through their constant repetition. Picturesque tales are told and retold: of fortunes lost when an ignorant visitor ate a tulip bulb (the focus of an execrable French play of 1880, Jacques Normand's *L'Amiral*) or of a long list of goods, including two lasts of wheat, four of rye, four fat oxen, eight fat pigs, twelve oxheads of wine, four tuns of beer, and so on, plus a ship to carry them in, all equal to the cost (which became for some the *actual* cost) of one bulb of the Viceroy variety. Tulips became so desired, we hear, that the most common bulb, which would previously have been tossed on the dung-heap (*Mesthoop*, a word repeated in most of the sources), became worth good money. Bulbs were said to have changed hands hundreds of times in an ever-rising frenzy of financial madness. This must, we are told, be an irrational, an insane, a crazy trade—indeed an evil one, for not only were fortunes invested in a ridiculous way, but those doing the investing were the wrong people, those who, because of their low social station, should not have been allowed to submit to the temptation of easy money. Everyone in the country was apparently involved. In fact, we hear of a wholesale social revolution, with weavers abandoning their looms *en masse* and riding around the countryside in carriages when they are not drinking the costliest wine on credit. They were not interested in flowers, we learn, but simply in "odious" gain. One influential eighteenth-century author, Johann Beckmann, tells us that no one ever received the flowers, or wanted to receive them: "How ridiculous would it have been to purchase useless roots with their weight in gold, if the possession of the flower had been the only object!" To want the bulbs for profit was at least understandable (and thus, in his view, rational). But it was all the more deplorable for that. Fortunately, retribution for the hubris of tulipmania was not long in coming: thousands, we hear, were ruined, and the economy of the Netherlands left in shocked disarray.[8]

These images appear in modern books on the subject, not to mention in the numerous Web sites, newspaper articles, and financial newsletters that have invoked tulipmania as a warning to investors in recent years. Yet the same tales of extravagance were told in the seventeenth century, often in exactly the same words. Critical reading of sources has not featured large in the study of this subject. If we trace these stories back through the centuries, we find how weak their foundations actually are. In fact, they are based on one or two contemporary pieces of propaganda and a prodigious amount of plagiarism. From there we have our modern story of tulipmania.

Most of the modern-day images of the tulip craze are based on Charles Mackay, whose *Extraordinary Popular Delusions and the Madness of Crowds* of 1841 is still in print and doing well. Mackay's title is less than unequivocal about his views of the irrationality of the trade, and some of the more picturesque stories—of tulips being eaten by the unsuspecting; of oxen, cheese, and rye being delivered for a Viceroy; of the universality of the trade—make their appearance here. Mackay's chief source was Johann Beckmann, author of *Beyträge zur Geschichte der Erfindungen,* which, as *A History of Inventions, Discoveries and Origins,* went through many editions in English from 1797 on. Beckmann was concerned about financial speculation in his day, but his own sources were suspect. He relied chiefly on Abraham Munting, a botanical writer from the late seventeenth century. Munting's father, himself a botanist, had lost money on tulips, but Munting, writing in the early 1670s, was himself no reliable eyewitness. His own words, often verbatim, come chiefly from two places: the historical account of the chronicler Lieuwe van Aitzema in 1669, and one of the longest of the contemporary pieces of propaganda against the trade, Adriaen Roman's *Samen-spraeck tusschen Waermondt ende Gaergoedt* (*Dialogue between True-mouth and Greedy-goods*) of 1637.

As Aitzema was himself basing his chronicle on the pamphlet literature, we are left with a picture of tulipmania based almost solely on propaganda, cited as if it were fact. Even the most authoritative Dutch accounts of tulipmania, Krelage's 1942 book and the articles in the late 1920s and early 1930s of the renowned economic historian N. W. Posthumus, are based essentially on images presented in the pamphlet literature. Although Posthumus, with some help from his fellow economic historian J. G. van Dillen and others, located some archival material on the tulip trade in Haarlem and Amsterdam, he published it without comment (and with many errors) and indeed seems not to have consulted it at any length when writing his pieces on tulipmania for the *Economisch-Historisch Jaarboek* and the *Journal of Economic and Business History*. While some recent accounts have made occasional reference to sources beyond the pamphlets or, in the case of Simon Schama, have presented contextualized and useful interpretations of some of those pamphlets, despite the wealth of writing on the subject we remain in largely uncharted territory.[9]

In fact, as we will see, the excitement generated by tulip bulbs fit almost none of the stereotypes. It is thrilling to imagine despairing tulip-sellers drowning themselves in canals, as Deborah Moggach does in her novel *Tulip Fever* (and as poetic license permits her to do). But even that exaggerated picture of the winter of 1637 taps into one of the chief images derived from the contemporary propaganda: that it was insane to want to pay large amounts for a tulip. If we take a calmer, more informed look at the tulip craze, we find a story that is different, but equally exciting. Not because people killed themselves over bulbs, or because they joined in the "madness of crowds," but because the story of tulipmania takes us into a fascinating world. This was a new world, a new country, with a new kind of culture, a new set of priorities, a new social system, a new impetus to its commerce and its society. Tulipmania opens a window for us into that culture and its values.[10]

When we delve deeply into the history of tulipmania, instead of merely exclaiming at its excesses, we begin to distrust the stereotypes. Although it was a craze, although it was a wonder, although it was much talked of at the time and ever after, most of what we have heard about it is not true. Not everyone was involved in the trade, and those who were were connected to each other in specific ways. The prices of some varieties of tulips were briefly high, but many never increased greatly in value, and it remains to be seen whether or not it was insane for prices to reach the levels they did. Tulipmania did not destroy the economy, or even the livelihoods of most participants.

But that does not mean that tulipmania was not a crisis. It might not have been a financial crisis, but it was a social and cultural one. In tulipmania, Dutch burghers confronted a series of issues that in any case gripped their culture: novelty, the exotic, capitalism, immigration, the growth of urban societies, and all the problems and excitement such issues raised. People in the 1630s and after found tulipmania a wonder, something to be marveled at, like a fireball, a child with two heads, or a plague of mice. But they also found it to be a warning. That warning, and the images it raised in the minds of those calling our attention to it, has always been treated as if it were a mere fact. Yet the reasons for the warning have scarcely been explored.

THE NETHERLANDS WAS NOT LIKE OTHER EUROPEAN LANDS. While most other Europeans lived in monarchies, the Dutch lived in a republic, a federalized state in which power lay chiefly with the towns and provinces rather than the court of the *Stadholder* (who was appointed, in any case, by the provincial authorities) or the States-General. While other countries were dominated by landed nobilities, the Dutch, at least in the prosperous west, were largely town-dwellers, led by oligarchies of wealthy merchants who, despite their money, did not form an aristocracy. While other populations suffered economically in the seventeenth century, the Dutch prospered, their high wages attracting immigrant labor from surrounding regions. Whereas their neighbors in Europe tended to rely, often precariously, on subsistence agriculture for their livelihoods, the Dutch relied on the Baltic grain trade to feed their population, freeing labor for specialized agriculture such as dairy farming; for rural industry, fishing, and overseas trade; and for a thriving manufacturing, processing, and commercial culture in the towns. With the rest of Europe enduring what is often described as a "general crisis"—economic, demographic, political, meteorological—in the first half of the seventeenth century, the burgeoning Netherlands was an unusual place indeed.[11]

Naturally there were many continuities in this society from the sixteenth to the seventeenth centuries, but in other ways changes were manifest. The long war of independence against the Spanish, which began in the 1560s and, after the hiatus of the Twelve Years' Truce from 1609 to 1621, was to continue until 1648, brought many of them in its wake. Although the provinces of the northern Netherlands, unlike their southern neighbors, succeeded in breaking away from their Spanish sovereigns during the revolt that encompassed both north and south, they were functioning as an independent nation long before the end of the armed conflict, indeed from 1579, when seven northern provinces formed what was originally a temporary military alliance in the Union of Utrecht. The Union defined in some measure the relationships between the center and the provinces—giving preference to provincial and local government—and circumstances placed the wealthy province of Holland, which paid far more toward the general budget than any other province, in a position of dominance over the rest of the country. In some ways, the rich towns of Holland, the province where tulipmania took place, and most particularly Amsterdam, were the most powerful parts of this rich nation, able to dictate economic and foreign policy for the whole country.

The war also helped to change the makeup of those towns. The tumults of the Dutch Revolt left Antwerp, previously the most important port in northern Europe, economically ravaged, and the blockade of the Scheldt estuary by the Dutch to frustrate Antwerp's Spanish occupiers did little to help the situation. One result for Antwerp and other towns in the southern Netherlands was a great emigration of merchants, with all their expertise, capital, and connections. Many of them, sometimes after a sojourn in the German lands, England, or elsewhere, ended up in the towns of the Dutch Republic. Antwerp was depopulated, but the northern Dutch towns grew enormously.

The resultant new faces, new money, and new ideas helped to revolutionize the Dutch economy in the late sixteenth century. The money and techniques of cloth merchants, not to mention the large number of linen weavers leaving the south at the same time, brought new life to the cloth industry of towns like Haarlem and Leiden. Between government intervention and private enterprise, overseas and intraregional trade blossomed in ports such as Amsterdam, Enkhuizen, and Hoorn; products from all over Europe, not to mention the East and West Indies, were exchanged, processed, and sometimes reexported from such towns. The foundation of the profitable East India Company (VOC) in 1602 and the rather less successful West India Company (WIC) in 1621 brought a host of new products into the country, but much of the trade was carried on by independent merchants who would invest in individual voyages, sometimes turning their attention to widely disparate products and locales. The unusual institutionalization of commerce in the Netherlands—the foundation of a chamber of assurance in 1598; a new commodity exchange in 1618; a public exchange bank, the Wisselbank, in 1609; and a lending bank in 1614—attracted capital and mercantile interest from all over Europe. Along with the favorable interest rates and the likelihood of the most up-to-date commercial information, this made a port like Amsterdam a promising place for any European merchant to do business. Although the economy suffered to some degree after the war resumed in 1621, the Dutch continued to succeed economically until midcentury. Capital was abundant, and opportunities for investment—trade, manufacturing, drainage projects reclaiming land from the sea, not to mention luxury objects such as paintings—were growing too. The mixing of peoples and interests in the big towns, though sometimes confusing, was also encouraged by the Revolt. Although a Calvinist-run society, the Dutch Republic in fact tolerated (with relative amounts of grudgingness) Catholics, other sects of Protestantism such as the Lutherans and Mennonites, and the Jews, who brought their contacts and capital to the Netherlands. Urban life, through both trade and immigration, was becoming more cosmopolitan and cultured. Amsterdam in particular was becoming a center of the world.

FIGURE 1. Artus Quellinus, design for western pediment of
Amsterdam town hall. British Library. The continents of the world
bring their goods to Amsterdam, including Asia's tulip.

Dudley Carleton, the English ambassador, commented on this in 1616
when he first went to Amsterdam, which at that time was just beginning
the great expansion that would result in the grand sweep of canals encircling the old part of the city. "I saw the whole town and observed this
difference from Antwerp, that there was a town without people and here
a people as it were without a town. Such are the numbers of all nations,
of all professions and all religions there assembled, but for one business
only, of merchandise. Their new town goeth up apace...." The Dutch
themselves were abundantly aware of their prosperity and the way that
the world's goods came to them from all over the globe. Although some-

times uneasy with their wealth, they were also proud, as we see from the triumphant frieze by Artus Quellinus on the western pediment of the magnificent Amsterdam town hall, finished in 1665 (see fig. 1). Quellinus depicted representatives of America, Africa, Europe, and Asia all bringing their local goods to Amsterdam. Asia, represented by a woman in exotic clothing and a turban, is accompanied by a camel, an ostrich, and three children. One of the children brings incense from the exotic east; the second holds a chest containing spices. The third carries Asia's own contribution to this exotic cornucopia: tulips.[12]

Quellinus saw tulips as glorious objects of trade. Tulipmania would probably not have happened in a society less commercially developed than the Netherlands. But in this case money intersected with aesthetics. As luxury objects, tulips fit well into a culture of both abundant capital and a new cosmopolitanism, a culture springing at least in part from the more aristocratic tastes entering the Dutch Republic from the south. Gardening, collecting, an interest in natural history, an interest in art: all these brought tulips to the attention of merchants in cities like Amsterdam, Haarlem, Delft, or Enkhuizen. Such interests also brought merchants into the sphere of more rarified circles, of the humanist fascination with nature that had already been flourishing in court circles elsewhere in Europe, such as the imperial court in Vienna. Tulips came to the Netherlands in part because of an interest in science, but they were embraced because such an interest was shared by more ordinary citizens with some money in their pockets. They came also because they must have inspired some of the same kinds of feelings as paintings, another object in which such people invested their money. And they came because they were in fashion.

The early modern Netherlands has not always had a good press from modern writers. In large part because of the themes and styles of seventeenth-century Dutch painting, some cultural critics have been quick to use the Dutch Republic as a kind of metaphor for capitalism, and in particular capitalism's discontents. Roland Barthes, in his essay "The World as Object," discerned in the Dutch a special aesthetic, "the art of the catalogue"; life in the Netherlands revolved around material and commercial concerns, the "patient weighing of property or of merchandise." Their art was all about surface and, he implied, their lives were too. "What have they to do with the *chronos* of passion? Theirs is the *chronos* of biology." The meatlike subjects of militia portraits, he wrote, look back out at you, the viewer, and in their painted eyes you too become merely "a matter of capital."[13]

Although other critics have been more nuanced in their vision of Dutch society, for many capitalism has weighed heavy on their minds. The Dutch, they feel, were obsessed with material goods—Hal Foster suggests that this amounted to "fetishism"[14]—and quite clearly, it is hinted, this was wrong. Foster writes of "the chill of the commodity," suggesting that (according to a Freudian analysis) objects were endowed with "a special luminous life" because of "the capitalistic gaze of the Dutch subject."[15] Norman Bryson, similarly, remarks of Dutch still life that "pleasure is disavowed, hidden by production; what replaces it is strain, effort, and the work imperative."[16] Dutch existence, despite the beauty of their still life, was apparently joyless, because wealthy burghers were overly burdened with their misplaced enthusiasm for capitalistic endeavor.

For most commentators, if not for Barthes, this materialistic sensibility is at least less than straightforward. Beginning with Simon Schama's *The Embarrassment of Riches* (1987), we see a series of more subtle analyses (including those of Foster and Bryson) of the ambivalence the Dutch may have felt about their objects.[17] Although the western provinces of the Netherlands had long been highly urbanized, the period after 1585 in particular saw unprecedented growth in the Dutch economy, leading to the northern Netherlands becoming what Jan de Vries and Ad van der Woude have (controversially) called "the first modern economy" and the most successful one in Europe.[18] The comparative suddenness of the northern Netherlands' rise to economic prominence is considered to have troubled Dutch society. It has certainly troubled modern scholars.

Behind such analyses lurks, almost inevitably, the tulip. If we are to see the Dutch as obsessed by objects, as soulless worshippers at the temple of Mammon, and especially as ambivalent consumers who had to be jolted into a realization of their own materialism, tulipmania and floral still life are bound to make an appearance. The tulip craze is cited by nearly all these commentators as the pinnacle of unconsidered capitalism, and the crash the inevitable correction bringing—if only temporarily—a questioning of capitalistic society. Although I would not agree with much of this image of tulipmania, which I think owes more to modern critics' opinions of capitalism than those in the seventeenth century, there is of course some truth in it. As we will see, a spate of pamphlet literature and satiric songs was published in February and March 1637, dedicated to ridiculing the idiocies of the tulip trade. Some of this indeed made reference to an older set of values, the values of Christianity and hopes for the afterlife. Moreover, there was also a reaction to such questioning, for not all were ambivalent. Some pamphlets actually made a case for capitalism, claiming that the critics were in fact simply jealous of those who had made money from the craze.[19] That this quarrel could exist does indicate a questioning of capitalism within Dutch towns. But texts have contexts, and too much has been made of these texts (or actually of the idea that such texts exist, as few seem to have read them) without considering the society in which they were written. Until this is done, until an in-depth analysis is made of what actually happened in tulipmania, it is difficult to say much of substance about the event or, by extension, about the society for which 1637 has been taken to be an emblematic and a defining moment.

A key to the problem here is articulated by Norman Bryson. In his essay "Abundance," he states that the old agrarian world portrayed by Pieter Brueghel the Elder depended on "its capacity to submit to a general morality of consumption and abstinence." Once the Netherlands found its new abundance, the idea of the general welfare disappeared. "Much of the complexity in Dutch still life will come from the collision between this traditional and community-based ethic, revolving round shared wealth and poverty, and the private ethic of the individual owner of property."[20] The question we need to ask is whether capitalism has to revolve entirely around economic individualism. If we assume that it does, and if we disapprove of that individualism (as some critics appear to do), we again risk applying modern visions of social relations to an early modern world. In fact, as we will see, despite the urbanized, craft- and trade-based economy of the province of Holland, social existence in towns like Haarlem, Enkhuizen, and even Amsterdam depended very much on a set of economic interactions and networks that had by their very nature to militate against the individualistic. Bryson is correct to suggest that a disturbance to these networks would cause agitation—and tulipmania was such a disturbance. What is less clear is whether this disturbance was due only to the excesses of capitalism.

By focusing chiefly on capitalism as a monolith and Dutch society as an undifferentiated mass, we lose sight of alternative lessons we can learn about the early modern world. Here is where examining tulipmania in a microhistorical way can lead us to new insights.[21] Precisely because early modern commerce was so rooted in other social, intellectual, and cultural systems and practices, it is only by looking at such systems and practices that we can understand all that this complex event can tell us. After the plea in 1991 by the art historian David Freedberg for more interdisciplinarity in the profession, and in particular more studies located at the intersection of art, science, and commerce, a more rounded consideration of early modern urban and commercial culture has started to emerge.[22] Scholars in history, art history, and the history of science have been exploring such areas as the history of collecting, the relation of print culture to early modern art and science, the social and economic analysis of the art market and the taste for painting, the connections between the existence and operation of social networks and the production of knowledge, and the way craftsmen's theory and practice came to influence the history of science.[23] In all this work, questions of representation, communication, interaction, and self-evaluation have resonated with the issue of commodification raised so often by analysts of the Dutch commercial scene. Commerce is perceived as a force to be reckoned with in the relationships that shaped early modern culture and society, but in the same way those relationships helped to shape the way that commerce itself was constructed.

In the wake of such studies, it becomes difficult to see early modern society, even in its capitalistic elements, as necessarily about individual interest. As the topics above will indicate, much of the work following Freedberg's call to action has dealt with the structure and interaction of communities. Whether we consider the history of collecting, the art market, the development of botanical knowledge, or any of a host of other subjects occupying Freedberg's juncture of history and art history, we find ourselves considering issues of social relations. As recent work in the history of science has shown, the membership of scholarly communities, their possible social breadth, their structure, and their ways of communicating knowledge are all crucial contexts for understanding the knowledge produced in the period. The way that ideas were communicated within social networks, and the porousness of such networks, has changed our way of understanding early modern communities and their knowledge. Where natural philosophy is concerned, we have come to understand the importance of nonprinted sources, of letters and conversation, and of the role that could be played by those traditionally conceived as social inferiors. To take only one example, the manuscript *Whale Book* by the Scheveningen fish auctioneer and fisherman's son Adriaen Coenen, recently edited by Florike Egmond and Peter Mason, makes it clear that Coenen's expertise gave him entrée in the 1580s into the highest circles of Dutch society, if not on equal terms. "It happened that I, Adriaen Coenen of Scheveningen, who write this, was on very good terms with the President of Holland, Mr. Cornelis Suys, Lord of Rijswijk, and often dined with him when I was in the Hague. For I had made a big book about all kinds of fish which greatly pleased Milord the President and which he liked to discuss and was very curious about. This book was often in his house, and when I went to dine with him, we studied and discussed after the meal with other gentlemen who were often guests there about all kinds of fish. . . ."[24] Egmond makes clear that in the early modern natural historical community a kind of modified social mixing could take place around a shared interest, although she also stresses that certain status markers—for example, the direction of exchange and lack of reciprocity—were preserved in the late-sixteenth-century Netherlandish collecting circles she is currently studying.[25] These issues of knowledge, expertise, and social and intellectual exchange were, as Freedberg indicated, intertwined with commercial concerns. But Egmond's talk of status markers and exchange points as well toward the noncommercial aspects of the operations of such communities. The line between commercial and noncommercial aspects of communities of learning is always a blurry one, much as those involved might like to sharpen it.[26]

This blurriness and social mixing should make it plain that, when we are dealing with issues of knowledge and its communication, we are not necessarily confined to discussing the learned. Early modern communities in general—communities such as the burghers and craftsmen of seventeenth-century Haarlem or Amsterdam—also found communication of knowledge to be crucial, whether that knowledge be social, aesthetic, or commercial.[27] One of the themes of this book is the way the sociocultural dynamics of Dutch towns in the 1630s often mirror the kinds of concerns historians of science more usually locate within the confines of the natural historical community. The most obvious example of this is the interest in matters of natural history among burghers and craftsmen whose main occupation was linen-weaving, brewing, insurance, sugar-refining, or innkeeping. As I will argue, this interest appears not to have been confined (as has always previously been argued, at least about tulip-mania) to the commercial possibilities thrown up by horticulture or the sale of rarities. But the parallels go much deeper than this. The enthusiasm for tulips, which took hold among sixteenth-century botanical collectors and seventeenth-century urban communities, gives us ample opportunity to examine the values and practices at Freedberg's intersection of art, science, and commerce. It also gives us the opportunity to look at the way groups that were not necessarily obvious locations of aesthetic values or natural historical practices in fact operated much like the more traditional *loci* of scholarly activity.

Historians of science, art historians, and historians, for example, are all interested in professionalization and ideas about authority within communities. In particular, the history of science has been preoccupied in recent years with issues of proof, trust, and witnessing, especially in relation to social status and relationships.[28] At the same time, art historians have noted the growth of a set of discourses about art within society that affected the art market and art collecting's role within a status society; once again, authority is claimed by access to knowledge and the ability to display it. This was naturally also true of those concerned with natural curiosities as well as *artificialia*.[29] But as we will see, "experts" could exist in a variety of contexts within early modern society; the guild structure, with its *vinders* regulating the trade, immediately springs to mind. Guilds, however, are longstanding organizations. Tulipmania gives us a chance to examine ideas about expertise, proof, and authority within a fluid and changing social scene. Although the social location of actors within tulipmania was naturally dependent in part on their profession, wealth, and social relations, the tulip craze, much like the natural historical community in the sixteenth century, gave artisans and burghers a new location and set of standards by which to judge status. This was not just a matter of wealth gained from tulips (if any was), but the construction of a hierarchy of expertise about this suddenly important area of both commerce and natural history. The trade quickly became organized, with commercial companies; "normal" trading practices (despite

the newness of the trade); and a semi-official board, the *collegie*, providing an (unenforceable) authority over transactions. These structures,
so hastily constructed, gave a badly needed framework of authority and
knowledge to this crossover between collecting and commerce.

That the structures of authority and expertise were badly needed is evident from the confusion engendered by the crash in tulip prices in February 1637. With little help from governmental authorities, enthusiasts
for tulips were for months left to find their own solutions to the problems
caused by refusals to pay for purchased goods. Those concerned were
urged to seek harmony through discussion, rather than through institutional means, and once again these attempts (though often unsuccessful)
took the form of arbitration with the assistance of experts. Historians of
Dutch culture will feel on familiar ground here. One of the most influential and overarching themes in the historiography of the Dutch Golden
Age is the idea that it was a *discussiecultuur*, a culture that attempted,
through discussion, mediation, and compromise, to rise above the difficulties created by a pluralistic and at times politically divided society.[30]
Thus tulipmania presents a microhistorical example of the subtle me-
diations and solutions sought by members of the *discussiecultuur* and
the profundity of the shock presented by its failure always to achieve its
ends. At the same time, readers interested in the ways that social life is
organized and mediated by a set of cultural practices will have much to
learn from this case, not least those historians of science fascinated by issues of proof, trust, and value. One of the functions of those playing roles
of authority within societies, including intellectual societies, is to help
to create or enforce a system of values, whether these values are social,
ethical, cultural, or commercial. These include an understanding of what
"value" actually is. Value is, in the end, a cultural construct, whether we
are talking about the value of a painting, the value of a tulip, or the value
of a person.

Communities find themselves at a loss when value is thrown into
doubt. Tulipmania did exactly this. By creating a novel set of cultural
values and potentially altering a longstanding social framework, tulipmania rendered unstable the whole notion of how to assess value. This
was particularly true in the 1630s because of already-existent social and
geographical mobility, but it was also true because of the cultural changes
that made tulipmania possible. And if there are disputes about value,

communities will look to experts or authorities to help resolve those disputes, yet the fluidity of this particular situation made this resolution hard to achieve. However, if we think about the importance social harmony seems to have played within these relatively small urban networks, we begin to recognize the factors that must complicate an analysis placing capitalistic greed at the center of the distress caused by tulipmania. Close reading of the attempts at resolving disputes over tulips suggests that honor, rather than simply money, governed the values of this community. This helps to explain why, even though the financial crisis affected very few, the shock of tulipmania was considerable. A whole network of values was thrown into doubt.

What tulipmania offers as a microhistorical subject, then, is a kind of laboratory in which to explore a set of issues in the history of art, the history of science, and the history of the social and cultural dynamics of early modern urban communities. It gives us a chance to look in microcosm at a society that was, indeed, grappling with its material values and the relation they bore to their social ones. And it lets us see how the themes prevalent in the current historiography of science and art can also yield fruit when applied within a society of amateurs. As microhistories should, this book thinks not just about local but also general historical themes. The localness of local history is, of course, also important. As will become evident toward the end of the book, the operations of particular networks and the quarrels they carried on—including the quarrel over the appropriateness of investment in tulips—had both a character with general resonance and aspects specific to this particular time, place, and set of actors.

In looking closely at tulipmania, we begin to gain an understanding of its context. We learn not only what actually happened in this famous but misunderstood event, but, more importantly, what that tells us about one of the most fascinating societies of the era. From tulipmania we learn something of what it was to live in this prosperous world, what dreams and enthusiasms this particular culture seemed to inspire. We learn about its connections, its focus on family and friends, its search for order and coherence in a changing world. We learn something, too, about its fears: fears of social breakdown, of confusions over status, of loss of honor, of the breaking of trust. Tulipmania teaches us, just a little, what it was like to live at this time. It teaches us what it was like to be someone like Barent Roelofsz Wanscher (to pick a name at random), to work, as he did, as an entrepreneur in linen yarn; to be a respected Mennonite consulted on affairs by coreligionists and Reformed alike; to socialize with neighbors and fellow-merchants; to live among other *bloemisten* on the Grote Hout-straat in Haarlem; and to have a little garden just outside of the northeast city gate, the St. Janspoort. It teaches us what it was like to buy and sell tulips and to confront your neighbors at the crash.

Fernand Braudel wrote in the preface to *The Mediterranean* about his desire to explore all the movements of history, from the briefest and most superficial events to the most slow-moving changes in the landscape and the gradual migrations of peoples. "I hope," he wrote, "that I shall not be reproached for my excessive ambitions, for my desire and need to see on a grand scale. It will perhaps prove that history can do more than study walled gardens." You can learn a great deal from studying the Mediterranean. But you can learn much from studying walled gardens as well.[31]

~~~~~~~~~~~~~~~~~~~~~~~~~~~~~~~~~~~~~~

ONE

Something Strange

JEHAN SOMER HAD, HE TELLS US, "SEEN A BIT of the world." Many of his contemporaries in Middelburg in Zeeland would, it is true, have had experience of travel for business, sailing down the coast of France to buy wine and salt. But Somer, a wealthy, well-educated, multilingual, well-connected young man—his father, David Somer, was *baljuw* (magistrate) of Middelburg—had spent two years, from 1590 to 1592, traveling for pleasure. The fact that he was disabled, walking with a crutch, did not prevent him from setting out to see the wonders of southern Europe and the Levant. After five months in Italy, he set sail with a Pole ("the Dansicker"), a Frenchman, and two Englishmen on the Italian merchant vessel of a Signor Patti through the Mediterranean. The voyage was not without incident. Not only did he nearly drown in Crete in July 1591, when desire for "good London" beer left him unconscious in the water under the boat of the German shipper who had offered him breakfast, but also, when heading back from the Balkans to Crete in mid-September, his ship fell to the Turks. Somer, along with his traveling companions, was forced into slavery on a Turkish galley.[1]

The Turks had attacked "with naked sabres in their hands" as Somer and the others came up on deck, and they were unable to resist. Their shipper, Patti, was released, but seven others from his vessel (five Slovenes, the Dansicker,

and Somer) were put to the oar. Somer was despondent. He fell into conversation in Greek with the other slaves, who encouraged him, saying he
was sure to be released soon. When he said he was not used to this kind
of work, they even gave him an easy berth on the outside of a five-person
bench where little effort on the oar was necessary. The galley made its
way to Alexandria, where Somer enlisted the help of a Greek slave who
had been on the galley for thirty years and had freedom of movement.
Pretending to be French, Somer was able to get in touch with the French
consul, to whom he had a letter of introduction. The consul promised to
investigate, and "the slave telling me this cheered me a little, but there
was but little joy in my heart, being so far from home, walking poorly,
with little money in my purse, but God strengthened my courage."[2]

The consul's initial inquiries about whether a Frenchman was being
held captive led the galley's captain to swear at him in Turkish (obligingly
translated into Italian for him by a Neapolitan). Somer, chained up, had
to listen as the captain railed at him, calling him a dog and threatening to
hit him unless he said how he had made contact with the consul. Somer
pretended to know nothing of the matter, and the following day the consul, now alerted to Somer's circumstances, was able to put the captain
in a better mood. Finally, having charmed the captain with a false story
about his origins, Somer, after some tense moments, was allowed to pay
twenty *chequini*, amounting to twenty-five gold crowns, for his release.[3]
He continued on his way, these experiences failing to mar his wonder and
fascination at the sights of Cairo, the Holy Land, Constantinople, Greece,
and the Balkans.

Jehan Somer had seen a bit of the world. True, his Middelburger roots
show up repeatedly in his account, as he measured the size of towns by
what was familiar to him: "FLORENCE is the size of *Brussels*," the Nile
"approximately as wide as the *Scheldt at Antwerp*. . . ."[4] In some ways that
made his trip even more exciting; here he was, able to report back to his
fellow-Middelburgers about the wonders of the South: the mountains
of Crete, the treasures of Venice, the towers of Constantinople. On his
return, he remained excited. What might seem strange after all these experiences, after all these thrills, was what he was excited about. Because
now he was excited about flowers.

Actually, Somer had already been excited about flowers while he was
on his travels. When he said he had seen a bit of the world, it was to estab-

lish his credentials to marvel at the Duke of Florence's famous Pratolino garden ("nowhere but in *Constantinople* have I seen the like of *Pratolino*"). On Candy (Crete) he saw tulips, white peonies, roses, yellow irises, and many other blooms—"there is no Island in the world where so many flowers grow as in *Candien* on Mount Ida"—and was amazed to find wild cauliflowers growing, especially as the Greeks did not know how to cook them and had no interest in eating them. But it was Constantinople that impressed him most with its omnipresent gardens and blossoms. "The Turks are great lovers of *Gardens* and *herbs,* and you would have to be a poor man not to have a *little Garden.* They spend much money on *strange plants* and *Flowers*[;] within *Constantinople* is a market, where they sell nothing other than flowers and herbs, which are brought there from the *Black Sea,* or *Mare Magiore,* and from other places, from Egypt to India."[5]

So perhaps it is not so odd to find Jehan Somer, returned from the thrill of his travels to the mundanity of life in Middelburg, still aflame with the exoticism of rare flowers. We hear in 1593 that he had the previous year brought back "strange bulbs and herbs . . . from Constantinople and from Italy," some of which he had been given at Pratolino by the Dutch herbalist of the Duke of Florence, Joost Goedenhuyzen, also known as Josephus de Casabona. A fellow Middelburger, the apothecary Willem Jasparsz Parduyn, wrote to Carolus Clusius that Somer had returned with a whole range of flowers, from dogstooth violets to auriculas, double narcissi, lilies, small tulips, crocuses, and many others. Somer himself only dared to write to Clusius, the most famous botanist of his age and the central node of horticultural activity in Europe, in May 1597. In his letter we can sense the urgency of his passion for flowers.[6]

Somer admitted that he would not normally have dared to "molest" Clusius with his letters, but he was encouraged to do so by three other correspondents of Clusius, Johannes de Jonghe, minister of the Reformed Church at Middelburg; Willem Jasparsz (that is, Parduyn); and Tobias Roels, the Middelburg city doctor. Somer sent Clusius a painting of a yellow fritillary, which had bloomed in his garden that year and was now "seeding beautifully," wishing only that he had more such flowers he could pass along. He reported on his martagon lily from Constantinople, which, along with a few others, was "blooming most beautifully" and had produced two or three offsets (small outgrowths of the bulb that can eventually be cut off and grown as bulbs in their own right). Somer was happy to send Clusius one offset, "along with other beauties which I expected yearly, which I will not fail to share with your honor liberally, for I assure myself that I shall receive something unusual each year; moreover I have already brought the same myself from Constantinople." Having made these offers, Somer probed further in his new relationship with Clusius, a kind of probing with which Clusius was more than familiar. "Since I understand that your honor also shares liberally with those who consider themselves connoisseurs (*liefhebbers*) of flowers, among whom I consider myself to be the very least, I pray your honor with friendship not to forget me, and to honor me with two, three, or four of your beautiful colors of tulips, yes, even if it were only one, for however small it is that comes from your honor's hand I shall receive with the greatest thanks."[7]

Somer's thrilled focus on one or two flowers within his Middelburg garden—the tall martagon with its many hanging curled pink flowers and prominent stamens; the small, checked, yellow fritillary with its drooping head—and the urgent desire to obtain even one of Clusius' prized tulip bulbs awakens us to a prevailing ethos among a certain group in late-sixteenth-century society. We know little of Somer's life, but the associates he mentions or who mention him in their letters suggest a community of *liefhebbers* engaged, within the walls of Middelburg and in gardens around the outskirts, in the fascinated pursuit of the cultivation of rare flowers. A whole group of people shared his floral obsession. What we need to understand is why.

Shipping flowers in from Constantinople, two-year sightseeing journeys on which bulbs and seeds could be purchased, owning a garden in the first place: these were things that did not come cheap. The professional elite of a town like Middelburg was, in the 1590s, in a good position to indulge these passions. Middelburg, located on one of the islands on the coast of Zeeland, had flourished in the late Middle Ages as one of the outports of Antwerp, the greatest center of trade in northern Europe, and as Antwerp's trade grew, so did the prosperity of Middelburg. In 1523 its economy was further stimulated by its merchants being awarded the imperial monopoly on the trade in French wine in the Habsburg Netherlands; in the sixteenth century almost 50 percent of its export trade was in wine. The same ships brought back raw salt from salt pans on the west coast of France for refinement. The town also profited from problems Flanders was having with the English, who from the late fifteenth century started exporting woollen cloth rather than sending raw wool to Flanders for processing; the reaction of Flanders—closing its ports to English cloth—led the Merchant Adventurers in 1582 to designate the more relaxed Middelburg as their staple.

The biggest boost to Middelburg's economy, however, as it was to the rest of the northwest Netherlands, was the immigration of sizeable numbers of merchants and artisans from the southern Netherlands after the fall of Antwerp to the Spanish in 1585. Whereas Middelburg's fortunes previously had been linked to Antwerp's, now Middelburg profited from Antwerp's decline. Before the immigration the town had already been one of the twelve largest in the Netherlands, with a population of more than 10,000; by 1630 it counted 30,000 inhabitants. Among those settling in Middelburg, or resettling there after a period in Antwerp, were merchants often more enterprising, with more capital and more widespread contacts than those of the old Middelburg elite. Thus one of the most intrepid and innovative merchants of the period, Balthasar de Moucheron, who made two unsuccessful voyages to try to find a northeast passage to China through the Arctic seas and was responsible for setting up a company at Middelburg specializing in the Caribbean trade, had moved from Antwerp to Middelburg. The blockading of the Scheldt estuary at Antwerp, which ultimately saw the movement of the economic center of the region from the south to the north, left Middelburg, with the exception of Amsterdam, in the best position to act as an *entrepôt* port. During the time that Jehan Somer was cultivating rare flowers in his garden, merchants were setting out northward for Archangel and southward for the Mediterranean and, increasingly, to the Indies. When the VOC was set up in 1602 to consolidate the Dutch trade in spices, porcelain, and other goods of high value from the Indies, Middelburg was the site of one of its chambers, attracting an initial capital investment of ƒ1,379,775.[8]

Middelburg's experience mirrors that of many of the major towns of Holland and Zeeland, the two provinces that chiefly benefited from the collapse of the south in the Dutch Revolt and the transfer of capital and expertise to the north. As it was a port, its inhabitants not only largely made a living from the sea but, in the 1590s, particularly after the establishment of Balthasar de Moucheron's trading company in the city, were also beginning to encounter the rarities and exotica brought back by shippers from the Indies and the Near East. The availability of both capital and rare and curious objects—and this, of course, included flowers—encouraged among the elite a culture of collecting, a concentration on the rare and the strange. Such a culture had already been prominent in the south, where collecting both art and antiquities, as well as developing urban gardens, had been popular among the educated class for some time. With the immigration of southerners to the north, their tastes as well as their capital moved to places like Middelburg (and, for that matter, Amsterdam, Leiden, and Haarlem). It seems no accident that many of the enthusiasts for rare flowers in Middelburg in the 1590s—the doctors Tobias Roels and Caspar Pelletier, the apothecaries Willem Parduyn and Reymer van de Putte, the merchants Jacques Noirot and Simon Parduyn—were southern by origin.[9]

In their correspondence, we see this group avidly awaiting the arrival of ships from the south and east, which might have exotic objects and flowers on board. In 1596, for example, Parduyn told Clusius of a ship newly arrived from São Thomé: "I have been on this ship to ask for something strange" (*wat vrempts*) and, he said, he would make sure to keep Clusius in mind if on other ships exotica (*yet vrempts*) could be found. In 1599, with the arrival of ships from Guinea, he sent Clusius "little creatures" off the ship (probably barnacles) and the beak of a bird (sadly deceased in transit), which was bigger than the bird itself, not to mention "a fruit or other plant unknown to me, not knowing what it is. . . ." He also borrowed a strange pineapple to give Clusius a look at it. The same curiosity inspired those of similar interests in other port towns, such as Amsterdam, Delft, Enkhuizen, or Hoorn, to become involved in the Indies trade. The apothecary Peeter Garet in Amsterdam concentrated on searching for rare plants on the East India ships, telling Clusius in 1602 that he had made the acquaintance of all the East India shippers, "who promise to bring me back strange kinds of all fruits, branches of trees, roots and herbs," complete with details of their names and powers. Clusius himself had been an early ship-follower; he was in England when Francis Drake returned from his circumnavigation of the globe in 1580 and hurried to talk to Drake and ask him for specimens, publishing in 1582 the first printed account of the voyage. After the foundation of the VOC in 1602, he even issued a memorandum to apothecaries and surgeons traveling on VOC ships instructing them to look out for "strange" botanical specimens, although it is not clear that anyone paid attention to his request.[10]

Middelburg, combining all the necessary factors of capital, interest, and the frequent arrival of exotica in its port, became at this time a remarkable center of floral interest. Some of this was botanical. The town doctor from 1584 to 1596, Matthias de l'Obel, was the author of one of the most important and frequently reprinted herbals of the period, and his colleague, Pelletier, who owned one of the most famous gardens in the province, was later to publish the first account of the flora of Zeeland, listing eighteen hundred plants. But l'Obel and Pelletier were part of the same circles of *liefhebbers* in Middelburg as Jehan Somer, Johannes de Jonghe, Willem Parduyn, Jacques Noirot, and other correspondents of Clusius, all of whom owned gardens (Parduyn mentioned "my principal walled garden, behind my house," implying he owned several). Middelburg was the home of a number of large gardens containing a variety of exotic flowers and trees. Jacob Cats, one of the most famous poets of the seventeenth-century Netherlands, reported later of the garden of his next-door neighbor in the Lange Noordstraat, Hortensia del Prado, built around 1613, that she had fruit trees "from all foreign lands," plants "from every foreign shore," and "flowers without name." Although most gardening enthusiasts would not have had gardens the size of del Prado's, or necessarily such features as her "hundred" fountains playing with fish, the existence of this "wood" or "open field" in the midst of the town speaks to the degree to which gardens were becoming a passion in Middelburg.[11]

At the same time, and surely influenced by this Middelburger floral culture, the town was an important site of the origins of floral still life painting (see fig. 2). Ambrosius Bosschaert the Elder, patriarch of the extended family later to include the floral still life painters Ambrosius Bosschaert the Younger, Balthasar van der Ast, and Roelandt Savery, came from Middelburg. Van der Ast, the younger brother-in-law of Ambrosius the Elder, went to live with the family in Middelburg after his parents died in 1609, and his own paintings were clearly influenced by Bosschaert, who trained him. As still life painting began to focus to some degree on depicting plants *naer't leven* (drawn from life), the presence of numerous gardens with the kind of exotica that turned up in Bosschaert's paintings

FIGURE 2. Christoffel van den Berghe, *Flowers in a gilt-mounted porcelain vase*, c. 1616. Courtesy of Sotheby's. Van den Berghe was one of a circle of painters of floral still life in Middelburg.

suggests Bosschaert's involvement in the circle of connoisseurs and his presence in their gardens. It has even been suggested that the portrait of the yellow fritillary sent by Somer to Clusius in 1597 might have been painted by Bosschaert because it featured as a motif in a number of his paintings. Tulips, more than other flowers, were prominent in the works of these painters.[12]

The gardens inspiring these interactions of connoisseurs and artists had changed substantially in the previous century. In the Middle Ages, both monasteries and castles had had gardens, chiefly for vegetables or herbs. Both monastic and castle gardens were laid out in quadrangles, and for the most part flowers did not make up an important part of their contents. Plants in the late medieval period and the first half of the sixteenth century were valued primarily for their usefulness rather than their beauty. Urban gardens, when they existed in the first part of the sixteenth century, had a similarly utilitarian purpose. From the map of Amsterdam of 1544 by Cornelis Antonisz we see that, with a few more decorative exceptions, the back gardens of the houses were more like miniature farms, with groves of fruit trees, agricultural outbuildings, and facilities for keeping animals. The first developments in sixteenth-century gardening in fact mirrored this stress on utility. The rise of humanism and interest in new medical developments, first in Italy and later in northern Europe, gave new impetus to the study of botany. Italian universities began the practice of founding special chairs of botany in their medical faculties, beginning with Padua in 1533. At the same time we begin to see the foundation of botanical gardens, chiefly associated with universities, to promote the teaching of medicine. Pisa and Padua laid out botanical gardens in the mid-1540s, followed by many other Italian cities by the 1560s. The trend in northern Europe took place later—Paris gained its garden in the 1570s—but by 1594 Leiden in the northern Netherlands had its own botanical garden, with Carolus Clusius as its first director and the Delft apothecary Dirck Cluyt, himself a respected expert on plants, as practical head of the garden.[13]

The appointment of Clusius, already an old man with a long career at the imperial court in Vienna behind him, as director of Leiden's garden was in itself both telling and influential. The university had actually wanted someone else, the renowned traveler, collector, and municipal doctor in Enkhuizen, Barent ten Broecke, usually known as Bernardus

Paludanus. His famous collection of curiosities, the first encyclopedic collection in the northern Netherlands, which drew princes and scholars alike to the small Zuider Zee port, would (the Leiden authorities stipulated) have made a fine accompaniment to the botanical garden. Paludanus' wife refused to move to Leiden, however, and the curators of the university began a long campaign to attract Clusius instead. But Clusius, as he had already shown in several works, shared the increasing disposition of many connoisseurs of plants in the later sixteenth century. For him, plants were to be valued not only for their use but also for their beauty. It is surely no accident that by 1608, the year before Clusius' death, the *hortus botanicus* in Leiden—presumably a site for medicinal plants—actually contained more than six hundred tulip bulbs. The tulip had no medical properties, but for Clusius that was unimportant. The tulip was beautiful.[14]

The palpable excitement of Willem Parduyn as he boarded Balthasar de Moucheron's ships in Middelburg in search of "something strange" must have been felt by all those who, like him, like Clusius, and like many others, followed the influx of a multitude of exotic plants into Europe in the sixteenth century. It was not just their beauty—the delicacy of the iris, the grandeur of the crown imperial—but their novelty that thrilled: "a plant unknown to me, not knowing what it is. . . ." With increased travel and the growth of trade after the long recession of the fifteenth century, the horticulture of Europe changed dramatically. In the herbals of the late fifteenth century, botanical authors described between five hundred and a thousand plants, relying chiefly on the observations of classical authors such as Dioscorides, Pliny, and Galen. By the time of the publication of Gaspard Bauhin's *Pinax theatri botanici* in 1623, on the other hand, the number of known plants had leapt to six thousand. Some of this enormous increase came from a new devotion to empirical observation, leading to the description of indigenous European plants, chiefly northern, which the Greek and Latin authors had never discussed. But much of the change came from rarities newly imported into Europe. It has been estimated that in the sixteenth century Europe saw the introduction of twenty times more plants than in the previous two thousand years. These included vegetables such as potatoes, runner and French beans, green and red peppers, Jerusalem artichokes, and tomatoes (arriving by 1550 and believed to be aphrodisiacs). But flowers also loomed large in this new horticultural universe. The common flowers of the Middle Ages were roses, lilies, carnations, violets, and cowslips, all depicted in the floral borders of illuminated manuscripts or on the flower-strewn backgrounds of *millefleurs* tapestries. These familiar flowers, as the works of floral still life painters testify, would fade into the background with the arrival of the more exciting, and frequently larger, exotica from Turkey, Asia Minor, Africa, America, and the East Indies. From around 1550 on, northern Europeans were introduced not only to the tulip, but to the hycacinth, the anemone, the crocus, the crown imperial, the iris, the narcissus, the ranunculus, and the fritillary. Contemporaries interested in plants were very conscious of this influx of new flowers. John Parkinson, justifying the writing of his *Paradisi in Sole Paradisus Terrestris* of 1629, remarked at the lack of flowers in the herbals that had so far appeared in English: "[John] *Gerard* who is last, hath no doubt given us the knowledge of as many as he attained unto in his time, but since his daies we have had many more varieties, then he or they ever heard of. . . ."[15]

The tulip naturally was a prominent figure in this transformation of the floral landscape of Europe, and Parkinson and others devoted increasing attention to it in seventeenth-century treatises about gardening. Although tulips originated in Asia Minor, Europeans came in contact with them in Turkey only a few decades before Somer was exclaiming in the 1590s over the large amounts of money expended on them in Constantinople. Whereas Europe's love affair with flowers was only truly launched in the later sixteenth century with the import of exotica, the Turks had had a longstanding enthusiasm for flowers. It appears both from literary evidence and from decorative motifs on buildings that the Turks were already familiar with tulips in the late eleventh century. After the Turkish conquest of Constantinople in 1453, the city's layout was reconceived by Sultan Mehmet II, incorporating elaborate gardens and parks, a redevelopment continued by his successors in the sixteenth and seventeenth centuries. Ordinary houses also frequently had interior courtyards with gardens, and private gardening on a small scale went on all over the city, fueled by a market devoted solely to plants and flowers. In an era when public gardens in Europe still lay in the future, Constantinople's population in the late sixteenth century could walk through the gardens of the mental hospital, admiring the fountain and promenades lined with roses, tulips, hyacinths, daffodils, carnations, and many other flowers. Bulbs were planted in the sultan's gardens on a grand scale; in 1574, for example, Selim II ordered the Sheriff of Aziz to send him fifty thousand tulip bulbs without delay, and similarly in 1593 Sultan Murad III wrote to a provincial governor ordering the urgent collection of a hundred thousand wild hyacinth bulbs, half blue, half white. Even on his visit in November 1591—a good time to buy bulbs, but not to see the flowers—Jehan Somer was rapturous over his view of Constantinople and its gardens from the water. With the towers of the city, the palace of "the Great Turk," and the shade of the cypresses planted along the rows of houses, it was "such a very beautiful sight," he wrote, "that everyone who sees it would say that it seems rather a Paradise than a City. . . ."[16]

Tulips were, in the course of the seventeenth and eighteenth centuries, to become even more important in Turkish culture. A Turkish traveler reported in 1630 that Constantinople contained eighty shops selling flowering bulbs supplied by three hundred growers. Under Sultan Ibrahim (1640–1648) the first chief florist was appointed, and in the following reign a council of florists was set up to regulate the quality of tulips and their sale. As the decision to fix prices in 1725 indicates, the Turkish fashion for tulip cultivation resulted in wildly rising prices, with one early-eighteenth-century tulip bearing the name of Sahipkıran, or "bankrupter." Tulips became so central to the culture of the court that a twentieth-century Turkish historian, Ahmed Refik, dubbed the era *Lâle Devri*, the Tulip Age. At this time, one might almost say the most important men in the empire were those with the greatest floral accomplishments. The Grand Vizier himself under Ahmed III, Ibrahim Pasha (1708–1730), was said to have more than five hundred thousand tulip bulbs in his garden and was given by Ahmed the nickname Schukjufé Perwera (tulip expert). Extraordinarily expensive court spectacles featuring tulips were one excuse for the Patrona Halil revolt in 1730 against the westernization of the state, which resulted in the execution of the Grand Vizier and Ahmed's abdication. Although the most prized tulips in Constantinople were very different from those so valued in Europe, having long pointed petals and a slim rather than rounded shape, ironically at least some varieties grown in Turkey had been imported from Europe, rather than the other way around. This reverse import trade, although not at first of any importance, seems already to have been in evidence at the beginning of the seventeenth century. When the United Provinces sent its first great embassy to Turkey in 1612, one of the many gifts taken along by the envoy, Cornelis Haga, was "200 bulbs of the best tulips," worth ƒ57.[17]

Popular mythology gives the credit for the introduction of the tulip into Europe to Ogier Ghislain de Busbecq, the Flemish envoy of the Holy Roman Emperor, Ferdinand II, to the Ottoman court. In the first of his published letters, dated September 1, 1555, Busbecq described his journey from Adrianople to Constantinople. "As we passed through this district we everywhere came across quantities of flowers—narcissi, hyacinths, and *tulipans* as the Turks call them. We were surprised to find them flowering in mid-winter, scarcely a favorable season. . . . The tulip has little or no scent, but it is admired for its beauty and the variety of its colors. The Turks are very fond of flowers, and, although they are otherwise anything but extravagant, they do not hesitate to pay several *aspres* for a fine blossom. These flowers, although they were gifts, cost me a good deal; for I had always to pay several *aspres* in return for them." In 1561, the botanist Conrad Gesner reported in his *De Hortis Germaniae* that in April 1559 he had seen in the garden of the Augsburg magistrate Johann Heinrich Herwart a plant that had been grown from seed from Byzantium or possibly Cappadoccia, which he described as similar to "a red lily." Gesner also saw tulips growing several years later, also in Augsburg, in the garden of the Fuggers, who, as bankers to many of the royal houses of Europe, were one of the wealthiest families extant in the sixteenth century. The assumption has always been made, for example by E. H. Krelage, the foremost authority on the history of the tulip in first part of the twentieth century, that the Augsburg tulips had been sent by Busbecq from Constantinople. However, although Busbecq was clearly interested in gardening and did send back bulbs and seeds, we cannot be sure either that he was responsible for the first tulips in Europe, or that the tulips in Augsburg were in fact the first. It is evident that tulip bulbs were making their way to Europe by a variety of routes and methods as trade in the Levant flourished in the mid-sixteenth century.[18]

One factor calling Busbecq's role into question is the dating of his letters. It was once believed that these were written either during or immediately after his embassy to Turkey, which ended in 1562, but it now appears that they were written in the 1580s, well after tulips became known in

Europe. It is also unclear whether the first tulips arriving in Europe were sent to Germany. L'Obel wrote in 1581, "It is a long time ago that, in Venice and Padua, we for the first time saw this Greek or Macedonian Lily . . . which were a beautiful purple color . . . after that we saw it in Florence and Genoa with a yellow and also a brown-red blossom." For that matter, there was little reason why the tulip should not have been known to Europeans earlier, as the areas where they grew in Asia Minor had been visited by Crusaders and merchants for centuries. The likelihood that it was trade, rather than Busbecq, that brought tulips to Europe is reinforced by the identification of wild tulips in Italy and Savoy that were closely related to the Asian varieties. Contemporary writers themselves recognized that at least some tulips (though not those considered the best) came from southern Europe rather than the Levant. Petrus Hondius, author of the country-house poem *De Moufe-Schans* (1614), said that the first tulips had come to the Netherlands from Narbonne, followed by the tulips of Bologna; only later, he said, did the Dutch become aware of the most beautiful tulips, from the east: Greece, Turkey, and Persia. It was certainly the case that the tulips depicted by the engravers working for people like Gesner, L'Obel, Dodoens, and Clusius had a very different shape from those popular in Turkey, being of a rounded, bell shape, rather than pointed and needlelike. It has been suggested that these tulips might in fact have been a wild species from Anatolia, perhaps sold more cheaply in the flower market of Constantinople than the more highly prized needle tulips, although others believe that they were a Turkish cultivated variety.[19]

The arrival of the tulip in the Netherlands is surrounded by a similar factual mist. As in the German lands, the northern and southern Netherlands were in contact with the Levant, chiefly through trade, and we hear stories of tulip bulbs appearing fairly early through these means, although quite some time after Gesner's encounters with tulips in Augsburg in the 1550s. In 1583 we hear from Clusius that a Mechelen merchant, Georgius or Joris de Rye, who had considerable botanical knowledge, had rescued some tulip bulbs that had been thrown away by an unsuspecting Antwerp merchant. The merchant had received the bulbs from Constantinople in a shipment of cotton cloth and, mistaking them for onions, had roasted a few and eaten them with oil and vinegar. Not surprisingly, from what we hear about the taste of tulip bulbs, he threw the rest into a pile of vegetable waste in his garden, where Rye happened to see them and recognize them for what they were. This resulted in Clusius himself being able to see several new varieties. Clearly this incident happened before 1583, but no date is given; the fact that Rye knew what he was looking at suggests even earlier contact with tulip bulbs, on his part at least. The earliest account we have of a tulip in the northern Netherlands is a bulb growing in the garden of the apothecary Walich Syvertsz in Amsterdam, who, at least later in the century, owned a garden outside the Jan Roodenpoort; again, no date is attached to this story, but we have no record of Syvertsz as a resident of Amsterdam until 1578. It is clear that trade made the arrival of tulips in the Netherlands at these early dates a possibility. The existence of Clusius made it a certainty.[20]

Carolus Clusius was himself from the southern Netherlands, born in Arras, which was then in Flemish territory (see fig. 3). He traveled extensively for his studies of plants, writing, for example, about the flora of Spain and southern Europe. He was also involved in the design of a number of private gardens, such as several belonging to his friend Marie de Brimeu, princesse de Chimay, and to the nobleman Jean de Brancion in Malines, where Clusius assisted from 1568 to 1573. In 1573 he was appointed director of the imperial botanical garden in Vienna, but when Maximilian II's son, Rudolf II, took the throne in 1577, he was dismissed, watching with grief as the medical garden was turned into a menagerie and his back pay proved difficult to obtain. Ultimately Clusius was persuaded to move, at an advanced age, to Leiden to take over the direction of the *hortus botanicus* in 1593. He died in 1608.[21]

Clusius was called by one friend, the Flemish neostoic philosopher Justus Lipsius, "the father of all the beautiful gardens of this land." His huge network of correspondents, with whom he exchanged both botanical information and seeds and bulbs, was responsible for much of the distribution of the tulip, not only through the southern and northern Netherlands, but also in Italy, France, and Germany. In this network, he was much more often the giver than the receiver. We know from Clusius' correspondence that he already possessed tulips before he went to Vienna. Several of his friends from the southern Netherlands had tulips from his store as early as 1570, well before the time of either Joris de Rye or Walich Syvertsz. The apothecary Jan Mouton in Tournai, for example, wrote to him in October 1570 to thank him for cyclamens, narcisi, and other flowers (some of which he had passed on to Jean de Brancion). "If

FIGURE 3. Jacob de Monte, *Portrait of Carolus Clusius*, c. 1584.
Leiden University Library.

I could be so much in his good graces," he begged Clusius in the polite
third person, "that it would please him to make the present of a large tu-
lypan (for through his grace & liberality I already have a small one). . . ."
Brancion wrote Clusius in July 1571 that he had collected "the seeds of
my tulipas" and replanted the bulbs and remarked that "George" had lost
the "large Yellow tulipa" Brancion had given him. Given that Clusius had
just spent years designing Brancion's garden, it is possible these bulbs
had also come from Clusius, although we know that Brancion himself on
at least one occasion in 1572 independently received bulbs and seeds of
"some turkish jollities," as a correspondent put it.[22]

When Clusius arrived in Vienna in 1573, through the contacts at the imperial court he was able to expand his horticultural universe. On arrival he encountered Ogier de Busbecq, who, expecting to depart for France the following year, gave him the seed of tulips he had received from Constantinople. He used these to conduct experiments on growing bulbs from seed, discovering, over six or more years, the kind of changes tulips undergo in these conditions and the kind of variations they can eventually produce: red, white, yellow, purple, and mixed and variegated colors. But, as Brancion's example has shown, it was not simply Busbecq's seed that came from Constantinople. Repeatedly Clusius mentioned in his letters tulips from "Byzantine seed," received by him, but also by the emperor and by private people, such as a noblewoman who sold him a bulb he called a treasure because of its rarity. It is clear that a constant stream of plants, seeds, and bulbs was coming into the imperial court from Turkey and that Clusius was redistributing these through his correspondence networks. These exchanges continued after Clusius lost his job and returned to Frankfurt, and indeed in Leiden and for the rest of his life.[23]

"I pray you to favor me (since you permit me to be so importunate with you) . . . to accommodate me with the seeds of whatever you have that is the most beautiful, including all the sorts of Tulipans," wrote the aged nobleman Saint-Maurice de Bellefontaine from Besançon in 1588. As we have seen from Jehan Somer's timid request for even one small tulip bulb in 1597, Clusius received such letters constantly. He was, in fact, more than generous with his bulbs and seeds: "no year passes," he told Joachim Camerarius in 1589, "without my handing out to my friends two or three hundred tulip bulbs which have borne a blossom." But such requests could be irritating. "Many people ask [flowers] of me. I give many of them away, although I also want my own garden to be beautiful. For why should I spend money and go to trouble, if I can experience no pleasure from my own garden? I would have to be insane only to drudge for others."[24]

But what did those others—Saint-Maurice, or Somer, or De Jonghe, or Brancion—actually want? Why did they feel so strongly about tulips? Justus Lipsius wrote amusingly in his neostoic treatise *De Constantia* of *liefhebbers'* immoderate love of flowers. "[T]hey do vaingloriously hunt after strange hearbs & flowers, which having gotten, they preserve & cherish more carefully tha[n] any mother doth her child: these be the

FIGURE 4. Peter Paul Rubens, *The Four Philosophers*, 1611.
Palazzo Pitti, Florence. Rubens portrays himself, his brother Philip,
and his friends Justus Lipsius (speaking) and Jan Wowerius, as
well as Lipsius' favorite dog, Mopsus. The closed tulips signify the two
members of the group who had died, Philip Rubens and Lipsius.

me[n] whose letters fly abroad into *Thracia*, *Greece*, and *India* only for a
little root or seede [.] These men will bee more grieved for the losse of a
newe-found flower, than of an olde friend. Would not any man laugh at
that Romane which mourned in blacke for the death of a fish that he had.

So do these men for a plant." But Lipsius himself, although advocating in *De Constantia* the use of gardens as places of rest, contemplation, and intellectual activity rather than focusing obsessively on rare plants, told Clusius when he sent him some tulip bulbs that these were "dearer to me than if you had sent me as many bulbs of solid gold or silver." What prompted such feelings?[25]

Some of the values of the *liefhebbers* are easily identifiable from their words as they plead with Clusius for a few of his precious bulbs or discuss what they sought as they boarded VOC clippers coming into Middelburg or Amsterdam. "Something strange" . . . "unknown to me" . . . "strange kinds of fruits, branches of trees, roots and herbs": it was novelty, exoticism, foreignness, unfamiliarity that drew these enthusiasts away from the traditional rose or violet. Somer did not long just for tulips from Clusius, but for tulips "of some strange colors" (*van eenige vremde colleuren*). It is easy now to forget that the tulip, so domestic, so *Dutch*, was at one time chiefly seen as "a strange and outlandish plant" (Rembert Dodoens), "foreign to us & a stranger" (Jean Franeau), among a host of flowers that were "strangers unto us . . . Out-landish flowers . . ." (John Parkinson). For Lipsius, this was not merely description but high praise. In *De Constantia* he expresses his wonder at the garden of his friend Charles Langius. "Againe, what plenty is here of flowers and hearbes? What strangenes and noveltie? In so much that nature seemeth to have compacted with in this little plot, whatsoever thing of price is comprised in this, or that new world."[26]

"Strangenes and noveltie" did not apply equally to every new plant brought into Europe in the sixteenth century. Horticulturalists, for the most part, did not wax rapturous about the glories of the runner bean. But the combination of novelty, exoticism, and beauty brought the tulip and other flowers into a complex of values about rarity, curiosity, and aesthetics that was a world away from the old values stressed by botanists and writers on gardening. Although this trend was gradually changing in the sixteenth century as natural history became a fashionable gentlemanly interest, horticultural writers had previously been interested only in the medicinal or culinary uses of plants. These views hung on into the seventeenth century, even as the aesthetic began to change. Thomas Hill's *Arte of Gardening* of 1608, for example, contained practically no flowers (certainly no tulips), and the roses, "lillies," peonies, and other flowers he did discuss were treated exactly like the herbs and vegetables. Although beauty was mentioned briefly, most of the flowers were given a long section detailing the "Phisicke helpes" they provided: "the oyle of Lillies doe greatly profit, by annointing on the belly, for that it healeth womens places, and softneth the humours there hardned." The fact that tulips had not been discussed by the ancient authors made the description of tulips doubly difficult, but a few uses were put forward, chiefly aphrodisiac. Joost van Ravelingen, who annotated the 1608 edition of Dodoens' *Cruydt-Boeck*, commented that "one can use the roots of Tulipans in salad with Oil and Vinegar as *Garlic*: for they taste good, or at least are not disgusting." He also found the consumption of tulip bulbs "very powerful . . . in increasing the desire to copulate." (John Parkinson in 1629 was a little more cautious: "for force of Venereous quality, I cannot say, either from my selfe, not having eaten many, or from any other on whom I have bestowed them," but since orchids were thought to have aphrodisiac powers, "I thinke this may as well have it as they.") But these attempts to find a use for tulips were, to say the least, half-hearted. John Gerard was already admitting in 1597 that nothing was known from the ancients about the "vertues of the *Tulipaes*," but that they "are esteemed especially for the beautie of their flowers." As we move further into the seventeenth century, we find that writers such as D. H. Cause have abandoned all question of utility. In his *Koningklycke Hovenier* he discussed the tulip first among all the flowers purely because it was so "outstandingly decorative."[27]

Beauty, in this case, was a matter of color. Although the shape and grace of tulips commanded attention—Parkinson wrote that "they carry so stately & delightfull a forme"—it was their color that gave them primacy even over other popular flowers entering Europe around the same time, such as the iris or the narcissus. In a poem from 1654 praising the author of the *Floriste françois*, the Sieur de la Chesnée Monstereul, Scudéry chided other flowers for thinking their colors might be matches for the tulip, when in fact the opposite was the case. The "unfortunate" narcissus, for example, was mistakenly in love with itself, but "your yellow color marks your extreme error." All the flowers—hyacinths, daisies, roses, peonies, carnations—whether from beyond the sea or not, "and a thousand others, as rare as they are beautiful," were instructed to "damp down your pride . . . Cede to the Tulip, & hide yourselves. She is incomparable, & nothing resembles her: She alone has more beauty than all of you together." Tulips had no scent, it is true (and if scent was what you liked, the carnation was preferable), wrote the professional gardener Pierre Morin. But some people wanted flowers "only if they are clothed in the richest colors, that is the most vivid ones, and diversified as well. These," Morin said, "will prefer the Tulip to the Rose or the Carnation."[28]

"Diversified" was the key to such a preference. Besides the brightness of the colors of tulips, their extreme variety produced a growing wonder in enthusiasts becoming more familiar with their own and others' tulips. Nature, wrote John Gerard in 1597, seems "to plaie more with this flower, than any other that I do know." Clusius noticed immediately that, particularly if tulips were grown from seed (a process that could take from five to ten years, during which time bulbs formed), they might eventually transform in color. Tulips grown from the seed of white tulips, which, Clusius found, were the most prone to variation, might continue to look like the mother plant, but also might suddenly change into plain or variegated versions of white, yellow, red, or purple. Yellows and reds might do the same, but were less likely to vary. Bulbs could also be propagated, and much more quickly, through the excision of offsets, which themselves could be planted, but these were less likely to change, at least for the same reasons as the flowers grown from seed. Cross-breeding, mutation, and disease could also produce new and different flowers, although these processes were purely accidental. The actual reasons for variation were not known to gardeners in the sixteenth and seventeenth centuries (the aphid-borne mosaic virus, which results in the variegated colors of the "broken" tulip, was not discovered until the twentieth century). This mystery itself added to the attraction, although for some it could be a worry, as tulips could grow worse as well as better.[29]

But it was the spontaneity of these changes, and their infinite variety, that so charmed the *liefhebbers*. "The more variety there is, the more beautiful the flowers are," we learn from the botanist Joost van Ravelingen's thrilled annotations in Dodoens' *Cruydt-Boeck*. "Every year one finds new varieties and sorts which no one has ever seen before. It is yellow, red, white purple, and (as some assert) blue: or two or three of the mentioned colors are mixed within one flower, that is in the middle, on the sides, or one or the other side of the petals, with speckles, stripes, or spots themselves beautifully embellished: sometimes the stripes are like flames, or winged, like bunches of feathers or plumage: Sometimes one color shines above the other: that is the white and the yellow have something red shining through: one seems like gold cloth, another silver cloth. . . ." The sense of wonder here is palpable. It was almost impossible for Van Ravelingen to describe all the variations on even one color, red or yellow, he found in the different flowers, but he felt he had to try. Various early yellow tulips were compared with "the rosiness of Gold," "the yellowness of Saffron," the "bleachedness of Lemons," and the color of "orange apples." The early red tulips were "thoroughly red, or reddish, that is dark red, beautiful light or high red, orange red, true red or vermilion red, blood red, carmine, incarnadine, or flesh-colored, sweet red, and dead or unsweet red, or yellow-brown: sometimes all these colors are mixed with yellow or with white, or other colors, which tend toward violets or blues . . . For you see these sort of Red Tulips, with gold-colored, yellow, white, or darker or lighter red, and also green and violet edges, stripes, rays, spots, and nerves, on the inside and on the outside, on the edges, on the back. . . . These varieties are more easily wondered at than described."[30]

We can see from both floral still life painting and the kind of flowers popular during the tulipmania that the excitement of variegation remained a paramount aesthetic consideration in the seventeenth century. An incident in 1635 in Haarlem demonstrates this. Two buyers, Pieter Jansz and Pouwels van Mackelenberch, only wanted flamed tulips and believed that only tulips like these were of value. Symon le Febure, who was supposedly selling them the tulips (he had actually already sold them to Jan Wynants, but that is another story), had told them, according to the unofficial broker Symon Sourijs, "that among the aforesaid group of *tulpaden*, were many beautiful flamed ones, which he himself did not know, and that the same flowers had cost him a hundred *pond Vlaams*," that is, ƒ600. (Not only were they beautifully marked, in other words, but they were new varieties and, consequently, even more praiseworthy and valuable.) The dissatisfied buyers, evidently now ducking out of a transaction gone wrong, were anxious to claim that this was not the case and that the tulips were nowhere near as wonderful as Le Febure had claimed. Witnesses, all of whom were active in the tulip trade, were called to recount what had actually been growing in Le Febure's garden. Salomon Seys, Abraham Rogiersz, Bastiaen Pouwelsz, and Jacob van Heede all swore that they had "with their eyes seen and found there many red and yellow tulips, and also many single colors, and no flamed ones, as four or five

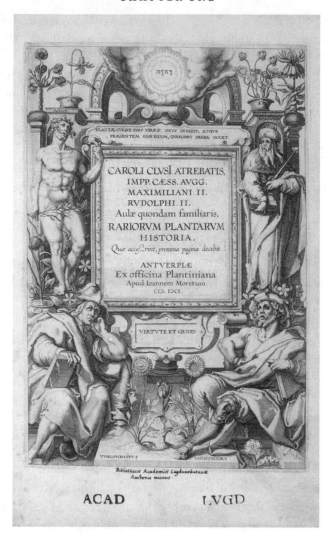

FIGURE 5. Title page of Carolus Clusius, *Rariorum plantarum historia*, 1601. Leiden University Library.

Cronen [which were single-colored], and five or six flamed Metermans, so that the witnesses all together with one voice declare, that the aforesaid whole group of flowers, was not worth twenty guilders." Plain tulips were as nothing; variegation was everything.[31]

Flamed, striped, or feathered tulips of these types quickly became the

FIGURE 6. Title page of Rembert Dodoens, *Cruydt-Boeck*,
1608 edition. Leiden University Library.

focus of attention in private gardens in the late sixteenth and early seventeenth centuries. We have seen from the townscape of Middelburg that Dutch towns were, toward the end of the sixteenth century, in the process of becoming more green. These developments were partly inspired by new reading matter, such as treatises by the botanists Dodoens, L'Obel, and Clusius (see figs. 5, 6, and 7), which were decorated with woodcuts displaying new and exotic plants and published mainly by the humanist Plantin press in Antwerp, and the less scholarly *florilegia,* books of engravings of plants, such as Emmanuel Sweerts' *Florilegium* of 1612 and Crispijn van de Passe's very influential *Hortus Floridus,* published in 1614 and reprinted with additions and in translation numerous times thereafter. Jan Mouton told Clusius that the reading of the botanist's *Rariorum aliquot Stirpium, per Pannoniam Historia* had inspired him to greed "in the way that a pregnant woman desires certain meats, etc., seeing the riches which you have brought to light." As an apothecary, Mouton was on the learned end of the market, and many enthusiasts of gardening, particularly as we move into the seventeenth century, would have been more attracted by the simple pictures of tulips, daffodils, and anemones available in Sweerts or Van de Passe. Despite the influence the rise of botanical gardens in the sixteenth century had on these developments, in the end the transformation of private gardens took them in the direction Clusius himself indicated in his own creation of the *hortus botanicus* in Leiden. Although utilitarian gardens with vegetables, kitchen herbs, and sometimes livestock did not depart from the urban scene, many urban gardens now took on a purely decorative function. This decoration, however, was a far cry from the lushness we now associate with the ideal private garden. As we can see from a famous engraving by Van de Passe (see fig. 8), they were by modern standards sparsely planted. Dutch gardens were known for their "neatness" and their comparative smallness. Plantings were made both in small, rectangular beds and in decorative patterns of swirls and knots, with large areas of bare ground surrounding rare and beautiful flowers like a frame around a painting. In most cases the owners of such gardens would have only a few specimens of these flowers. Because of their small numbers and the way they were planted, it was generally easy for owners to keep careful track of each flower and what it was; some owners kept garden books with the exact details of their floral treasures.[32]

As gardening became fashionable, first in the south, then in the northern Netherlands, it became the norm for members of urban elites to own one or more gardens. The pattern of city growth in the period of high immigration to the north alerts us to the increasing importance of gardening to urban culture. In Amsterdam, when the great canal ring

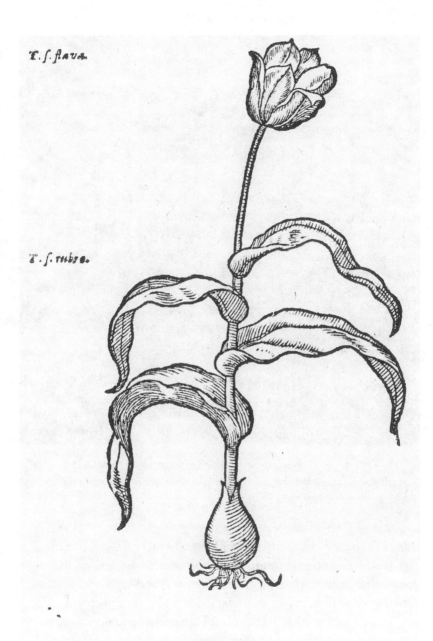

FIGURE 7. *Tulipa serotina flava* from Clusius, *Rariorum plantarum historia* (1601). British Library.

FIGURE 8. Crispijn van de Passe, *Spring*, from *Hortus Floridus*, 1614.
British Library. Note the widely spaced planting, typical of such gardens.

was built to extend the city beyond its medieval boundaries in the first half of the seventeenth century, the fashionable houses on the three great canals, the Herengracht, Keizersgracht, and Prinsengracht, were constructed with deep gardens behind them. The multiplicity of gardens depicted on the 1625 map by Balthasar Florisz van Berkenrode (see fig. 37, chap. 3) shows clearly that the rich elite that bought properties on these canals in the first expansion of 1614 wished to join in the fashion for gardening. Indeed, they were almost required to do so, as a city ordinance of 1615 specified that on the Keizersgracht, the 180-foot land parcels had to preserve 80 feet of land unbuilt. But Amsterdam gardens were not only to be found behind the new houses. Already in the mid-sixteenth century wealthy Amsterdammers were buying land for gardens outside the city walls: outside the St. Anthonispoort to the east, and particularly outside the Regulierspoort to the south, around the area of the present-day Rembrandtplein. This area, known as the *paden* for the long paths leading away from the city, was the site of various gardens owned by figures known to be *liefhebbers* of tulips early in the seventeenth century, such as Abraham de Goyer and Abraham Casteleyn, both of whom were also active in the tulipmania of the 1630s. Both men, indeed, were living in the *paden* in the 1630s, according to the tax register of 1631, and De Goyer was, presciently, already building up an empire of gardens on the Walepad, on the Weespad, and along the Singel through a series of land transactions starting at the beginning of the century. In Haarlem, where the town did not extend its city walls until 1680, large numbers of people lived outside the St. Janspoort and Kruispoort to the north and the Grote Houtpoort and Kleine Houtpoort to the south (see figs 9 and 10). Both these areas were important sites not only for the occupants' own gardens, but for the gardens of many wealthy town-dwellers, who would walk the ten minutes or so necessary from the center of town to enjoy their flowers in the spring and summer. The Rosenprieel (rose arbor), located outside the Kleine Houtpoort, was a favorite location for such gardens. An elegant example was sold by Grietgen Hendricxsdr in 1639 for *f*900: "a beautiful, pleasant and enjoyable garden, with a new well-built building within it, outside the Kleine Houtpoort . . . graced with many beautiful flowers, various large fruit trees . . . with a beautiful painted gallery with many painted seats with various histories, and many other agreeable features . . . [including] on the north side of the said Garden a particularly pleasant little play house. . . ."[33]

By mentioning pleasure gardens like Hendricxsdr's in the late 1630s, we have at first glance moved away from the botanical intensity of the gardens of apothecaries in cities like Middelburg, Tournai, or Brussels in the sixteenth century. Hendricxsdr's garden was one of fashion, with its painted gallery and playhouse for pleasant afternoon gatherings in summer, the kind of garden party scenes depicted by painters like Dirck Hals or Esaias van de Velde. Yet in getting this taste of the future, we have not necessarily moved so far from the ethos of the late-sixteenth-century *liefhebbers*. As we will learn later on, the fashionability of garden owner-

FIGURE 9. North side of Haarlem, with the St. Janspoort and
Kruispoort. Detail of Pieter Wils, map of Haarlem, 1649. British Library.
The map is oriented with the north on the left side.

{ 48 }

FIGURE 10. South side of Haarlem, with the Kleine Houtpoort and Grote Houtpoort. Detail of Pieter Wils, map of Haarlem, 1649. British Library.

ship did not necessarily preclude a *liefhebber*'s knowledge of and passion for flowers. Whether in the green enclaves behind the tall Amsterdam townhouses or the long array of walled gardens lining the Grote Houtweg in Haarlem, seventeenth-century enthusiasts were planting, experimenting, admiring their flowers.

In the late sixteenth century, as we have seen, flowers were already becoming central to the whole enterprise of gardening. Jan Mouton commented that in the area around Tournai, where he lived, most people were no longer general lovers of plants: "loving only what has beautiful flowers, according to their judgment, & having no use for the rest." And as tulips increasingly were praised for their exciting colors and patterns, gardens could become not only flower gardens but tulip gardens. Christiaen Porret, a learned Leiden apothecary who inherited many of Clusius' bulbs after his death in 1608, complained in 1610 that being a *liefhebber* was not what it used to be. He told his fellow floral enthusiast Matteo Caccini in Florence that he was able to maintain his garden with the help of "several connoisseurs" among his friends who had helped him liberally, but that, except for himself, most of the old *liefhebbers* of Clusius' time were dead. "The rest only have common flowers[,] except for tulips. Some of them are well furnished with those." This kind of specialization was attacked by Petrus Hondius in his poem *De Moufe-Schans* in 1614. Hondius is usually accused of complaining about the stupidity of the passion for tulips. In fact, he himself was a *liefhebber*, mentioned repeatedly as a breeder of tulips by Joost van Ravelingen in later editions of Dodoens' *Cruydt-Boeck*. He was eloquent about their variety and beauty: "All my art and all my knowledge are much too limited to measure the colors of Tulips"; painters would have to use all their powers to give these colors names. His own garden at his patrons' estate at Terneuzen had five or six beds of tulips, but, he said, it was silly only to breed one flower when it lasts only a few weeks per year, leaving the garden otherwise empty of color. He planted flowers that would bloom all year round, so that every week there was something new to be seen, but, he said, many others had gardens stocked purely with tulips. This was going too far: "here in the Netherlands so many idiots can be found who, in their gardens, can praise this flower alone."[34]

It is surely no coincidence that Mouton, Porret, and Hondius all had the same complaint about their fellow enthusiasts. Hondius dedicated this part of his poem to Porret, one of his friends and correspondents. Porret in his turn, like Jan Mouton, had been a friend and confidant of Clusius. He, like Clusius, was in touch with Matteo Caccini in Florence and with other *liefhebbers*. Although with Porret we are moving into the seventeenth century, in his example we still see the kind of communication and discussion of flowers so evident in the letters of Jehan Somer and others. Somer, we will recall, only wrote to Clusius at the urging of his fellow floral enthusiasts in Middelburg, one of whom had already communicated with Clusius about Somer's existence four years earlier. The tulips so prized in this period were, according to Dodoens, "only to be found in the gardens of the *liefhebbers*." That statement implies that this was a relatively exclusive world, something that, given the expense of maintaining a garden, should not surprise us. But its exclusivity is not the only feature we should note. It is also important that it *was* a world.

In this chapter we have considered how such people came in contact with tulips and what sorts of values made them fond of them. But these contacts, these values, are the result of a sociable universe that in itself demands exploration. Tulips did not become objects of desire in isolation; tulipmania, ultimately, was a cultural construct. Before investigating the complex of ideas and social relations that fueled this event in the seventeenth century, we should think a little about its roots in the sociability of the sixteenth.[35]

It was actually 1602 when Jean de Maes, Clusius' nephew, wrote to his uncle about L'Amoral de Tassis. L'Amoral was the son of the postmaster in Brussels and, De Maes was excited to report, had "many rarities, among others the double-flowered Jonquil, which he has in his Garden, which several have seen, I mean people worthy of trust, among others Sʳ le Conseiller vanden Brande, Monsieur du May also, have assured me of it." De Maes went to see him and learned that L'Amoral himself was planning to write to Clusius, to send him a bulb of the martagon pomponii "to start an acquaintance," as well as to send him portraits from life of the rare plants that he had in his garden. "This is the first time in my life that I have spoken to him, for the purpose of knowing whether it was true that he had the double Jonquil as I had heard. Several people claim to have it, but he actually does. I find him a very decent gentleman."[36]

De Maes' remarks about L'Amoral give us a picture of the world of the *liefhebbers* in one large Flemish town. L'Amoral's double jonquil was the talk of the Brussels elite. Conseiller vanden Brande was, clearly, a *regent*, and L'Amoral himself came from a family of officials and was soon after to become a courtier at the imperial court in Prague. The thrill of this rarity had some chasing to see it, others claiming themselves to possess it. (We know that Du May, one of the visitors of the jonquil, was a *liefhebber*; he had just sent Clusius, via Jean de Maes, three different anemones, offering at the same time anything he had in his garden and thanking him for the pale yellow martagon Clusius had sent, which he had handed on to De Maes, already having six or seven of the same thing. De Maes reported a great loss in Du May's tulips that spring.) De Maes, who had never met L'Amoral, found his curiosity about the existence of a double jonquil a sufficient reason to pay him a visit, and L'Amoral took the time not only to discuss the flower with him, but to show him others, such as a *pan porcin*, "white as snow," which had been sent to him from Italy, and a very beautiful double *heparica* of a "celestial blue." De Maes' relationship with Clusius was also useful to L'Amoral, who clearly wanted to expand his contacts in the horticultural world (although it appears that L'Amoral also happened to be the great-nephew of Jan Boisot, another *liefhebber* and an old friend of Clusius'; Boisot's sister was also a collector of flowers). Having De Maes write to Clusius about L'Amoral first eased his own path, and the gift L'Amoral proposed to send to Clusius—portraits of all his rare plants—was wonderfully appropriate, as it entailed the transfer of information not only to another *liefhebber*, but to the botanist best equipped to bring this information to the attention of everyone.[37]

We see here a busy and, most importantly, a *social* world of visits, letters, and exchanges with *liefhebbers* both within Brussels and elsewhere. Although Clusius, while he was alive, formed a central node of this community, it is clear that discussion and exchange of flowers was constant among other floral enthusiasts, not only in the towns of the southern and northern Netherlands but in England, France, the German lands, and Italy. Among countless examples, the Florentine nobleman Matteo Caccini, one of the great floral connoisseurs of Italy, corresponded with the Leiden apothecary Christiaen Porret and exchanged plants, including ones Caccini had received from Constantinople. Some of these Porret redistributed to other *liefhebbers*; in 1611 he gave some of Caccini's flowers to Jerome van Wingen of Tournai, "a man very curious about plants, animals, and other rarities, and well furnished with them," who wanted to make Caccini's acquaintance and to acquire some narcissi.

Part of the point of these exchanges was knowledge. Connoisseurs in different towns talked, when they could, about rare and unusual plants, what they looked like and how to grow them; Jan Mouton in Tournai mentioned discussing a rose without thorns with Boisot in Brussels in 1587; Boisot talked of the names Jean de Brancion was giving to his flowers. Clusius regularly heard from his correspondents about how their flowers were faring: Boisot reported in detail in 1582 the appearance and origins of his three best tulips, not to mention three grown by his sister, which were "among the most beautiful I have ever seen." Jean Robin, "herboriste" of Henri IV of France, traveled through Flanders in 1602, visiting gardens of churchmen, apothecaries, and other gardeners in multiple cities, discussing and collecting great numbers of plants and deliberately talking to as many *liefhebbers* as he could. Jacques Plateau, who spoke to Robin in Tournai, was curious about why he had gone to the trouble to travel all over the country when he could have acquired many of these plants from the same source. But it was clearly useful for Robin, who needed many contacts for his own knowledge and ability to supply the king's gardens, to cast his horticultural net as widely as he could. For Robin the need was professional, but for wealthy amateurs it was also more than fruitful to develop the sense of a community of floral connoisseurs. The 1618 edition of Dodoens gave the credit for the existence of furthering of flowers—"every day one sees remarks on something new, worthy of being drawn"—to "the diligence of the lovers of plants."[38]

The correspondence between Porret and Caccini is also telling in other ways: an apothecary (albeit one related to Christoffel Plantin) was exchanging gifts with a nobleman. The humanistic community of *liefhebbers* was one of social mixture, although, it must be said, mixture on a fairly high level. As we have already noted, owning a garden and acquiring rare plants and flowers required a healthy income. Although it is impossible to find out the true extent of the fashion for gardening, we can learn something about who was considered to be part of a horticultural community through references in letters and particularly the acknowledgments of *liefhebbers* we find in works such as the herbals by Dodoens and L'Obel. Crispijn van de Passe clearly saw the enthusiasts for tulips of the early seventeenth century as such a cohesive group that he

FIGURE 11. Adriaen van de Venne, scholar showing an aristocrat
a tulip, 1623. Koninklijke Bibliotheek, The Hague.

made a special register, updated in later editions, of *liefhebbers* (the word
he used) in Amsterdam, Utrecht, Haarlem, Leiden, Delft, Rotterdam, The
Hague, Gouda, Dordrecht, Brussels, Antwerp, Lille, Valenciennes, Stras-
bourg, Cologne, Frankfurt, Vienna, and Prague. For Dordrecht, Vienna,
and Prague he was forced simply to list "unknown Liefhebbers," but he
apologized to anyone he had not included, saying that "this comes from
the fact that they are unknown to me, I hope that with time I will come to
know of them." Although the various lists overlap in several ways—the
prominence of apothecaries and doctors, naturally interested in plants,
for example—it seems fair to say that the names we find in L'Obel and Dodoens are more likely to come from noble families than later lists like Van
de Passe's. L'Obel's and Dodoens' contacts, not to mention most of Clu-

sius', were in the southern Netherlands, where, by the time of the Dutch Revolt, noble families were more prominent than in Holland and Zeeland. A fair proportion of these southern connoisseurs were also well-off professionals or merchants, however, and it was particularly the immigration to the north of this section of the gardening community that was responsible for much of the interest prompting Van de Passe's register from the mid-1610s. L'Obel's list in 1581 includes a variety of nobles, highborn officials, and wealthy people, many of whom were also in touch with Clusius: the Prince de Chimay; Marie de Brimeu (later princesse de Chimay); Philips de Marnix van Sint Aldegonde, an important figure during the Revolt; Matthias Laurin, treasurer-general of Flanders; Jan van Hoboken, *greffier* of Antwerp; Jan van Brancion; Jan Boisot; Jan Mouton; Joris de Rye; "and other good friends." When Jean Franeau, a southerner, came along in 1616 with his long poem praising flowers and particularly the tulip, he said that tulips were cultivated by "*les grans*," many of whom he named. The prevalence of nobles was so great that Franeau even felt compelled to explain that aristocrats could cultivate these precious objects without fearing the threat of *dérogeance*, losing their noble status for being involved in trade. This was, after all, *agriculture*.[39]

Van de Passe, like Franeau, was part of a somewhat later generation, and his registers of around 1615 concentrated on the north, particularly Utrecht, Amsterdam, and Haarlem. They contain names we will come to know in the 1630s, such as Abraham Castelyn, Outger Cluyt, Abraham de Goyer, Volckert Coornhart, and Andries Rijckaert in Amsterdam, or Andries de Busscher, Balthasar de Neufville, Pieter Bol, and Johan Quackel in Haarlem. With the exception of Cluyt (a doctor and the son of Dirck Cluyt, Clusius' apothecary assistant in the Leiden *hortus* and himself a well-traveled botanical collector), all the others on this list were merchants. Yet, as we will be discussing later, the sense of a community of *liefhebbers* does not desert this group despite its somewhat different social origins and the probable lack of correspondence with the great humanistic botanists of the era. In the seventeenth century, in France, England, and Italy, as well as the Netherlands, there continues to be a culture of sociable exclusivity about the tulip connoisseurs. This is clear in the writings of Nicolas de Valnay and the Sieur de la Chesnée Monstereul, Parisian advocates of tulip culture and, in the case of Valnay, an officer at court; but in other ways it was also true of the less courtly tulip connoisseurs in Haarlem in the 1630s. Valnay wrote in the 1680s that the way to learn to love flowers was to "confer with a Curieux, have his flowers, visit your gardens and his together, and remember some of what is said." The image could easily come from a hundred years earlier. So, in many ways, could La Chesnée Monstereul's plea, in a special chapter of his *Le Floriste françois*, that the tulip should not be allowed to become common property. To make them available to everyone would, he said, "take away the most praiseworthy interaction to occur among Men, & deprive them of the sweetest society there is among people of honor. How much does their rarity give in knowledge to curious Spirits? how many agreeable visits? how many sweet conversations? & how many solid discourses? This is certainly the sweetest life in the world . . ."[40]

The existence of such a community of like-minded people was naturally useful for the spread of botanical knowledge and an important factor in the rising interest in flowers in general. But, as Valnay and other lauders of the communal aspect of tulip culture could testify, the concentration of a well-off group on the acquisition and cultivation of one precious and fragile object was not necessarily a recipe for longstanding harmony. Alongside the continuing wonder at the beauty of new and better flowers lurked a competitive impulse to acquire those flowers or to outdo one's fellows in their propagation. Lipsius, weighing up in *De Constantia* the pros and cons of gardens for pensive neostoics desiring to avoid the conflicts of the world, found an obsession with flowers a hypocritical way to spend one's supposed retirement from society. Those who get "new or strange" flowers, he wrote, only boast of them, and "His companions doe grudge and envie at him, yea some of them return home with a heavier heart, than ever did *Sylla* or *Marcellus* when they were put backe in their suit for the Pretorship. What should I call this but a kinde of merrie madnesse? not unlike the striving of children about their little puppets and babbies."[41]

The comparison with children quarreling over dolls would not have pleased the many enthusiasts involved in disputes over flowers. Our Middelburg *liefhebbers*, for example, so supportive of Jehan Somer's tentative desire to make contact with Clusius, were at the same time in competition with each other for Clusius' favors, as Johannes de Jonghe indicated in a letter to Clusius in 1596. The city doctor Tobias Roels had begged De Jonghe to give him a martagon from Constantinople, promising that he would share whatever Clusius sent him later. But, he complained, De Jonghe "is not behaving either with justice or trustworthiness," for in fact "he is keeping it all for himself alone." This minor incident was only one of many, and a token of an impulse prevalent throughout the flower-loving part of Europe. In Italy in the seventeenth century, for example, because of the failure by the Prince of Caserta to provide one promised bulb of a pink narcissus, the Monsignore Acquaviva became obsessed with buying plants to make him envious, determined at the same time never to give the prince "another thing in my life." And in France Valnay wrote in the mid-seventeenth century about the struggle to get one of the chief tulip connoisseurs of Paris, a M. Lombard, to pass along some of the stock of what Valnay called "the only beautiful tulips there are in the world." Lombard himself had had to coax a mere one of these out of another connoisseur, M. Laure, and now "Monsieur Lombard did not want to communicate them to anyone, which augmented the desire & the price." Only age persuaded him to accept several thousand *écus* for his "treasure," and after a long series of "sales, exchanges, and accommodations," by the 1680s the main stock of the best Parisian tulips was in the hands of Valnay and a few others.[42]

"Which augmented the desire & the price": Lombard's behavior raises another issue that complicates the vision of a harmonious world of tulip connoisseurs. Particularly because tulips *were* so desired, they could not in fact be compared with Lipsius' silly dolls. They were far too valuable for this. The appropriate behavior for dignified gentlemen pursuing a learned pastime within the context of a humanistic community was to exchange willingly; gifts, not sales, were the means of prosecuting these interlocking personal and intellectual relationships. But exchange, and friendship too, becomes more strained when the objects in question are not mere tokens, but expensive and coveted. Market forces began to intrude on a world that otherwise (despite its many merchant members) was not of the market. In the circumstances, the commodification of the tulip was unavoidable. That did not make it less troubling for the *liefhebbers*.

One result of tulips becoming a valuable commodity was their lack of security. Burying valuable items in the ground, even in a walled, locked garden, is not safe. Clusius and other tulip connoisseurs suffered numerous thefts. Usually the culprit was a servant or a gardener, or so the victims suspected, but it was often impossible to be sure. Clusius, who had the most to steal, was repeatedly robbed, in Vienna, Frankfurt, and Leiden, losing bulbs every year between 1580 and 1584, with further thefts in later years. In 1581 his servant disappeared along with some very important plants, which were then sold, along with some chests of bulbs that turned up for sale in Antwerp with the bulbs labeled in the servant's own handwriting. The following year he had to report that most of his prized and variegated tulips had been stolen. Frustratingly, he saw some of his flowers thereafter in the garden of an aristocratic Viennese lady, who denied having bought them from Clusius' servant, even though no one else bred such flowers besides Clusius. In Leiden in the 1590s he was robbed several times, to the point that in 1596, having lost more than a hundred of his most beautiful tulips, he nearly gave up on the idea of having a garden. His friend Marie de Brimeu offered him the use of her own garden, plus "a couple of good dogs" and a guard to spend nights in the garden until the thief was caught. But she herself lost her best tulips from her garden in Liège in 1602, and every single flower from the same garden in 1603. The same stories were told throughout the community of *liefhebbers*: Jan van Hoghelande's gardener copied the keys to his Leiden garden and stole everything he was intending to plant in 1591; Jan Mouton, old and ill in 1585, finally was able to hobble to his neglected garden but found "many losses among my rare plants." Gardeners, more than anyone, knew the value of these rare bulbs and flowers. The availability of bulbs on a wider scale, coupled with the development of new and rare breeds, must have made the desire to steal irresistible for some just as the value of the rarest was rising. L'Obel, depressed over constant thefts, sighed in 1601 that "goodness and sincerity are deteriorating. . . ."[43]

But with tulip bulbs so valuable, issues of goodness and sincerity arose even when outright theft was not at stake. Just as values of cooperation and exchange were called into question by the competitiveness of some tulip connoisseurs, a certain change of ethos was necessary within the culture of *liefhebbers* to accommodate the infiltration of the market. This was a shift of values, but perhaps not so great a one as some have claimed. It is evident that, from at least the mid-1570s, people were selling rare plants and flowers in Europe. Clusius mentions sellers of hellebore in Vienna in 1576, for example, and in the 1580s we hear from Jacques Plateau of public sales of flowers in Brussels. By the turn of the century

Jean de Maes was remarking repeatedly on the presence in Brussels of French plant sellers such as a M. Nicolas from Paris, or Falquin Baltin, who arrived in 1601 with large numbers of dogstooth violets, hyacinths, narcissi, and other exotic plants.

Although purchasing flowers from such tradesmen was different from the traditional exchange relationships of the *liefhebbers,* this certainly did not stop the *liefhebbers* from buying. Camerarius bought seed from a seller in 1574, and Clusius wrote that he would like not only seed but a catalogue of the rare plants the man had available. Jean de Maes was clearly not pleased by the presence in Brussels of what he called *tracasseurs* (plaguers) selling flowers such as pale yellow martagons, but his account of the problems "*amateurs*" had had with them suggests that sales were in fact brisk.[44]

In some ways the exclusivity of the world of the *liefhebbers* was offended by this trade, especially as the sellers, particularly local ones, were increasingly not to be found among the connoisseurs of flowers. (Baltin, it is true, at least claimed to have a forty-year acquaintance with Clusius.) Jacques Plateau said in 1586 that tulips of various colors were now fairly common in Brussels, because "several artisans [*mecaniques*] are selling them publicly"; in 1602 Jean de Maes, also in Brussels, said that "practically everyone in this town" was selling flowers. For the elderly humanist Clusius, this was something of a betrayal of his social and cultural values. It was true that the humanistic botanical community was a mixed one—apothecaries corresponding with noblemen, the minor noble Clusius with princes—but this community did not extend to the lower orders. In 1594 Clusius wrote to Lipsius about his depression over the state of affairs. Too many people were getting involved with flowers, selling them, and asking Clusius for presents. For him, it was too much. "This pursuit [gardening] will in the end be cheapened, my dear Lipsius, because even merchants, yes even artisans, low-grade laborers, and other base craftsmen are getting involved in it. For they can see that rich men sometimes hand out much money in order to buy some little plant or other that is recommended because it is so rare, so that they can boast to their friends that they own it. To hell with those who started all this buying and selling! I have always kept a garden, sometimes for my own pleasure, sometimes so that I might serve my friends, who, I saw, took pleasure in that pursuit. But now, when I see all these worthless people, sometimes even those whose names I have never heard, so impudent in their requests, sometimes I feel like giving up my pastime altogether."[45]

Clusius felt that his world of *liefhebbers* was getting too wide; everyone was asking him for flowers, and some people were even selling them. He wanted the community to remain small and limited to a certain social level. But these views were not necessarily shared by other *liefhebbers*. Jean de Maes had plenty of complaints about the sale of flowers in Brussels by the *tracasseurs* (the word Clusius used was *rhizotomi*, root-cutters). But this was not because of the act of selling, but rather because they appeared to be cheating their clientele. The Frenchmen selling pale yellow martagons will probably have deceived their purchasers, he said in 1602, in the same way that they did with the yellow cyclamens, which have since proven to be "vulgar." They had promised rare plants from the Pyrenées; "time will tell us if they are Imposters." This is quite a different sentiment from Clusius'; in moderation, the commodification of flowers was, for someone like Jean de Maes, a reasonable, even a useful development, as long as the sellers were honest.[46]

These values could extend to the behavior of *liefhebbers* themselves. It was not unknown for connoisseurs to buy from each other, even in this early period. Marie de Brimeu, for example, proposed buying yellow fritillaries and double jonquils from Dirck Coornhart in Amsterdam in 1601; Coornhart's son, Volckert, is one of Van de Passe's *liefhebbers*, and it is evident from other documents that he was simply following up on the activities of his father. More telling, however, is the example of Jan Boisot in Brussels. A longstanding *liefhebber* and friend of Clusius and other botanists, Boisot was thinking in mercenary terms around the same time that Clusius was bemoaning this development. Of one flower he had received from Lille, he remarked in 1592 that "if this bulb would continue to flower like this every year it would be of great value." In 1599 he and other connoisseurs were the subject of complaint by Jean de Maes, who was taking up serious gardening. "You have to buy everything. Friends are not friends in this profession, on the contrary, no one is looking these days for anything other than profit. Even Monsieur Boisot, who has such a great abundance of [flowers] that it seems as if the whole orient is spread out at his place, is so cheap, that he would rather give an *écu* than one Hyacinth bulb."[47]

In the tulipmania, we are often told, the values of the *liefhebbers* were swept aside by the crass commercialism of an unthinking mob. This came, we hear, from the lack of understanding of those buying and selling flowers, who, had they stuck to the pure values of the connoisseurs and experts, would never have lost their heads to the lure of profit. But if we look at the *liefhebbers* of the sixteenth and early seventeenth centuries, we can see that this story is not so simple. Their aesthetic values, their concept of rarity, their thrill when they found "something strange" was always paramount—but so was it in 1636, as it had been fifty years earlier. Their desire to form a community of information, discussion, and exchange was always an ideal—but so, as we will see later, was it in 1636. The commodification of the tulip began long before the tulipmania, and although it represented a transition from the values of someone like Clusius, it was, nevertheless, part of the experience of being a *liefhebber*.

In 1618, Joost van Ravelingen wrote about which tulips were the most prized in the northern Netherlands. "Here in this country people value most the flamed, winged, speckled, jagged, shredded, and the most variegated count for most," he wrote. But his next words are telling: "and the ones that are the most valued, are not the most beautiful or the nicest, but the ones which are the rarest to find; or which belong to one master, who can keep them in high price or worth."[48] As these words show, we are here in the midst of a complex of ideas about beauty and rarity, but also about the market. "Something strange" could also be—indeed almost certainly would be—something expensive. This was as true for art as it was for tulips. In the next chapter we will find out how.

TWO

~~~~~~

Art & Flowers

AUGUST 17, 1635, FOUND THE NOTARY JAN DE VOS standing outside the house of Marten Kretser in Amsterdam. He was there to make an *insinuatie*, an oral warning or request made on behalf of a client, usually as a prelude to further legal action. In this case, De Vos represented Jan Hendricxsz Admirael in a transaction that was already foundering in problems. Four days earlier informal arbitration (*uijtspraecke van goede mannen*), itself a sign of difficulties, had determined what should happen next, and Admirael was irritated that it was not going along as planned. On August 16, in the presence of the professional gardener Willem Willemsz, Admirael had brought Kretser "certain tulip bulbs," just as the arbiters the two men had chosen had agreed, though he still owed Kretser ƒ180 in addition to the bulbs. But Kretser was not fulfilling his part of the bargain. In return for the bulbs and the money, he was supposed to have sent Admirael "eleven paintings by various masters plus a print by Lucas van Leyden," but, De Vos announced to him, "you, the insinuated one, have only put one of the paintings in his hands and are refusing under an unfounded pretext or through a frivolous objection to deliver him the rest of the paintings and the print." Admirael demanded prompt delivery of the pictures; only then would he pay the additional ƒ180.

People being insinuated were supposed to give an answer, although frequently it was something deliberately bland, such as "I hear and see" or "I want a copy" of what the notary had said. In this case, Kretser was more forthcoming. "I have never refused to make the delivery," he said, "and I am still prepared to do so." But he demanded that Admirael make a money guarantee that the bulbs would ultimately be found to be the ones that Admirael had sold, and which were described in the decision of the arbiters. These were not idle requests. It was August, and the bulbs had probably been out of the ground for several months: small brown onions that could produce a beautiful, flamed red and yellow tulip, *or* a drab and unexciting plain yellow one. There was no way for Kretser (or, for that matter, for Admirael) to know.[1]

We must presume that Admirael decided the paintings and (what was clearly most important to him) the print by Lucas van Leyden were worth the trouble, as no further account of a quarrel appears in the archives. The case, like so many conflicts over tulips both before and after the crash of February 1637, raises numerous issues about trust, proof, and the nature of business transactions in seventeenth-century Holland. Here another question also intrigues us: why were tulips being exchanged for *paintings*? What did it mean for people like Admirael and Kretser to be interested in both? What did these objects mean to them? How did tulips fit into the world of art and art collecting? And how did this overlap between the two relate to the tulipmania of the 1630s?[2]

Neither Admirael nor Kretser was a stranger to either tulips or paintings. We do not know very much about either one of them, but we do know that. Admirael, who lived on the Prinsengracht (in what is now Prinsengracht 525), was a wealthy man; in 1636 he was in the process of building eight houses, and when he remarried in 1643 the amount of money carried forward for his children from his previous marriage was ƒ10,000 (see fig. 12). It is not clear what Admirael's profession was. When he married he was listed as "clerq," but in 1643 he was referred to as "father of the limecarriers"—a similar title to one held earlier by his father, presumably denoting a leader in the plaster trade. Admirael was a new name; at the time of his first marriage in 1627 he was still known as Jan Hendricxsz van der Bent, and it seems it was his father, Hendrick, who chose the new name. (Jan Hendricxsz's son Barend, however, had reverted to Van der Bent by the time of his father's death in 1662).[3]

FIGURE 12. Far left: house purchased by Jan Hendricxsz Admirael in 1643 (now Prinsengracht 483). Rijksdienst voor de Monumentenzorg, Zeist.

The prosperous Admirael was to be found everywhere in the tulip trade in Amsterdam in the 1630s. He owned two gardens, one behind his house on the Prinsengracht, the other further north, in the Rozenstraat, at an address referred to as *inden Bloemhof* ("in the flowergarden"). Besides selling to Kretser, he seems to have been involved in a variety of transactions ("diverse purchases and sales of tulips") with the broker Cornelis van Breugel. In December 1635 Admirael sold an offset of a Pargoens Schilder to Willem Hendricksen Verwer; in the spring of 1636 he became involved in the sale of tulips to the engraver Simon van Poelenburch; and in January 1637 he sold "various Tulpa" from his garden to the merchant Pouwels de Hooge. He was also involved in out-of-town trade: he bought tulips from the Alkmaar innkeeper Wouter Bartholomeusz Winckel, whose estate sale in February 1637 yielded the highest prices recorded for tulips, and from 1636 onward he was embroiled in a quarrel over some tulips he had sold to the rector of the Latin School in Alkmaar, Wilhelmus Tiberius (also known as Puteanus). Admirael was close to another major tulip dealer, Jeronimus Victory (originally Vittori), an Italian who had turned his attention from insurance and freighting ships to floral matters in the 1630s. Victory acted as arbiter in various disputes between Admirael and Van Breugel, and in September 1635, Admirael bet Victory a tulip bulb, the Generael Gouda, that within six months the fortress of Schenckenschans (at that time in the hands of the Spanish enemy) would be regained by the Dutch Republic, a bet Admirael would have narrowly lost had the bulb not turned sickly within a month and the wager been abandoned.[4]

But, as in the Kretser case, in many of these transactions tulips were intertwined with art. Several of Admirael's contacts were artists or art lovers. For example, Simon van Poelenburch, himself very active in the tulip trade—we even find him selling tulips while living in Paris in 1617—was an engraver; his sister Maria was married to the well-known Haarlem engraver Jacob Matham, the stepson of Hendrick Goltzius. In 1639 Admirael had dealings with the art dealer Hans van Conincxloo, dealings which, it has recently been conjectured, involved the exchange of art for tulip bulbs. And Admirael himself bought art: at the important Jan Basse sale in March 1637 he bought a portrait and four small paintings, and toward the end of his life, in 1660, we hear that drawings had been stolen from his collection and that he transferred a number of his paintings to the

Reformed church in Diemen. Admirael's desire to trade tulip bulbs for Kretser's paintings and print was clearly part of a longstanding interest in art.[5]

Of Marten Kretser's passion for art we can have no doubt. His possession of the eleven paintings and the Lucas van Leyden print should tell us something about that. But in the 1630s he is something of a nebulous figure. We know that he was from Amsterdam and that when he married in 1626 he lived on the Keizersgracht; when he made his deal with Admirael, he was 37. Like Admirael, he owned a garden with tulips and was clearly buying and selling from it; several deals in Haarlem in 1636 involved tulips he had bought or that were presently in his garden. In 1635 he (along with Rembrandt) was a buyer at the major sale of prints and drawings from the estate of Barend van Someren. Kretser's later activities in the Amsterdam art world, however, become clearer to us. Possibly having trained as a painter, he eventually became one of the more important "gentleman dealers" of the mid-seventeenth century in Amsterdam. In 1645 he seems to have undertaken to supply the market, making a contract with the artist Pieter van den Bosch to paint any pictures Kretser ordered him, from dawn to dusk in winter and from 7 A.M. to 7 P.M. in summer, for a salary of ƒ1,200. Kretser also acted as an expert appraiser on several occasions in the 1650s. But he was chiefly known as a collector. His famous collection of paintings, which he sold in 1650, contained works by Titian, Rubens, ter Brugghen, Bassano, Rembrandt, Poelenburgh, Lastman, Honthorst, Mor, Dürer, Fabritius, Asseleyn, and many more. Indeed, the same year saw a laudatory poem by Lambert van den Bos, the *Konst Kabinet van Marten Kretzer*, which spent 120 stanzas praising Kretser's taste in art. Bos called him a "Lover of Art" and a "Maecenas." He was one of the directors of the Amsterdam theater in the 1640s; in 1653 he founded a Brotherhood of Painting, a society of one hundred painters, poets, and lovers of poetry and art, which met for the first time on October 20, 1653, and was, in turn, praised in several poems by Jan Vos and Thomas Asseleyn. For us, these activities were in the future, but in the 1620s and 1630s we see Kretser moving in this direction, as his dealings with Admirael suggest. He was also moving in the same world as other tulip buyers and sellers. The godfather of his daughter Maria in 1635 was the tulip grower and silk merchant Abraham de Goyer, whom we have already met. And in 1633 the godfather of his daughter Christina was none other than Hans van Conincxloo—who, like Kretser, became embroiled over paintings and, it is conjectured, over tulips, with Jan Hendricxsz Admirael.[6]

One thing we can conclude from these recurring relationships is that the group of tulip dealers and buyers was closely knit. We will be exploring this later on. But for now, the first thing we learn from the experiences of Marten Kretser and Jan Hendricxsz Admirael is the interconnectedness of tulips and art. The collecting of art seemed to go with the collecting of tulips. This meant that the tulip craze was part of a much bigger mentality, a mentality of curiosity, of excitement, and of piecing together connections between the seemingly disparate worlds of art and nature. It also placed the tulip firmly in a social world, in which collectors strove for social status and sought to represent themselves as connoisseurs to each other and to themselves.

An interest in collecting was, at the beginning of the seventeenth century, a new and increasingly fashionable activity for European elites (see plate 8). Collecting has often been seen as a taste beginning with the great princes of Europe—the collection of Rudolf II, who had gathered together a circle of artists at his court in Prague, was the most celebrated of his age—but it is now becoming clear that at the same time, from the mid-sixteenth century on, aristocrats, wealthy merchants, and professionals such as doctors and lawyers were also forming similar collections, even if they were not as packed with natural and artistic wonders as Rudolf's *Kunstkammer.* In chapter 1 we saw such collections in the making, as apothecaries, doctors, and city officials in Middelburg and Amsterdam boarded ships from the Indies in search of exotica. This was hardly limited to the towns of the Netherlands—similar language was used by the Duke of Buckingham, who told his agent, Balthasar Gerbier, to collect "any thing that Is Strang"—and, as numerous recent studies have shown, collections of both artifacts and natural exotica flourished in Italy, France, central Europe, and England. But Buckingham's instructions to Gerbier, who frequently operated in Flanders and the Netherlands, were in fact à propos. Because of the trade with the Indies beginning at the end of the sixteenth century, the northern Netherlands became known as a center of collectibles. As princes, aristocrats, and wealthy burghers throughout Europe began to adhere to

FIGURE 13. A famous seventeenth-century cabinet of curiosities belonging to Ole Worm. Ole Worm, *Museum Wormianum*, 1655. Leiden University Library.

the fashion of collecting art, artifacts, *naturalia*, and exotica, they dispatched buying agents like Gerbier to the Netherlands. In 1608 a group of Venetians visited Amsterdam to purchase curiosities; in 1609 Rudolf II authorized the purchase of Indian exotica, flowers, shells, crabs, and ethnographic rarities; in 1612 Pierre Desmartin, curator of the king of France's cabinet, requested permission from the States-General to export a variety of "rarities" he had bought for the king. Such items were becoming available in specialist shops. The premises of apothecaries, many of whom, as we have seen, had both a personal and a professional interest in rare plants, also often became places to buy curiosities of many other kinds, and other shops with both art and rarities began to appear in Dutch towns. The schoolmaster David Beck wrote in his diary in 1624 of visiting the *Const-winckel* (art shop) of "de Jonge" Mieroop and seeing there "Antiquities, rarities, coins, shells, Vessels, Jewels, little paintings etc." The visit was one of politeness—Beck gave Mieroop five old coins and Mieroop reciprocated with a print of Hendrick van Nassau by W. Delf and a few shells—but Beck is clear in his identification of the place as a shop, not simply a collection. Many visitors to the country recounted visits to such shops. In 1663 the English traveler Philip Skippon went to the shop of Christopher van der Mulen in Rotterdam, where "we saw *Brasilean* spiders teeth, rattles of *Indian* snakes, the rind of an *Indian* apple," and a host of other curiosities.[7]

Visitors to the country often remarked on the widespread ownership of pictures and other collectibles. A German on a diplomatic mission with the Duke Ludwig Friedrich zu Wurttemberg wondered in 1610 at the "many beautiful paintings in individuals' homes, And the many Indian rarities. . . ." Where pictures are concerned, in modern scholarship about collecting it is practically impossible to escape remarks such as John Evelyn's statement in 1641 that "'tis an ordinary thing to find a common Farmor lay out two, or 3000 pounds in this Commodity, their houses are full of them. . . ." But most of the recent work on the art market, based largely on inventories, has suggested that Evelyn was unlikely to have known what was in the homes of common farmers and that in fact it took wealth to collect pictures. The same was true of other kinds of curiosities, if they were collected on any kind of scale. However, modest ownership of pictures and rarities was within the capability of self-employed merchants and master craftsmen due to the increase in purchasing power that came with the flourishing Dutch economy in the first half of the seventeenth century. In the mid-seventeenth century in Delft, around two-thirds of the population owned paintings of some kind, and it is estimated that average ownership of paintings at this time among the burghers of the Holland towns ranged between five and eleven simple pictures.[8]

What was needed to make a real collector, as opposed to someone who happened to have some curiosities and pictures, was not only wealth and the opportunity offered by the trade of the Netherlands, but also the *desire* to collect and the knowledge of what was worth collecting. Many theories have been offered about what drives people to collect. One view prevalent in accounts of seventeenth-century Holland is a search for social status. Collecting came later to the northern Netherlands than it did to the previously wealthier, and more aristocratic, south. Numerous paintings depicting collections by artists like Frans Francken or Willem van der Hecht testify that by the late sixteenth century *liefhebbers* of art and collectibles in Antwerp were becoming a self-conscious group, one that even identified itself by this name (*liefhebber der scilderyen*) as its members joined the painters' St. Lucas Guild even though some were not painters (see plate 8). One of the motivations of these southern merchant collectors, as we can see from their self-presentation as elegantly dressed nobles in *Kunst-kammer* paintings, was to appear aristocratic even though they were not: collecting was, in the end, an activity still identified with the elite. As we saw earlier with flowers and rare plants, not to mention with trade, these southern trends proved influential for later developments in northern collecting. While it was not true that all collectors of paintings, rarities, or both were southerners, analyses of the origins of collectors in the north in the early seventeenth century suggest that a sizeable proportion were immigrants from the south; indeed it has been claimed that practically all collections of paintings from the period 1590–1630 belonged to displaced Flemings. Some, like the extremely wealthy Jan Nicquet, brought their collections with them. Along with paintings, however, southerners also imported the view that collecting was an elite enterprise, a sign of social success. Thus someone wishing to climb the ladder of society would feel it necessary to have a collection to show that he also had taste. A well-known, if controversial, example of this use of collecting as a means of grasping at status is Rembrandt. Rembrandt's large collection of art— he was a major buyer at the Amsterdam Weeskamer (Orphan's Chamber) auctions in the first part of the seventeenth century—as well as natural history objects, shells, and ethnographic curiosities was clearly a subject of fascination for him, as we can see from its frequent appearance in his art. But as R. W. Scheller has argued, it might also have been designed to further a project (perhaps evident when he married Saskia van Uylen-burgh, who was above him in station) of acquiring social and professional status by emulating the wealthy merchants of his day. (If so, the plan did not work.) In the same fashion, one of the most famous merchants' collections of the period, belonging to the brothers Gerard and Jan Reynst, far from being painstakingly built up through the Reynsts' taste and contacts, was simply bought wholesale in the 1630s from the Venetian nobleman Andrea Vendramin as a tool for social enhancement. Despite the fact that most of the collection therefore failed to say much about the Reynsts as collectors, it had its desired effect; it was so renowned that it was visited by a variety of notables, including, in 1638, Amalia van Solms, the wife of the stadholder Fredrik Hendrik.[9]

Most art historians have considered such collections to be art collections, because they usually contained paintings. The passion of Dutch art historians, beginning with Abraham Bredius in the early twentieth century, for printing inventories has not led to a correction in this view, as usually anything other than traditional art objects has simply been omitted. But in fact a collection like the Reynsts' was as well known for its natural curiosities, minerals, and ethnographic curiosities as it was for its paintings or sculpture. Many Dutch collections in this period followed an Italian and German organizing principle: they aimed for the all-encompassing, the encyclopedic, a collection that, in theory, would contain representatives of all aspects of the known world, items to spark thought and associations and learning. Of course, such a goal was beyond the capabilities of even the wealthiest collector, and it was not only funds but also opportunity that limited the possibilities for true encyclopedism. The vagaries of what actually turned up in the ports of Holland or in the auctions or lotteries of the towns, or what items caught the fancy of merchants in foreign cities, or what a friend happened to send from his own collection, or what type of items the collector himself preferred: all this, chance rather than policy, determined what entered the collections of the Dutch Republic.

Yet in other ways one *can* discern policy in such collections. It was simply that the encyclopedic was replaced, in practice, with the cult of the exotic. As many writers on collecting have pointed out, wonder was the chief emotion to be incited by these displays, and that wonder came from certain aesthetic and intellectual predilections among collectors. In principle, collections were divided between *naturalia* and *artificialia*, items to be found in nature and items that were man-made, such as art or ethnographic materials. A truly representative collection would be full of dull items as well as exciting ones, but what we find in Dutch collections of the era is not dull—and, on the whole, not Dutch. Collectors were interested in items they had not seen before or that were unusual or strange; things from foreign climes; specimens that seemed freakish or odd, or that were spectacularly beautiful; and things, if man-made, that had taken amazing skill and technical prowess to produce. The bird of paradise is a famous example of some of these categories. Colorful, beautiful, and strange, stuffed specimens of birds of paradise ended up in many Dutch collections. These beautiful birds from New Guinea and the Moluccas, with their long, sweeping tail feathers and colorful feathered collars, so different from the common birds of the Netherlands, had something even more thrilling about them: they had no feet. The theory was that, unable to perch, they were condemned to remain perpetually in flight. No wonder excited Dutch collectors had a place for them in their cabinets. In the end, the truth came out: native sellers of specimens were cutting off the feet to make the birds easier to pack. Here aesthetic considerations took over from the wonder of the exotic. The footless birds were actually better, according to one dealer in curiosities, Jan van Wely, who had sold a footed one to the emperor: "the indians are very right to cut off the foot along with the leg, because it is the ugliest part of the bird. . . ." It hardly mattered whether it was bizarre or it was beautiful, because both qualities gave the bird of paradise, footed or not, a place in Dutch cabinets.[10]

When Christiaen Porret died in 1628, his cabinet was put on sale, providing us with the first printed sale catalogue for a collection in the Netherlands and a good picture of what might appear in such collections. Porret, whom we met in chapter 1 as a friend of Carolus Clusius, correspondent of a variety of plant lovers, and grower of tulips, was an apothecary in Leiden at the sign of the Three Kings. He had good intellectual credentials, including familial relationships with the Plantin–Van Ravelingen printing dynasties. He was also a relatively wealthy man; in 1600 his goods were estimated for tax purposes at ƒ8,000, in 1602 at ƒ10,000. This wealth is reflected in the breadth of his collection, which was sold in 719 lots, many of which consisted of multiple objects (such as one lot of sixty watercolors of fishes and animals). The title of the catalogue advertises the "Singularities or Rarities and Exquisite Collector's Items [*Sinnelickheden*] Of Indian and other foreign Sea-Horns, Shells, Earth and Sea creatures, Minerals, and also strange Animals, plus several artfully made handicrafts and paintings." Perhaps as fitted an apothecary, the concentration of the collection was on *naturalia*. Besides innumerable shells and beautiful mineral samples, Porret enjoyed such possessions as the tooth of a rhinoceros; a chameleon; "an Indian bird's beak, red, black, and yellow"; a small crocodile; a large crocodile; and the feet, head, skin, and eye of an emu, not to mention natural curiosities the cataloguer was unable to name, such as "A wonderful Nest of a strange little Creature." Porret also owned many watercolors of plants: fifteen of irises, fifteen of lilies, sixteen of crocuses and fritillaries, fifty of narcissi and hyacinths, seventy of tulips, twenty of anemones, fifty-three of poisonous mushrooms and thirty-two of edible ones, plus a large book full of pictures of flowers and herbs. But Porret's collection did not stint on the *artificialia*. For a start, it included ten European paintings, a number of pictures from the Indies and China, and two Dürer prints. Like many collectors, Porret evidently loved ingenious machines, such as the "ivory Sphere or Globe/with various balls/turning within each other/on a pedestal/or foot of ebony" (he had another very similar). Exotic handicrafts—cloth from the Indies, paper from Persia, a Chinese flowerpot in the shape of a lion, a turban cloth, Hungarian and Turkish shoes—rounded out the collection.[11]

The division between *artificialia* and *naturalia* in a collection like Porret's is not necessarily a categorization that would have been made at the time. Certainly the cataloguer of the collection for Porret's sale made no such division, and except for a somewhat vague grouping together of the paintings, and, later, the watercolors of plants and animals, there is little sense given of any clear typing of objects (although admittedly in such a catalogue we are not hearing the voice of the collector himself). The question of the relationship between art and nature—a question that the cultivated tulip frequently raised—was in any case a vexed onc in the early modern period. Since the classical period it had been a commonplace that art and nature were in opposition to each other, yet just what these two categories meant to each other was a matter of contention. Aristotle had said in his *Physics* that art imitated nature, but it was a constant question whether art should settle for imitation (which implicitly valued nature more highly) or whether it should go further, inventing rather than merely copying what was before the artist. A classic and influential exposition of these questions, known to all educated Europeans in the period, came from Pliny. In his story, two Greek artists of the late fifth century BC, Zeuxis and Parrhasius, were in competition with each other to produce the most "successful" picture, and that success consisted of a convincing realism. Zeuxis painted a picture of grapes so realistic that birds flew up to the wall where it was hanging. But Parrhasius' subsequent picture of a curtain proved so convincing that even Zeuxis was fooled, asking for the curtain to be drawn back so that he could see the painting he presumed was hiding behind it. He ended up bowing to Parrhasius' superior talent, since Parrhasius had been able to deceive an artist and not, as Zeuxis had, merely a flock of birds.[12]

This story emphasizes doubly the superiority of art to nature. Not only could Zeuxis fool the birds, but his view that it was more worthy to be capable of fooling man than nature only reinforced the point that man was central to any valuation of either nature or art. In the centuries following Pliny, artists made a strong case for the superiority of their craft to the creative powers of nature. The popular comparison during the Renaissance between the creative genius of artists and that of God added influence to these ideas. It was not just that artists, like Zeuxis, could imitate nature, but that they actually could improve on nature; the skill artists showed, in invention or, perhaps even more, in the ability to select what was the most beautiful, was thought to rise above the natural objects they imitated. In this way, one could even suggest that artists had risen above God. Erasmus wrote in 1522 that "We are twice as pleased when we see a painted flower compared with a real one. In one we admire the cleverness of Nature, in the other the inventiveness of the painter," although he was careful to add to this "in each the goodness of God." The ability of artists to select and invent when depicting nature was much emphasized in contemporary discussions of pictures of flowers. The best painted flowers were those that were idealized versions of the originals and thus improvements on nature. It was common to praise floral still life painters for their ability to surpass nature: thus the poet and statesman Constantijn Huygens wrote in verses on the Flemish floral painter Daniel Seghers, "Nature as judge, concede defeat in the contest:/The painted flower rendered the real one a shadow." Jan Vos said the same about Seghers in 1654, pointing out that although spring "shows off, for a little while, with your paintings," "ZEEGERS" created, whenever it suited him, a living spring of flowers with his colors. "The Arts," he concluded, "are sometimes much stronger than Nature."[13]

But for all these comments in favor of art, nature—including the tulip—proved a valiant opponent. Seghers could provide just as potent an argument for the other side. Perhaps Seghers painted the most beautiful flowers on canvas, advocates of flowers wrote, but he could never properly render their natural beauties. The professional gardeners John Rea and his son-in-law Samuel Gilbert preferred real tulips to their portrayal by "Pater Zegers, a Jesuite in *Antwerp*, famous for painting flowers"; Rea, for example, commented of a tulip called the Agate Hanmer, "Her Native Beauties shaming Art,/Once did that famous Jesuite try/To copy out her Majesty; But falling short of his desire,/He left his Pencil to admire."

A religious tint was naturally a frequent aspect of such claims. By challenging nature, artists were, of course, challenging God, the creator of nature, much as attempts were made to separate one from the other. One of the tulip songs published after the crash of February 1637, *De Rechte Bloem-Prijs* (The Just Price of Flowers), made this point, using the term *principael*, usually employed to distinguish an original art work from its copies. "The Flower is principal, the rest are just Copies:/Take artful Needlework or beautiful Paintings,/It is simple imitation, for the Purple of the Paintbrush/Compared with the Purple of the flower is by far the worst part." This was because "God Himself dresses the flower in her beautiful colors." Despite the long tradition of artists challenging God and nature with their talent and their *ingegno*, in the seventeenth century some voices continued to maintain that art could do nothing to imitate the wonders of nature.[14]

But the mixture of artifice and natural beauty in a collection such as Porret's is in itself suggestive. Although (or perhaps because) the distinction between art and nature had for so long been a cultural trope, scholars, artists, gardeners, and architects of the late sixteenth and seventeenth centuries took a particular pleasure in confusing or blurring these categories. A favorite form was to create objects of art that looked like *naturalia*. Bernard de Palissy was working within precisely this tradition when he produced his beautiful, illusionistic ceramics: shiny platters with lifelike, life-sized lizards and snakes in three-quarter relief. Garden designers, particularly in some of the mechanically sophisticated gardens in Italy such as Pratolino in Florence or the Villa Aldobrandini at Frascati, fashioned unreal animals to decorate the landscape and used machinery to produce such effects as rainbows and the singing of birds. Jehan Somer, visiting Pratolino in 1591, wondered at the artificial giant's body with a marvelous grotto inside studded with sea creatures spouting water: "I don't think one could find anything more in the sea" than one could find inside the giant, a thrilled Somer wrote.[15]

This mixing of art and nature is even more telling when we look at natural objects that have been made into *artificialia*. Porret had several of these: besides "a big piece of white coral, painted red and gilded," he had "a half Egg of an Ostrich, on an ivory foot, made in such a way as to serve as a Goblet." These kinds of ostrich-egg cups, with their combination of egg and pedestal, were common in European collections, as well

FIGURE 14. Cup made from a nut (*Coccus de Maldiva*) mounted
in silver, an example of nature improved by art. In Clusius,
Exoticorum libri decem, 1605. Koninklijke Bibliotheek, The Hague.

as in churches, where they served as reliquaries or were wrapped with
metal bands and hung from the ceiling. Another piece of *naturalia* that
often served as a kind of art object was the coconut (and sometimes the
more oblong Seychelles nut), which, like the ostrich egg, was mounted on
a metal pedestal to make a reliquary, goblet, or bottle or even fashioned
into artifacts resembling ships or animals. The nautilus cup, a great pearly
polished nautilus shell transformed into a beaker, was a feature of many
a luxurious cabinet (see figs. 14 and 15). Eggs, nuts, and shells were not
only mounted on metal stands and decorated with metal ornamentation
but were also carved or engraved. Philip Skippon, on his travels through
the Netherlands in the 1660s, visited the collection of "one *Cliver*" in Middelburg, where, among other mainly natural rarities, he saw an "ostrich
egg with faces carved on it." One analysis of 530 coconuts from the early
modern period found 185 portraying scenes from the Old Testament and
100 from the New, 15 with pictures of angels and saints, 180 with non-
sacred motifs, 25 with owls, and 25 with other animals. Whether we look
at coconuts, ostrich eggs, nautilus cups, or other, similar objects, such as

a candelabra made with reindeer horns, we can see the fascination early modern craftsmen and collectors felt with a conscious mixing of art and nature. This was also, however, a kind of triumph of art over nature. When artists felt compelled to decorate a nautilus shell with pictures of other shells, it suggested that the nautilus shell alone was not good enough and that only man could make perfect what nature had left wanting. As we will see later, tulips could from some points of view be considered similar to these half-natural objects, if one believed that tulip breeding was in fact a form of art.[16]

But a wholly natural object could itself be artful: beautiful things were *constich* (artful, ingenious), and not only those obviously made by

FIGURE 15. Nautilus cup, 1651. Foot made by
Willem Claesz Brugman; shell carved by Joan Belkien.
Stedelijk Museum Het Prinsenhof, Delft.

man. Tulips could also fall into that category, although, as we will see later, this was for more reasons than merely their beauty. One of the chief seventeenth-century French writers on the tulip, Nicolas de Valnay, made the comparison explicit. He gave the credit for the influx of rare flowers into France to Louis XIV, who protected "the Arts," of which the stocking of beautiful gardens was certainly to be counted, and his rhapsodizing over the marvelous qualities of tulips drew him into an explicit, and favorable, comparison with works of art. Tulips, he said, gave constant variety compared with pictures, medals, and porcelains—collectibles (in the later seventeenth century) that were more in fashion and that, no matter how long you looked at them, never changed an iota. Flowers were better designed and better constructed than anything that could have been dreamed up or executed by the *Académie de peinture*, and bulbous flowers like tulips had the advantage of actually multiplying under the care of their owner, something you could, regrettably, never claim for a painting. You could give a tulip to a friend and still keep its offset for yourself, a useful trait in a society of collectors, which, as we have already noted, was knit together by exchange relationships and gifts. In a final flight of fancy, Valnay even made a claim for the antiquity of flowers, choosing the side of the ancients in the quarrel between the ancients and the moderns. No matter how old your medals and coins were, he said, they were always modern compared to flowers: flowers "are from the creation of the world." What Valnay said about paintings and medals could be repeated for porcelains and all the "other rarities that are in vogue": no matter what collectible flowers were compared with, they would always end up holding first rank among all the "pleasures of sight."[17]

Valnay might perhaps have wished to provoke, and certainly his dare to the *Académie de peinture* would have won him few friends. But it was actually far from surprising that he grouped tulips and other rare flowers with luxurious objects of art. Even Clusius, the premier botanist of his era, did not limit his interest to flora; his request to VOC doctors and apothecaries to look for rare plants asked for "diverse sorts of strange fish," and he was known to reciprocate gifts of plants with medals or other man-made curiosities. Christiaen Porret's collection was simply an indoor corollary of the garden he cultivated not only for his business but also, as we have seen, because of his private passion for tulips and other exotic flowers. In the same way, Paludanus' famous cabinet in Enkhuizen, visited by the

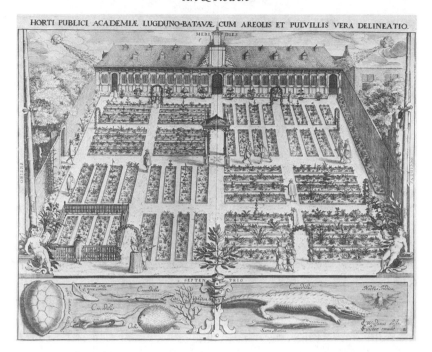

FIGURE 16. *Hortus botanicus* in Leiden, with arcade containing a collection.
Willem Swanenburgh after Jan Cornelisz Woudanus. Atlas van Stolk, Rotterdam.

likes of Prince Maurice of Nassau, Duke Friedrich von Württemberg, and
scholars ranging from Clusius to Peiresc, encompassed a garden as well
as a collection, and it is no accident that he not only was thought fit to
head the new botanical garden in Leiden, but that the university wished
him to bring his collection as well. When Paludanus failed to take up the
appointment, a collection to accompany the Leiden *hortus* was nevertheless erected in a covered gallery running across the back of the garden (see
fig. 16). No matter what one's priorities were in collecting—whether one
wished for an encyclopedic inclusiveness or the selection of rare specimens for admiration, study, and display—a flower garden made a suitable partner for a cabinet of curiosities.[18]

Abraham Casteleyn clearly thought so. Casteleyn, prominent in the
tulip world from early on (he was one of Crispijn van de Passe's Amsterdam *liefhebbers* around 1615 and was involved in tulip transactions from
the beginning of the century), died in late August 1644. When the notary,

the witnesses, and his three executors arrived at his house on the St. Pieterspad on the Singel to inventory his goods, they made special note of
four things: the money left in the house, his documents about property
ownership, his tulips, and his *naturalia*. The money tells us something
about him; a little more than ƒ36,230 was found in the house, enough
to buy several grand houses on one of the main canals of Amsterdam.
(There was, as it turns out, another ƒ12,630 in his account in the Wisselbank.) Casteleyn, who was unmarried and had no children, was leaving a
fortune to his heirs, one of whom was his brother Isaac, who also figured
in the tulip trade. Because he died in the late summer, his tulips were
in the house, not the garden; tulips had to be lifted from the soil after
they had bloomed in early summer and only replanted around the end of
September. The tulips were in an upstairs room (the same room as most
of the money), laid out in labeled drawers and little boxes. Significantly,
Casteleyn kept details about them in the room below, in the same place
as documents about the expensive houses and gardens he had bought
and sold; the inventory records "Fourteen books with the description of
the tulip bulbs." When the notary came to list which bulbs were in the
house, always checking against Casteleyn's records, the bulbs took up
thirty-eight pages of the inventory. Seven years after the crash of 1637,
tulip bulbs were still among Abraham Casteleyn's greatest treasures.[19]

So, it is certain, were his shells. The notary and witnesses were in Casteleyn's house for days, not only writing down painstakingly the name
of every bulb, but laboriously counting every single shell. Christiaen
Porret's collection had contained so many shells that the "foreign Sea-
Horns" and "Shells" got prime billing on his sale catalogue; but Casteleyn had practically nothing but shells, plus some other sea creatures
and a crocodile. (Virtually his only *artificialia* were "an Indian tobacco
pipe" and a portrait of the king of Sweden.) The notary counted 2,389
shells. This collection was so important to Casteleyn that, days before
he died, he called a notary to his deathbed to make precise conditions
about its fate. His "rarities of little shells, little horns, and other rarities" were to be shut up in a chest with three different locks, and each of
his executors would have a key for one of the locks; only when the three
men were together could the chest be opened, so that no one executor
could tamper with or sell the collection. No potential buyer might see
it without all three executors present. For four years it was to be main-

tained as a complete whole and only to be sold in its entirety; only if "a reasonable price" could not be obtained for the collection by the end of four years might his relatives consider selling it off bit by bit. Casteleyn obviously had strong feelings about his collection as a collection, about its integrity as a unified whole.[20]

Was this a coincidence, this pairing of tulips and shells? Why were these the two things most important to Casteleyn? One answer, as we have already discussed, invokes the thrill of collecting, a thrill made obvious by Casteleyn's arrangements for his collectibles, such as the fourteen-volume register of tulips and the trays of bulbs with careful labels such as "Drawer D: Nº. 5:" or the chest with three locks for his shells and sea creatures, one of his last concerns on this earth. Shells were growing in popularity at the same time as the cultivation of tulips, and for many of the same reasons (see fig. 17). Although the local shells of the North Sea coast held little interest for collectors, the exotica brought back from the East and, later, West Indies by VOC and WIC ships did. Larger, rarer, more curiously shaped, more colorful than the more familiar Dutch varieties: it was the same story with shells as with tulips. The Dutch had to wait for Georg Everhard Rumphius' *D'Amboinsche rariteitkamer* of 1705 for a scholarly treatment of exotic shells, but the passionate shell-collecting we find at the end of the seventeenth century had already begun in the late sixteenth. We have reports of visitors to large shell collections at the beginning of the seventeenth century. Among those owning collections of shells in the 1620s and 1630s were the painter Jacques de Gheyn III and the engraver Christoffel van Sichem. Filips von Zesen reported in 1664 that in Johan Volkersen's house on the Keizersgracht was a collection, chiefly of shells, worth ƒ100,000. Moreover, Philibert van Borsselen showed consciousness of a community of shell-collectors when he dedicated his *Strande* (Beach) of 1611 to his brother-in-law Cornelis van Blijenburgh "and all Fellow-Shellfanciers." Van Borsselen's long and tedious poem in alexandrines was a paean to Van Blijenburgh's shell collection and, by extension, the infinite variety, beauty, and exotic uses of shells, which were, in the end, the creation of God.[21]

Van Borsselen actually claimed to have little use for tulips, at least in comparison with shells. No flowers were really good enough for him, whether lilies, marigolds, hyacinths, roses, carnations, or violets. But he was definitive that, where shells were concerned, "No Tulipa I ever

FIGURE 17. Abraham Susenier, shell still life, c. 1659.
Dordrechts Museum, Dordrecht.

saw could compare to them/No matter how rarely they might be veined
and glowing," whether clad in "gold cloth" or "with gold mixed with the
glistening of silver thread," whether "here the Sun seems to give her red,
there the Moon her white. . . ." Such a rapturous description belies his
supposed contempt for tulips, even if shells were apparently even better.
Casteleyn was not the only collector, in the Netherlands or elsewhere, to
turn his attention to both tulips and shells. For a start, someone we have
already met, the late-sixteenth-century Middelburg apothecary Willem
Parduyn, who corresponded with Clusius and encouraged the young
Jehan Somer, had both tulips in his garden and shells in his cabinet of
naturalia. Jacob Marrell, the Utrecht painter of floral still life and tulip
portraits, who also traded in tulips, had both bulbs and shells in his collection, and indeed when his estate was inventoried in 1649, the notary
grouped the eight drawers of bulbs and three of shells together in one en-

try, as if they were part of the same cabinet. In France, one of the greatest collectors of the age, Louis XIII's brother Gaston d'Orléans, not only had one of the best-stocked gardens in Europe (and commissioned Nicolas Robert's beautiful series of botanical paintings on vellum, the *Vélins du Roi*) but also a large collection of shells. Some of the most prominent professional gardeners of the period had collections in which shells featured. Both the elder and younger John Tradescants, gardeners to the high nobility and eventually to the English crown, were well-known collectors; a 1656 catalogue of "Tradescant's Ark," their museum at Lambeth, contains more than 120 types of shells, and a portrait by Thomas de Kritz portrays John Tradescant II with some of the more exotic specimens. But perhaps the best example of this confluence of tulips and shells comes from Pierre III Morin, who not only came from a family of important professional florists but also was a famous Parisian collector. John Evelyn, who visited his oval garden in the Faubourg St-Germain in 1644 and 1651, remarked that he, "from an ordinary Labourer, in that profession [gardening], arived to be not onely a most Extraordinary *Florist* [that is, *amateur* of flowers] but so greate a *Vertuoso*, that his Collection of Shells, Insects & other natural Curiositys emulats the most famous in *Paris*, not forgetting the goodly Vasas of Purcelan, Branches of Corall, on which is carved a p[r]etty large Crucifix greatly esteemed; besides his folios of *Tailles-douces* of Alber [Dürer], Lucas [van Leyden] & the best antient Masters, some Pictures," and so on. Evelyn said in 1651 that Morin "had abundance of incomparable shells, at least 1000 sorts which furnish'd a Cabinet of greate price. . . ."[22]

Observers of the zeal with which collectors strove to acquire both tulips and shells also drew comparisons between the two. Balthasar Gerbier, by now Charles I's agent at Brussels (where similar passions reigned) wrote in the same breath of the "trickes" of "tulip and cockle-shell-lovers." A tulip song from 1637, pretending to praise the tulip but actually attacking it, pointed out, in a common trope, that one should value God, not things on earth. The author wrote of three earthly temptresses: "flamed Tulips . . . speckled shells . . . [and] precious gold." Naturally, with both tulips and exotic shells so rare, gold was bound to enter the equation as well. Shells, no less than tulips, were expensive; indeed, one shell was given the name "Speculation-goods." The best known of these direct comparisons of tulip- and shell-collecting came from the volume of emblems by Roemer

Tis miſſelĳck waer een
geck zĳn gelt aen leĳt.

FIGURE 18. Emblem on the folly of shell-collecting. Roemer
Visscher, *Sinnepoppen*, 1614. Koninklijke Bibliotheek, The Hague.

Visscher, *Sinnepoppen*, from 1614. In two successive emblems, Visscher
ridicules the taste for shells and tulips (see figs. 18 and 19). The fourth emblem, showing exotic shells lying on a beach, is labeled, "It is bizarre what
a madman spends his money on," with verses below pointing out that we
used to give shells to children to play with, but now they were the price of
jewels. The fifth, depicting two fat tulip blossoms, comments darkly, "A
fool and his money are soon parted." The text of the tulip emblem makes

FIGURE 19. Emblem on the folly of tulip-collecting. Roemer Visscher, *Sinnepoppen*, 1614. Koninklijke Bibliotheek, The Hague.

the comparison explicit: "This Emblem is not so very different from the previous one, springing as it does from the same reason, so enough will have been said in the previous one; for a strange little shell or a new little flower, it's nothing other than poppycock (*tuylery*); but the shell-lunatics don't have to waste so much money or buy or maintain the gardens of the Flowerlovers." *Tuylery* was perhaps a little pun; a *tuil*, besides meaning a joke, also means a bunch of flowers.[23]

If contemporaries noticed the twin interests of people like Abraham Casteleyn, it was not so surprising. Many floral still lifes from the early seventeenth century paired the tulip and the shell. The Middelburg origins of the most important painter of these pictures, Balthasar van der Ast, remind us once again of this milieu, the seaport with its gardens of exotic flowers and rarities arriving on the ships of the VOC. But the coincidence of place—and one could make the same argument of Paludanus in Enkhuizen—still does not explain why it is *these* particular items that so captured the enthusiasm of late-sixteenth- and early-seventeenth-century collectors. What did tulips and shells have that was so compelling?

We have already examined some reasons why tulips appealed to their owners, the chief one being the excitement of their great variability and variety, the changeability that led John Gerard to label the flower "*Tulipae infinitae . . .* in number and variable colours infinite." Gerard said that "each new yeere bringeth foorth new plants of sundrie colours not before seene: all which to describe particularlie, were to roule *Sisiphus* stone, or number the sandes. . . ." But this was obviously not the case with shells: although the variety of *types* clearly was attractive, individual shells naturally did not change, and indeed it was part of their appeal that, unlike so many other natural rarities, which had a tendency to rot or fade, they were extremely easy to preserve. Although it is impossible to get completely inside the minds of early modern collectors, the kind of comments made about both tulips and shells, and the sort of objects one finds in both collections and still lifes, hint at a different reason why collectors found them appealing. Collectors, I would argue, lived in a particular aesthetic universe. That universe, at least in part, was made of marble.[24]

The contents of cabinets of curiosities show that veined and streaked stones such as marble, agate, and jasper were favorites of early modern collectors. In Porret's collection, for example, we find many objects made of these stones, usually simply oblong, rectangular, oval, or spherical pieces of polished stone, such as "Four Jasper and Agate stones, round like balls," "A flat oblong beautiful piece of Stone, like Marble," or "Twenty oval pieces of Agate, Jasper, and others." Paludanus' collection, which was much larger than Porret's, had, it was reported in 1592, forty-two sorts of marble, ninety-nine types of agates and cornelians, and sixteen knife handles of agate and jasper. There were even special collections entirely of agates, such as that of the goldsmith Antoine Agard in Arles. Marble was popular in decoration in the period; we see the kind of marble spheres Porret owned in various records of auctions; *pietra dura* furniture of marbled marquetry was popular among those wealthy enough to afford it, and marble floors were a status symbol of the time in the Netherlands, even if they were not as common as Dutch genre paintings would suggest.[25]

Agate was praised by one contemporary writer as "full of pleasure, because of the variety of its colours." But this variety, and the look of marble, was just as valuable in objects that were not actually made of stone. It seems that it was the coloration of marble, rather than its cool, smooth texture, that was so exciting for collectors, and this could be found in a variety of other items, including other types of *naturalia*. One lot in Porret's auction, for example, was "a Snake skin, beautifully marbled." Butterflies, another favorite collectible—Pierre Morin had a large collection, which Evelyn particularly admired, saying they "present you with a most surprizing & delightful tapissry"—had the same look, and one 1634 book on insects referred to "adamant, ruby, pyrope, opal" as a means of conveying their particular qualities. Shells quite clearly fell within the same marbled category as these other objects. Van Borsselen made this clear enough in *Strande*, where he mentioned numerous "marbled little shells," including those with this quality enshrined in their Latin names, such as *Cochlea fontana marmorata*. Pondering shells in general, he rhapsodized, "Who has ever seen such a jewel,/Who has ever seen such Coral, such Marble, such Agate?" Snake skin, butterfly, shell: all shared the same aesthetic space and shone, it was thought, like polished stone.[26]

When Philibert van Borsselen gave tulips their due (before dismissing them in favor of shells), one of the words he used to describe them was "veined," or "veined through" (*door-adert*). Clearly we have not left the aesthetic space we have just described. The veining and streaking of marble, agate, or jasper was, once again, a favorite comparison for tulips. John Rea, describing the variety of tulips, wrote that they were composed of "divers several glorious colours, variously mixed, edged, striped, feathered, garded, agotted, marbled, flaked, or speckled, even to admiration. . . ." The marbling of the tulip was reflected in many of the names given to the flowers. The informal French classification system for tulips (which was not, it is true, used in the Netherlands, although some of these names were adopted there, as well as in England) was based on similarity to marble and gemstones. Tulips that had broken, changing from a plain color to one striped and streaked in the way Rea described, were called by the French *panachées* (once fixed, they were *parangonnées*), and among the types of *panaches* were the Agates, the Morillons (rough emeralds), and the Marquetrines (referring to marquetry work). When the Sieur de la Chesnée Monstereul made a list of tulip names in 1654, he included fifty-five of the Agate class alone, and in the Netherlands we find, in various tulip books, names such as Agaat Bisschop, Agaat Fenis da Costa, and Agaat van Enckhuysen. Other French tulips were *marbrées* or *jaspées,* and in the Netherlands names like Ghemarmerde [marbled] de Goyer, Ghemarmerde van der Eyck, Ghemarmerde van Willem Willemsz, and so on, were usual. Tulips were not a collector's item simply because they were expensive but because they were part of the same aesthetic universe as shells and many other items so prized in early modern collections. Tulips, like shells, could be stone.[27]

In some ways this is a story of the superiority of nature to art. It was the hand of God, or of Nature (depending on how you wanted to look at it), that had painted tulips with their glorious veined markings, in the same way that shells and snakeskins had been decorated without the hand of man. But the subject of craft, and man's craftmanship, raises its head again here. The use of the past participle as an adjective—marbled, *marbrée, ghemarmerde*—suggests a process that has been completed: the tulips are not marble, but they have *been marbled.* In other words, they have been turned from plain to patterned, like marbled paper. And indeed a connection with marbled paper seems to have existed. Paper with the swirling patterns of marble arrived in Europe around the end of the sixteenth century from Turkey, the same place as tulips and so many other exotic flowers. The Dutch were early enthusiasts for the paper, which was a much-valued collector's item (Paludanus, for one, had marbled paper in his collection, and Porret had "a book from Persia with paper of various beautiful colors, bound in blue, and gilded," plus two platters made "in the manner of the Turkish paper"). During the seventeenth century the manufacture of marbled paper began in the Netherlands, and, like tulips, it eventually became associated with the country, although from the start in Germany it was known as "Turkish paper." The resemblance between the paper and stone was made early on—Sir Thomas Herbert noted in his travel journals that such paper "resembles agate or porphyry"—and one of the earliest patterns to enter Europe, from the early seventeenth century, was known as Agate. Interestingly, Evelyn, who wrote a manuscript description of the technique of marbling, identified one design as "Pennaches (as the French call it)," thereby linking the aesthetic concept with the existence of tulips said to be *panaches* or *panachées*. Perhaps the best evidence that tulips were considered in the same class as marbled paper comes, yet again, from tulip names. The Viennese noblewoman Anna Maria von Heusenstain, in one of her frequent letters to Clusius demanding gifts of flowers, reported that one tulip she still lacked was "das tirckhish papir." But perhaps this is not necessarily a linking of the tulip with the man-made—a subject we will come to later—as tulips were also connected to other, naturally marbled objects. One French tulip was called a *Coquille marbrée*, a marbled shell. Thus we have stone, linked to paper, linked to flowers, linked to shells: all suggesting, at the very least, a world of marbled collectibles whose aesthetic values resonated constantly against each other.[28]

Tulips, then, although for most of the year outside in the garden, fit into some of the same categories collectors used for the objects in their cabinets and collections. The love of shells and the love of tulips was much the same. They were also expressed in similar ways. Collectors were not only interested in having collections; they identified with them, they loved them, and they wished to glorify them, to pore over them, and to preserve them. Van Borsselen's brother-in-law, Cornelis van Blijenburgh, is one example, loving as he did to contemplate his collection (and its existence as a production of God as well as of himself) closeted in a remote turret in his house. The codicil to Casteleyn's will, showing that to the last he was concerned that the collection he had built up should not be broken apart, is another. Collections were naturally intended to incite wonder at the creation of God and the ingenuity of man, but they also involved the thrill of possession, the search for social status, and the wish to be known and to be remembered. The desire for the preservation and publicity of collections can be seen in poems like Van Borsselen's about them, in the many catalogues of cabinets of curiosities that became available in this period, and also in pictures.

As secular painting began to take over from religious pictures in the Netherlands in the late sixteenth and early seventeenth centuries, we see the proliferation of still life paintings. Many of these still lifes (most obviously the *Kunstkammer* or *cabinet d'amateurs* paintings mentioned earlier, which pictured cabinets of curiosities) can be directly connected to the collecting impulse so prevalent at this time. One major subject of still lifes in the seventeenth century was groups of shells, and it is evident from details in some of them, such as boxes in which shells were kept, that we are looking at particular collections. The most obvious case of the human element of collecting, the identification of the collector with his collection, is that of Jan Govertsz van der Aer of Haarlem, who lived from around 1544 to 1612 and who had at least eight portraits painted of himself with his shell collection. In 1608 he was painted by Cornelis Cornelisz sitting in front of a variety of exotic shells and surrounded by figures representing the arts and sciences. Similarly, Hendrick Goltzius' portrait of him from 1603 shows him with more of his shells and holding a large (marbled) *Turbo marmoratus* in his hand (see fig. 20). Clearly this was a man who wanted to be remembered, and who wanted his shells to be remembered along with him.[29]

If fixity and memory are special goals of collectors, tulips might seem a rather strange item to collect. Their ephemerality was one of their chief qualities, and, because the excitement and unpredictability of their changes were part of their attraction, tulips seem in some ways to have little in common with the virtual immortality of shells. Butterflies, though also perishable, could be preserved longer. (Evelyn noted that Pierre Morin, displaying his butterfly collection, told him "how he preserv'd them from decay, of all which he promised to publish a Treatise.") But we can reflect somewhat on this desire for fixity even in the case of tulips if we think about pictures. Even more than shells, flowers were portrayed in still lifes during the period of tulip worship, and tulips were almost certain to play a starring role in these pictures. In some ways, it was the very evanescence of tulips that appealed. Certainly, many still lifes, including floral still lifes, were intended to remind the viewer of the ephemerality of human existence. Both writers and painters in the seventeenth century were much occupied with the ideas of *vanitas* and *memento mori*, and, leaving aside works more directly related to death and the afterlife, there is scarcely a gardening manual or book about flowers that does not make the obligatory comparison between the brevity of the life of flowers and the shortness of human life. "Man is just a flower, who blooms in

FIGURE 20. Hendrick Goltzius, *Portrait of Jan Govertsz van der Aer*, 1603.
Museum Boijmans van Beuningen, Rotterdam. Van der Aer's pride
in his shell collection is clear from this and other portraits.

the morning/And at the end of the day is surrounded by death," carolled
Jean Franeau. "... Flowers ... teach us, that human life is like a flower
of the field, which soon vanishes," wrote Emmanuel Sweerts, claiming,
somewhat less than convincingly, that this was the reason for publishing what amounted to a sales catalogue of his flowers. John Parkinson
commented on the many lessons one could learn from flowers, including
"the mutabilitie ... of states and persons ... [since] where many goodly
flowers & fruits did grow this yeare and age, in another they are quite
pulled or digged up, and eyther weedes or grasse grow in their place, or

some building erected thereon, and their place is no more known." Even those with their minds on something other than plants found the comparison irresistible. Thus in the rhetorical competition that took place in Haarlem in 1635, Matthijs JonckHeer of Vlissingen submitted a poem on the subject of beauty, which pointed out that "The beautiful earth planted with many flowers has, it is true, a beautiful lustre, but it is only for a time. . . ." In his discussion of Dutch still life, Norman Bryson has complained that in most analyses of these paintings "ritual invocations of *vanitas* sometimes constitute the sole critical act." It is hard to deny that many still lifes, including floral still lifes, were indeed intended as a reminder of death (see figs. 21 and 22). This is obvious in pictures like Ambrosius Bosschaert's *Vanitas,* which shows a bunch of tulips next to such symbols of ephemerality as an hourglass, with an inscription above reading, "Beauty, riches, power, joy, art, and the fame of high position, Yes, all that is of the world, will pass like a flower" (a reference to Psalm 103:15). But increasingly it has seemed worth asking whether this passing of earthly joys is necessarily reflected in all seventeenth-century pictures of flowers.[30]

The question of whether or not we should see a picture of a vase of flowers as an allegory is part of a much wider debate that has now occupied art historians for some time. Still life, perhaps less than most other types of painting, provides few clues for the spectator about its ultimate point. It is obvious that a vase of flowers alongside a skull, a bubble, an hourglass, a smoking candle, or other symbols of the temporary refers to the frailty of human life and the need to concentrate on the more permanent joys to be found in heaven. But it is much less certain what we should make of a vase of flowers on its own, or a vase of flowers with small insects, or a vase of flowers surrounded by exotic shells. Does every occurrence of an object necessarily denote a particular symbol or set of meanings? One group of art historians has continued to emphasize the allegorical, didactic, essentially moralizing nature of Dutch art in the seventeenth century. Another group—while, in most cases, not entirely abandoning the idea of the allegorical—has chosen instead to stress the representational aspects of still life and other forms of Dutch art at this time. Dutch painters, such scholars suggest, wished to explore the materiality of the world, a subject of particular interest to a culture with a capitalist power base and a consciousness of the importance to its

FIGURE 21. Simon van de Passe, *Memento Mori*, 1612.
Museum Boijmans van Beuningen, Rotterdam. Both the skull
and bones and the floral still life evoke a theme of *vanitas*.

society of the existence and exchange of goods. Still lifes, according to this interpretation, are representations of the material world, but representations consciously setting some objects in relationship to others to convey particular cultural messages, albeit ones less direct and, perhaps, less literal minded than those suggested by a purely iconological interpretation. Some of these scholars have further called attention to the way the objects portrayed in still lifes are transformed by their representation on canvas; the artist was, in essence, making a statement about the power of art and craft (linked, it has been argued, to the power of science and technology) to remake the world of objects.[31]

The rise of floral still life certainly took place at a time when both secular consumption and scientific interest in the world were rising. Some scholars of still life draw connections between an objective interest in the natural world—in plants, insects, and animals—and the origins of

FIGURE 22. Jacques de Gheyn the elder, *Vanitas*, 1603.
Metropolitan Museum of Art. The tulip is only one of a series of
symbols depicting the evanescence of life on earth, with
Democritus and Heraclitus laughing and weeping at the spectacle.

FIGURE 23. Adriaen van de Venne, symbol of widowhood, in
Jacob Cats, *Houwelijk*, 1625. Author's collection. In the illustrations
in this book, the tulip is the coat of arms of the maiden.

floral painting. Floral still life, for these writers, stems at least in part
from late-sixteenth-century representations of nature, as well as a fashion for naturalistic ornamentation. These are joined in works such as
Joris Hoefnagel's beautiful, miniaturistic paintings of insects and flowers for Rudolf II, which, in the main, are not considered to be allegorical
(although they could be), but rather stemming from a more "scientific"
outlook that is shaped nonetheless by the transformative power of craft
(see fig. 24). Such an outlook fits well both with the passion for natural
history we have seen ranging from the apothecaries of Middelburg to
courts such as Rudolf's. Moreover, the kind of illumination and illustra-

FIGURE 24. Joris Hoefnagel, *Allegory on the Brevity of Life*, 1591.
Palais des Beaux-Arts, Lille. Although sometimes allegorical, Hoefnagel's
still lifes are also examples of "scientific" naturalistic representation.

tion Hoefnagel was responsible for was in itself a collector's item for one
of the grandest collectors of the age. At the same time, a variety of art
historical voices make other links between still lifes and collecting. They
urge us to think of still life paintings themselves as collections. This can
mean a variety of things. Most abstractly, the still life painting itself is a
collection because it brings together rare objects and sets them in a relationship with each other, in the same way as a real collection would do.
This is as true of floral still lifes as any other. Since, as all writers on the
subject stress, the exotic flowers usually portrayed in such pictures could
never have been placed in a real vase together, as they bloomed at different times of the year, by picturing them, the artist collected them in the
only form they actually *could* be collected. Still lifes have also been called
collections because the logic of the relationship among the different objects is not immediately apparent and requires the logic of the collector's
creativity to explain them.[32]

A more straightforward way in which still lifes could be collections
is that they actually are pictures of the contents of people's cabinets. Al-

though some of the *Kunstkammer* pictures from Antwerp in this period, showing collections of art, antiquities, and other curiosities, seem to be pictures of real cabinets, most pictorial displays of curiosities or of flowers were not (see plate 8). Where flowers are concerned, this seems almost certain, since the same flowers are sometimes used repeatedly in different paintings. Yet still lifes appear at least to have entered the spectrum of collecting, a spectrum that begins with the kind of pictures of natural objects we heard about in chapter 1, such as the picture of the yellow fritillary Jehan Somer sent to Clusius. We need to explain why a tulip magnate like the silk merchant Abraham de Goyer had eight floral still lifes on his walls, or, more curiously, why the Alkmaar schoolmaster Dirck Essings and his wife, Helena Meyers, had not only a garden full of tulips (which were named in the inventory of Meyers' estate), but also "xxvi painted tulpaes each separately painted on a little board." To some degree, and for various purposes, collectors did have pictures made of their collectibles. Jan Govertsz van der Aer's pictures of himself surrounded by his shell collection place him in the center of his own collection. But it is perhaps no less a sign of identification or possession that Somer had a picture made of his fritillary or that another correspondent of Clusius, Jacques Plateau, who was a collector as well as a plant lover, had portraits made not only of his "double white Narcissus," but of other items in his cabinet, such as "the portrait of a very strange fish" or of "a very strange Parrot." In one letter alone Plateau sent twelve such "portraits." These pictures were made for the enlightenment of Clusius, but it was common enough for collectors to have their collectibles portrayed for their own pleasure. Jan van Hoghelande in Leiden, for example, employed a female painter to depict his flowers, and John Evelyn reported of Pierre Morin's butterfly collection that "some of these, as also of his best flowers, he had caus'd to be painted in miniature by rare hands, & some in oyle." Parisian collectors frequently had drawings made of their specimens, and it was normal, according to J. Laurent, for the "Grands Fleuristes" of Paris to have their flowers painted along with a record of their names. The Dutch were known to do the same (see plate 9).[33]

As in the pictures of Jan Govertsz van der Aer's shells, paintings of flowers are a way to celebrate one's possessions. If *vanitas*, the evanescence of earthly joys, is relevant here, perhaps it is relevant in the inverse of its usual function. Rather than reminding the spectator of what will pass away, perhaps it reminds us of what has already faded. Still lifes allow a stilling of time, a fixity, a preservation of what is in fact transient. This is true of all material things, of all collectibles, but it is more true of flowers than of medals or jewels. A floral still life gives the opportunity for the impossible: the preservation of what will certainly fade. Indeed, such a picture allows a fantasy of a desirable but never attainable reality in its presentation of flowers that bloom at different times of year—again, a gathering together of riches against the commands of time. The purpose of the paintings of tulips commissioned by the great Parisian collectors was, Laurent reported, so that they could "enjoy them for the whole year."[34]

Pictures of flowers, like pictures of shells, are found in some fashionable collections, allowing collectors and *liefhebbers* a preservation and fixity of what is precious. With so many other similarities between shells and tulips—their scientific interest, their rarity value, their beauty—it is not surprising that we see them so often portrayed together. Balthasar van der Ast, the most celebrated painter of shells of the period, and part of the Middelburg circle of painters associated with the Bosschaert family, painted many still lifes of tulips and shells. Thus it was not just a cynic like Roemer Visscher who placed these two items in conjunction. But similar as shells and flowers were in the minds of different onlookers—a waste of money for the cynics, but for the collectors a source of value and indeed of self-worth—I would argue that tulips go beyond shells in their desirability and meaning. Again we can refer to painting for our argument. Tulips, as we have seen, appear not only in still lifes. They also had portraits. In this, they were like people.

Tulip portraits were different from floral still lifes because of their very plain, focused presentation (see fig. 25). Generally the tulip is presented alone, neither standing in a vase with other flowers nor depicted with its bulb, as it would have been in a botanical illustration. Rather than placing the tulip in a context, with a background scene or a table on which a vase is placed, the tulip, unusually, is portrayed against a plain white or cream background. Sometimes a name is written underneath, and sometimes a price. Tulip portraits were often painted on vellum, a highly expensive material, and consequently both more exquisite and of much higher value than such a work would have been on paper. The fact

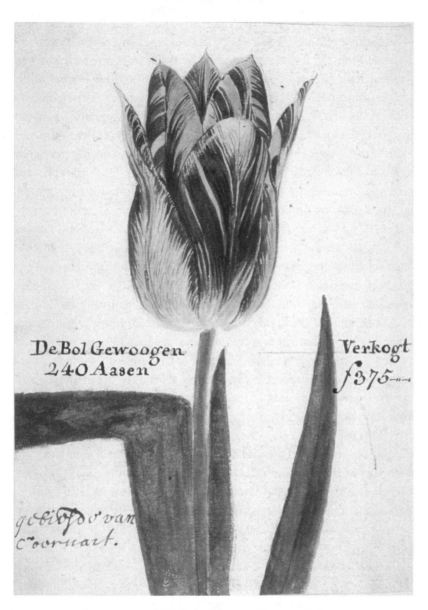

DeBol Gewoogen
240 Aasen

Verkogt
ƒ375--

gebiesd van
coornart.

FIGURE 25. *Gebiesd van Coornart*, tulip portrait from
the tulip book of P. Cos. Wageningen UR Library. The bulb
is named for the *bloemist* Volckert Coornhart in Amsterdam.
This tulip book lists weights and prices at sale.

that this material was used also raises the already-live issue of the purpose of these pictures. The use of vellum brings tulip portraits into the realm of high art, a notion supported by the employment of artists to paint such pictures who might well have commanded high prices (Judith Leyster, Antony Claesz, Pieter Holsteyn, Jacob Marrell). It has generally been argued that tulip portraits (often loose, though sometimes bound in books, of which around fifty are known) were made as sales catalogues by enterprising growers wishing to display their wares during the eleven months of the year that the tulips were not in bloom. Although this was clearly sometimes the case—tulip books were painted for the grower P. Cos in Haarlem (unknown, except for the name on the tulip book itself) and, by Marrell, for Francesco Gomes da Costa in Vianen—it was certainly not always true. The prices on the portraits were frequently not ones actually being charged, but a record of wonder: they matched the prices charged at the Weeskamer sale of the late Wouter Bartholomeusz Winckel's tulips in Alkmaar on February 5, 1637, generally thought to have been some of the highest amounts charged for tulips in the period. (This link with Alkmaar was actually acknowledged in one tulip book, labeled *Tot lof der eedele tulpa*, "in praise of the noble tulip"; see plate 1.) The prices charged in Alkmaar appeared in at least one broadside criticizing the trade (see fig. 33 in chapter 3) and seem to have been copied out onto tulip portraits, perhaps for the delectation of happy owners of the same type of bulb. The purpose of these tulip portraits is still something of a mystery, but given the tradition we have just noted of *liefhebbers* and collectors of flowers commissioning pictures and albums of their rare blooms, not to mention the material qualities of these works, their potential association with collection and the identity of collections seems significant. In at least one Haarlem inventory such drawings were described as hanging, framed, on a wall.[35]

Most scholars of portraiture agree that the early modern period, starting with the Renaissance, is a time of greatly increased production of portraits. A variety of reasons have been given for this, generally focusing on both the needs of court culture and propaganda and, more crucially for us, a growing individualism and self-reflection. The Netherlands in the seventeenth century saw more portraits, across a wider social scale, than ever before. Some of these, like the famous *schutterij* (civic militia) portraits such as Rembrandt's *Night Watch* or the Haarlem portraits of

FIGURE 26. Anon., pencil drawing of a man looking at a tulip book apparently
portraying tulips in his garden. Courtesy of Haboldt and Co., Paris.

Frans Hals, are group portraits, but they nevertheless demonstrate both
group solidarity and the individuality of each member. In thinking about
tulip portraits as potentially part of this genre, we need to consider what
the functions of portraits were. Certainly they allowed for the fashion-
ing of a subject's identity and for a potential admiration or even emula-
tion of that identity, as the many contemporary collections of portraits
demonstrate. But portraits also served (like still lifes) to fix in both time
and space something that was ephemeral and changeable. Subjects of
portraits recognized this. Hans Maler's portrait of Matthäus Schwarz
from 1526, for example, includes the inscription, "On February 20 1526

I Matthäus Schwarz had this form at Schaz. I was then exactly 29 years old." (Schwarz also had portraits painted to commemorate his giving up drinking in 1542 and his taking it up again a year later.) Similarly, Holbein's 1517 portrayal of Benedikt von Hertenstein tells us that "this is the form I took when I was 22 years old" (see fig. 27). In general, portraits commemorated and captured qualities that—as Leonardo da Vinci pointed out—might otherwise suffer from the depredations of time. Time might also bring absence or, eventually, death, and portraits played a role here as well. Early modern people were well aware of the value of portraits as a substitute for someone who was absent. Family members distributed pictures to each other and had copies made of portraits of dead relatives. As one sixteenth-century aristocratic lady wrote her husband, who, while on campaign in the Netherlands, had sent her his portrait, "For me, the time of your absence now passes with far less pain than at first, for I will now delight in this image until your homecoming."[36]

It might seem far-fetched to put tulip portraits in the same categories as these. Art historians are undecided about whether or not it is possible to have portraits of inanimate objects, or indeed of animate, nonhuman ones. Richard Brilliant, for example, excludes pictures of cars on philosophical grounds; identity, for him, is necessary for a portrait, and identity must include self-consciousness and the ability to interact socially, which we cannot claim for a car. But other scholars point out that in the sixteenth and seventeenth centuries, the term "portrait" referred in general to representations of specific things and could thus include animals or plants, for example, as well as people. We have seen this already in references to pictures of individual plants: Jehan Somer sent the "portrait" (*contrefeytsel*, the same word used to describe the portrait of a person) of his yellow fritillary to Clusius; when other *liefhebbers* had pictures of their flowers made, they called them *portraicts* or *portraictures*. Besides the similarity in the name, we can see a similarity in function between portraits of people and of plants. The clear function of many pictures as substitutions for flowers that were not continually present before the eye reminds us of the substitutive function of portraits of dead or absent relatives or friends. Students at Leiden, for example, made explicit in a petitition to the university authorities in the early seventeenth century their desire to use the watercolor collection of the curator of the botanical garden, Dirck Cluyt, numbering more than a thousand pictures, as a means of

FIGURE 27. Hans Holbein, *Portrait of Benedikt von Hertenstein*, 1517. Metropolitan Museum of Art. Von Hertenstein tells the viewer that this was his form at the age of 22.

study in the wintertime, when no plants were available in the garden. In Paris, a collection of pictures of plants compiled by Guy de la Brosse at the Jardin des Plantes incorporated the commemorative function of portraits; it recorded a number of plants that had died during the previous winter. In other cases, a picture could be simply a substitute for having the object itself, a solution for collections attempting to be encyclopedic, and one used by a variety of collectors. The large number of pictures of flowers in Christiaen Porret's collection may well have served such a function, and most early modern collecting followed similar patterns. It is evident that, by linking pictures of plants with both portraits and collecting, we can begin to understand the kind of identification owners had with their flowers. Portraiture meant, in many ways, possession.[37]

We could develop this connection of tulip portraits to their owner's identity by thinking of portraits of creatures that, in the view of their owners, were somewhere between human and nonhuman. In the seventeenth century and, even more so, in later centuries, aristocrats were fond of capturing their pets on canvas. This is evident in portraits of court dwarves by artists such as Bronzino and Velazquez. But more to our purpose is the portrait of the dog (see figs. 28 and 29). As standards of living rose in the early modern period, dog ownership for purposes of pleasure rather than work moved down the social scale, and we have what one scholar has labeled "obsessive pet-keeping" by 1700. The dogs that were beloved were useless ones, meant for play rather than work: like exotic flowers, they were luxury objects. In the Netherlands in the seventeenth century there was a mania for dog-collecting, reflected in paintings like those of the aptly named Hondius (his *Dog Market* of 1677 shows sixteen different breeds). In 1634, for example, the Leiden *schout* (sheriff), Willem de Bondt, organized a solemn funeral, involving a procession of other dogs, for his dog Tyter, an event that, admittedly, was ridiculed in a satirical poem by the playwright Joost van den Vondel. One English traveller noticed this mania: "In Holland they love their dogs extreamly, & give them names of Men & saints. . . ." John Caius' *Of English Dogges* (1576) commented with disgust on this kind of affection for and identification with dogs in the English setting, remarking of spaniels, "it is a kinde of dogge accepted among gentles, Nobles, Lordes, Ladies &c. who make much of them vouchsafeing to admit them so farre into their com-

FIGURE 28. Alexandre-François Desportes, *Blonde et Diane*. Musée de la Chasse et de la Nature, Paris. The names of the dogs are carefully noted on the portrait.

pany that they will not onely lull them in theyr lappes, but kysse them with their lippes, and make them theyr prettie playfellowes. . . ." This infatuation with dogs—"to beare in their bosoms, to keepe company withal in their chambers, to succour with sleepe in bed, and nourishe with meate at bourde"—translated into dog portraits, both as companions to man and, increasingly, on their own. Joris Hoefnagel, for example, made eight portraits of dogs that are assumed to be the favorite pets of his patron, Rudolf II; in the late seventeenth century French artists such as Alexandre-François Desportes and Jean-Baptiste Oudry painted portraits of hunting dogs, and in the eighteenth century John Wootton portrayed dogs such as Lyon, Casey, Mina, Die, Gill, Tapster, Lusette, Madore, Rossette, Mouche, as well as Horace Walpole's dog Patapan. Dogs were to be commemorated, and indeed to be remembered when they were gone, as the eighteenth-century fashion for odes to dogs and epitaphs for them

FIGURE 29. Diego Velázquez, *Portrait of Don Sebastián de Morra*, c. 1648.
Permission of Museo del Prado, Madrid. Velázquez, along with Bronzino and
others, portrayed court dwarves in a way comparable to portraits of pets.

also indicates. Dogs were possessions, although they had individuality, as
we can see in their names, which were sometimes inscribed on their portraits. Lipsius, for example, whose three dogs were, besides his garden,
among his chief passions (Mopsus was his favorite), had portraits made

of all three, complete with their names and poems about them. Mopsus also appears in Rubens' group portrait of Lipsius and friends, *The Four Philosophers* (see fig. 4 in chap. 1). This naming of dogs, as well as portraying them, demonstrates their owners' identification with them. As some linguists who write about naming have pointed out, no one names something—as opposed to classifying it—without deeming it important or expending some form of emotion upon it.[38]

Is it possible, then, to compare tulips with dogs? It might be argued that dogs are individuals, whereas tulips are not. In response one might point out that each tulip sort must begin with a single bulb, which might not reproduce itself, and would remain in the hands of the breeder (and some linguists would say that if you name your dog Fido, he is just one of a subset of all the world's Fidos). In any case, we have seen that collectors had strong feelings about their tulips. Perhaps this is the same kind of passion people felt for their dogs: beloved objects that would not always be there but could always be at hand or be remembered (to return the following year, in the case of the tulip) through the painting of a portrait. In both cases, moreover, we see an identification of owners with possessions through the giving of names. As on some dog portraits, tulip portraits generally provide us with a name: Admirael Grebber, Bruyn Purper da Costa, Generael de Goyer, Duck van Schapesteyn, Paragon Casteleyn, Oudenaerde, Geel en Root van Leyden, Switser, Coornhart (see fig. 31). Something like seven hundred tulip names were used in the Netherlands around the time of the tulipmania.[39]

These names do not seem mysterious to us, as we are used to individual breeds of flowers being given names, such as the Princess Diana, the P. G. Wodehouse, or Tranquillity, all names of present-day roses. A tulip called the Pim Fortuyn was "baptized" in the Keukenhof on May 6, 2003, exactly one year after the politician's murder. But these kinds of names were new in the late sixteenth century. Most flowers were known to nonbotanists by a general vernacular name, without great attention to different breeds, and attempts by botanists to classify plants remained in chaos before the work of Linnaeus in the later eighteenth century. This was not so much a problem with flowers that then had few varieties; William Turner's *The Names of Herbes* of 1548 gave only one name for each plant, arranged alphabetically, and according to Gervase Markham, who published *The Second Booke of the English Husbandman* in 1615, "You shall understand then that

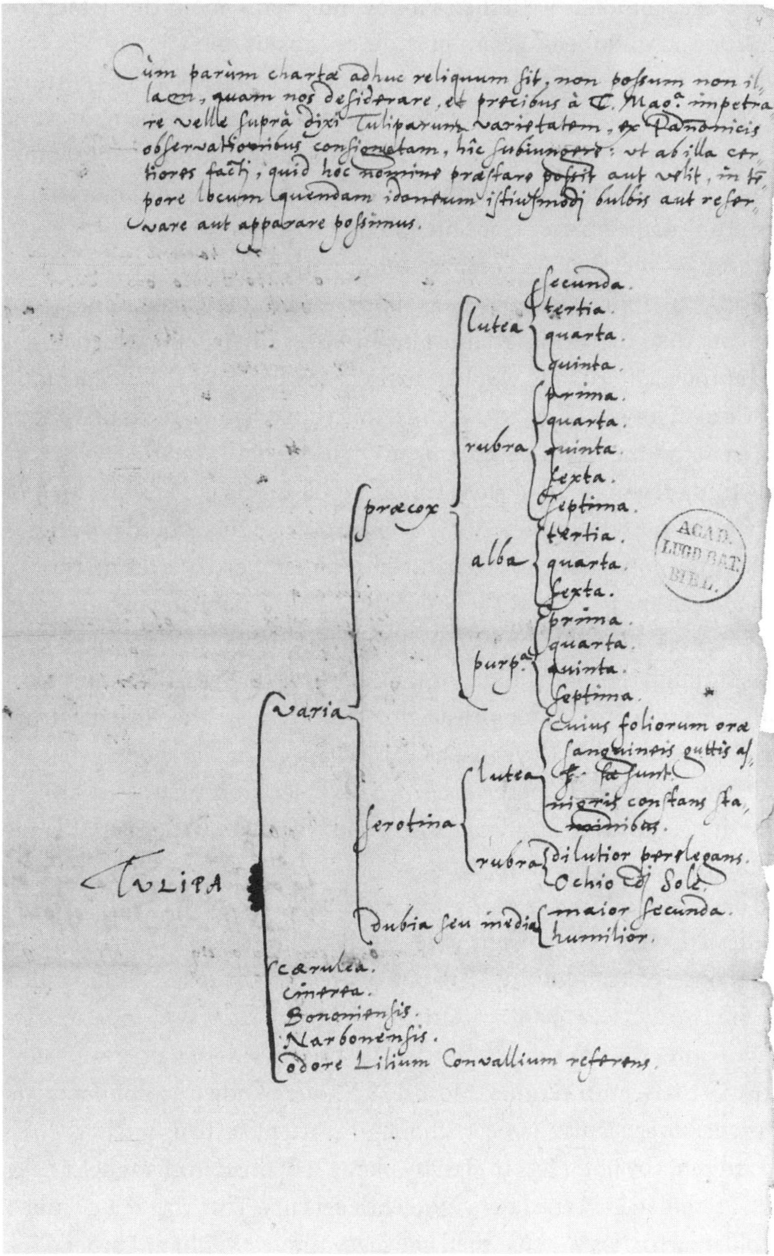

Cùm parùm chartâ adhuc reliquum sit, non possum non il
lam, quam nos desiderare, et precibus à T. Mag.ᵒ impetra
re velle suprâ dixi Tuliparum varietatem, ex Pannonicis
observationibus consignatam, hîc subiungere: ut ab illa cer
tiores facti, quid hôc nomine præstare possit aut velit, in te
pore locum quendam idoneum istiusmodi bulbis aut reser
vare aut apparare possimus.

FIGURE 30. Attempt to classify tulips by Welsenis in a letter
to Clusius. Permission of Leiden University Library.

Roses are generally and aunciently but of three kindes, the Damaske, the red, and the white. . . ." But new flowers, and flowers with many varieties, posed different demands (see fig. 30). Most of the botanical and gardening writers of the period stuck to descriptive names; thus Parkinson, writing on daffodils in 1629, gave names such as "The French Daffodil with great flowers" or "The greater late flowring French daffodil." Latin names were no different, so that Gerard's daffodils in 1597 had names like *Narcissus medio purpureus praecos,* or in English "Timely purple ringed Daffodill" (there was also the "More timely purple ringed Daffodill" and "The very hastie flowring Daffodill"). Clusius similarly classified tulips as *praecox, serotina,* and *dubia* or *media,* according to their time of flowering, and his followers, like Parkinson, tried to stick to this sort of classification, but with difficulty. Because of the yearly multiplication of new types of tulips, by 1629 Parkinson was having to describe fifteen varieties of the "early White Tulipa" alone, including such "names" as "whitish without, with some purplish veins & sports, & of a lively blush within" (all this also expressed in an equally long Latin name).[40]

But although this proliferation of flowers demonstrates the problem of classifying a rapidly changing and hybridizing plant, the naming practices of those dubbing flowers "Generael de Goyer" or "Zomerschoon" are very different from those classifying them into groups of early or late blooming, red or yellow, and so on. Naming flowers was like painting their portraits or having their bulbs—indeed, it was even better, for it was taking full possession of them and impressing one's own identity upon them. If the collector identified with his collection, he could not fail to identify with that part of it that, he believed, he had created himself. La Chesnée Monstereul wrote a whole chapter of his *Floriste françois* to explain the principles of French tulip nomenclature. The name, he wrote, should be "appropriate to the form, color, & perfection of the Tulip; if it is not the case that the person who raised it gives his own name in addition, which is permitted; thus Monsieur Robin gave the name Agate Robin to an Agate Tulip which rectified, & to one (being more embellished) the name has been given of Agate Royalle. . . . And thus each must name Tulips by judgment, & not by whim." Yet La Chesnée Monstereul then went on to cite the variety of different names that breeders, enthusiasts, and collectors have given their tulips: names of towns where they were bred, names of favorite subjects, names of romances, names of heroes of the past. In other words, these names were given by whim, and not by judgment. He dismissed the Dutch by saying, "The Hollanders have another method of naming Tulips; they give them the names of Army Generals."[41]

The Dutch did in fact have a number of tulip names beginning with "Admirael" and "Generael," demonstrating, perhaps, one of the higher ranks this country, on a war footing, wished to give its noble flowers. (There were, however, a few Dutch tulips with names like Princesse, Duc, Comte, and Duchesse, probably originally French or southern Nether-landish; and in England we eventually find tulips called such names as President and even Superintendent.) But La Chesnée Monstereul made a common mistake about these naming practices. Although later on we find flowers with the names of real admirals—some eighteenth-century hyacinths had names like Amiral Tromp and (with a bow to the English) Amiral Vernon—none of these seventeenth-century tulip names were those of real heroes. Instead they were the names of towns, of breeders, and, particularly, of *liefhebbers*. Admirael da Costa referred to the tulip grower Francesco Gomes da Costa of Amsterdam and Vianen; Generael de Goyer was, of course, named for Abraham de Goyer; and Admirael van En-chuysen recalled the town, Enkhuizen, where the tulip was probably bred. But many other kinds of names were also used. Without the system of Ag-ates, Morillons, and so on, which the French adopted more fully than the Dutch, Dutch *liefhebbers* named flowers for their looks (Ghemarmerde, Silver Laeckens [silver cloth], Goude Laeckens [gold cloth], Laprock [rag skirt]) or in praise of the flower (Zomerschoon [summer beauty], Schoone Helena [beautiful Helena], Semper Augustus, Cedonulle [ceding to noth-ing]). They named them for associations of the namer—very often their home, as in Oudenaerde or Gouda (short for Generael der Generaels van Gouda). But very often *liefhebbers* named them after themselves (see fig. 31): the Otto de Man (Otto de Man of Delft), the Saeyblom van Casteleyn (Abraham Casteleyn of Amsterdam), the Beste Grebber (Frans Pietersz de Grebber of Haarlem), the Purper en wit van Busscher (Andries de Busscher of Haarlem), the Coornhart (Volckert Dircksz Coornhart of Amsterdam), the Anvers Victory (Jeronimo Victory of Amsterdam), the Columbijn en wit van Poelenburg (Simon van Poelenburch of Amsterdam), and many more.[42]

The unusual practice of naming cultivars in this way had existed for a very short time in Europe and was a source of wonder for commentators

Grebber.

FIGURE 31. Pieter Holsteyn, tulip portrait, *Grebber*.
Courtesy of Sotheby's. The flower is named for the Haarlem
painter and *bloemist* Frans Pietersz de Grebber.

on the tulip trade. The earliest name I have found is a tulip called Varia Brakel, named by Jean de Brancion, mentioned in a letter of 1582; *drap d'or* (gold cloth) I have seen for the first time in 1592. By the time of Emmanuel Sweerts' *Florilegium* of 1612, which advertised tulips from Amsterdam sold there and at the fair in Frankfurt, still practically no tulips had real names. They were called names like "Tulip with light purple stripes"; only one, the Goude Laeckens, had a name, and even these were just called "d'orée" in the French section of the tetralingual text. Already in the late sixteenth century, however, the tradition of naming flowers after the person laying claim to their discovery or breeding had begun. In 1584 we hear mention of a fritillary in Orléans that, according to a correspondent of Clusius, was "called in this place Caperonia from the name of the one who first made it known in that city: who was an apothecary excellent in the knowledge of simples named Caperon." Crispijn van de Passe's tulip appendix to his *Hortus Floridus* (c. 1615) lists tulips named after a number of known *liefhebbers* in Amsterdam and Haarlem, such as Cattelijn (Casteleyn), Cromhaut, Quackel, Garret, Cornhert, and De Goyer.[43]

In thinking about the meaning of names like these, we must consider the contemporary consciousness about naming and identity that must have reigned in Dutch society at this time. The seventeenth century in the Netherlands was a time of naming. This was true, first of all, for objects, since the newly flourishing trade with the East and West Indies brought so many new objects to the country that the diplomat and Renaissance man Constantijn Huygens wrote that many had no names. But it was also true for people. In the seventeenth century people's names were in flux. Names consisted of a first name and a patronymic (Salomon Pieterszoon, abbreviated to Pietersz), with, perhaps, a family name added on (Salomon Pietersz Seys). The use of the family name increased greatly during the seventeenth century; in 1622 in Alkemade only 18 percent of male heads of households had a family name, but by 1680 this figure was 60 percent. Family names appeared most rapidly in towns and in the western provinces Holland and Zeeland: in other words, exactly the kind of places where tulips were popular. This was also another case of southern influence; in 1600 in Amsterdam 80 percent of bridegrooms of southern Netherlandish descent already had family names, but only 14 percent of those born in Amsterdam did. But even those with family names used them fluidly. It was common for someone to be referred to, and to refer to himself, sometimes as Pieter Gerritsz and sometimes as Pieter Gerritsz van Welsen. Salomon Seys (like Van Welsen, active in the tulip trade in Haarlem) never signed his name, as he was, very unusually for this cohort, illiterate though still well-off; but he was referred to in documents fairly often as simply Salomon Pietersz. His distinctive mark, similar to fishbones without a fishhead, makes it clear that it is always the same Salomon.[44]

As with the names of tulips, Dutch people in this period were creative with their names. Those without family names were sometimes hard to distinguish from each other; nicknames helped distinguish one Pieter Willemsz from another. Jan Michielsz, a rabbit-seller in Haarlem who was on the make in the tulip trade in 1636, was sometimes known as Jan Conijn (Jan Rabbit). One is tempted to associate one Jacob Heyndricksz, also of Haarlem, with the trade as well, because of a reference to him in a government document as "alias bolletgen dirck" (alias Little Bulb Dirck). And it would be hard to forget about Gerrit Willemsz, mentioned twice in the resolutions of the burgemeesters of Haarlem as "Gerritgen met zyn Gatgen" (presumably meaning Little Gerrit with his Little Arse). But this inventiveness with naming extended to the family names the seventeenth-century Dutch chose for themselves. Probably the best-known example is that of a tulip: that is, of Claes Pietersz, who in the 1620s became Claes Pietersz Tulp, the Dr. Tulp of Rembrandt's *Anatomy Lesson of Dr. Tulp*. Tulp, like many of those taking on new names in the period, chose one from the sign or gablestone identifying his house on the Prinsengracht. Similarly, the brewer and regent Cornelis Guldewagen of Haarlem (see fig. 34 in chapter 3), who became embroiled in a singularly ill-advised transaction involving 1,300 tulip bulbs in February 1637, acquired his name from his family's house on the Grote Houtstraat, De Vergulde Wagen (the gilded wagon). There are many similar names, resulting in people named things like Jacob Pietersz Olycan (oil can), Pieter Jacobsz Indischeraven (Indian raven, that is, parrot), Gerrit Ghuersz Doodshooft (death's head), Pieter Dircksz Spaerpott (savings bank), and Pieter van Alderwerelt (all the world; one of his two houses on the Herengracht in Amsterdam sported a globe on the roof). We can tie these names to a process of identity formation: it is clear that people of this period were making conscious choices about what name to use. The father of Jan Hendricxsz Admirael, whose tulip deal we examined at the beginning of the chapter, chose to change his name to Admirael; his grandson chose to dispense with it and to return to the old family name of Van der Bent. Similar choices are evident in the case of Anthony Jacobsz, one of several apothecaries and merchants involved in a tulip company in Enkhuizen. His father was plain Jacob Fockemsz, but Anthony's brother decided to be Frederick Jacobsz Pronck, and Anthony himself wavered between Anthony Jacobsz and Anthony Jacobsz Apesteijn.⁴⁵

Naming, then, was in the minds of the kind of merchants and *liefheb-bers* who also raised and sold tulips. The novelty of naming themselves, and of naming tulips, at the same time as the market for tulips was beginning to heat up is another piece of evidence, like the painting of still lifes and tulip portraits, that helps us to understand the mind-set of the *liefhebbers*. As the Haarlem historian Schrevelius wrote in 1648, "many loved the Tulipa, [and] gave her names and titles of honor." Naming tulips was part of these people's identity as collectors. Naming was, in the first place, a central task of collecting: it was not enough to have things, but one had to know what they were, and collectors across Europe went to considerable lengths to find out what their specimens, whether local or exotic, ought to be called. But where tulips were concerned, the question of identity became more complicated. A collector then was not only concerned about having a flower and knowing what it was; he wanted, if he could, to have something new, something no one else had or could have. We will recall that one of the selling points used by Symon LeFebure of Haarlem for the flamed tulips he hoped to sell to Pouwels van Mackelenberch and Pieter Jansz was that there were "many beautiful flamed ones, which he himself did not even know." Novelty was the key. And La Chesnée Monstereul stressed the right of "un Curieux," when "a Tulip has *panaché* [become multicolored] through his work, & . . . , having continued for two years without changing, rectifies: if it is unique, & he has never seen anything similar (which has happened to several), then he can give it whatever name he pleases. . . ." The very laying down of these kinds of conditions shows how precious the right of naming was felt to be. To give a tulip a name—and in particular to give it one's own name—was to bind a collector's own identity as well as his money into his love of tulips. With collecting itself a way of raising one's own status in Dutch society, having the power of naming collector's items could be a powerful statement in the world of the *liefhebbers*.⁴⁶

We have linked the tulip to the mind-set of the collector in a variety of ways. Tulips, and paintings of tulips, were invoked in debates about the relationship between art and nature. Tulips were prime examples of a broadly held aesthetic sense on the part of collectors of *naturalia* and *artificialia*. Tulips appeared in collections, and the names that collectors gave them were part of a developing sense of identity on the part of *liefhebbers* that was mirrored in their own concomitant self-baptism. But tulips can be linked with collecting, and with art, in another fashion. For tulips were not only thought to be similar to art; in some ways they were thought actually to *be* art.

We have seen that, at least according to La Chesnée Monstereul, a *curieux* in Paris was allowed to name his new tulip only "if it had *panaché* because of his labor." It was a matter of discussion in the seventeenth century how much of a role man actually had in the changing of a variable tulip. As we have seen, this was a question of the relationship of art and nature, and although many writers, such as Petrus Hondius, suggested that gardening was a means of praising God for his creation, others, such as Samuel Gilbert, admitted that man had a role to play as well: "Assisting Nature by industrious Art." In fact, although this was not widely acknowledged at the time, there was little assistance man could ultimately render. No one in the period knew anything about the various processes, be they hybridization or breaking through the mosaic virus, that changed a plain tulip to a flamed or striped one.

Botanists and gardening writers such as Parkinson and Van Ravelingen speculated on the possibility that broken tulips were diseased; Parkinson said that "this extraordinary beauty in the flower, is but as the brightnesse of a light, upon the very extinguishing thereof, and doth plainly declare, that it can doe his Master no more service, and therefore with this jollity doth bid him good night." La Chesnée Monstereul was more contemptuous, writing that attributing beauty in tulips to sickness was analogous to "the way that a person in agony turns different colors when through a contagious malady he approaches death." But there was no real way to test these theories since the nature of the illness, if there was one, was not known. However, experiments such as those conducted by Clusius or Jacques Garet in London on growing tulips from seed suggested that there were indeed ways for man to use his craft to intervene in the processes of nature.[47]

Probably because of the influence of Clusius' work, the focus of much of the discussion about the way to change tulips concentrated on the seed. Although the outcome of the laborious seven-to-ten-year process of growing variegated tulips from seed remained uncertain in every case, growers felt they were achieving something simply by sowing only the seed of tulips they considered to be superior and by removing all but the best bulbs from their gardens. But the tedium of these methods—described by Nicolas van Kampen, an eighteenth-century commercial grower in Haarlem, as "unpleasant" and "useless"—did not escape the seventeenth-century owners of tulips. The concept that man's art could change nature soon led to more direct interventions in natural processes. Man could, it was thought, actually create a new tulip.[48]

Some of these promised shortcuts to the wonderful flames and stripes so coveted by collectors remained close to natural processes. The theory that broken tulips were actually ill led John Rea, for example, to suggest that one should deliberately damage the bulbs of "more vulgar" tulips by digging them up just before they flowered and putting them in the sun "to abate their luxury, and cause them to come better marked the year following," a method he claimed to have used many times with success. But many other procedures to alter tulips entered much more obviously the realm of art. Like an engraver carving designs on a nautilus shell, gardeners set about by intrusion to change their flowers. Among the methods suggested were cutting two bulbs in half and sticking the halves together to combine the best qualities of each; soaking the bulbs or seeds of flowers in ink, paint, or colored water to induce the flowers to be flamed with that color; or even burning the ground with a concoction made of pigeon dung. From these would come, it was claimed, new, exotically colored blossoms. Other methods were suggested to make flowers bloom earlier or later in the year, or to grow double flowers.[49]

It is true that we know about many of these methods chiefly from those making fun of them in their works. John Parkinson had little use for such ideas, which he called "meere tales and fables. . . . The wonderfull desire that many have to see faire, double, and sweete flowers, hath transported them beyond both reason and nature, feigning and boasting often of what they would have, as if they had it," he wrote. It was, he said, "the more to be condemned, that men of wit and iudgement in these dayes should expose themselves in their writings, to be rather laughed at, then beleeved for such idle tales." The methods proposed to "cause flowers to grow yellow, red, greene, or white, that never were so naturally" would simply not work: "when they come to the triall, they all vanish away like smoake. . . ." But the simple fact that Parkinson, John Evelyn, Sir Thomas Hanmer, and others felt it necessary to write against such views indicates that some took them seriously; we find such proposals in books like the *De Florum cultura* published by Giovanni Battista Ferrari in 1633. Even those ridiculing such methods, moreover, did not necessarily abandon the concept that the art of man could change the works of nature. La Chesnée Monstereul had little use for the man who had destroyed his garden by burning it with pigeon dung, but he still affirmed repeatedly that "it is a certain thing that the Curieux can embellish Tulips through Art. . . . they will see what Art can do, in achieving the things that nature has begun."[50]

By discussing the growing of beautiful tulips in the context of a debate over the superiority of art to nature, authors like La Chesnée Monstereul were consciously placing tulips in the category of art. A tulip was a man-made object; if it could not literally be classed among the *artificialia*, it was, at the very least, an item that was, like a coconut-shell goblet, half-art, half-nature. Both the language used by gardening writers and the names given to tulips make clear a mental association between the flowers and the products of art and craftsmanship.

We have already seen that tulips existed in the same aesthetic space as collector's items made of agate, jasper, or marble, or items that looked like them, such as marbled paper. The marbled paper is significant precisely because it was made by man, not a work of nature like the stone it imitated. In the same way, tulips, and the gardens in which they were planted, were constantly compared to enamel, to luxurious cloth, to elegant clothing, to shining carpets, and to beautiful embroidery. Gardens, with an intricate design of flowers, were consciously constructed to imitate the effect of a carpet of colors or a tapestry, and both printed and manuscript descriptions made the comparison. Giovanni Baptista Ferrari, for example, describing the layout of the gardens of Francesco Caetani, Duke of Sermoneta, near Cisterna, explained that each section was devoted to several colors of flowers, with one dominant color, producing an "orderly carpet of flowers." Similarly, Marie de Brimeu, princesse de Chimay, used the word *tapisserie* (tapestry, carpet) repeatedly in her correspondence with her friend Clusius to praise the gardens he had laid out for her: "the riches of your tapestries truly surpass by far those of gold & silk, as nature surpasses artifice." The word was, in fact, her usual way of describing the beauties of gardens; she referred to Clusius' garden in Frankfurt simply as *vos tapisseries* (your tapestries). John Parkinson, thinking about the particular suitability of tulips for garden design, said that "the place where they stand may resemble a peece of curious needle-worke, or peece of painting." The metaphor of carpets and embroidery became standard for the description of gardening, and indeed it was sometimes no metaphor. Pierre Vallet, who designed the engravings for a book describing the gardens of Henri IV, was in fact a professional embroiderer, and the swirls and patterns of his parterres and beds were intended, apparently, to double as designs for needlework.[51]

Not only did the patterns of tulips in a flower garden look like tapestries, but an individual tulip, with the variety of its colors, was itself compared to luxurious cloth. We have already seen that some of the earliest tulip names reflected this particular imaginative leap. Nearly the oldest known tulip name was a reference to gold cloth (Goude Laeckens), and we quickly encounter Silver Laeckens, Saey-blom (say-flower), and Sjery nabij (nearly silk), names that also soon appeared in French and in English translation. In the same way, Clusius made repeated comparisons in his writings on tulips of a flower resembling silk shimmering with red and yellow threads, or another looking like silver silk and being known for that reason as *Silberfarb*. These kinds of cloth were the most elegant and expensive known in the period. Silk was a material reserved for the elite, and cloth shot through with gold or silver thread was the height of luxury; the most fashionable brides at court, such as Louise Christine van Solms (sister-in-law of the stadholder Fredrik Hendrik) or her niece, Fredrik Hendrik's daughter Louise Henriette, wore dresses of silver tissue. Works praising tulips, such as Franeau's *Iardin d'hyver*, were often replete with clothing imagery; Franeau imagined the goddess Flora as a "craftsman tailor," writing of tulips that were embroidered, bordered in silver, dressed in silk mantles, and "full of artifice." The association of tulips with coveted types of cloth put tulips in the realm of the elite. Like embroidery, which was labor-intensive and thus expensive, fine clothing in the seventeenth century was one of the most highly visible status symbols of the age. But it also linked tulips back to collecting and to art.

One of the items often found in cabinets of curiosities was fine textiles; Porret's *Kunstkammer* contained a variety of pieces of exotic cloth, such as "a large beautiful cloth from the Indies, with various colors." And when Franeau compared tulips to elegant clothing, he said that it was the work of nature—but also the work of the Flemish elites (*"les grans"*) who grew tulips in their gardens.[52]

Aesthetically, then, tulips were thought to look like man-made objects. They were, in fact, considered by some as essentially the product of human ingenuity and craft, and they were at their best if they resembled the most elegant materials available to elites and visible within the cabinets of collectors. (One Dutch gardening text said that the best tulips were "like satin"; this was a practical matter, a means of identifying which to use for the collection of seed, not a flight of fancy by someone writing an elegy to tulips.) Tulips were like art. But we can take this comparison, so clearly present in the minds of contemporaries, one step further. The same kind of critical comment made about art in the period was also made about tulips; tulips, like art, were a subject for connoisseurs.[53]

Art historians studying the seventeenth century in the Netherlands do not have an easy time discovering the aesthetic principles governing the contemporary judgment of art. Compared to a later period, few critical works are available to give us a window into the minds of either artists or collectors in the first half of the century (Seymour Slive has called the Dutch "unusually inarticulate" about their own art in the period). Yet, with these qualifications, we can see that the same words were used to describe beauty at the time in both paintings and tulips. Karel van Mander, the southern-born Haarlem artist who wrote the only early-seventeenth-century Dutch text about contemporary art, used the first section of his *Het Schilder-Boeck* (1604) to talk about the qualities to be found in good paintings. The words he favored (*aerdigh, fraey, schoon*) to talk about beauty, and the same values about harmony of form and clear, bright colors, were also used by those talking about the beauty of tulips. Van Mander also wrote about the importance in paintings of a smooth rendering of the surface, which would engage the eye, a quality he described with the word *netticheyt*; at the same time, Van Ravelingen's annotations to the 1618 edition of Dodoens tell us that the tulip was "much honored in all lands for the *netticheyt* of its petals." But perhaps the most important aesthetic quality praised in both paintings and tulips was *verscheyden-*

heydt: variety. The idea that art (and, for that matter, nature) should show diversity dates back at least to Pliny, and it formed an important principle in the Renaissance for art, music, and literature. For Karel van Mander it was crucial. Since art should found itself on nature, he said, and "nature is beautiful through variety," both in colors and in forms, art should strive for as much diversity as possible. The best paintings, Van Mander advised, resembled a field of flowers drawing the eye, like a bee, darting from one point of sweetness to another. While Van Mander appealed to flowers to make his point about variety, John Parkinson made it clear that variety was just as important for those occupied with flowers in a more concrete sense. "There are not onely divers kindes of Tulipas, but sundry diversities of colours in them, found out in these later dayes by many [of] the searchers of natures varieties, which have not formerly been observed: our age being more delighted in the search, curiosity, and rarities of these pleasant delights, then any age I thinke before." It was the variation of tulips—from each other, from mother bulb to offset, from year to year—that made tulips so much more compelling than other flowers: as Van Ravelingen put it, "the more varied the flowers are, the more beautiful they are."[54]

The very fact that a critical vocabulary was being applied to tulips at all, however, tells us something further about their relationship to art. The seventeenth century was a period when elites were not only becoming more interested in collecting art, but also in talking about it. We have already seen that collecting both *naturalia* and *artificialia* was an activity mainly for the well-off, and that becoming a collector was a means to enhance one's social status. It has recently been pointed out, however, that, although the passage of visitors through collections was a means of the collector displaying his wealth, since most paintings, at least, were not very expensive, it was more important to be able to *talk* about art. This would allow the *liefhebber* to demonstrate his own appropriateness as a participant in the community of connoisseurs, which, increasingly, overlapped with the elite community in general. Although these arguments have so far been made only about Antwerp, the importance of art, the art market, and collecting in Holland, as well as the increasing existence of art dealers and those capable of appraising paintings, suggest that the same phenomenon existed in the north. Certainly it was the case that wealthy merchants in the period frequently took lessons

in drawing and painting from artists, giving them the knowledge to develop a good eye.[55]

While art collectors and connoisseurs were increasingly applying
critical standards to art in this period, however, the same process was
happening with the tulip. In the late sixteenth and early seventeenth centuries, *liefhebbers* and writers about flowers were relatively undiscrimi-
nating about tulips, finding all types, more or less, cause for admiration
and wonder. But relatively quickly, such enthusiasts began to develop a
hierarchy of varieties and a set of characteristics of the best flowers. *Liefhebbers* like Jan Boisot were already talking in the 1580s about "my best
kinds of Tulip," and writers on gardening saw their task in part as providing a kind of guidebook to the best flowers since, as Parkinson explained,
"many that have desired to have faire flowers, have not known either what
to choose, or what to desire." The idea that those capable of buying Parkinson's elegant folio volume needed to know "what to desire" suggests
that, like a connoisseurship of art, which not only gave pleasure but at
the same time provided an *entrée* into the elite, knowing which were the
right tulips to praise was part of a kind of gentlemanly self-fashioning.
Just as art collectors in the seventeenth century were taught who the best
painters were by books like Abraham Bosse's *Sentiments sur la distinction
des diverses manières de peinture* (1649), so that they could, at the very least,
flaunt their knowledge in company and make sensible purchases from
dealers, so were *liefhebbers* of tulips aided by books on gardening. "The
distinction between the species is very necessary to know," Nicolas de
Valnay advised, presumably for much the same reason as Bosse's readers
needed to know about which painters were which. Writers like La Chesnée Monstereul and J. B. Reyntkens duly provided chapters with such titles as, "What the Tulip should be, in its Colors, Panaches, and Form," or,
tellingly, "How one must judge whether a *Tulipant* is beautiful, or not."
The beauty of a tulip was not self-evident, but culturally constructed.
Valnay, in his turn, informed his readers that the most beautiful tulips
were the *bigeares*, which had stripes of brown, red, violet, or other colors
on a yellow background; that the colors should be as far from red as possible; and that the more lustered and the more "satined" the flowers were,
the better. He also gave instructions on the proper form of the flower,
the best color for the base, and the appropriate size and color of the stamens. These standards were linked in part to breeding, but they were

also—like the very desire of the ignorant but aspirant gardener to know "the best tulips"—naturally a matter of fashion. Like styles of clothing, flowers went in and out of mode in this period; with novelty such a key to their popularity, oldness was tantamount to drabness. Already in 1590 we find Boisot telling Clusius that a type of narcissus had already been thought in Brussels to be "vulgar here for a long time." John Rea justified the publication of his *Flora* in 1665 because Parkinson's *Paradisi in Sole Paradisus Terrestris* (1629) was no longer any use, containing, as it did, mainly flowers that were out of style: "a multitude of those there set out, were by Time grown stale, and for Unworthiness turned out of every good Garden." These "obsolete and overdated flowers," as Samuel Gilbert put it, were often the ones that had grown too common to suit the taste for rarity as well as novelty. Thus, for example, Rea wrote of a Passe Oudenaerde, a Dutch tulip dating from before the 1630s, that "it is common . . . and so little esteemed. . . ." For connoisseurs, these standards solidified over time into what ultimately came to be known as "florists' flowers," with the firm specifications for shape, color, texture, and markings enforced by the development of flower shows in the eighteenth and nineteenth centuries.[56]

Knowing about flowers, like knowing about art, was a badge of cultivation, of status, of participation in a world that could afford the expensive and had the cultural capital to be able to talk about it. Not surprisingly, during the 1630s the issue of expertise in the tulip trade was a live one. With tulips ranging in price, knowing what was a "good" tulip was important. Thus, for example, in August 1637, two Haarlemmers involved in the tulip trade, Salomon Seys and Rogier Alleman, were involved in a lawsuit over the quality of bulbs. Alleman had sold Seys two "bad flowers" (*slechte bloemen*) and was condemned by the court to give him instead two Admirael de Mans that were of sufficient quality. Seys, at the center of a variety of tulip deals, knew what a good Admirael de Man looked like. It was likewise an excuse for Susanna Sprangers (sister of the important Amsterdam art collector Gommer Spranger), when trying to extricate herself from a bad deal with Lambert Massa (buyer of art at auction, connected with various art dealers, and brother of an important Muscovy merchant who was painted by Hals), that she knew nothing about tulips: "having no knowledge of the flowers nor knowing the worth of them. . . ."

(Her excuse was that they had been bought by her late husband, Dr. Outger Cluyt, son of the curator of the Leiden *hortus*, Dirck Cluyt.) But though a matter of business, tulips were also a talking point of the elite. Among those consulted in 1637 in a case about tulips bought from the bankrupt Wassenaer florist Antony van Flory was Arent Fabricius, high in the Admiralty, who had visited Flory's establishment with the nobles the Heere and Vrouwe van Raephorst. Fabricius declared that the tulips he had seen there "were so bad and of such small Importance, that he, the witness, would not have wanted to give 100 guilders for the whole mass piled up and pressed together."[57]

When the elite of Amsterdam or Haarlem talked about tulips, visited florists' gardens, and showed knowledge of their subject, what did this say about them? Did it put them in the camp of the *liefhebbers*, the connoisseurs, the collectors of *artificialia* and *naturalia*, who knew a beautiful object when they saw it? Or did it show that they were part of the tulip trade, interested in tulips because (like brewing, cloth manufacture, dyeing, sugar refining, the Muscovy trade, wine-selling, or any of the other trades they turned to for their income) they made a good investment and a more than handsome profit? This question has been addressed, rather unthinkingly, in the old story of tulipmania that has come down through the years. It is usually said, indeed in the most authoritative works on the subject to date, that "the real tulip amateurs," "the true *cognoscenti*," kept out of the tulip trade, which was, instead, left to the unthinking public who knew nothing of tulips. In other words, one must make a division between the *liefhebbers* and the merchants, a division between those who collected tulips as a form of art and those who thought of them as an item of trade. Yet we have already seen in chapter 1 that the tulip not only was commercialized very early, but that even the sixteenth-century *liefhebbers* did not necessarily hold themselves aloof from purchase rather than exchange of bulbs. In this chapter, we have seen that, in the period of tulipmania, tulips remained within the orbit of the *liefhebber* and the collector. Tulips and tulip gardens were the cognitive parallel of collections of art and *naturalia*; tulips fit into the aesthetic universe of collectors; tulips were discussed as if they were art. And—as Nicolas de Valnay pointed out—they might as well have been art. For we cannot in fact see, on closer examination, a clear distinction between "the true *cognoscenti*"—the art collectors—and those who traded in tulips. It is impossible to draw the distinction some authors have wished to make between collectors and traders, because in many cases these people were the same.[58]

An example we are already familiar with is Abraham Casteleyn. Casteleyn was a longtime figure in the tulip world: Crispijn van de Passe accounted him a *liefhebber* around 1615, and an eight-page list of rare tulips from 1617 spoke of the "Tulippe Cattelijn" as one of the "most esteemed Tulips." In 1611 Casteleyn mediated for his friend Volckert Coornhart (another longstanding member of this group) in a dispute with one Jacob Elbertsen Smeersmouter over tulips that had turned out less beautiful on blooming than they had appeared before purchase. Casteleyn, like a number of other art collectors, bought large numbers of anemones at a sale of plants to benefit the estate of a gardener, Pieter Pietersz, in 1626. Numerous tulips portrayed in tulip books are named after him; he was clearly an active *liefhebber* and breeder of plants. And he was active in the trade in the 1630s: the cloth merchant Jan Jansz Schoft of Enkhuizen, for example, not only visited Casteleyn in late 1634 or early 1635 to buy tulips but made it clear that Casteleyn was actively involved in selling to others (Casteleyn refused to sell bulbs at a lower price, saying that he had charged someone else more). Yet, as we have seen, this apparent tulip dealer was himself a collector, both of shells and rarities of the sea and, it seems, of tulips. There is no division between *liefhebber* and tulip trader apparent here.[59]

Indeed, it seems that these two roles went together. The example of Casteleyn—or, for that matter, of Jan Hendricxsz Admirael or Marten Kretser—was not an isolated one. In Amsterdam, at least, where the sources are more definitive, we know that a significant group of tulip buyers also bought art at auction. This group of buyers, who attended the public auctions held by the Amsterdam Weeskamer, were a relatively close-knit group who would probably have known each other, if through no other way, from their attendance at the auctions, which have been described as "a social activity" and a form of entertainment. Among the merchants active in the Amsterdam tulip trade who bought art in these circumstances were Abraham de Schilder, Abraham Casteleyn, his brother Isaac Casteleyn, Jan Hendricxsz Admirael, François Schot, Cornelis de Bruyn, François Hendricksz Coster, Jan Pietersz Neckevelt, Volckert Dircksz Coornhart, Lambert Massa, Adam Bessels, Dirck Glaude, Abraham de Goyer, Michiel Kistgens, Abraham Versluys, Reijmont de Smith, Carel Quina, and Marten Kretser. Many other such collectors were connected to tulip buyers by marriage or through trading connections. Some of these men, moreover, had further connections to art and collecting. Besides Kretser, Admirael, and Massa, whom we have already encountered, there was, to take only a few examples, Adam Bessels, who was married to Margaretha Reynst, sister of the major collectors Gerard and Jan Reynst; her great-uncle, Jean Nicquet, was also a major collector whose collection passed to his son Jacques (for whose will Bessels acted as executor); or Abraham de Goyer, who himself owned a respectable sixty-five paintings, including a Rembrandt, as well as a large collection of pamphlets; his son, Barent, was a painter. As we will see in chapter 3, there are other such examples, and multiple connections among these men.[60]

Because in Haarlem regular public sales of paintings, like the Barent van Someren, Gommer Spranger, or Jan Basse sales in Amsterdam, were not permitted (a subject of some disquiet among painters), it is not so easy to obtain a list of buyers of art who were also involved in the tulip trade. But it is clear from other documentation that ownership of pictures was also common there, and that there were several major collectors (although it should be noted that large collections of natural rarities have not so far been found in Haarlem inventories, unlike in VOC port towns like Amsterdam or Delft). We know from Karel van Mander that a tulip buyer like Nicolaes Suycker de Jonge was already an art collector in 1604, and we see from his 1641 inventory that he was a major collector, owning pictures by Pot, Blommert, Goltzius, Jan Mostaert, and Dirck Hals; he himself was a painter (as well as a tax-collector), and Jan Mostaert, after whom Suycker's brother was named, had been his great-uncle. Another person involved in the tulip trade, the wealthy lawyer Paulus van Beresteyn (see fig. 32), who was painted by Frans Hals, owned a Maarten van Heemskerk and a Goltzius; he was the son of a major art collector, Aernout van Beresteyn, whose collection was also mentioned by Van Mander, and the whole family was known as important in the arts. Other documents hint to us an active interest in paintings among tulip buyers and sellers (hardly surprising in Haarlem, a town noted for its high concentration of painters). Those involved in the tulip trade quarrelled over paintings as well as tulips—Rogier Alleman sued Andries de Coningh "over sale of paintings" in 1638, for example, both being figures

FIGURE 32. Frans Hals, *Portrait of Paulus van Beresteyn*, c. 1620. Louvre. Beresteyn was an art collector as well as a *bloemist*.

in the tulip trade—and we know that a variety of people connected with tulips, such as Andries van den Broecke, Willem Gael, Daniel Olthoff, and Cornelis de Bruyn, attended various lotteries and sales of pictures (legal and illegal) that occurred in the 1630s. One such lottery was held, illegally, in 1636 by the painter Frans Pietersz de Grebber, who was subsequently prosecuted for breaking the prohibition on public sales of paintings. De Grebber, like some of his buyers, was very active in the tulip trade; he even, tantalizingly, is reported to have bought a "book with *tulpaden*" in 1639 for which he was sued for nonpayment.[61]

The involvement of De Grebber and Suycker points to an even closer connection between tulips and art. Several important (and several less important) artists also bought and sold tulips. De Grebber himself was no minor figure, but had probably the largest studio in Haarlem, in which he trained people like Judith Leyster, who later painted several tulip portraits. It is also clear that the famous still life painter Willem Claesz Heda was involved in the tulip trade. He was arbiter of numerous disputes about tulips in the 1630s, a sign that he was considered something of an expert on the trade. Several tulips are named after him, such as the Parasette van Heda and the Sr. Peneselbe van Heda, showing that he was also raising tulips. And we find continued interest in tulips on his part, extending to a dispute in 1654, when he was accused of planting someone else's tulip bulbs in his own garden. Other less important Haarlem artists to be found buying and selling tulips include Simon van Poelenburch (by this time living in Amsterdam), Willem de Poorter, and Joost Jansz Haverbeeck. One of the Haarlem tulip companies included as a partner the Amsterdam artist Matthijs Bloem. In Utrecht, Jacob Marrell, who painted the important tulip book of Francesco Gomes da Costa, was himself not only a tulip dealer but one of those who gathered in Utrecht on February 7, 1637, to elect representatives to a meeting of tulip traders in Amsterdam to discuss the collapse of the trade. In The Hague, Jan van Goyen famously spent considerable sums on tulips in the last weeks of the craze. And other *bloemisten* were closely connected to painters: Cornelis de Bruyn, for example, was married to Catharina Saverij, daughter of the painter Jacques Saverij; in 1639 he was accused of cheating her uncle, the artist Roelandt Saverij, out of some of his paintings at the end of his life. A series of art dealers were also connected to tulips: Abraham de

Cooge and Jan Serange in Delft, David Jorisz in Haarlem, plus, of course, Marten Kretser in Amsterdam.[62]

These many interconnections of art and tulips show us that it is actually not so surprising that Nicolas de Valnay in Paris should have compared tulips to paintings and porcelains or, for that matter, that Marten Kretser should pay for Jan Hendricxsz Admirael's tulips with eleven paintings and a Lucas van Leyden print. Nor was this interconnection entirely confined to high-flying collectors and dealers like Kretser in Amsterdam. From 1637 to 1641, a lawsuit raged in Utrecht between Joost Dareth, a gunmaker, and the illiterate ebony worker Aert Ottensz van Renswoude (usually known as Aert Otten). Otten bought half the tulips and bulbs in Dareth's garden for ƒ250 plus two paintings, one by Adam Willaerts, the other by Carel de Hooch. He also bought, in advance, whatever offsets that would grow on the other half of Dareth's bulbs for the next three years, for ƒ150 per year. For the first year's installment on the offsets, he intended to pay, again, with paintings: two by Hendrick Blommaert (one an annunciation), a battle scene by Joost Cornelisz Droochstooth, and another picture by Carel de Hooch. There was also some question of a *wintertgen,* or winter scene, by Anthony Verstralen, which Dareth claimed was part of the transaction, but which Otten said had actually been sold to Dareth separately for ƒ9. After the fall in price of tulip bulbs, Otten was unhappy about continuing the deal, but the pictures were already in Dareth's possession, and Otten found himself unable to get them back. There was also the matter of a pair of pistols, which Otten had earlier taken to Dareth to be cleaned but which Dareth had instead sold to a third party; Otten was countersuing for those, as well as for his paintings. Over the years the case grew increasingly bitter and complicated, but what is striking is the degree to which it seemed not to be about money, but about the possession of paintings, and in particular the *wintertgen,* a picture worth less than ten days' pay for a skilled laborer. It is tempting to see this case as one less about tulips and more about the love of paintings. At the very least, we must say that it was about both.[63]

It is evident, then, that we cannot separate out the "good" buyers of art and tulips, the connoisseurs who, borrowing from the language of the period, had a right to be interested in rare flowers, from the merchants who, again according to this tradition, were "bad" because they were interested in tulips as a commodity. In many cases the "good" and the "bad" were the same. The role of commerce here is, for us, a problematic one. It is hard to determine exactly why people bought tulips, even if they were collectors of art—and of course there was a commercial element even to collecting, however much the values of exchange and civility were also involved. Paludanus, for example, bought and sold curiosities for his collection in Enkhuizen and must have made some kind of profit from the transactions. For tulips, for rarities, for paintings, the question remains whether the reason for purchase was decoration, collection, or profit (although it must be said that paintings, at least, did not rise in price over the course of the seventeenth century, rendering their value as an object of speculation fairly negligible). Commerce, as we have observed, was a feature of the tulip trade almost from the beginning. As trade in tulips heated up, some buyers, at least, wanted whatever could command the highest price. The fact that by this time some tulips could change hands several times before they flowered makes it clear that at this point tulips were valued by some only for their profitability. But the continued emphasis on beauty—the lawsuits over "bad flowers," which did not fit the aesthetic standards of the era—reminds us that beauty and profit go hand in hand. Rarity helped to create a fashion that then defined the standard of beauty; this, in turn, led to a high price. This is the reason for the constant changes in the fashion of flowers. Once a particular tulip was cultivated too widely, it became "obsolete and overdated," as Samuel Gilbert phrased it, and consequently could not fetch such high sums. It must then be replaced by something newer, which consequently was claimed to be more beautiful. The same forces we see acting here in gardening were also at play in the world of art, where specialization in Dutch secular painters of the seventeenth century helped to define a niche in an increasingly full market. It was not ultimately a successful strategy, as specialization itself helped to keep prices down by providing more competition and a greater choice in product. Moreover, for a variety of reasons the market for art contracted in Holland after the middle of the century. And where flowers were concerned, too many changes in fashion led to a degree of boredom as tulips as a group became more common and less a source of wonder. The result of this was the rise of the hyacinth as the eighteenth-century flower of mode.[64]

For our tulip buyers and *liefhebbers*, however, this moment was still far away. Tulips at the height of their popularity joined with other precious

collectibles in a complex of aesthetic, personal, and commercial associations. The public they appealed to was the same public that collected art
and rarities. One tulip song even claimed that it had eclipsed these items,
moaning that "Those who previously had an interest in paintings, in
books,/In the great sciences, that is now all finished,/They would rather
see nothing stand before them but a tulip." As we have seen, however, this
was not in fact the case. Paulus van Beresteyn did not stop buying paintings because he was buying tulips. Actually, the plague epidemic of 1636
stopped him from buying either. But that is another story.[65]

THREE

Bloemisten

THE TRADE IN FLOWERS WAS "ALL THE RAGE," the Wynants family said later, at the beginning of February 1637. Pieter Wynants, a prosperous Haarlem merchant of forty-one, had invited his family to Sunday dinner on the first of February, not many days before prices in tulips fell. As the brothers, sisters, and cousins sat around Pieter Wynants' table, of course they were talking about tulips.

The dinner Pieter provided would have been a good one. These were not poor people. Pieter Wynants' wife, Margarieta Verschuyren, was the sister of a Rotterdam burgemeester, and his sister Barbara Jacobs Wynants in 1633 had married Laurens Jacobsz Reael, son of a former Secretary of the Admiralty. Pieter himself was in textiles, one of the two main industries of Haarlem, the other being beer. He had f40,000 to leave to his children when he made a codicil to his will in 1641 (reflecting an increase from f30,000 in his will of 1638). He was involved in the manufacture and sale of linen cloth and thread (*garen*), and his guests, mainly his relatives, were mostly involved in the same industry. The friends and relatives around his table that Sunday were all in their late thirties and early forties. Pieter's brother, Hendrick Jacob Wynants, thirty-eight, also a cloth merchant, was there, as was their widowed elder sister, Elsken Wynants, forty-three. They were joined by their first cousins, Hendrick Jan Wynants, thirty-five, similarly in textiles, and his sister Barbara Jans Wynants, thirty-nine, who was also a widow. (With the plague raging for nearly the past two years, young widows and widowers were even more common than usual in Haarlem.) The party was completed by Geertruyt Cornelisdr Schoudt, widow of Abraham van der Hulst, and her relatives by marriage, Jacob de Block, a dyer, and his wife, Trijntgen Lamberts (or so she was mentioned in the account we have available; her full name was actually Catharina Lamberts Schouten).[1]

The Wynants family and their guests had more in common than their age and comparative wealth. They were also all Mennonites. The Mennonites, the most important Protestant sect in the Dutch Republic outside the Calvinist Reformed Church, believed in behaving in accordance with the example of the early church, rejected infant baptism, refused to take oaths, and refused to bear arms. This meant that they were barred from serving in government office or, usually, from taking part in the *schutterijen*, the civic militias. Although these barriers necessarily reduced their local influence, at least in government, Mennonites were frequently wealthy, and although they might have lived plainly, that did not stop them from having their simple clothes and furniture made of the best materials. Mennonites were also a substantial presence in the population, especially when one considers that the Reformed Church, which had control of the government and most positions of responsibility, never achieved anything like a majority position in terms of actual numbers. In Haarlem in 1618 it is estimated that Mennonites made up about 14 percent of the townsfolk (figures from around the same period suggest that about 12.5 percent were Catholic and only around 20 percent Reformed; the rest were either in smaller religious groupings such as the Lutherans or Jews or were simply part of the religiously undecided who made up more than half the population of Haarlem). Although compromises were made by some Mennonites to the dominance of the Calvinists—some invested in the VOC, for example, whose ships were armed with cannon, and others married into regent and therefore Calvinist families—most retained their overall loyalty to their particular group. Pieter Wynants might have married the sister of a burgemeester, but, like so many of his religious compatriots, he left money to the Mennonite church. Not surprisingly, then, as we will see, Mennonite families were also strongly interconnected.[2]

During the dinner, Pieter Wynants' cousin Hendrick Jan several times suggested to Geertruyt Schoudt that she might like to buy a pound of tulip bulbs. These were Switsers, which, along with Coornharts, were the most popular sort of bulbs in late 1636 and 1637. Switsers, which were red and yellow striped flowers named after Swiss mercenary soldiers and celebrated by various poets, including Andrew Marvell, would have been in bulb form at the beginning of February and, for their own good health, buried in someone's garden. Schoudt would have to take the bulbs on trust, although as she was through various ties closely bound to the Wynants family, this was perhaps not such a problem.[3]

Geertruyt Schoudt was not the first person Hendrick Jan Wynants had sold to that day. He offered her the Switsers at a discount: she could have them for 50 guilders less than he had sold similar ones to "doctor Plas"— Gregorius van der Plas, the city doctor—that is, for f1,400 instead of Plas' f1,450. But Schoudt was not buying. Finally the dyer Jacob de Block intervened. "Go ahead, I'll back you for eight days, so you won't lose anything by it," he said. Hearing that De Block was willing to stand *borg* (guarantor) for her, Schoudt was persuaded at last and made the purchase. But Hendrick Jacob Wynants, seeing that his cousin had sold her bulbs that he wanted for himself, said to Hendrick Jan, "What are you doing?" and then addressed Geertruyt Schoudt. "Truytgen, give them to me, I'll give you forty *rijksdaalders* [f100] or f100 profit right away." Jacob de Block, her guarantor, had no use for this extra offer, however. "Don't do it, Truytgen," he said. "You'll get more than that [if you wait and sell them later], and I'll back you for eight days, so you won't lose anything." Even Jacob de Block's wife, Trijntgen Lamberts, chipped in with her own "Don't do it, Truytgen," pointing out that Schoudt would have more money—presumably to pay for the bulbs in the summer—when she inherited her share from the estate of her brother-in-law, Jacob van der Hulst, who had recently died. "We'll back you for eight days." De Block, however, evidently thought that Geertruyt Schoudt would be unable to pay and thus he, as her backer, would have the Switsers for himself; he admitted as much to Hendrick Jan Wynants when they happened to meet again on February 4 on the regular barge service to Amsterdam. "Yes, that's how it will turn out, that I'll end up benefitting from them myself."[4]

Evidently once the prices fell, fewer than eight days later, Jacob and Trijntgen were not so eager to stand by their promises. That was why

Geertruyt Schoudt asked all the Wynants cousins to come before a notary on February 20 to explain what had happened. Schoudt now owed ƒ1,400 to Hendrick Jan Wynants and had, it seems, no means, or certainly no desire, to pay it. Quarrels over her brother-in-law's estate would mean that she would not inherit for years, and her guarantor for the tulip purchase was now reneging on his promise. Geertruyt Schoudt's story was just one of many featuring disappointment and broken promises during this period—and not just after the beginning of February 1637. We will come to those other stories in time. What interests us for the moment is something else: the small circle within which Hendrick Jan Wynants was selling his tulips. This was neither a haphazard trade nor a wild one.

When the tulip trade is mentioned, it has been traditional to stress not only the apparent insanity of paying high prices for flowers but also the apparent universality of the desire to do so. "... [T]his mania, like a contagious illness, infected the whole Low Countries, & passed into France," wrote Jean de Parival in his *Les Délices de la Hollande* in 1665, and this interpretation, as well as the implicit judgment upon it, has been a constant in most later accounts of the trade. Besides the problem immediately presented by Parival's statement—the fact that it was only parts of the province of Holland, not all of the Netherlands, that became really interested in flowers—we are still left with the implication that everyone in the country, from high to low, was selling tulips.[5]

This is indeed the theme of a few of the satiric songs and pamphlets that were produced in some quantities around the end of 1636 and the beginning of 1637, mostly after the fall in price, and most, but not all, in opposition to tulips. One, by Steven Theunisz van der Lust of Haarlem, *Troost voor de ghescheurde broederschap der rouw-dragende kap-broertjes*, lists myriad crafts and professions that all united under the fool's cap of the tulip. These included not only those in the cloth trade—weavers, yarn merchants, bleachers—but also students, shoemakers, painters, barbers, chimney-sweeps, apothecaries, bakers, brewers, shopkeepers, butchers, and many more. Everyone, "pious and impious, thieves and whores, Haarlemmers and Amsterdammers," was said to be buying and selling tulips.[6]

These kinds of comments have had their effect on later accounts of tulipmania. Several later-seventeenth-century writers assured the reader, in words plucked almost verbatim from productions of people

like Van der Lust, that "through all of Holland the trade was practised /
old / young / Woman and Man / Daughter and Servingmaid / Farmer and
Nobleman / yes Lettercarriers / Shippers / Messengers / Turfcarriers / Chimney-
sweeps bought Tulips / everyone left his work. . . ." As we learned in the
introduction, this picture of an all-encompassing tulipmania was picked
up by the influential late-eighteenth-century account by Johann Beckmann. Beckmann in turn provided the information for Charles Mackay's
Extraordinary Popular Delusions and the Madness of Crowds of 1841 and,
through him, for most of the twentieth-century accounts of tulipmania,
all of which, even the most authoritative, serious history, seem to suggest
the universality of the tulip craze.[7]

Yet Beckmann painted a picture based on no documentary evidence.
"Oft did a nobleman purchase of a chimney-sweep tulips to the amount
of 2000 florins," he wrote, "and sell them at the same time to a farmer;
and neither the nobleman, chimney-sweep or farmer had roots in their
possession, or wished to possess them." Where did he get these images?
Beckmann's choice of professions for his examples about tulipmania—a
nobleman, a farmer, a chimney-sweep—is telling. From the long list of
professions provided by Steven van der Lust, a few had already been dis-
tilled out by Aitzema, Abraham Munting, and others in the later seventeenth century, and by the time we get to Beckmann, we have only a few
to represent everyone, with that tell-tale chimney-sweep providing the
splash of color every time amidst the duller nobleman and farmer. Beckmann's debt to his predecessors is obvious. But that picture is founded
on propaganda. If we turn our attention to what the archives, rather than
what the pamphleteers, have to tell us about tulipmania, things look
rather different.[8]

In the first place, there were no chimney-sweeps, farmers, or noblemen. At least, I have found none to date. Although people in a range of
professions were involved in the tulip trade, Beckmann, not to mention
Aitzema and others, has simply plucked these chimney-sweeps out of
the air. Yet if we are going to understand tulipmania, we have to be more
specific than this. We have to find out who was actually involved in tulipmania, and, just as important, what lay behind the mere names one can
cite from using documents as simple anecdotes. As with the tale of Geertruyt Schoudt and her purchase of tulips at the home of Pieter Wynants,
we have to consider how tulip buyers and sellers (who called themselves

bloemisten or *floristen*) were actually connected to each other, and what those connections might have meant to the operations of the trade. This chapter aims to tell that story.[9]

The story also needs to be told to place tulipmania in context. We have already reflected in preceding chapters on the role sociability played in the circulation of knowledge and, moreover, the way that possessing such knowledge could lead to social or professional success. This was true of natural philosophy, of art, and of commerce, as well as the intersection of all three. Tulipmania offers us a microcosm of such a "community of information" and an opportunity to witness the beginnings of its crystallization into something more organized and hierarchical. The need in all these areas for successful participants to be in the know, and the respect and authority accorded to those who were, makes tulipmania an avenue to consider the role of information and expertise in social and intellectual organization.

To work out the details of this particular community, however, is not necessarily easy. I have looked at records of all the known sales and quarrels about sales, hoping to identify as many of the buyers and sellers as possible. We know, from a meeting in Amsterdam on February 23, 1637, of representatives of those involved in the trade, that a selection of major cities in the province of Holland contained florists or *bloemists*, nearly all of whom, it should be said, were not professional florists but simply took part in the trade alongside their normal occupations. Many bought or sold only one bulb. The cities that sent representatives on February 23 were Haarlem, Leiden, Alkmaar, Utrecht, Gouda, Delft, Vianen, Enkhuizen, Hoorn, Medemblik, and the region De Streek; Amsterdam was also represented at the meeting but refused to sign the accord reached on the day. These deputies—several attended from each city—themselves represented many more in their own areas. In Utrecht, for example, a meeting was held on February 9 to choose three representatives of the "lieffhebbers and traders of the said flowers" to go to Amsterdam on February 23; thirty-six attended that meeting (see fig. 53 in chapter 4). It was not possible for me to investigate every city thoroughly for the purposes of this study. But by looking chiefly at two of the main cities in the trade, Amsterdam and Haarlem (whose estimated populations in 1635 were something more than 120,000 and 42,000, respectively), and one somewhat smaller town, Enkhuizen (whose estimated population in

1622 was 22,000), we are able to get a good picture of the trade in the 1630s. The question is who, in these cities, was actually involved. I have identified approximately 285 in Haarlem—at the time recognized as the center of the trade—who bought and sold flowers, around 60 in Amsterdam, and about 25 in Enkhuizen. More specificity would naturally be desirable. But counting these tulip traders is difficult; some bought and sold, some merely made bets with tulips, some (not included in my figures) had tulips named after them, were arbiters in disputes about the flowers, or were regular witnesses to transactions, making it likely, but not certain, that they were also involved in the trade.[10]

Moreover, when making these assessments, we have to face the problem that the archival record does not provide us with information about every transaction. Sales of tulips tended to be recorded in various circumstances. When the sale was made, some kind of contract was generally drawn up, either on a small slip of paper (called a *coopcedulle*) or in a legal document made by a notary and given to each party, as well as recorded in the notary's own bound volumes of contracts, wills, inventories, *insinuaties*, affadavits, and so on. If the sale was made at an auction, either at an inn or more official auctions held by the Weeskamer (the orphan's chamber, which looked after the interests of children who had lost one or both parents), the sale would also be recorded by a secretary. We do not have a full record of these transactions; there are many more to be found in the notarial record than elsewhere, but where auctions are concerned, we run up against a wall. Although I have found documentation of the existence of auctions, the actual sales records, which are available for the Weeskamer art sales in Amsterdam, are no longer extant for sales such as the Jan van Damme, David de Milt, or Pieter de Jonckheer Weeskamer tulip auctions in Haarlem (Van Damme, a gardener by profession, left tulips that brought in a staggering ƒ42,013:5), nor are they for the Weeskamer sale of the tulips of Wouter Bartholomeusz Winckel in Alkmaar on February 5, 1637, in which the prices were so high that they were printed on a broadside as a kind of wonder, but which unfortunately did not record the names of the buyers (see fig. 33). Some of the buyers in the Winckel sale, and many others involved in tulip transactions, can, however, be located precisely through quarrels about them, quarrels that occurred both in the period of rising tulip sales and after the fall in prices. As we will learn later, many of these arguments were pursued in the first

FIGURE 33. Broadside, *Lijste van eenighe Tulpaen verkocht aende meest-biedende*, 1637. Wageningen UR Library. This publication used the prices at the Winckel auction on February 5, 1637, in Alkmaar to ridicule the trade.

instance with threats by notaries, such as the *insinuatie* by Jan Hendricxsz Admirael that began chapter 2. Many of the names of those participating in the tulip trade are known from notarial records, although until now there has been no real effort since Posthumus' research in the 1920s to locate any new notarial materials nor, rather astonishingly, any attempt to find out something about the character of those identified in the documents. But the trail does not end with the notarial archives. Tulip buyers and sellers also took their claims to court, both before and after February 1637. Although civil court records from this period are sparse for the main cities concerned, we do have the rolls of the Kleine Bank van Justitie of Haarlem, a kind of small claims court, as well as similar civil courts for places like Hoorn and Enkhuizen. These, particularly in Haarlem, provide us with new names of people suing about tulip transactions, many of which, in the period after the fall in prices, were actually claims for a percentage on much larger original sums. The Kleine Bank thus gives us access to both smaller and larger transactions.

Using these records, then, with certain reservations, we can take a look at the kind of population that was interested in tulips. Was it really the case that everyone, high to low, was a *bloemist* in the 1630s? In fact, as the numbers mentioned above indicate, the people involved in tulipmania formed a fairly small group. Although the sources prevent us from knowing about every person who bought or sold tulips, the same names seem to recur in various different contexts. The one contemporary pamphlet that actually names names, Jan Soet's *Dood-Rolle ende Groef-Maal van Floortie-Flooraas* (The Death-Roll and Wake of Floortie-Floraas), contains hardly a *bloemist* who did not appear elsewhere in the manuscript record (see fig. 56 in chapter 5). Although we can only throw up our hands in despair when confronting a lawsuit like the one which came up in the Kleine Bank van Justitie in Haarlem in 1636, in which the essentially anonymous Jan Pietersz sued the equally anonymous Pieter Jansz over the sale of a Gouda bulb, such cases are surprisingly rare: generally tulip traders are identifiable and often substantial citizens. While some bought or sold only one tulip, others pop up everywhere, even in transactions taking place in other towns. Some even formed companies to deal in tulips. And if we look at the tulip traders as a group, we can see that, far from being an indiscriminate social group, they were in fact often connected to each other, and some were more important, and more expert, than others.[11]

The dinner at Pieter Wynants' house, although in some ways perhaps an unusual event, makes a case in point. The guests were all part of the same religious group, one that was something of a closed society. Many of them were related to each other, including, not surprisingly, Geertruyt Schoudt, the buyer, and Trijntgen Lamberts, the wife of her *borg* or guarantor, Jacob de Block. All three obviously knew the Wynants family well enough to be invited to Sunday dinner. On the same day, however, Hendrick Jan Wynants had also sold a pound of Switsers to the Haarlem city doctor, Gregorius van der Plas, who, far from being either a Mennonite or in the cloth trade, moved instead in Catholic and artistic circles (besides his medical contacts, he was closely connected to the Catholic goldsmith Dominicus van Lijnhoven, who, in turn, was brother-in-law of the well-known Catholic painter and *bloemist* Frans Pietersz de Grebber). Thus we must not jump to hasty conclusions about connections among our *bloemisten*.

Not long ago the Dutch historian Simon Groenveld suggested extending the concept of *verzuiling*, or pillarization, in Dutch society back to the period of the Dutch Republic. Pillarization is a familiar concept to the Dutch today. It defines a state of affairs, generally acknowledged to have existed in the Netherlands since about 1850 (though now disappearing again), in which sections of the population, often defined by their religion, pursued most of their daily activities within their own community, with separate schools, community organizations, political parties, and shops. Groenveld, however, wished to identify traces of pillarization in the sixteenth through eighteenth centuries. For the period that concerns us, up to 1650, he reserved his analysis to churches, rather than extending it, as he did for the following hundred years, into the realms of schools and charity work. Groenveld himself was hesitant about applying the word "pillarization" to the formation of churches, and critiques of his analysis have pointed to the excessively flexible definition of *verzuiling* that he applied to Dutch society in the Republic. But even if we cannot use this word to describe Dutch society at the time of the tulipmania, it is salutary to think of the way that individual Dutch in this period—in common with all early modern town-dwellers—operated within particular networks and lived within particular interacting communities and worlds. Tulipmania gives us a window into these networks, just as the networks themselves show us something about how tulipmania itself could take place.[12]

If these buyers and sellers of tulips were not farmers, nobles, or chimney-sweeps, who were they? They were not farmers because on the whole tulip traders were urban, not rural. We have records of one or two buyers or sellers coming from villages near Haarlem or Hoorn, such as Reynier Hindlopen, *schout* (sheriff) at Hoogwoude, a village outside of Hoorn. We also hear occasionally of auctions taking place at village inns, such as a sale at the inn of Huybert Huijgen in Velsen, where Cornelis Thijsz sold a Viceroy to Jan Abrahamsz, a baker, for ƒ1,000 on January 1, 1637. But these accounts are rare; tulipmania, like most other trade, was an urban phenomenon in what was, in any case, the most urbanized society in Europe in this period. As for noblemen, there were none to be found in the records. This was in part because of the low numbers of aristocrats in western Dutch society in the seventeenth century; the province of Holland, at least, was for the most part ruled by *regenten*, the wealthy burghers who held office in the major towns. As the tulip trade *was* a trade—and we will see, when we look at the professions held by those involved with tulips, that flowers were a sideline for many involved in commerce—it is not so surprising to find that it is merchants and skilled craftsmen, rather than nobles, who are found in the records of tulip transactions.[13]

Finally, those involved in tulips were not chimney-sweeps. Actually, chimney-sweeps are only the most picturesque of the lower-class professions cited by pamphlet literature and chroniclers as part of tulipmania. Weavers, in fact, are the people most frequently associated with tulipmania in these texts. As we will discuss in chapter 5, many of the satiric songs, and even those ending up in popular general songbooks of the era like the *Haerlems Liedt-Boeck* of 1643, focus on weavers. The pamphlets of the period most often cited subsequently (and indeed used by many as factual representations of the trade), the three dialogues *Samen spraeck tusschen Waermondt ende Gaergoedt*, consisted of conversations between two weavers. Yet weavers, and laborers in general, do not feature much in the archival materials, where the preponderance of the middling sort is striking. Posthumus, the only author who has looked in any detail at the manuscript record, admittedly addressed this question in the 1920s, attributing the absence of artisans to the abandonment of the use of notaries to record transactions as the trade heated up. But even if this were the case, one would expect artisans to turn up in the archives more than they do. If artisans failed to use notaries late in 1636, we should still find some of them trading with merchants (who did use notaries) earlier on, and certainly to be approaching notaries as lawsuits seemed a likely recourse in 1637; yet neither seems to have happened. And although the small claims court, the Kleine Bank van Justitie, which Posthumus did not investigate, brings many more people to our attention, it does not substantially change our picture of the tulip trade. One might expect to find mainly smaller fry there, at least in 1636, since the court dealt only with claims of less than fifty guilders. But this court was also populated with burghers, some quite substantial. The former burgemeester Johan de Wael, for example, appears frequently in the 1630s, and the people in-

volved in suits about nonpayment for tulips are again not usually identifiable as laborers. A few people's professions are not evident, and there
were indeed a few *bloemisten* who seemed to come from lower trades;
we might have found more if such a source had been available for Amsterdam as well as Haarlem. But on current evidence, the preponderance
of middling *bloemisten* must stand, even in the Kleine Bank. Indeed, the
court ended up dealing with far larger tulip transactions in 1638, once it
was decided in Haarlem that defaulters should pay litigants a fee of 3.5
percent of the original purchase price. The Kleine Bank van Justitie is a
good place to encounter tulip traders in the mid-1630s, but a poor place
to find weavers, chimney-sweeps, or the like.[14]

But if we do not find tulip buyers and sellers at the bottom of urban
society, we also are hard put to locate many at the top. On the whole,
those involved with the flowers seem to have come from a stratum below
that of the *regenten*, the holders of office in city government. The federal
Dutch system gave primacy to the towns, which sent representatives to
the provincial government (the States), and from there to the national
assembly (the States-General). Legislation not only originated from these
deputies but everything (including, for example, a tax on tulips proposed
by the States of Holland in the autumn of 1636) was referred back to the
towns for discussion and recommendations. The leaders of the towns
were therefore important not only locally, but also nationally. They were
usually chosen by co-optation, meaning that towns were led by an oligar-
chy consisting entirely of members of the Reformed Church and, for the
period we are looking at, men of northern origin rather than immigrants
from the south. Those *de facto* restrictions meant that some of the richest
members of the local society were not, in fact, part of the government.
Mennonites (such as the Wynants, or the Moens family in Amsterdam)
could be extremely wealthy, and southerners are now credited by historians with having done much to transform the Dutch economy into the
wonder of the seventeenth century, yet they were largely excluded from
official power in the localities. However, those who did attain local office
were certainly in the top stratum of society, both in wealth and in local
influence and respect.[15]

Among our tulip traders, only one in Amsterdam was to become a
regent, albeit one of the most important. Jan Munter eventually served
as burgemeester, but had started life as a Mennonite and was related to

many of the other Mennonites who became involved in tulips. He and his brother-in-law Pieter Dircks arranged in September 1636 to buy all the tulips belonging to a couple in Amsterdam, Claes Jansz and his wife, Marritje Machiels. In Haarlem, *regenten* were similarly sparse among the *floristen*. Only five people who can be connected with tulips held the top offices of burgemeester, *schepen* (alderman, with legislative or judicial duties), or member of the *vroedschap* (city council); in Enkhuizen, where far fewer were involved in tulips, three were in top offices. Haarlem's total would have been even smaller if two of the four, Cornelis Guldewagen (see fig. 34) and Johan de Wael, had not tried to go into the tulip business in a big way only days before the fall in prices. Guldewagen and De Wael were both brewers—De Wael in the brewery De Zon (the Sun), and Guldewagen, initially a soap merchant, in the brewery De Vergulde Hart (the Gilded Heart)—and as such were right at the top of Haarlem society. De Wael had already been burgemeester of Haarlem in the 1620s, and Guldewagen was co-opted into the *vroedschap* in 1625, had already been *schepen* twice in the 1630s, and on June 5, 1637, was appointed treasurer of Haarlem; he achieved the post of burgemeester for the first of many times in 1642.

Their high position could not protect them from the vagaries of biology and economics. Guldewagen and De Wael transplanted 1,300 bulbs to Haarlem from the garden of the bankrupt florist Anthony de Flory in Wassenaar in early February, hoping, it seems, to make a profit for themselves and for the curators of Flory's bankrupt estate. But then the prices abruptly fell. They fought a rearguard action in May, protesting that the bulbs in any case were sickly and had been so even in Flory's garden (his gardeners also said they should never have been transplanted at that time of year, an argument perhaps directed at Flory's curators, with whom they were apparently in business). The outcome is unknown, although it was still dragging on in 1639; the Haarlemmers threatened to take the curators to the high court, the Hof van Holland, but I have found no such case in the court's records. Although the numbers of *regents* who bought and sold tulips seem to have been few, the outrage Guldewagen and De Wael appear to have felt is worth noting. Their influence in the city government may well have shaped Haarlem's official reaction to the tulip crash, since it was at the request of these two men, plus the clogmaker Hendrick Lucasz (also very active in the trade), that the burgemeesters

FIGURE 34. Frans Hals, *Portrait of Cornelis Guldewagen*, c. 1660.
Krannert Art Museum, University of Illinois, Urbana-Champaign.
Guldewagen, one of the *regenten* trying to influence policy after the crash,
is shown here in his full prosperity more than twenty years later.

and *vroedschap* of Haarlem wrote on June 16, 1637, asking for the Hof van
Holland's temporary settlement of tulip affairs to be withdrawn.[16]

Even if most of those who took part in the tulip trade were not of the
regent class, large numbers were substantial citizens. Because of the timing and nature of the tax registers that were compiled in various towns,
it is not always easy to tell how wealthy they were. It is generally believed

that these assessments underestimated people's wealth. In Amsterdam in 1631, when a 0.5 percent tax on property was assessed on those with more than ƒ1,000, twenty-four of the sixty known tulip buyers and sellers were on the list of around four thousand well-off Amsterdammers. The wealthiest of these was the sugar refiner Abraham de Schilder, who was assessed as having property worth ƒ60,000. (For comparison, altogether 322 residents of Amsterdam had fortunes assessed at between ƒ50,000 and ƒ500,000; 231 of these were at De Schilder's level, between ƒ50,000 and ƒ100,000. The number of residents who had between ƒ20,000 and ƒ50,000 was 584.) Other wealthy Amsterdammers involved in the tulip trade included Reymont de Smith (ƒ25,000), Adam Bessels (ƒ30,000), and Volckert Coornhart (ƒ20,000). These are substantial sums, though nowhere near the assessments of the richest men in Amsterdam in 1631, Jacob Poppen (ƒ500,000); Guillielmo Bartholotti (ƒ400,000), who, although not himself known to have taken part in tulip sales, was the son of a known *liefhebber* and related by marriage to several of the *bloemisten;* or Balthasar Coymans (also ƒ400,000), whose relative Jasper Coymans was caught stealing baskets of bulbs out of a Keizersgracht garden in 1631.[17]

The figures would no doubt be higher for many of the Amsterdam tulip traders if the tax assessment of 1631 had been made several years later. Although several of these *bloemisten*, notably Adam Bessels, Abraham de Goyer, Carel Quina, Jeronimus Victory, Abraham Versluys, and Volckert Coornhart (if he had lived past August 1636) were in their fifties and early sixties in 1637, most others were in their mid-thirties; the average age of the Amsterdam tulip cohort in 1637 was thirty-eight. Most had recently married and had had at least one child by 1637, meaning they were recently established in life. In 1631, six years earlier, these would have been young men, mostly not yet married, and some (such as Dirck Arentsz Bosch, scion of a very wealthy Mennonite family, or Jan Jeuriaensz de Meijer, a furrier) would have been only in their teens, Bosch aged sixteen and De Meijer aged seventeen. So the 1631 tax records probably underestimate the wealth of the Amsterdam *bloemisten* in 1636–1637.[18]

Finding out about the wealth of those in Haarlem is also complicated. The tax records date from 1628, 1650, and 1653, and, except for 1650, assess only the annual rent, or potential rent, of any houses owned by those assessed. The earliness of the 1628 Kohier and the lateness of the assessment in 1653 make it difficult to come to any overall judgment of the wealth of tulip buyers and sellers there. Certainly no one named in the tulip trade comes close to being able to afford the most expensive rent on a property in 1628, the combined house and brewery of Claes Adriaansz Verbeecq, which amounted to ƒ1,400. The most expensive property owned by any *bloemist* in the 1628 Kohier is a house, owned by Pieter Vrients, whose rent was assessed at ƒ380 a year. Thirty-two of our tulip traders owned houses assessed at more than ƒ100, but this fact is deceptive, because Haarlem was a town where renting rather than owning was the norm, and many of the tulip traders owned numbers of cheaper houses that they also rented out, meaning that the value of individual properties does not tell us enough about one person's wealth. Nicolaes Suycker den Jonge, who was clearly very well off, for example, owned houses assessed at ƒ256, ƒ215, ƒ140, ƒ94, ƒ80, ƒ65, ƒ52, ƒ48, ƒ44, ƒ33, and ƒ18. One means of judging whether a Haarlem tulip trader was wealthy is to look at the area in which he had his own residence (although that is not always easy to ascertain). Following a 1989 analysis of these records by neighborhood, we can identify twenty-four *bloemisten* as owning houses in "rich" neighborhoods and another ten in "wealthier than average" ones. But we are still faced with the problem of the date of the records, which means that many names that might figure in 1637 are missing. The average age of the *bloemisten* in Haarlem is similar to that in Amsterdam—thirty-nine—so that we still have the problem of judging a man's wealth at thirty-nine on records that present us with his wealth at age thirty. And when we get to 1653 we find a number of well-off former tulip traders, but this tells us little about their circumstances in the 1630s, only that they failed to go bankrupt during the tulip craze. So again the records do not give us much help—although that last point, the failure to go bankrupt, is one we should bear in mind for later.[19]

In the end, then, our analysis of the social level of our tulip traders must remain somewhat impressionistic. But we still can make a judgment. This is perhaps easiest if we look at the professions of those involved in tulips. Overall we can say that in Amsterdam those buying and selling tulips ranged from middle-level to well-off merchants, often pursuing international trade. In Haarlem, where industry rather than seaborne trade was the chief occupation of the merchant class, we find a large number of manufacturers; several men from the professional classes such as lawyers, surgeons, doctors, and notaries; four artists and five silversmiths; and a variety of craftsmen. However, one should not be fooled by the designation of craftsman into thinking that these people were all poor. Skilled craftsmen—and numbers of this group were officers of their guilds—could be very wealthy men. For example, one person who sold a tulip, Abraham Anthonisz de Milt (who was related to a variety of other tulip traders), was a baker, but he lived in a house worth ƒ5,000 on the Kleine Houtstraat, owned another on the same street worth ƒ2,000, and, when he died, his estate was valued at ƒ26,927. Similarly, the professional gardener Jan van Damme, who died on January 18, 1636, owned two houses and had just sold a third when he died; his estate (largely consisting, admittedly, of tulips) was worth ƒ44,013. The designation of craftsman also did not necessarily indicate someone's actual profession at the time, but frequently simply the craft in which he was trained; a "baker" could actually be a grain trader or a "shoemaker" a merchant in leather. As for Amsterdam, practically everyone we can identify with tulips was at least a middle-level merchant, and even in Haarlem and Enkhuizen the numbers of merchants, wealthy manufacturers, professionals, and artists and high-level artisans made up a sizeable proportion of those who bought and sold tulips.[20]

But if we are to understand why these people, and not others, became enmeshed in the tulip trade, if we are to see what lessons we can learn from these groups about the nature of early modern communities, we need to think not just about the breakdown of the population of tulip traders into different subdivisions, but how the individuals interacted with each other. Precisely because the group of tulip traders is not particularly large, we would expect there to be strong connections among the different people involved. Did different people from the same family, from the same profession, from the same religion, from the same neighborhood buy and sell tulips? Was the scene from the Wynants dinner table repeated in rooms across urban Holland?

To begin with, in some extended families we are able to find several tulip traders, which is even more remarkable when we think of the relatively small numbers of people trading tulips at all. In the Netherlands at this time, business worked very much on a family basis. The first people a merchant would trust, the first people he would go to for capital investment, the first people he would ask to guarantee his debts, and the first people he would be likely to join in business ventures would be his own relatives, a group often known as the *vrunden* or *vrienden*: the friends. One's actual friends were also in some ways equated with one's family, but in general, a family was closer and more reliant on each other than its members were on outsiders. The close ties of the *vrunden* could easily entail a kind of cooperation in business, so that brothers and brothers-in-law, in particular, often went into business together or joined together in the same individual ventures, such as investment in a particular long-distance voyage. We can see this even in the non-tulip activities of some of our *bloemisten*. Lambert Massa, for example, who was a Muscovy merchant and a Haarlemmer living in Amsterdam, initially served as an agent for his older brother Isaac (now known for having written an account of Russia in the Time of Troubles and for having been painted by Frans Hals, sitting smiling beneath a tree beside his wife, Beatrix van der Laen). In the 1620s Lambert Massa also joined together with another brother, Christiaen, in his investment in a variety of voyages to Archangel. Similar bonds can be seen in the potash business set up in 1640 by the brothers Jacques and Pieter de Clercq and their nephew Abraham Ampe, the son of their sister Levyna de Clercq. The Amsterdam sugar refiner Abraham de Schilder, who sold tulips in a public auction in 1633, at one time owned a refinery on the Singel with his wife's uncle, Andries Rijckaert (whose name in turn we find attached to various tulips he must have bred). These kinds of family/business relationships are common in seventeenth-century Holland.[21]

If we cast our eye down the lists of tulip buyers and sellers, in fact, we become entangled in whole webs of family connections. In Utrecht, for example, the *bloemisten* included several sets of brothers: Pieter and Johan van Gelder, Anthony Verbeeck and Jacob Verbeeck de Jonge (not to mention their father, Jacob Verbeeck den Oude), Bastiaen Hendricksz van Gheesbergen and his brother David, and Daniel and Matthijs Hoorns. Furthermore, Daniel Hoorns, a silk merchant, was the brother-in-law of another silk merchant, Hendrick van Hardenberch; the notary Johannes Luyt and the shoemaker Cornelis Stevensz Pauw were married to sisters, Maria and Stephania van Voorst. The strength of family connections in Haarlem is no different. With a longer list of tulip traders, we find even more interrelationships, and more complicated ones. Again, there were brothers—Pieter and Cornelis Bol, Cornelis and Abraham de Bruyn, Willem Gerritsz Schouten and Gerrit Gerritsz Schouten, Jacques and Pieter de Clercq, Pieter Alleman de Jonge and Rogier Alleman—and at least twelve sets of brothers-in-law: the Allemans and Sacharias Reyns, Andries de Busscher and David van der Cruijs, Bouwen Fransz and Jacob Teunisz Ram, Gerrit Nannincx Deyman and Simon van Poelenburch, Frans Pietersz de Grebber and Dominicus van Lijnhoven, Jacob Grimmaris and Jan Salomonsz Schapesteyn: and on and on. We also have more complicated relationships; for example, Cornelis Bol's niece (and his brother Pieter's daughter) Josina Bols was married to the son of Dirck Boortens; Abraham de Milt's daughter was the sister-in-law of Andries de Busscher: again on and on. Amsterdam, though providing a smaller pool, had its own sets of *tulpisten* brothers-in-law. These relationships—and there are many more—are in some ways not surprising. Many people in early modern towns were interrelated. But it still seems significant that so many connections existed among precisely the cohort that was buying and selling tulips. Other families and names play no part: we need to think about why.

The connections are even more weblike when we weave in another factor: religion. We have already witnessed the buying and selling over a Sunday dinner of a Mennonite family in Haarlem. The fact that the Wynants were Mennonites is important. Mennonites were always closely intertwined with each other, even though there was sometimes some outmarriage, or conversion, as in the case of Jan Munter, or, for that matter, of Barbara Jacob Wynants, the sister of Pieter and Hendrick Jacob Wynants—her marriage to the regent Laurens Reael will probably have meant some kind of religious compromise on her part. Mennonites appear in disproportionately large numbers among the *bloemisten*, and, more than other groups, they seem to have been particularly interested in selling to each other.[22]

Picture a scene from Haarlem in January 1637. It was the home of Jacques de Clercq, thirty-eight, part of the wealthy De Clercq family, which specialized in selling potash for the bleaching industry. Sitting in his house was De Clercq's brother-in-law, Pieter Moens, the son of the enormously rich Amsterdam linen merchant Anthony Moens (his wealth was assessed in 1631 at ƒ320,000). Along with him was the fifty-three-year-old linen yarn merchant Barent Roelofsz Wanscher, a man of tremendous influence in Haarlem, with his finger seemingly in every pie. Moens and Wanscher were bargaining hard with each other over tulips.

They did one deal in which Wanscher had to pay Moens *f*100, and then fell to negotiations over another. Unable to come to an agreement on a price, they turned to Jacques de Clercq for arbitration. Although a year later De Clercq was to fall out with Moens over the inheritance from his father-in-law's estate—Moens is recorded as saying of De Clercq that "no greater Thief was ever caught"—at this point his word was worth something to both parties. De Clercq pronounced a price Moens must pay Wanscher: *f*350 plus a *rijksdaalder* (*f*2.5) for De Clercq's maid and another *rijksdaalder* for Moens' coachman, but Moens could subtract from the sum the *f*100 he was already owed by Wanscher for the other deal. As Wanscher had De Clercq swear to this account before a notary in 1639, we can conclude that Moens, like so many others, ultimately resisted payment.[23]

These men were, not coincidentally, all Mennonites. The religious connection seems to have been of substantial weight when Mennonites were looking for people to trust with their money. We find in Amsterdam the grain merchant Anthony de Man (who himself was brother-in-law of the Mennonite *bloemist* and cloth merchant Dirck van de Cooghen) buying "diverse Tulips of various sorts" from the young Dirck Arentsz Bosch, son of the wealthy Mennonite merchant Arent Dircksz Bosch. (In 1637, by the way, Bosch married the stepdaughter of a sister of Trijntgen Lamberts, whom we found urging Geertruyt Schoudt to buy tulips at Pieter Wynants' dinner table.) We find Bosch also selling an Anvers, a Terlon, a "Gemarmelde Goijer," and 1,000 *asen* of a tulip called Pels to the Mennonite Jan Pietersz Neckevelt, a neighbor of De Man's (although Neckevelt bought from Calvinists as well). We find the Amsterdam cloth merchant Jacob Abrahamsz van Halmael (later to set up a cloth business with Dirck van der Cooghen) selling tulips worth *f*1,800 to the Haarlem brewer Abraham van Meeckeren and his mother, the brewer Maria Vlaminghs, in return for an equivalently valued amount of Swedish barley. The transaction between these Mennonite merchants, on January 12, 1637, was, however, hastily canceled on February 10. (Van Meeckeren had already sold some of the tulips to the Haarlem locksmith Jan Salomonsz Schapesteyn, but Halmael, probably unwisely, agreed to take the money from Schapesteyn directly when it was due.)[24]

But when Pieter Moens and Barent Roelofsz Wanscher sat bargaining in the house of Jacques de Clercq, they were demonstrating more than the propensity of Mennonites to trade with each other. All these men were connected not only by religion and by southern origin, but also by operating in overlapping networks of *vrunden*. Moens was De Clercq's brother-in-law; Wanscher was De Clercq's close associate, the official guardian of the interests of his first wife, Sara van Middeldonck, and later of his daughter Geertruyd after Sara's death. And the web of *vrunden* stretched much more widely than this. As figure 35 shows, a whole host of Mennonite *bloemisten* was spread through Haarlem, Amsterdam, Rotterdam, and Utrecht—all connected, and almost always by ties of blood. Jacques de Clercq himself bought and sold tulips, but so did his brother Pieter in Haarlem, his brother-in-law Pieter Moens in Amsterdam, his nephew Cornelis Verdonck in Rotterdam, his nephew Abraham Ampe in Haarlem, his sister Levyna's nephew Andries Pietersz van den Broecke in Haarlem, his brother-in-law Jacob Verbeeck den Oude and his sons Jacob and Anthony Verbeeck in Utrecht, his stepbrother-in-law Jan Munter in Amsterdam, his wife's uncle Johan Moens in Haarlem, and his future son-in-law Bastiaan van de Rype in Haarlem. Then there are the more indirect connections, with Jacob Abrahamsz Halmael, Dirck van der Cooghen, Severijn van den Heuvel; right back, finally, to Geertruyt Schoudt, whose tulip purchase began this chapter. Since many other families seem to have had nothing to do with the tulip trade, such a web of connections is striking. The existence of this network in the tulip trade resonates with several themes of seventeenth-century Dutch society we have already discussed: the importance of family in business and the influence of religion on nonreligious activities. It also gives one cause to think about how other types of interconnections influenced the course of tulipmania.[25]

For we find other commonalities among the *bloemisten* than simply linkages of family and religion. Identifying those commonalities gives us clues to the way that the exchange of tulips took place. Did it matter, for example, where people lived? In both Amsterdam and Haarlem, there were certainly clusters of tulip buyers and sellers (see fig. 36). For example, of the *bloemisten* in Amsterdam whose addresses I know, at least five—Jan Hendricxsz Admirael, Abraham de Schilder, François Schot, Adam Bessels, and Jeronimus Victory—lived within two streets of each other (Schot and Bessels on the east side of the Keizersgracht and De Schilder on the west, Victory on the west side of the Herengracht, and Admirael on the east side of the Prinsengracht, all around the area between the Huidenstraat and the Berenstraat). Another small cluster is on

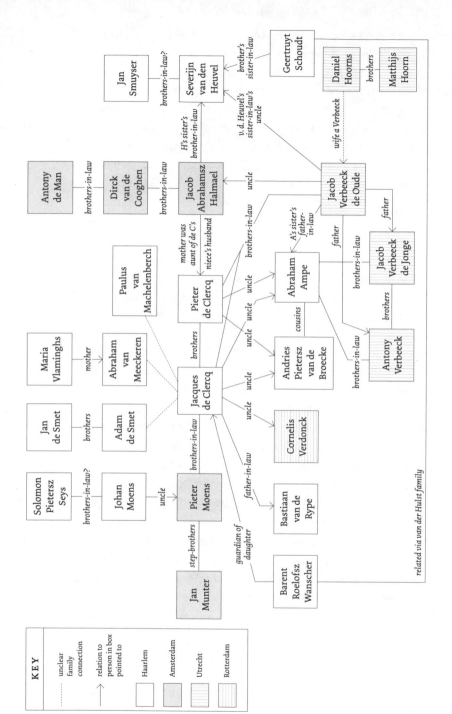

FIGURE 35. Diagram of connections among some Mennonites in the tulip trade.

KEY

·········· unclear family connection

⟶ relation to person in box pointed to

☐ Haarlem

▨ Amsterdam

▥ Utrecht

▦ Rotterdam

Solomon Pietersz Seys — *brothers-in-law?* — Johan Moens — *uncle* — Pieter Moens

Jan Munter — *step-brothers* — Pieter Moens

Jan de Smet — *brothers* — Adam de Smet — *brothers-in-law* — Jacques de Clercq

Maria Vlaminghs — *mother* — Abraham van Meeckeren

Paulus van Machelenberch

Jacques de Clercq — *brothers* — Pieter de Clercq

Pieter Moens — *guardian of daughter* — Jacques de Clercq

Jacques de Clercq — *father-in-law* — Bastiaan van de Rype

Barent Roelofsz Wanscher

Jacques de Clercq — *uncle* — Andries Pietersz van de Broecke

Jacques de Clercq — *uncle* — Cornelis Verdonck

Jacques de Clercq — *uncle* — Abraham Ampe

Pieter de Clercq — *uncle* — Abraham Ampe

Pieter de Clercq — *mother was aunt of de C's* / *niece's husband* — Jacob Abrahamsz Halmael

Pieter de Clercq — *brothers-in-law* — Jacob Verbeeck de Oude

Andries Pietersz van de Broecke — *cousins* — Abraham Ampe

Abraham Ampe — *A's sister's father-in-law* — Jacob Verbeeck de Oude

Abraham Ampe — *brothers-in-law* — Jacob Verbeeck de Jonge

Abraham Ampe — *brothers-in-law* — Antony Verbeeck

Antony de Man — *brothers-in-law* — Dirck van de Cooghen — *brothers-in-law* — Jacob Abrahamsz Halmael

Jacob Abrahamsz Halmael — *H's sister's brother-in-law* — Severijn van den Heuvel

Jan Smuyser — *brothers-in-law?* — Severijn van den Heuvel

Severijn van den Heuvel — *brother's sister-in-law* — Geertruyt Schoudt

Severijn van den Heuvel — *v.d. Heuvel's sister-in-law's uncle* — Jacob Verbeeck de Oude

Jacob Abrahamsz Halmael — *uncle* — Jacob Verbeeck de Oude

Jacob Verbeeck de Oude — *wife a Verbeeck* — Daniel Hoorns

Daniel Hoorns — *brothers* — Matthijs Hoorn

Jacob Verbeeck de Oude — *father* — Jacob Verbeeck de Jonge

Jacob Verbeeck de Oude — *father* — Antony Verbeeck

Jacob Verbeeck de Jonge — *brothers* — Antony Verbeeck

related via van der Hulst family

the Herengracht just south of the Leliegracht, where Wynand Schuyl, Reymont de Smith, and François Hendricksz de Coster all lived, along with Schuyl's fantastically wealthy brother-in-law, Guillielmo Bartholotti, whose house is now the Nederlands Theatermuseum. Altogether nine *bloemisten* we know of lived on the Keizersgracht, six on the Herengracht, and four on the Prinsengracht, all relatively near each other. The tall, grand houses along these canals were by this time the province of the elite in Amsterdam. As the canals were dug and the city started to expand westward into the newly forming canal ring—the first stage began in 1609—wealthy merchants increasingly left the old city on the eastern side of the Dam to take up residence on the new canals, especially the prestigious Keizersgracht and Herengracht. These houses, moreover, unlike those in the crowded old town, were built with capacious gardens behind them. A cluster of tulip buyers here confirms our impression that in Amsterdam this was a trade mainly of the well-to-do. But another area of concentration, around the Zeedijk and the Geldersekade, where four tulip traders seem to have been living in 1637, also housed a large number of merchants.[26]

There was another node of flower traders in Amsterdam who, perhaps not surprisingly, lived surrounded by gardens. Several of the *bloemisten* we have already met—Abraham Casteleyn, Abraham de Goyer, Simon van Poelenburch, and the wealthy professional gardener Willem Willemsz—lived just outside the city gates at the Regulierspoort, around the area of the current Rembrandtplein and Thorbeckeplein. The land around the Reguliershof was at this time a stretch of gardens; De Goyer, we recall, had begun amassing plots of garden land from the beginning of the seventeenth century. Willemsz's land there will have been partly commercial, as indeed was that of De Goyer, at least eventually. Jeronimus Victory, the Italian merchant-insurer turned florist—unlike the other flower traders we are examining here, he turned flowers into his profession and was called a "Blommist" in the documents describing his property at death—bought a garden and dwelling on the Regulierspad in November 1632, although he actually lived on the Herengracht. His 1647 inventory lists two further gardens bought in this area, on the Nieuwepad and the St. Jorispad, in 1641 and 1642. The gardens of the wealthy and the plots where commercial gardeners operated were in close proximity to a number of important tulip traders, including Abraham de Goyer, who,

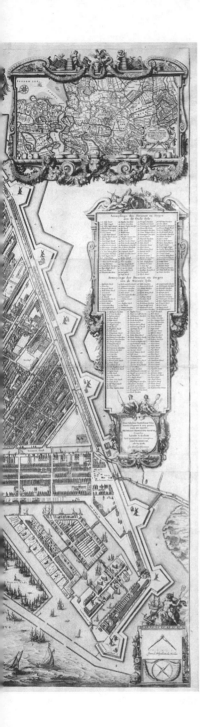

FIGURE 36. Balthasar Florisz Berckenrode,
map of Amsterdam, 1647 copy of 1625 map.
Gemeentearchief, Amsterdam. Here marked
with clusters of the homes of *bloemisten*.

though a silk merchant, was said to have made more than ƒ20,000 on tulips in one year.[27]

This kind of close proximity of tulip traders is also notable in Haarlem (see fig. 37). Haarlem in the 1630s was a city bursting at its seams. Unlike Amsterdam, which early in the seventeenth century began making plans for an expansion to deal with its growing population, Haarlem made no changes to its city boundaries during the period we are discussing. The heart of the city was crowded, with a maze of narrow streets opening out into several grander thoroughfares and into the broad Grote Markt, dominated by the Grote or St. Bavo Kerk on the east and the city hall, newly expanded, on the west (see figs. 38 and 39). On the eastern edge of the town was the river, the Spaarne, with a few residential districts on the opposite bank. Haarlem had little room for urban gardens, so people began building houses and gardens outside the city gates, the Kruispoort and the St. Janspoort on the north, and the Grote Houtpoort and Kleine Houtpoort on the south. Even more striking is the expanse of walled gardens, belonging mainly to merchants living in town, which stretched out in the same areas on the north and south sides of town. Many of the people named in connection with tulip sales owned gardens, sometimes several, outside the city walls.

Bloemisten were scattered across Haarlem, which in any case, like Amsterdam, could be traversed on foot in twenty minutes. Once again, however, we can identify certain clusters that would put tulip traders in contact with each other. For example, the few houses to be found on the perimeter of the Grote Markt contained five or six tulip traders, including the printer Vincent Casteleyn; the tinsmith (later brewer) Willem Schoneus (see fig. 41); and the inn Den Ouden Haen, whose innkeeper, Allert Schatter, sold at least one tulip and which was itself the site of tulip trading. Surrounding streets in this wealthy area of town housed numbers of other *bloemisten*, such as Cornelis Double on the Warmoesstraat; Johan van Gellinckhuysen, Bartholomeus van Rijn, and possibly Andries de Coning on the Anegang; Symon Jansz Kan on the Nobelstraat; and Paulus van Beresteyn on the Zijlstraat. But the most striking clusters we can find are the large numbers of tulip buyers and sellers who owned houses on the northwest side of town and those who owned gardens on the southeast. The Kruisstraat, a fairly short street crossing only two others in its course leading out of town on the northwest, was lined with the houses of people involved in tulips: Pieter Jansz Alleman, Jeuriaen Jansz, the baker Theunis Jansz, Ysack Jansz (a maker of parts for looms who was a partner in a tulip company), Pieter Jansz Jonckheer, Abraham Ampe, Pauwels van Camere, Jan van Clarenbeeck, and Nicolaes Suycker. If one continued walking down the Kruisstraat out of the Kruispoort, one would encounter even more *bloemisten*: Rogier Alleman, Jan Jansz Holleman, Aert Huybertsz (also part of Ysack Jansz's tulip company), Bartel Louisz, Jan Quakel (who owned a lane outside the Kruispoort to the west side of the Kruisweg, the Quakelslaan), Salomon Seys, Pieter Vereecke, and Stoffel de Way. Five minutes' walk away, outside the St. Janspoort, were six or seven other tulip traders, including Jan Wynants, the innkeeper of De Penningsveer, which was located in the area.

The cluster of gardens owned by *bloemisten* on the southeast side is just as striking. The popular district for gardens was the Rosenprieel, just across the canal encircling the city outside the Kleine Houtpoort. A host of tulip buyers and sellers would make the short walk to their gardens on a spring evening or a summer day and would likely encounter others with an interest in tulips, often with gardens immediately adjacent. Gerrit Nannincx Deyman, for example, besides living next door to a house owned by his brother-in-law Simon van Poelenburch on the Spaarne, owned a garden in the Rosenprieel next to one owned by Lucas Wery, which itself was neighbor to a garden belonging to Andries Mahieu. Otto Fransz van Flodorp owned a garden in the same district next to one owned by Adam de Smeth; on one side of Flodorp was a house and garden belonging to Barent Cardoes, and next to him was one owned by Pieter Bol. Dominicus van Lijnhoven owned a garden in the Rosenprieel next to Jan van Clarenbeeck, and so on. In short, the entire district was populated by gardens owned by tulip buyers and sellers. A smaller number could be found a few minutes to the west, outside the Grote Houtpoort, and a similar, smaller figure outside the northern gates.

This kind of proximity of those interested in tulips might, conceivably, lead to sales. We find a variety of tulip sales between people living on the north side of town. For example, in 1636 Jeuriaen Jansz, a baker on the Kruisstraat, aged around fifty, sold the second offset of a Gouda to his next-door neighbor, Pieter Jansz Alleman (father of two other *bloemisten*,

1. St. Jansweg
2. Kruisweg
3. St. Janspoort
4. Kruispoort
5. Kruisstraat
6. St. Jansstraat
7. Grote Markt
8. Anegang
9. Grote Houtstraat
10. Kleine Houtstraat
11. Kleine Houtpoort
12. Grote Houtpoort
13. Rosenprieel
14. Kleine Houtweg
15. Grote Houtweg

FIGURE 37. Pieter Wils, map of Haarlem, 1649. British Library. Here marked with some locations of *bloemisten* mentioned in the text.

FIGURE 38. (*overleaf*) The Grote Markt in Haarlem, facing west toward the town hall. Cornelis Willemsz Blaeulaken, after Pieter Jansz Saenredam, in Samuel Ampzing, *Beschrijvinge ende Lof der stad Haarlem*, 1628. Noord-Hollands Archief, Haarlem.

Hier siet gy dat Paelleys dat Willem Graef en koning   Nu is het Raedhuijs
Heeft tot syn Hof gesticht en koninklyke Woning   De Raeden besig syn o[..]
Gelyk soo voor als'na het Grafelyke Hof   Daer recht gewesen [..]
Te Haerlem is geweest tot onser eeren lof   En daer die Word ge[..]

van der Steden weg en Hoek kan een Land bestaen al waer de goede seden
..ed te plegen   Al waer der Wetten tucht met voeten word getreden
..eede twistomstaet Gelyker wys de siel het lyf is levens band
..icht te buyten gaet So is gerechtigheyt het leven van een Land

FIGURE 39. Pieter Jansz Saenredam, *Choir and North Ambulatory of the St. Bavo or Grote Kerk, Haarlem.* J. Paul Getty Museum, Los Angeles.

Rogier Alleman and Pieter Alleman den Jongen). Jansz, though a baker, was clearly heavily involved in the tulip trade. We have a record of a further transaction by him in his own neighborhood, when Jansz bought an offset from Heindrick Bartelsz, who lived outside the Kruispoort; Bartelsz himself had bought it from Ysack Jansz outside the St. Janspoort. (Neither Jansz nor Bartelsz was happy about the weight of their bulb, which had been sold by the *aes*, and in August 1636 were investigating the matter.) And when Jeuriaen Jansz died in 1643, we find that his well-off estate, which included a well-stocked house on the Kruisstraat and another half a house on the Kleine Houtstraat, a fair amount of silver, and eleven paintings, still contained tulips in the garden. The fact that flowers were being inventoried in 1643 suggests that they were still thought to be valu-

FIGURE 40. The Grote Houtstraat in Haarlem, looking north. Cornelis van Noorde,
1779, after Nicolaes Hals. Noord-Hollands Archief, Haarlem.

FIGURE 41. Home of Willem Schoneus, tinsmith (later brewer) and *bloemist,* on the Grote Markt in Haarlem. Now known as the Hoofdwacht. Rijksdienst voor de Monumentenzorg, Zeist.

able. In fact, the Weeskamer took the trouble to hold a separate sale of flowers when Jansz's household goods were auctioned for the sake of his orphaned children, bringing in ƒ114:5.[28]

In late August 1636, soon after his investigation into the offset he had bought from Heindrick Bartelsz, Jeuriaen Jansz was lying ill with plague.

FIGURE 42. Jan van Goyen, drawing of the Kleine Houtpoort with the Grote Houtpoort in the distance, 1640. Noord-Hollands Archief, Haarlem.

He clearly wished to put his affairs in order (not uncommon in this plague time), although in fact he was not to die for another seven years. One of his outstanding problems was the failure of his next-door neighbor, Alleman, to collect and pay for the offset he had bought. At the end of August collection was well overdue since, for horticultural reasons, tulips were dug up after their flowering in May or June and by September ought for their own health to have been returned to the ground. Alleman had also refused to show up to witness the bulb being lifted, although he did send his brother-in-law, Claes Jonas; perhaps the offset proved unsatisfactory, as Alleman then refused to cooperate. Because Jansz lived next door to Alleman, the quarrel must have been conducted essentially over the garden wall. Jansz even had a journeyman in his bakery, Jan Casier, swear before a notary that Jansz had gone to Alleman and asked, "with politeness, too," to come and pick up the bulb and, when that failed to have any effect, sent his wife on the same errand. Every time Alleman was approached, however, he refused to accept the bulb. Proximity here probably helped to make the sale; it may also have made the quarrel more seething.[29]

But there are other kinds of proximity than the physical. We have already discussed family and religion, but there is also proximity of interests. Earlier in the chapter we gave some thought to the breakdown of professions and trades in some of the cities where tulip sales took place. We saw that, on the whole, middle-level merchants and skilled master craftsmen made up the tulip-trading population, with a scattering of very wealthy and potentially poorer people mixed in. But if we look more closely at the actual professions of the tulip traders, we can find plenty of opportunities for contact. It might be harder to identify those contacts in Amsterdam, where most of the traders were international merchants of one kind or another. The multiplicity of their dealings, which might change in nature—from cloth to grain to spices to wine—from one ship's voyage to the next, makes their likely interactions mostly opaque for us. Certain merchants, such as Adam Bessels and Lambert Massa, were identifiably involved in the Muscovy trade, for example, and would no doubt have been acquainted, but they could well have been in touch with most of the other tulip buyers and sellers in Amsterdam on other trading matters at one time or another. International merchants will have seen each other daily on the docks or at the *beurs,* the open-air Amsterdam stock exchange.

In Haarlem, dominated less by merchants in international trade and more by manufacturers, the breakdown of known professions is startling. The Wynants Sunday dinner, which gathered together three cloth merchants and a dyer, tells the tale. Of 167 *bloemisten* whose profession could be identified, by far the largest single grouping—forty-six—were merchants involved in the cloth trade. Thirty-four were cloth merchants, dealing variously in linen, linen yarn, woolen cloth, and flax, but mainly concentrating in linen and linen yarn. A further ten, at least, owned bleacheries, and one, the Jacob de Block who guaranteed Geertruyt Schoudt's tulip purchase at Pieter Wynants' dinner table, was a dyer. The specialty of another ten merchants is unclear, but they also could have been involved in the cloth trade. These men would have traded together, imported batches of yarn from Silesia together, and met together in the guild: several were officials, such as Jan van Clarenbeeck, *vinder* (officer) of the *twijnders'* (yarn merchants') guild, or Cornelis Bol den Jongen, Andries van den Broecke, Pouwels van Mackelenberch, and Pieter Vrients, who were among the official inspectors of the yarn trade around this period. Far from being weavers, then, a large proportion of the *bloemisten* in Haarlem were actually cloth merchants—the employers, not the employed, in the cloth trade. And this group would have been in constant interaction with each other, both professionally and socially. There were, moreover, other clusters of occupations whose members would know each other from their guild and their social interactions. The bakers, for example, of whom I have counted eighteen, were the next largest group after the cloth merchants. Three of these were officers of their guild during the period. Brewers, who were overall the wealthiest members of Haarlem society and who would have certainly moved in the same social circles as the cloth merchants, provided ten known *bloemisten*. Another popular profession among the tulip traders in Haarlem was innkeeper. We find similar clusters elsewhere. Cloth was the most important profession in Utrecht as well (we know of six cloth merchants who were *bloemisten*, of whom four specialized in silk). In Enkhuizen the apothecaries dominated: the Enkhuizen tulip company was made up of three apothecaries, as well as a spice merchant and a dyer.[30]

What should we make of these concentrations of professions, of family members, of religious groupings, of people living in the same neighborhood? Naturally in some cases proximity must have influenced sales. This was clearly true with some family or religious connections—Mennonites such as the Wynants, Moens, and Wanscher families spring to mind—and we find a number of cases of geographical closeness apparently leading to sales on the north side of Haarlem, besides the case of Pieter Jansz Alleman and his unfortunate neighbor Jeuriaen Jansz. But on the whole it is surprising how little we can correlate individual sales with the commonality of interests we have detailed here. It seems that, for the most part, cloth merchants did not particularly sell to cloth merchants or bakers to bakers; it happened, but it was not a noticeable pattern. Nor did people usually sell to their relatives. This is explicable when we think about the idea of the *vrunden*: if the family's fortunes were in some ways the responsibilities of all, a family member would be less likely to sell *to* a family member—to make a profit from him—than to sell *with* him, or buy *with* him, to join together in making a profit in the same way as brothers-in-law or other relatives might have joined together in freighting a ship to the Baltic or in manufacturing silk cloth.

Michiel Kistgens and Jan de Haes, brothers-in-law (and Mennonites), are one example of this dynamic. Among the numbers of Amsterdam merchants whom the Haarlemmer Hans Baert was chasing for payment in June 1637 were Kistgens and De Haes. On January 18 the pair had bought for ƒ1,250 an Admirael van der Eyck bulb weighing 180 *asen*. The bulb was at that moment growing in the garden of Jan Woutersz in Haarlem, and, like so many, they seem to have been reluctant to pay for their purchase. Earlier, as we have already noted, another pair of brothers-in-law in Amsterdam, Jan Munter and Pieter Dircksz, had arranged with Claes Jansz and his wife, Marritje Machiels, on September 16, 1636, to buy "all the Tulip bulbs offsets and seedlings whatever they might be called which presently stand in the garden behind the house [of Jansz and Machiels] ... both in the earth and planted in pots," to be paid for and collected when the flowering season was over. It is impossible to tell how many tulips this entailed, but given the price paid, 14 *pond Vlaams* (that is, ƒ84), Munter and Dircksz were getting a fairly good deal. In the event, once the prices fell, the pair canceled the transaction with full agreement of the sellers.[31]

It was not only individual sales that might be affected by family or other connections. Some of the companies that were formed to sell tulips in this period were also clearly based on the interconnectedness of their members. For example, one of the newly formed companies in Haarlem was made up of six partners, of whom three, Theunis David Kop, Lenaert Prior, and Pieter Wynants (not to be confused with the Mennonite Pieter Jacobsz Wynants) were all immigrants from the "land of Gulich" (Jülich), two from the same town of "Glabbich" (Gladbach), now Mönchengladbach, near Düsseldorf. It is difficult not to conclude that the commonality of their place of origin, so far away from Haarlem, must have contributed to their consorting with each other in this business venture. Other companies formed because of their family relationships. The wealthy Reymont de Smith helped out his relative, François Heldewier, when Heldewier and his wife emigrated from Brussels to Amsterdam in 1635 with no means of support. In making the contract, Heldewier said that his "sorrowful and indigent state" was to be transformed by De Smith's decision to begin a tulip company for which the capital was provided by De Smith and the work done by Heldewier, who got his clothing, housing, and living expenses paid as a salary; the bulbs remained the property of De Smith and all the profit went to him. Heldewier made clear in the contract that De Smith was acting because Heldewier was his "blood relative." In the same way, another tulip company based mainly on family relationships, but one with more equality than De Smith's, was the company in Enkhuizen. Of the five partners, the three who were apothecaries all were connected: Barent ten Broecke (the nephew of Paludanus) was linked both to Anthony Jacobsz, also known as Anthony Jacobsz Apesteijn, who was married to ten Broecke's sister Claesgen, and to Jan Jansz Apotheeker, who was the guardian of the children of ten Broecke, who died in 1636. Again, the bonds of profession and personal relationships surely helped make the formation of this company possible. We also should note the way personal or informal connections were at times transformed through the trade into clearly organized business relationships.[32]

But although relatives and those connected to each other sold *together,* if the identifiable groupings in society who were involved with tulips regularly affected their sales to others, it is not apparent from the records of sales that remain to us. What, then, should we make of the clusters we find? If neighbors did not necessarily sell to neighbors, linen merchants to linen merchants, or brothers to brothers, how did they interact? How did these connections actually affect the shape of the tulip trade? Although we cannot do more than speculate, looking at the data through a different lens can be illuminating. Linen merchants might not have limited their sales to each other, but their predominance in the trade in Haarlem, and that of various other interrelated groups around the country, might reflect a different type of interaction. They might not have sold to each other—but they probably talked.

Tulipmania was in many ways an event dependent on talk. Communication was vital. Even in the 1630s, tulips were not readily available, and the kind of discussions of flowers, not to mention visits to rare blooms in the spring and early summer, that we saw among the sixteenth-century *liefhebbers* continued as prices for tulips rose during the 1620s and 1630s. Those who were interested in the flowers would have had to know about how they were grown, what the different varieties—which in any case kept changing—looked like, who owned which tulips, and, of course, what kind of prices were being charged for them. Standards for what made a particular shape or pattern of tulip superior or inferior to another would also have been developed in discussion with other *bloemisten,* as would the appropriate price—thus leading to the kind of comments we have already heard, that a particular tulip was not worth five *stuivers* or some other paltry sum. One can imagine a whole culture of communication about tulips during this period, mainly based in individual towns, but also extending (as we see from tulips in one town being sold in another, or the networks of tulip buyers crossing city walls, as the Mennonite web did) across much of north Holland.[33]

Some information, it is true, was available in other forms than talk. Tulip books might have helped those with access to them to identify the markings of different tulips, an exercise that must have been extraordinarily difficult, as the smallest variation in the striping or flaming on a white or yellow background would have resulted in a tulip being given a new name. As for the availability of tulips for sale, in at least in a few cases this was advertised. If the Weeskamer in a town held a sale to benefit the estate held in trust for orphaned children, the auction would be advertised in a variety of cities in hope of attracting a sizeable number of buyers. We can see this in the sale of the flowers belonging to the gardener David de Milt; the accounts for his estate include entries in the summer of 1638 for the cost of printing and posting of bills advertising the auction (as well as for the free beer evidently provided during the sale). When the tulips of another deceased gardener, Jan van Damme, were auctioned by the Weeskamer in Haarlem, the *weesmeesters* paid out from the estate *f*3:17 to pay for the posting of bills in Gouda, Utrecht, Leiden, Delft, The Hague, Rotterdam, Alkmaar, and Hoorn. This advertising makes it easy to understand the ability of the Weeskamer auction in Alkmaar on February 5, 1637, to attract Haarlemmers, as well as people from other towns, who had to travel a comparatively long way to buy bulbs at some of the highest prices recorded in the period.[34]

But although the Weeskamer sales were advertised, and although there were certainly other organized auctions of flowers, such as one held by Abraham de Schilder in Amsterdam in 1633, most sales of tulips were either arranged between individual parties who met up in taverns or private homes or occurred during what appears to have been semi-organized trading in inns, as we also find with other goods. There was a regular market for birds, for example, in an inn run by Joost Joostensz Plavier (himself a *bloemist*) in the Schagchelstraat in Haarlem. To know where to get tulips, or to get the tulips one wanted, to be able to arrange purchases, or to know what one was buying: all required communication.[35]

The discussion that took place around tulips helps to explain some of the commonalities we find among different tulip buyers and sellers, even if they were not buying from or selling to each other. The network of interconnected Mennonite families; the presence, in a fairly small group of buyers, of people with close connections to each other, whether business or personal; the predominance in Haarlem of merchants connected to the manufacture of cloth; and the clusters of *bloemisten* in particular areas of Haarlem or Amsterdam: all these are testimony to what must have been a great deal of talk. It is regrettably impossible to prove conclusively that this is why we see these clusters without seeing many sales within the clusters themselves. But it is easy to imagine the situations: a conversation on the corner of the Keizersgracht and the Wolvenstraat, at a christening, at a function of the *twijnders* guild, at a gathering of the civic militia. Where people congregated, information was passed on that was necessary to initiate a tulip sale. Certain locations, popular places for *bloemisten* to meet, would thus have been nodes where this information was transferred. Schrevelius, the historian of Haarlem of the following decade, acknowledged this in his *Harlemias* of 1648: "in inns and Booksellers' shops the young *blommisten* learn the price and worth of the flowers."[36]

For people interested in flowers, gardens naturally functioned as one of these nodes. *Bloemisten* spent a lot of time in gardens. The gardens behind houses and, in Haarlem, outside the gates of town were walled, but, as we saw in the sixteenth century, visiting other people's gardens was evidently a popular activity for *bloemisten*. The sociability of the *liefhebbers* is a theme in the literature about flowers. This is connected to exchange and the role of personal relationships, but also to the acquisition of knowledge. La Chesnée Monstereul's suggestion that "agreeable visits," "sweet conversations," and "solid discourses" were reasons to keep tulips the exclusive property of experts has resonance in some of the gatherings we witness in Haarlem in the 1630s. Sir Thomas Hanmer noted in 1659 that in the spring "the Florists fly about to see and examine and take the chiefe pleasure of gardens, admiring the new varietyes that Spring produces. . . ." Although we cannot claim that all the meetings in Haarlem were exclusive, in terms of the formation of expertise they did lead to a kind of exclusivity. Specialization in tulips had its effect on sociability, and vice versa.[37]

Certainly incidental details in many documents about quarrels over flowers suggest as much. We can tell that in the spring and summer months those interested in tulips must have spent a good deal of time standing around with others in gardens, talking about tulips, witnessing transactions, even conducting auctions. Much information could be gleaned in this way that might have affected individual sales. So we hear in one document, for example, that the carpenter Aelbert Jansz, the gardener Roger Rogiersz, and Salomon Seys, co-owner of an inn and apparently a tulip entrepreneur, just happened to be in the garden of Pieter Bol when the art dealer David Jorisz, clearly checking the provenance of a bulb, pointedly asked Bol if he had sold a particular Gouda bulb to Jan Arentsz (the answer was no). Similarly, when someone like the baker Harman Govertsz Aeckerman wanted to establish the facts of a transaction with Andries Pietersz van den Broecke, he called on the testimony of Aert Huybertsz, Roelant Veruvestraeten, and Ysack Jansz, all of whom were active enough in the trade to be partners in tulip companies (Huybertsz and Jansz in one, Veruvestraeten in another). Van den Broecke was clearly not so well known to them; he is referred to in the affidavit as "a certain Young man." They had all been present on July 21, 1636, in the little garden house (*thuijn-huijsgen*) in Huybertsz's garden, along with Van den Broecke, who had bought an Admirael van der Eyck planted in Utrecht from Aeckerman the previous winter. Aeckerman asked Van den Broecke why he had not yet taken delivery of the bulb; he said it was because his "buddy" (his *macker*) had not wanted to receive it, but that he did want it and had the money whenever his *macker* was ready. Aeckerman's acerbic reply, that he had sold the bulb to Van den Broecke, not his *macker*, was heard by them all. In these kinds of gatherings, the quality of bulbs must also have been discussed. Thus the declared judgment of Salomon Seys, Abraham Rogiersz, Bastiaen Pouwelsz, and Jacob van Heede, who on various days in the summer of 1635 visited the garden of Symon le Febure, that the tulips he had there were not worth twenty guilders all together.

PLATE 1. Anon., title page of tulip book,
Tot lof der eedele tulpa, ca. 1635–1640.

PLATE 2. (*facing page, top*) Anon., *Satire on tulipmania*,
second half of seventeenth century.
Musée de Bretagne, Rennes.

PLATE 3. (*facing page, bottom*) Jacob Gerritsz
Cuyp, *Bed of Tulips*, 1638. Dordrechts
Museum, Dordrecht.

PLATE 4. (*above*) Pieter Brueghel the Elder,
Spring, mid-sixteenth century.

PLATE 5. Conrad Gesner, *Tulip in Garden of Johann Heinrich Herwart*, 1559. Universitätsbibliothek Erlangen-Nürnberg.

PLATE 6. (*top*) Ambrosius Bosschaert the elder, *Vase with flowers and shells in a window*, c. 1618. Royal Cabinet of Paintings Mauritshuis, The Hague.

PLATE 7. (*bottom*) Hans Bollongier, *Tulip still life*, 1639. Rijksmuseum, Amsterdam.

PLATE 8. (*overleaf*) Frans Francken II and workshop,
with Jan Brueghel II, Archdukes Albrecht
and Isabella in a collector's cabinet,
c. 1626. Walters Art Museum Baltimore.

PLATE 9. (*left*) Jan Philips van Thielen, *Tulip
still life*, first half of seventeenth century.

PLATE 10. (*above*) Michiel Jansz van Mierevelt.
Double portrait with tulip, bulb, and shell, 1606.
Galerie Sanct Lucas, Vienna.

Semperaugustus.

PLATE 11. (*left*) Pieter Holsteyn, tulip
portrait, *Semper Augustus.*

PLATE 12. (*above*) Jan Brueghel II,
Satire on Tulipmania, c. 1640.
Frans Hals Museum, Haarlem.

PLATE 13. Hendrick Gerritsz Pot, *Floraes Mallewagen*, c. 1640. Frans Hals Museum, Haarlem.

If you spent enough time in gardens, it seems clear, you would learn all about the tulip trade.[38]

Another focal point for information about tulips and the trade was the tavern. Taverns in this period were in any case normal places for economic transactions, the discussion of business, and the making of deals. Inns in Amsterdam such as Het Witte Wambeijs and De Menniste Bruyloft on the Oudebrugsteeg, not to mention a host of taverns in Haarlem—Den Ouden Haen or 't Haentje on the Grote Kerkhof next to the Grote Kerk, De Toelast on the St. Jansstraat, De Syde Specx on the Spaarne, De Bastaertpijp, De Coninck van Vranckrijk, and others—were the site of discussion about tulips and tulip trading, at times in continuous auctions, which were sometimes called *comparatiens* or *collegiën* (see fig. 43). The contemporary pamphlet *Samen-spraeck tusschen Waermondt ende Gaergoedt*, probably written by its printer, Adriaen Roman, represents the situation of a newcomer into such an inn. Gaergoedt, the greedy half of the dialogue who attempts to corrupt the wiser Waermondt into participation in the tulip trade, advises him:

> You will go into an inn, I will tell you the names of a few, though
> I know few or none where there are no collegiën; once there, you
> will ask if there are no Florists there. When you come to their
> room, and because you are a new person, some will quack like a
> duck; some will say: a new whore in the brothel, and so forth; but
> you mustn't let it bother you, that always happens.

This account is propaganda against the trade and as such must be taken with a large grain of salt. It is hard to believe that the tulip traders themselves would have been moralizing against their own activities. What we can learn from such an account, however, is the apparent regularity of attendance at such an event (although this, too, could be moralizing, emphasizing the supposed abandonment of gainful employment). More reliable sources, in the form of notarial documents discussing individual transactions, make it plain that *tulpisten* were certainly to be found at times gathered together in inns, talking about tulips, and sometimes holding sales, either as auctions or individual transactions. As we will discuss later, the *collegie* seems to have been regarded more as a kind of

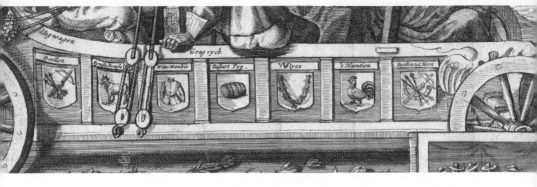

FIGURE 43. Crispijn van de Passe, *Floraes Mallewagen*, 1637, detail.
Atlas van Stolk, Rotterdam. The wagon bears the signs of
inns prominent in the tulip trade, such as the Witte Wambuis in
Amsterdam and the Bastartpijp and the Haentje in Haarlem.

general authority over the trade, making adjudications about disputes, rather than necessarily as the running auction depicted in some of the pamphlets. But it is clear from these sources that if you wanted to learn about tulips, about who was selling what, where the best tulips were, what was desirable and what was worthless, an inn was a place to find a kind of consortium of knowledge. A node of the transfer of information such as an inn was also a way of establishing a kind of hierarchy of expertise.[39]

That was the experience of the baker Jeuriaen Jansz, whom we have already encountered. In late May or early June 1636 he bought the offset of an Admirael Lieffkens—a flower that happened to be standing in the garden of Marten Kretser in Amsterdam—from the shopkeeper Heinrick Bartelsz. Bartelsz himself had bought it from Ysack Jansz the previous winter for ƒ6:10 per *aes*, 2 *stuivers* per *aes* less than he was now charging for it, and now he was selling it on to Jeuriaen Jansz before he himself had received it. Jeuriaen Jansz wanted two days to think about the purchase, and during that time he went into the inn of Cornelis Arentsz Kettingman, where he encountered "the Collegie and gathering of various *tulpisten*." It was "recounted and forthrightly said, that they certainly knew, that the said *tulpa* Admirael Lieffkens had been visited and lifted from the earth before its proper time. . . ." Because of this, the bulb, which was being sold by weight, was not as heavy as was being claimed by Ysack

Jansz. Thus Bartelsz, who was now selling the bulb on, had, they said, been "deceived"; not knowing how much this offset actually weighed, no one could honestly sell it for the price Bartelsz had been charged. Bartelsz, hearing this from Jeuriaen Jansz, was "highly displeased" about both the deceit and the loss of the profit he should have had on the bulb from his now fully informed buyer. But if Jeuriaen Jansz had not gone to Kettingman's inn, both of them would have been deceived. Taverns must frequently have served in this way as places to check on the latest information about particular offsets, bulbs, and flowers.[40]

Gardens and inns were places to come into contact with other *bloemisten*; they were nodes where information about tulips could be transmitted. But the people associated with such places were themselves nodes. We cannot be surprised to find, in Haarlem at least, a fair representation of gardeners in our breakdown of the known professions of tulip buyers and sellers. With eleven people known to have been involved in gardening, frequently with others working for them, they represent one of the larger single groups involved with tulips. Among those were several who were able to make good money from tulips, such as David de Milt and Jan van Damme, both of whose early deaths make the details of their estates available to us. Pieter Bol and his brother Cornelis Bol den Jongen, besides other enterprises, seem to have engaged in commercial gardening, as did Jan Cornelisz Quakel, whose family owned a considerable amount of land outside the Haarlem city walls. Barent Cardoes had worked for years for Pieter Bol, and others we have encountered, such as Gillis de Milt, Pieter Jansz Winckel, Rogier Rogiersz, and his brother Abraham Rogiersz (a *vinder* of the guild of market gardeners), are also to be found buying and selling tulips, talking in gardens, and judging tulips.[41]

The natural inclination of professional gardeners to make money on flowers is perhaps not worth comment. More important for our argument are the innkeepers. If tulipmania was partly a matter of the transfer of information, that fact would help to explain not only the clusters of *bloemisten* that existed, but something of their character. Some people would naturally come into more contact than others not only with tulips, but with talk of tulips. They might have worked in trades that had a great deal of contact with the public—especially those in contact with tulip growers, buyers, and sellers. Innkeepers are the obvious place to start. The inns where *bloemisten* congregated, and where auctions and *collegiën*

FIGURE 44. Extant sign of a Haarlem inn involved in the trade, the Toelast, on the St. Jansstraat (now Jansstraat 64). Author's collection.

were held, placed innkeepers right in the middle of the network of information about tulips. Innkeepers were good witnesses for those seeking legal solutions to their problems about tulips, because they saw so much of the tulip trade within their own walls. In one example, Teunis Dircxsz Mes, innkeeper in the Toelast on the St. Jansstraat near the Grote Markt, appeared before a notary on behalf of Jan Willemsz Cortoor, a merchant selling woollen cloth, describing Cortoor's purchase in his inn of a Gouda bulb from the wine-seller Jan Smuyser for ƒ600. With so much contact with the trade and so much information at their disposal, it is not surprising that innkeepers also represent such an important section of the known tulip buyers and sellers in Haarlem. We know of eleven innkeepers or owners of inns who were themselves *bloemisten*. Rogier Alleman and his wife, Maeycken Verschuyll, innkeepers in De Druyff, both got involved in tulip deals, as did a variety of others, including Allert Schatter, innkeeper at Den Ouden Haen; Jan Wynants, innkeeper of the Penningsveer outside the Janspoort; Pleun Jansz van Doorn, innkeeper of the Halve Maan on the Kruisweg outside the Kruispoort; and Huybert Fransz, innkeeper in the Schipper. The family of Jan Cornelisz Quakel owned at least one inn, De Gulde Druyff, and two very active figures in the tulip trade, Salomon

Seys of Haarlem and Cornelis van Breugel of Amsterdam, bought an inn in Haarlem together, the Stads Herberge, outside the St. Janspoort, in 1636. Relatives of innkeepers might also be influenced by the information they heard through this conduit. Jan Joosten Plavier, a Haarlemmer who bought tulips in Middelburg, was the son of Joost Plavier, innkeeper in De Sijde Specx, and the brother of Joost Joosten Plavier, innkeeper on the Schagchelstraat.[42]

But people would not have talked about tulips simply in gardens and inns, or around the family dinner table, or even on the street corner. If we look closer at which professions in Haarlem featured largely in the tulip trade, we can see more locations where information about tulips might have been discussed. After merchants in the cloth industry, the occupation most strongly represented in our lists of *bloemisten* is the bakers. Bakers could be wealthy—as we saw when discussing the well-to-do Abraham Anthonisz de Milt—and were certainly not out of place among the other skilled craftsmen and merchants participating in the trade. Eighteen bakers, including three officers of the bakers' guild in these years, are known to have bought and sold tulips in Haarlem. Again, they mostly did not sell to each other. One baker, Steffen Jansz, sold to a fellow-baker, Heyndrick Pietersz. But otherwise their deals were conducted across trade lines: Jan Abrahamsz, for example, bought tulips from, among others, the *regent* and yarn merchant Jan van Clarenbeeck and sold to another leading yarn manufacturer, Cornelis Coelembier; Abraham Theunisz bought from the artist Joost van Haverbeeck. Bakers came into constant contact with members of their community. As people came in and out of their establishments buying bread, one can imagine them talking about local issues and the gossip of the neighborhood, which would, as prices rose, include the tulip trade. Although bakeries, unlike inns or gardens, were not necessarily places where tulips were bought or sold, bakers would have had plenty of opportunity to learn about tulips from their customers.

The same could be said of shopkeepers, and again we find five of these—one of the larger clusters—among the *bloemisten*. Such shopkeepers, like their baker counterparts, could be substantial members of society. In 1637 the shopkeeper Aert Thomasz Ducens was an officer in one of the *schutter* companies (the civic militia), a position reserved for the more respected and socially acceptable citizens. He had a garden and

FIGURE 45. Jan Steen, *The Leiden Baker Arend Oostwaert and his wife Catharina Keyzerswart*, 1658. Rijksmuseum, Amsterdam.

both bought and sold tulips; he sold three bulbs to the southern textile merchant Severijn van den Heuvel, one of which was planted in the garden of the prominent tulip trader Pieter Woutersz, a master tailor. Shops, like bakeries, were nodes where information about tulips could be passed on. We might even be able to extend this discussion of the transfer of knowledge about tulips to professionals who came into similar contact with the public. Doctors and surgeons, for example, feature here: the official city doctor, Gregorius van der Plas, bought from Hendrick Jan Wynants, and five surgeons (Cornelis Coper, Gerrit Nannincx Deyman, Johan van Gellinckhuysen, Tymon Maertensz, and Jacques Hens) also took part in the trade. Of course, their information might easily have come from other relationships; Van der Plas was good friends with the goldsmith Dominicus van Lijnhoven, who in turn was brother-in-law of Frans Pietersz de Grebber; Gerrit Nannincx Deyman was brother-in-law of Simon van Poelenburch in Amsterdam; all were *bloemisten*.

The names of notaries also have a certain significance on our lists of buyers and sellers. Notaries were at the center of a certain section of the tulip trade. When they were not out serving *insinuaties* on those involved in quarrels, inventorying the houses of the dead, or visiting those wishing to make a will who were too ill to leave their beds, they stayed in their houses and allowed the world to come to them. Streams of people wishing to make declarations (*verklaringen*) that might help themselves or others in legal cases, to make wills, to arrange prenuptial agreements or contracts made their way to notaries each day. Although not all transactions concerning tulips were made before notaries, many were; simply by virtue of the traffic passing through their houses, notaries must have known all about tulips, all about the sales, all about the disputes, as they must, indeed, have known much of the affairs in their neighborhood generally. Several notaries took the plunge with tulips. In Alkmaar, Cornelis de Haes arranged legal contracts involving tulips and later was to be found acting in lawsuits when his clients were unable to collect the money for tulips they had sold. Despite the part he played in these quarrels as a notary, he himself behaved in exactly the same way after buying from Wilhelmus Tiberius. It was the same in Haarlem. The *regent* Jacob Steyn, at this time secretary of the city as well as a notary, who recorded contracts concerning tulips in his distinctive sloppy hand, was unable to resist buying tulips from David de Milt. His fellow notary Egbert van Bosvelt in his turn bought both flowers and food and drink in 1636 from Gerrit Tielemansz but failed to pay for them; Tielemansz had to take Van Bosvelt to the Kleine Bank van Justitie to get his money, and even then he received less than a quarter of what he demanded. As for a third Haarlem notary, Wouter Crousen de Jonge, we know of no sales or purchases by him, but we can imagine how the talk of tulips set him daydreaming. In a presumably quiet moment in the summer of 1635 he began doodling in his ledger, practising his initials and his signature, over and over, but also drawing three small, simple, faintly smudged tulips (see fig. 46). As a notary, how could he help but hear about tulips in 1635?[43]

It was in the spring of 1636 that an official of the city of Haarlem, Cornelis van Teylingen, called what may have been at least a semi-official inquiry into the tulip dealings of Cornelis Double. Eight *bloemisten* came before our doodling notary, Wouter Crousen de Jonge, to talk about their experiences in the previous summer. Some had bought from Double; others were witnesses to his double-dealing. From this investigation, we can see how both nodes of information and hierarchies of knowledge operated in the tulip trade. All these men, when asked about Double's cheating over tulips, were in a position to call into play the pool of knowledge about tulips and tulip-dealing that their community had developed over time.

Bartholomeus van Rijn, thirty-six, had bought a Coornhart and a Blijenburger from Double in the "dry bulb time" between flowering and replanting of the bulbs in the early autumn. He planted them again to "enjoy" them on their next flowering, but instead the plants did not make their expected appearance above ground. Van Rijn was suspicious. He had heard a rumor that Double had been selling bulbs that were "falsely bored through," so, in the presence of a witness, Jan van Radingen, who was an arbiter in a number of tulip quarrels, he dug the two bulbs up again. His suspicions were confirmed. His bulbs did indeed have holes bored in them, meaning they would never grow or produce flowers. Double clearly had calculated that by preventing the bulbs he sold from thriving, he could make a profit on their sale yet keep the market from being debased by the multiplication of bulbs through offsets. Indeed, by preventing the bulbs he sold from even flowering, he could make the bulbs he kept for himself even more valuable. Van Rijn was not having it. He went to Double's brother-in-law, Jan Cuyck, demanded his money back—and got it.[44]

Next to come before the notary was Andries de Preyer, around twenty-six. Preyer, a linen merchant, was very active in the tulip trade. He had had a similar experience with Cornelis Double to that of Bartholomeus van Rijn. Having bought a Gouda bulb from Double for a little more than ƒ30 in the summer of 1636, he found that "no proper sprouting came to light." He took care to have the bulb dug up before witnesses: Jan Dircksz

FIGURE 46. The notary Wouter Crousen de Jonge doodling
tulips, 1635. Noord-Hollands Archief, Haarlem.

Ossecoop lifted it in the presence of Cornelis Coper, Dirk Witvelt, Symon Suery, Cornelis Lourisz, and Reynier Huybertsz, all of whom were also present in March 1636 as Preyer gave his testimony. They in turn confirmed that they were there when the bulb was lifted and that, "having visited the same and found it to be falsely bored through, and not suitable ever to bear any flower, or to bring forth any growth," they decided to take action. They went together, taking the bulb with them, to the inn of Allert Schatter, Den Ouden Haen, where Cornelis Double was, and, "showing him and putting the said bulb in his hand," they witnessed an argument between Double and Preyer. Double admitted that the bulb had come from him and suggested that he could come to a settlement. The group of aggrieved *bloemisten* "exhorted him out of friendship to point out and Name" the man from whom he had himself earlier bought or received the bulb, so that he would not himself suffer any financial damage, but Double refused to do this, saying that he would rather put the whole business behind him and simply settle himself (evidently he was the person actually at fault). In the end Double paid Preyer ƒ93. Of this, ƒ20 was a fine; the remaining ƒ43 was profit for Preyer above the ƒ30 he had previously paid.[45]

The invocation of a sort of floral posse to confront Double was one way of dealing with the problem of Double's bulbs. Stoffel de Way chose a variation on this theme. De Way, twenty-six, was another prominent *bloemist*, involved in numerous transactions and no doubt well known to all those central to the flower trade. Like the others, he had bought bulbs in the summer of 1635: a Nonswith from Double, and an Oudenaerde from Pieter Govertsz, who, in turn, had bought it from Double. But at the appropriate time the bulb of course failed to sprout. De Way had heard a "common Rumor" about Double: that the bulbs he sold had holes bored in them. Concerned, he dug the bulbs up, with Pieter Govertsz as witness. Like the others, they were, he said, "so badly, viciously, and falsely bored through" that they would "never more . . . bring forth a flower." De Way's solution (appropriately enough when we think about the power of information in this world) was publicity. He took the bulbs to an inn run by a man called Steven and "let them be visited by many Tulipists and *bloemisten*," who all "uniformly judged them to be falsely bored through." De Way followed this up by going to complain of the "deception" to Double's "Vrunden," which, given the importance of reputation in this community, led to rapid reimbursement, again by Double's brother-in-law Jan Cuyck.[46]

One theme we can draw from the experiences of these men with the reprehensible Double is the existence of the kind of common pool of information we have posited in identifying certain nodes for the tulip trade. Those standing around talking in gardens or sitting around talking in inns came to know what they were talking about. If transactions were going on, they would know what they were; if tulips were of poor quality, they would know that too. They knew the actors in the trade and where the tulips were located. They spoke a language they all could understand, and their references assumed a shared, if exclusive, knowledge. Thus in several cases in the Kleine Bank van Justitie in Haarlem, we hear people (actually, the court's secretary, Michiel van Limmen, himself a *bloemist*) referring simply to tulips in "the garden of Poelenburch in Amsterdam" or to "Corennaert in Amsterdam." We can hardly expect the average inhabitant of Haarlem to have been familiar with Volckert Coornhart in Amsterdam or with Simon van Poelenburch's garden there, for all that Poelenburch, at least, had grown up in Haarlem. But these were clearly names well known to the litigants, and also to the scribe who wrote them down in this form. (Van Limmen actually did not know as much as he should have about his own transactions: he sued Tymon Maertensz to try to force him to disclose in whose garden the Gouda he had bought from him was actually planted.) To have possessed the general knowledge of the tulip community would have been constantly useful, allowing more careful dealing and, as in the Double case, an ability to flush out cheating. The linen merchant Bastiaen van de Rype, for example, divulged in a court case in September 1636 that he not only was owed money for a bulb called Jan Gerritsz bought by Stoffel de Way, but that De Way had sold the bulb on to another man, Pieter Willemsz. He was able to use this information about other people's transactions to help settle a dispute he was having with De Way over completely different bulbs.[47]

Such knowledge was not merely useful; it also made for a kind of exclusivity or communal feeling among the *bloemisten*. We see in the Double case a sense of general outrage over the plight of certain cheated customers. Not only were various *bloemisten* willing to be present to judge the condition of the bulbs being lifted, but they followed through, where Andries de Preyer was concerned, by going together to confront Double themselves. The image of Stoffel de Way sitting in a tavern with his ruined bulbs, visited by knowledgeable tulip folk who pronounced on Double and his double-crossing, also suggests a kind of informal society of *tulpisten*, in which those who counted passed judgment on the affairs of the trade. We have suggested that people who lived in the same neighborhood, were part of the same extended family, or were in the same trade might have talked about tulips to each other or to those they came in contact with in their trade. Perhaps those who might not have known each other otherwise came in contact because of their common interest in tulips. The deliberate massing of evidence against Double certainly suggests a sense of commonality despite the varying other contacts of some of those involved (though several were, of course, linen merchants). Some of those who joined the *bloemisten* were simply casual buyers and sellers, perhaps people who only ever possessed one bulb. Others, however, were experts and seem to have been acknowledged as such.

One type of expert is a businessman who has chosen to become a partner in a tulip company. I have found six companies set up specifically to buy and sell tulips; two were in Amsterdam, three in Haarlem, and one in Enkhuizen. There is also evidence of the existence of other partnerships or groups selling together, as in the case of Hendrick Woutersz, who referred in several lawsuits to having to consult his "fellow partners" or "comrade" about the outcome of the suits. The companies will be discussed in more detail in chapter 4, but here we can note that within the companies themselves there was also a consciousness of a hierarchy of expertise. Most of the firms contained tulip experts. In the five companies for which we have contracts, four designate one person who will do all the buying and selling; the other partners simply provided capital. In Enkhuizen, this person was the dyer Cornelis Cornelisz Varwer; in one Haarlem company, Roelant Veruvestraeten was to run the business, while in another, a partnership between Jan Govertsz Coopall and Cornelis Bol den Jongen, Coopall performed this function. Reymont de Smith, whom we encountered previously, employed his impoverished relative, François Heldewier, as the active partner in his Amsterdam tulip business. We also have evidence that certain people who were more expert in tulips bought and sold as brokers on behalf of others. In January 1637 the Haarlem baker Gerrit Symonsz Tetrode sued the brewer Gerrit Gerritsz Schouten for failure to pay for "Brokerage" (*Makelaerdi*) on tulips bought for him, and professional brokers, such as Cornelis de Vogel or Pieter de Ketelaer, also acted for clients in handling tulip deals. If those making a business of selling tulips were at the center of nodes of information about them, it is evident that those who took the main responsibility for sales within tulip companies will have been particularly prominent experts within the community of *bloemisten*. Jan Govertsz Coopall bought, sold, and acted as an arbiter in lawsuits about tulips. When he died of the plague in November 1636, the secretary recording his death in the burial register noted, unusually, his nickname: "the prince of the tulips."[48]

But those not connected to tulip companies could themselves acquire the reputation of being at the center of everything to do with tulips. Although here we must speculate—we do not normally find such endorsements as the one Coopall received on his death—we can imagine that certain figures who turn up everywhere in the tulip trade would have been central to the community of *bloemisten*. Several of these we have encountered in various circumstances in this and previous chapters. In Amsterdam, for example, Jan Hendricxsz Admirael, who quarreled with Marten Kretser over the artworks Kretser was exchanging for flowers, seems to have been busy selling to many of the Amsterdam tulip community. His many deals suggest to us that Admirael must cut something of a figure among the *tulpisten* of Amsterdam. Similarly, Abraham de Goyer was described by the poet Gerrit Jansz Kooch as "a great *bloemist*, who had a very large garden outside the Regulierspoort on the Singel. . . . The same Goyer said to me," Kooch wrote much later, "that he had sold in one year from his garden twenty thousand guilders in flowers. With that he spent ten thousand guilders on a beautiful country house in Maarssen and reinvested the other ten thousand in flowers." Similarly, Abraham Casteleyn was sufficiently known as a tulip salesman that those interested in tulips were traveling from Enkhuizen to buy flowers from him. And the fingerprints of Cornelis van Breugel, who dealt extensively with both Admirael and Jeronimus Victory, appear to mark many transactions over tulips in Amsterdam. Haarlem also had its kingpins in the tulip trade. Several of them—Rogier Alleman and Jacques de Clercq, for example—were selling in Enkhuizen in addition to their activities in Haarlem. Others, such as Hans Baert, repeatedly dealt in tulips in Amsterdam. Within Haarlem, figures like Stoffel de Way, Pieter Woutersz, Andries de Preyer, and Salomon Seys—most of whom made the mistake of buying from Cornelis

Double—seem to have stood right in the middle of the community of *bloemisten*, with numerous purchases and sales. Seys, for example, found himself in the midst of complicated transactions between Rogier Alleman and Pieter Woutersz, bought from Joost Jansz van Haverbeeck, and apparently even dealt bulbs with far-away Groningen, as a lawsuit of 1640 indicates. He sold tulips to Jacques Bertens, Franck Pietersz de Jongh, Gerrit Pietersz, and Pieter Jansz Ryck, and was involved in a complex affair with Jacob Baerckensz and Aert Huybertsz, which also appears to be about flowers. He was arbiter for a variety of lawsuits about tulips in the Kleine Bank van Justitie; he represented Hans Lailepel in court in a case against Dirck Jansz in 1638; he swore to the poor quality of the tulips of Symon le Febure; he was to be found chatting to *tulpisten* in the garden of Pieter Bol in 1636. He evidently knew people on the Amsterdam tulip scene and went into business with Cornelis van Breugel, who lived there, buying a Haarlem inn with him in 1636. If we wanted to look for a tulip expert in Haarlem, Salomon Pietersz Seys would be one of the first names that would spring to mind.[49]

This was literally true in cases when people wished to establish normal practice. The existence of experts is not merely a matter of our counting transactions: the community at the time identified its own, a process that must have been crucial when it came to locating the best information about tulips and to making and enforcing rules in a new trade. Salomon Seys was once again in the midst of this process. In 1639, as part of a lawsuit being brought by Dr. Johannes Stevilda of Leeuwarden in Friesland, Seys, along with Hans Baert and Jan Quakel, swore before a notary how the Haarlem tulip community dealt with the problem of bulbs that bloomed differently from the way they had appeared when they were sold. Seys, Baert, and Quakel said that "the custom is, and always was," that the buyer was not required to receive a bulb in this circumstance—a statement that was surely of comfort to Stevilda, who must have been a buyer in precisely this position. Similar statements were requested by out-of-towners as part of lawsuits after the fall in prices, when experts were asked by lawyers for descriptions of the way people in their town reacted to the fall in price. In Haarlem, David Clement, Willem Gael, Daniel Olthoff, and Pieter Joosten de Sanger provided such an account; in Alkmaar, Adriaen Jansz Cruidenier gave his version of the lack of cooperation after the crash; and in Enkhuizen, the baker Olfert Roelofsz and the apothecary Jan Sybrantsz Schouten made a declaration about the price of a pound of Switsers in late January and early February 1637. The lawyers conducting these suits, such as Salomon de Bray in Haarlem, knew that in these men they had people at the center of the culture of tulips. Clement and his companions said in the summer of 1637 that they had been "in the past winter present at many and various sales of flowers and also have made many and various sales of flowers, buying and selling, involving many thousands"; Schouten in Enkhuizen said in 1638 that he knew how much Switsers cost in the winter of 1637 because "in that time he wrote out with his own hand various documents of purchase and sale of the said Switsers at the said price. . . ." If there were nodes of information in tulip culture, we can find them here.[50]

The choice of particular people to pronounce on local practice was naturally an endorsement of their local standing within a trade. This was not limited to tulips; in other professions, when a question arose about how things should be done, a representative with acknowledged expertise would be called on to declare what was normally done. Thus a selection of members of the yarn industry were asked in 1645 to declare that yarn was normally packed in paper. The selection of officers in guilds and elections of inspectors for the trades was a similar acknowledgment of expertise. For the most part it appears that the designation of experts in tulips was more informal, but on at least one occasion it was explicit. As we have already noted, on February 23, 1637, after the fall in prices that occurred toward the end of the first week of the month, representatives of the *bloemisten* of twelve towns or districts met in Amsterdam to decide how to proceed. The Amsterdammers refused to sign the agreement, rendering their names unknowable to us, but those from Haarlem are all names familiar to anyone reading the notarial documents and lawsuits: Willem Schoneus, Jan van Clarenbeeck, Pieter Gerretsen (who was actually Pieter Gerritsz van Welsen), Cornelis de Bruyn, and Barent Cardoes. We must assume that their presence in Amsterdam was no accident. As we have noted, the delegation from Utrecht, François Sweerts, Bastiaen Hendricksz van Gheesbergen, and Anthony Verbeeck, went to the meeting because they were elected by thirty-three other tulip traders (see fig. 53). As in Haarlem, one must assume that those with more knowledge, as well as those with more influence, would have attended such a meeting.[51]

In the sixteenth and early seventeenth centuries, someone like Carolus Clusius—although there *was* no one else like Carolus Clusius—was a node of information about tulips too. So were Christiaen Porret, Matteo Caccini, Joachim Camerarius, René Morin, Pierre Morin, and all the *liefhebbers* spread across Europe. For tulips to flourish and spread, there had to be a community of information, a network of communication, to convey both expertise and a shared longing for tulips to a wider, if not very extensive, group. In previous chapters I have suggested that there was a continuity of interest and appreciation of tulips from the *liefhebbers* to the *bloemisten* and that, in fact, in some cases it was impossible to identify whether someone was one or the other. In some ways, tulip trading was simply an extreme and more capitalized form of *liefhebberij*. Although this argument is easier to make among the on average wealthier tulip-buyers of Amsterdam, who also can more easily be associated with art collecting, in other cities artists and art-collectors also played their role in tulipmania.

But even though it must be assumed that the fascination of tulips for some was their value rather than their beauty, there are other continuities with the world of the *liefhebbers*. As we have seen in this analysis of the composition of the tulip community, information and expertise were as crucial to the world of the *bloemisten* as they were to sixteenth-century naturalists. Information served both aesthetic appreciation and business—and in any case, as I have already argued, business was in some ways just as much a feature of the art world as it was of the tulip trade. To be able to deal in tulips one had to be able to understand them: the nature of the flowers, how they grew, what the different varieties were, not to mention who owned which tulips and what transactions had recently taken place. The flow of information limited and shaped the trade. As we have seen in this chapter, the claim made from the earliest days that tulipmania engulfed all of Dutch society seems to be based on propaganda rather than fact. The interest in tulips was relatively socially limited, not only by wealth or social station, but also by one's interaction with a variety of networks. These networks could be those of family, of religion, of profession, of neighborhoood—but ultimately they were networks that carried information about tulips and those who owned them. Those who knew more were the most central to the trade.

This is just as true for art collectors, among whom we encounter many of the same issues, including the nebulous distinction between aesthetic appreciation and conspicuous consumption we can find in the tulip trade. It is true that, unlike tulips, art in seventeenth-century Holland was relatively stable in price, which meant speculation in art was fairly pointless. However, again the dynamics of the art world share much with those of the floral community. As we have noted, the ability to discuss art, to appear the expert, was beginning in this period to be useful both commercially and socially. In 1993, Donald Posner described the artistic culture of seventeenth-century France, stressing the necessity of having the right "jargon," as one contemporary described it, when looking at paintings. One author, Abraham Bosse, gave his readers advice about how to buy paintings and how to prevent oneself from being swindled; another, Pierre Lebrun, wrote in 1635 giving advice about how simply to talk about art without looking a fool. In the Netherlands, this type of artistic treatise was rare to nonexistent; for the period of tulipmania, the *Schilderboeck* of Karel van Mander was virtually all that was available. But there were clearly ways for people who were not artists to get to know about art. Buyers could, and did, call in what were deemed experts—professional artists—to judge the value of paintings. But once again we must stress the importance of sociability. Some buyers trained themselves as artists; others interacted socially with artists; and then there was the sociability of collectors. As John Michael Montias showed in his book on art auctions in Amsterdam, buyers of art at auction in the first half of the seventeenth century formed clear networks and would have got to know each other in any case from their constant reappearance at sales.[52]

Comparing this kind of activity with that of the *liefhebbers* of plants in the sixteenth century reveals a certain crossover between the groups, both in social terms and in its aspirations to urbanity (despite the more learned character of some botanical experts in sixteenth-century Flanders). But such a crossover is also evident when we look at those who stood talking in gardens outside the Kleine Houtpoort. With the development of standards by which flowers could be judged, *bloemisten* were treading the same aesthetic-commercial territory as someone like the art collector Marten Kretser or others called in to value paintings or to judge their quality. Frequently such valuers were practitioners, who were thought to be the true experts. The same circumstances characterized quarrels over tulips, and it was especially important that one's knowledge about flowers be up to date, given the constantly changing nature of the tulip and its different breeds. An expert like Salomon Seys, asked to pronounce on quality or practice, had to have command of considerable recent information about both value and taste. For Seys and others like him, this was useful knowledge not only because it helped his activities as a trader, but also because it added to his status within a particular community, a community that could have been made up of collectors of *naturalia* or of art collectors but in fact concentrated on tulips. The display of his knowledge would add to his prestige among those valuing such knowledge. Thus even if tulipmania is thought to be chiefly a matter of commerce, its dynamics cannot be divorced from the social and cultural history of communities of knowledge.

It is also intimately intertwined with the Dutch culture of the period, with its stress on harmonious practice (a stress that, in any case, pervaded intellectual communities as well). By discovering the hierarchical nature of the world of the *bloemisten*, we learn that the trade itself was to some degree subject to a kind of informal order and authority. Respect for expertise in its turn brought about the development of rules concerning the tulip trade. It also helped to influence who might enforce them. As we will see in chapter 4, although the courts were usually a last resort in quarrels, the influence of the tulip experts infiltrated even there. Many cases in the Kleine Bank van Justitie in Haarlem were resolved by arbitration, and by and large the people appointed as arbiters were themselves experts in the matters under dispute. Among the forty-four people we know of who in a more or less official capacity helped in the settlement of tulip disputes in the 1630s, more than half (twenty-six) are known to have taken part in the trade themselves, and as there must have been many transactions of which we are not aware, the figure could actually be much higher. Certainly it was the practice for those knowledgeable about a subject to pronounce on it in these circumstances. Thus we find names we know well acting as arbiters, such as Hans Baert, Jacques de Clercq, Jan Dircksz Ossecoop, Simon van Poelenburch, Jan Quakel, Willem Schoneus, and Salomon Seys. As experts, they were also guides and makers of rules.

This was even more the case in the *collegie* (see fig. 47). We have heard of these gatherings in inns as places where *bloemisten* could learn about the latest news of the quality of tulips, of the provenance of bulbs, and of recent transactions, not to mention places where auctions took place.

FIGURE 47. The *collegie* or *comparitie* in Haarlem,
as portrayed in the Crispijn van de Passe's cartoon, *Floraes
Mallewagen*, 1637, detail. Atlas van Stolk, Rotterdam.

But the *collegie* was also a kind of committee, presumably of tulip experts,
who appear to have made rulings on the trade. When the baker Jeuriaen
Jansz was having trouble in August 1636 getting his next-door neighbor,
Pieter Jansz Alleman, to accept and pay for an offset of a Gouda Alleman
had purchased, Jansz pointed out the way the *collegie* had dealt with a
problem with the other offset of the same bulb. In that case the offset had
been sold to Jan Govertsz Coopall, who could not be present when it was
dug up and sent the professional gardener David de Milt to judge the bulb
instead. De Milt, who clearly knew a good deal about flowers, rejected the
offset, much as Alleman was now doing. But, Jansz pointed out, "the *collegie van de blommisten*, to whom the case was submitted, let it be known
that the said Coopall must accept the offset, which he did, and he has
honorably and virtuously paid for the said offset," which, Jansz implied,
was what Alleman ought to be doing as well.[53]

Although we do not know who made up the *collegie*, by making rulings
of this sort, it seems to have been the embodiment and culmination of the
culture of knowledge and expertise on which the tulip trade was based.
Both expectations and rules were articulated through its judgments, not
to mention through the presentation of cases to them by the *bloemisten*
for adjudication. Depositions like Jeuriaen Jansz's demonstrate attitudes
that we were already in a position to note in the Double case. Andries

de Preyer, hearing about Double's rumored boring through of the bulbs, gathered together a committee of experts who, their suspicions confirmed, trooped to Den Ouden Haen to confront Double and force him to pay compensation. Stoffel de Way's appeal to his community was even more dramatic: sitting angrily in a Haarlem tavern in March 1636, displaying his ruined bulbs to the many "Tulpaen and bloemmisten" who visited and inviting them to pass judgment on Double's "deceit." Given that this publicity forced Double, or at least his "Vrunden," to pay up, De Preyer and De Way correctly assessed that more knowledge about tulips also meant more power over the community of *bloemisten*. The *collegie* is only a step further toward the formalization of these ideas into institutions.[54]

Yet while the *collegie* represented an establishment of authority through knowledge, the sparse evidence we have of its operations suggests that its power remained nebulous. It was a power gained through the force of peer pressure. The smallness of the community in itself made this power possible. Yet it had no real ability to force people to behave in a particular way. This was evident in a quarrel over a bulb bought by the surgeon Jan Gellinckhuysen from the baker Henrick Jansz Hal. At the end of May 1636, an auction was held in the garden of the clogmaker Henrick Lucasz. During this auction, Hal put up for sale, at so much per *aes* (a measure of weight), the offset of an Engelsche Admirael that had come from the garden of Jan van Damme and was now standing in the garden of Jan Govertsz Coopall. The last bidder was Gellinckhuysen, but he evidently thought better of his decision to buy, saying, "I wish to be freed, through *wijnkoop*." In other words, he wanted to pay for drink for Hal and, with that payment, extricate himself from the deal he had made. Hal said in response, "If that is the way the *collegies* do it, or the way that people sell goods by the *Aes*, then you will be free, but I consider you to be the buyer. . . ." The dispute was supposed to be settled several weeks later, on June 16, when both parties met in the inn Den Vergulden Kettingh. Witnesses reporting on the event said that Hal stressed that even though the *collegie* had "repeatedly asked him," when he was selling the bulb, to let Gellinckhuysen off the sale, he had not wished to do so. The witnesses heard Gellinckhuysen agree: "that is the truth: you would not free me."[55]

Jan Gellinckhuysen made an agreement and then wanted to break it. Henrick Jansz Hal, in turn, would not do what the *collegie* repeatedly requested, and there was little they could do about it. Through the influence of information, the development of networks within the community, and the force of precedent as sales continued, a combination of formal and informal institutions might keep a community trading tulips under control. But the examples of both Hal and Gellinckhuysen should have been—indeed, perhaps were—specters haunting those taking part in such a high-priced trade. In a small and interconnected community of buyers and sellers, quarrels, disputes, and broken promises would have an even more shocking effect. Perhaps the *collegie*, the courts, or even the gentle words of arbiters could bring a quarrel to an end under normal circumstances. But what if the circumstances suddenly were not normal? What would happen then?

~~~~~~

FOUR

Grieving Money

DIRCK BOORTENS AND PIETER GERRITSZ VAN Welsen were trying to keep things civil. They were trying hard. It was April 14, 1637, and tulips had fallen in price more than two months earlier. The two men had made a contract for an astonishingly large amount of money—ƒ11,700—but, despite the crash, they were determined to see things through.

Both had reason to know a good deal about tulips. As their lengthy statement before a notary in April made clear, Boortens, a bleacher and cloth merchant of sixty-one, had some experience in the flower trade. He had sold large numbers of tulips planted in his garden to a variety of people—not to mention that his son, also Dirck (conveniently a lawyer), was married to Josina Bols, daughter and niece of two men very active in the tulip trade, Pieter Bol and Cornelis Bol den Jongen. As for Pieter Gerritsz van Welsen, he was to be found buying, selling, and talking about tulips in the company of various other prominent *bloemisten,* such as Jacques de Clercq and Jan Quakel. He was in Alkmaar in the summer of 1637 inspecting the much-vaunted tulips of Wouter Bartholomeusz Winckel, auctioned for tremendous sums on the previous February 5. Most tellingly, Van Welsen had been one of the representatives of Haarlem at the meeting of florists in Amsterdam on February 23 to discuss the future of the trade. Neither man, then, was a fool about flowers. And, as they were anxious to point out, they were both "people of honor."[1]

The contract Van Welsen and Boortens made was dated surprisingly late: March 17, well after the fall in prices of tulips in early February 1637. Boortens clearly wanted to get well away from the tulip trade, but Van Welsen, evidently a more adventurous sort, thought in March he could still make it pay. He agreed to buy from Dirck Boortens "a good group of tulips" in Boortens' garden, plus an Admirael Liefkens and a Sayblom owned by Boortens but located in the gardens of Pieter Bol and Guilliame Storm, respectively. Van Welsen was to come and see them several days later to make sure they were healthy; having done so, and having found some that were not in the best condition, he agreed to a new price of ƒ11,400, a discount of ƒ300. This sum would be paid in three installments, as often happened with houses, beginning with a payment of ƒ4,000 in June 1637, when the tulips would be ready for collection, and if anything happened to the tulips in the meantime—theft, alteration, spoilage—that would be Van Welsen's problem. But what made this particular contract so interesting, and so potentially problematic, was the clause indicating that many of these bulbs had already been sold by Boortens "to many and various persons and people." By buying these tulips from Boortens, Pieter Gerritsz van Welsen would be assuming the responsibility to deliver them to their new owners, as well as the ability to collect the money from those owners when the time came to lift the bulbs from the ground.[2]

The problem, of course, was that "after that, not long ago, a great and extreme fall and reduction in the said tulips has come" so that "the people who bought the said tulips, pound goods and offsets from the said Dirck Boortens do not want to receive them nor pay for them." It is inexplicable why the notarial document claimed that it was only "after that"—after the contract had been signed on March 17—that tulips had fallen in price, since no one could have known better than Van Welsen, a representative at the Amsterdam meeting on February 23, that they had done so in early February, before the contract was ever made. But whatever the reason, these two men were holding firm with their agreement. Boortens was not required to give any reductions in price nor get embroiled in any lawsuits or quarrels; he was freed from all that by his deal with Van Welsen. And indeed, the two men claimed with pride that, precisely because they *were* "people of honor," they could deal with each other peaceably.[3]

Too good to be true? Of course it was. Dirck Boortens and Pieter Gerritsz van Welsen tried to be civil, but they could not keep it up for long. In June 1637 the degree of noncompliance among Boortens' buyers must have become manifest. A further notarial document of July 9 took quite a different tone from earlier, saying that "already certain great difficulties and quarrels had come to pass over the payment of the sum of Eleven thousand four hundred ca[rolus] g[uldens]"—and "great difficulties and quarrels" was a considered correction in the document to the original wording, the more subdued "differences." Now the two were appointing arbiters to avoid further problems. As the month wore on, they even found it necessary to say that if the arbiters could come to no agreement, they would turn to a super-arbiter, the wealthy Mennonite Balthasar de Neufville. And if arbitration failed, Boortens and Van Welsen were evidently prepared to take the matter further, having brought in two lawyers before the high court, the Hoge Raad: Cornelis van Hyselendoorn and Pieter van Luchtenberch. In the event they were able to settle—how, we do not know. But it is interesting to see how quickly "people of honor" could break their promises.[4]

Actually, we should be amazed that Boortens and Van Welsen stuck to theirs as long as they did. This was a time of broken promises. The fact that they tried their best to accommodate each other, that they chose arbitration among a variety of alternatives in attempting to solve their differences, and, indeed, that they stressed that "people of honor" would find their own way to peace and accord will be telling for us in our examination of the tulip trade. In this chapter we will consider why *bloemisten* like Boortens and Van Welsen behaved as they did, and what this experience actually meant to them. We will look at how the tulip trade actually worked and, perhaps culturally most important, begin to think about what the ramifications were when contracts made "in good faith" led only to "great difficulties and quarrels."

Commerce, as we have seen, was nothing new to the world of tulips. In the sixteenth century, the *liefhebbers* who so avidly studied exotic flowers and reported on their yearly progress in their gardens were admittedly uneasy about the commercialization of what, for them, was a matter of scholarly courtesy and exchange. Yet Clusius and his friends paid close attention to the horticultural wares on offer in the markets of places like Brussels or Frankfurt, and it is clear from their correspondence that they not only looked, but bought as well. There were respectable flower merchants, such as Emmanuel Sweerts, whose *Florilegium* of 1612 portrayed the flowers available both at the Frankfurt fair and at his shop in Amsterdam, and, for that matter, *liefhebbers* allowed themselves to be concerned about price. In 1610 the Leiden apothecary Christiaen Porret, friend of Clusius, remarked in the midst of discussing seeds and bulbs requested by the Italian *liefhebber* Matteo Caccini that "varied tulips are still in great esteem here and, depending on what they are like, are still worth here 8. 10. 12. 15. 20. 25. and more than Fifty florins each." This litany of prices did not stop Porret from exchanging flowers with Caccini rather than selling to him, but our investigation of the identity of those who sold tulips even in the 1630s makes it clear that there is no easy line to be drawn between the supposedly artistic and selfless *liefhebber* and the apparently profit-hungry tulip salesman. Both existed in the same people, and indeed it is because of the love of the object itself, not to mention the fashion for owning tulips, that prices rose. We can thus, if we are so inclined, date the beginnings of the commercialization of tulips long before any sign of a tulipmania.[5]

By around the time that Porret was writing, certainly, it was not only itinerant salesmen, such as the Falquin Baltin who visited Brussels in 1601, who had tulips for sale. The first thirty years of the century, particularly in Amsterdam, with the expansion of the city and the creation of the gardens of the canal ring, were good times for gardeners. These included professional florists who grew flowers for a wealthy market. Someone like Pieter Pietersz, whose death in 1626 prompted a public auction of his wares, would have profited handsomely from the trade (and certainly Willem Willemsz, a florist outside the Reguliershof in Amsterdam much involved in the tulip craze, was accounted wealthy enough to appear in the fairly exclusive tax registers of 1631, worth ƒ2,000, only a third less than his neighbor, the silk merchant Abraham de Goyer). Pietersz's sale, mainly of anemones with a few irises and tulips thrown in, brought in ƒ637:17, and some of the most active buyers are familiar names from the tulipmania ten years later: Abraham de Schilder, Abraham Versluys, Abraham Casteleyn, Jeronimo Victory, Marcus Cornelisz Flora, and Adam

Bessels, as well as the Leiden botanist Dr. Pieter Pauw. Although some of these were themselves florists, or later became so, others, as we have seen, were merchants heavily involved in other activities such as sugar refining or the Muscovy trade. We can already find such merchants selling each other tulips around the time of Christiaen Porret's correspondence with Caccini. In Haarlem, for example, Andries Mahieu was offered in 1611 rather less than he wanted by the cloth merchant Heyndrick Jacobsz Coninck for all the offsets in his garden. Similarly, in Amsterdam, Volckert Coornhart, whose involvement in tulips continued until his death in late July or early August 1636, became embroiled in a problematic transaction in 1610. The purchaser, Jacob Elbertsz Smeersmouter, had failed to pay the ƒ136 he owed, because a tulip he had actually bought from Coornhart's father had come up in his garden looking less beautiful (and therefore worth less money) than it had appeared at the time of sale. Coornhart, in his strenuous efforts to recover the money in 1611, used an intermediary, yet another familiar name: Abraham Casteleyn, who went to Elbertsz's house to discuss the problem with him and tell him this sort of behavior was unacceptable. But it was not only the names that were familiar, but the issues, too: uncertainty about bulbs, which could change from year to year; the linkage of beauty to value (not to mention the importance of value at all); and the problems raised by the unwillingness of participants to follow through on the contracts they had made.[6]

One of the things that first struck Sir Dudley Carleton, British envoy to The Hague, when he arrived in the country in the spring of 1616, was the raptures expressed everywhere about tulips. He was not impressed. "The tulip gardens are in their flower," he wrote to his friend John Chamberlain, "but we are not yet taken with that delight with which they are here so much transported." Carleton's remarks, however, indicate how popular the flowers were among the wealthy in the 1610s, a popularity echoed by Roemer Visscher's 1614 emblem ridiculing the high prices for tulips ("a fool and his money are soon parted"; see fig. 19 in chapter 2). Nor were those recommending flowers for their beauty in this period blind to their monetary worth. Jean Franeau, for example, in his poem praising the gorgeous flowers bred by the Flemish gentry, pointed out that "he who considers the profits that some make every year from their tulips will believe that there is no better Alchemy than this agriculture." The author of a French pamphlet of 1617 on desirable bulbs, which promises, paradoxically, to be both "Compendious" and "Abridged," lists for the eager buyer a "Register of the most esteemed Tulips which are sought after at present & of great value, & worthy to be sought out at whatever price they are."[7]

When David Beck, a schoolmaster and poet in The Hague, began his diary for 1624, he was recovering from the death of his wife three weeks earlier. The diary consists of his daily round of walks, visits, singing of psalms, writing of lessons for his pupils, and seeing his children. On the first day of January—well before any tulips would have been blooming— he mentions the three-hour conversation he had with two friends, one a church official, on matters that would have concerned them: "Sermons, Ministers, Schools, Schoolmasters, Writers and Writings. . . ." But they also talked "finally about Tulips, Flowers, and the Flower-fools." To talk in January about the "Flower-fools" suggests, perhaps, that even at this early stage bulbs might have been exchanged in the winter; even if this was not the case, clearly in the 1620s those interested in tulips were a feature of the landscape, a source of wonder for the unmoved. Certainly at the same time as Beck was writing, the chronicler Nicolaes van Wassenaer, who by necessity had to leave out most of what was happening around him, found tulips worthy of comment in his monthly published newsletter of European affairs, the *Historisch verhael alder ghedenk-weerdichste geschie-denissen*. Unlike Beck and his friends, however, Wassenaer was not consumed with amazement at the "Flower-fools," but rather seems himself to have been one of them. In April 1623, June 1624, and April 1625, Wassenaer, more accustomed to talking about politics and the Thirty Years War, reported on the latest tulips and what was being said about them. His first comments on this subject proposed that people of different humors had different interests, so that cholerics were enthralled with weapons and wars, and melancholics with hell, devils, and necromancy, and attracted to solitary places such as mountains and deep cellars. The sanguine, on the other hand, were attracted by beautiful flowers, and most particularly by tulips, whose variety incited admiration at the omnipotent strength of God. Wild tulips in Asia, he said (in language familiar to us), "ornament the land so that it appears through the variety of colors to be the most costly Carpet in the World." His words were, perhaps, an excuse for his enthusiasm about tulips against naysayers among his readers, people like David Beck.[8]

Wassenaer, in his three years of reports on the tulips, showed some familiarity with a few details about the market for the flowers, presumably in Amsterdam. In 1623, for example, he gave an eyewitness account of the garden of the *liefhebber* Adriaen Pauw, pensionary of Amsterdam and lord of Heemstede: "I saw a Garden full of many different Tulips/in the middle of them was a Cabinet surrounded with mirrors which threw back the reflection of the Flowers so elegantly/that it seemed like a Royal throne." Wassenaer seemed particularly taken with the Semper Augustus, a red and white flamed flower, which "this year" (1623) "is the principal . . . never did a Blommist see a more beautiful one than this: no Tulip has ever been in greater esteem. . . ." His discussions of the Semper Augustus suggest that the market for tulips at this point was still very much a matter for a small band of *liefhebbers*. He reported that the Semper Augustus was so prized that one had been sold for a thousand guilders, but that the owner thought himself cheated, since with two offsets he could have sold the whole thing for three times the price the following year. The following spring, in 1624, Wassenaer remained entranced with the Semper Augustus. There were only twelve of them in existence, he reported, and they would cost *f*1,200 apiece, except that the owner of all twelve could not resolve himself to sell them, realizing that only while he had the market cornered would the price remain high. However, he said, other speculators (the word he used) talked up the merits of a variety of other flowers, such as the Testament Clusii, Testament Coornhert, Mortarum van Casteleyn, and Jufferkens van Marten de Fort (named after a *liefhebber* in Haarlem), and sought out a tulip similar to the Semper Augustus, the Par Augustus, which he accounted the mere "bastard" of the real thing. Other familiar tulips were also beautiful, he was however willing to admit, tulips such as the Lacken, Oudenaerden, Domvilles, and Croonen. Prices for the Semper Augustus, at least, seemed to be rising in 1625: in his last report on the tulips Wassenaer said that *f*2,000 and *f*3,000 had been offered but that the owner still could not make up his mind what to do. In any case, the spring of 1625, after a cold January and February, provided "many beautiful colors" that, again, "serve for us as a means to admire the miracle of God/which shows itself in such a small thing."[9]

The kind of prices Wassenaer mentioned were (as is clear from his tone) highly unusual before the mid-1630s. The much lower sums mentioned by Porret for the period around 1610 are confirmed by one or two transactions from 1611, in which a tulip called the Caers op de Candelaer (Candle on the Candlestick) sold for ƒ20 and sometime later in the spring was resold for ƒ24. As sometimes also happened later, whole beds of tulips were sold at once, and in the same season of 1611 four beds were sold at a price of ƒ200. (This might not have encompassed large numbers of tulips, given that gardens of the period included so much bare ground between the flowers). Although we lack recorded prices for the 1620s, the sort of prices we find in the recorded sales of the period from late 1634 on are initially much lower than those in Wassenaer's reports on the Semper Augustus. For example, a sale around October 30, 1635, saw a Saeyblom van Coningh sell for ƒ30 and a Latour for ƒ27. Given a lack of data, we cannot be entirely sure about when prices really started to climb, but for the few tulips for which it has been possible to construct proper price series, it appears that the last part of January and the beginning of February 1637 showed a much sharper rise than previously. We should note that many bulbs were sold by weight rather than by individual bulb, because a heavier bulb was more likely to contain offsets, which would in subsequent years produce new bulbs and consequently more profit. Some more valuable bulbs were weighed in *asen* (an *aes* or ace was 0.048 grams), others in pounds. So how much did prices rise over these weeks? Although there was no single "market" price, since tulips were not sold at a central place (and there could be serious regional variations), from individual transactions we can tell that some of the changes in price were dramatic. If we look at a tulip called the Groot Gepluymaseerde, for which we have three comparable prices from the period, the bulbs rose from a value of ƒ0.07 per *aes* on December 28, 1636, to ƒ0.15 per *aes* on January 12, 1637, more than doubling in price in two weeks.[10]

These price rises must have taken place in an atmosphere of growing excitement. As we move through the mid-1630s, we can tell from the growing number of contracts involving tulips, and quarrels about their sale, that this relatively new luxury item was capturing the attention of those interested both in their beauty and in their worth. It was already the case in 1634 that *liefhebbers* and enthusiasts were traveling to other towns to buy tulips, and over the next two years, most particularly in the summer and autumn of 1636, we read more and more often in the manuscript record about *bloemisten* and their activities. They congregated in gardens and talked about tulips, discussing who had the best varieties and who was selling to whom. They talked to each other on street corners and, in the case of Geertruyt Schoudt, at the dinner table. They met each other in inns, where all sorts of things were commonly for sale, but it will have become known to the community that in certain taverns tulip traders might be found. For those involved, although their daily occupations certainly did not cease, the world of tulips and *bloemisten*, with its own hierarchy of experts and authorities, the standards of practice in trade established by brand-new custom and the declarations of the *collegiën*, and the new social connections and exploitation of old ones surely contributed to a sense of a new social experience and the thrill of comradeship. At the same time, the rise in prices as more people grew interested in having bulbs will have added its own excitement and feeling of optimism. Although, as we have already discussed, the numbers involved in tulipmania never reached the all-encompassing picture painted by many authors, the very fact that neighbors seem to have talked to neighbors; colleagues with colleagues; shopkeepers, booksellers, bakers, and doctors with their clients gives one the sense of a community gripped, for a time, by this new fascination and enthralled by a sudden vision of its profitability.

Profitable it was. Tulips of all varieties continued to be traded, with some of the more luxurious varieties, such as the Viceroy, Admirael van Enchuysen, or Admirael Lieffkens going for high prices at the end of 1636 and the beginning of 1637. Switsers, one of the most popular bulbs of the period, went from a price of ƒ125 per pound on December 31, 1636, to a high point of ƒ1,500 per pound on February 3, 1637, a twelve-fold increase. Geertruyt Schoudt, by buying Switsers on February 1, 1637, promised to pay almost at the top of the market (ƒ1,400, including Hendrick Jan Wynants' discount of ƒ50 on what he had charged the city doctor Gregorius van der Plas earlier in the day). In Enkhuizen, for the sake of a lawsuit apparently being brought by a buyer in Leeuwarden in Friesland, the baker Olfert Roelofsz and the apothecary Jan Sybrantsz Schouten swore in May 1638 that the prices for Switsers had indeed increased in this manner, although someone involved in their deposition was inclined to exaggerate. They said that "in the end of the month January, and until mid-February a[nno] xvj^{c}xxxvij [1637], within this Town, a pound of Switser bulbs were not only sold but daily bought and sold, worth, and rose up from the sum of six hundred to eight or nine hundred carolus gul[den]s." The more moderate "eight to nine" actually replaced a crossed-out "thousand," and, moreover, the deleted words "or more" are still visible just after. Reijier Wyarde, the lawyer from Leeuwarden, was perhaps trying his luck for his client just a little too far. But even without exaggeration, the rise in price remained astonishing.[11]

And contemporaries *were* astonished. In some ways they were too astonished, for many of the prices recorded were not extraordinarily high, especially if one looks before the final few weeks of the craze. For example, on December 31, 1636, the Mennonite merchant Jacob Abrahamsz van Halmael made a deal with Jacob Luijcasz Cock of Zwolle in which Cock delivered Halmael linen worth ƒ1,000, and Halmael (who was apparently fond of these kinds of exchanges of goods for tulips, something he also arranged with his coreligionist Abraham van Meeckeren over a load of Swedish barley) would in return deliver tulips when they were ready. The individual tulips were not so expensive in the grand scheme of things: a Lieffkens at ƒ130, a Groote Gepluymaseerde at ƒ110, a Paragon Lieffkens at ƒ130, a Rood en Geel van Leyden at ƒ40, a Jan Symonsz at ƒ35, a Lion at ƒ70, and so on. What transfixed pamphleteers in 1637, and has continued to fascinate writers on tulipmania ever since, were the prices reportedly paid at an auction in Alkmaar on February 5, 1637, by the Weeskamer for the benefit of the orphans of Wouter Bartholomeusz Winckel. Although we have no independent confirmation of the veracity of these prices—no list of items, buyers, and prices exists such as we find for Weeskamer auctions in Amsterdam—some time afterward a broadside was printed containing a list of prices reputedly paid (see fig. 33 in chapter 3). Many of these were no more than other prices for bulbs in recent weeks—a Paragon de Man for ƒ260, a Cos for ƒ205, a pound (1,000 *asen*) of Macx bulbs for ƒ300—and the average price overall for single bulbs in the main auction was ƒ792.88. But the attention of those reading the broadside was no doubt captured by a few much higher prices: a Viceroy for ƒ4,203 and, particularly, an Admirael van Enchuysen with an offset, which reportedly sold for ƒ5,200. It was also noted on the printed sheet that the total sold in tulips and other flowers and plants was around ƒ90,000. Although we cannot be sure of these prices, it is clear from the behavior of the *weesmeesters* and guardians of Winckel's children that they considered the bulk of Winckel's estate to be planted in the ground.

In July 1636 the children's uncle showed greatest concern about lifting of the tulips, and in August the guardians appointed by the Weeskamer were ordered to administer his goods and "especially" the tulips he owned and had bought or sold. The emphasis on "especially" (*special[lijk]*) is telling. The Alkmaar auction remained a byword for the tulipmania in the pamphlet literature and in later accounts, and, as we have noted, the prices recorded in tulip books next to portraits of beautiful blooms were usually those from this particular auction.[12]

What made the auction in Alkmaar so interesting, and ultimately so problematic for the guardians of Winckel's children, was that it was held in the middle of winter. No tulips were available for inspection, and, for that matter, no bulbs could be taken away. Everything remained in Alkmaar until the summer, and, importantly, none of the high prices that so dazzled spectators were actually paid on the spot. This was in the nature of the flower trade, which was fundamentally shaped—as indeed were attempts to enforce it—by the seasons. Tulips, depending on the type, bloom in April, May, or June, and last only for a short period, perhaps a week or two. After they had blossomed, it was thought imperative to lift the tulips out of the ground, dry them off, and keep them wrapped up indoors. Otherwise they might be damaged in the ground. When September came, the tulips were replanted, and they remained in the earth until after the next flowering season the following summer.

This seasonal rhythm gave a special feeling to the trade, as for much of the time the goods were not actually in one's hands, being necessarily buried in the ground. If a bulb was sold to another party, it would still stay underground until the summer, so that sometimes, if bulbs were sold on, the tulips would be found in the gardens of third or fourth parties—and the same problem of immoveability faced those who sold property where tulip bulbs were planted. Thus, for example, when Cornelis de Bruyn sold a bleachery with a garden in Santpoort to Claes Engelsz Boon in January 1638, he felt compelled to specify in the sales contract that the tulips in the garden remained his property and that he must be allowed to visit them until the proper time to dig them up. The same problems beset anyone buying or selling a bulb outside of the "dry bulb time," as the summer months were called. Any transactions taking place in the summer were relatively straightforward: the seller delivered the bulbs and the buyer paid on receipt. (Of course, problems might arise if the buyer had not actually seen the bulbs in flower before purchase.) During the rest of the year, whether the sale was made by personal contract before a notary, by private agreement, in a Weeskamer or unofficial auction, or at an inn, in nearly every case the agreement was made, but all parts of the transaction itself were deferred to the summer. A seller promised to deliver the bulbs when they were ready to be lifted, and the purchaser—who usually would take a look at the tulips when the time came—promised to pay on delivery. That meant that if someone bought an Admirael van Enchuysen for ƒ5,200 at Alkmaar on February 5, 1637, he did not actually receive it on that day, nor did he pay for it. And given the date of the auction—around the time of the crash—he probably never did.[13]

Deals, it is true, did not always work this way. Cock's deal with Halmael, in which Halmael received ƒ1,000 worth of linen, entailed immediate delivery of the cloth, with merely a promise of delivery by Halmael "when it is time to pull up the Tulips or Bulbs." Similarly, sometimes delivery of bulbs took place without full payment being made. The apothecary Jan Schouten of Enkhuizen bought an Otto de Man bulb from Rogier Alleman of Haarlem but failed to pay the full amount; in September 1636 he received a visit in Enkhuizen from Alleman and two other prominent *bloemisten* from Haarlem, Stoffel de Way and Jan Goossens, demanding that he pay the ƒ60 owed. But the case of someone like Pieter Willemsz Groes of Enkhuizen is much more typical. Groes, a master shipwright, bought from the Enkhuizen dyer Dirck Maes an assortment of bulbs for ƒ5,000 on November 15, 1636, with the notation that it was "to be paid *according to Custom* on the delivery of the said flowers. . . ." With neither goods nor money customarily handed over at the time of sale, both sides therefore ran a risk in the tulip trade. Trust and honor had to play a major role in a trade like this.[14]

How did the tulip trade actually operate? Groes' agreement with Maes before a notary, with a contract, was one way of making a sale. People with tulips would conclude a deal with someone who wanted to buy, sometimes using one or more informed parties as a *seghsman*, an arbiter who helped to come to a fair price that pleased everyone. A notary might write out a contract declaring the terms, or sometimes the buyer and seller would simply write out a bill of sale, called a *coopcedulle*, recording the agreement made in simple terms (see fig. 48). We have a collection of *coopcedullen* for the transactions between Pieter Willemsz van Rosven

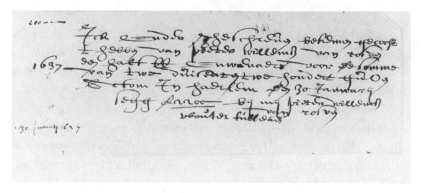

FIGURE 48. *Coopcedulle*, or IOU, in which Wouter Tullekens of Alkmaar buys a half pound of Coornhart bulbs from Pieter Willemsz van Rosven of Haarlem for ƒ2,200. Regionaal Archief Alkmaar.

in Haarlem and Wouter Tullekens in Alkmaar between mid-December 1636 and the end of January 1637. For example, on a small slip of paper Tullekens would record that "I the undersigned declare that I have sold to pieter Willemsen van Rosven a Cent of 530 asen planted in the garden of frans pietersen grebber for the sum of seventy-two gulden actum In haerlem the 15 January 1637 I say 72:0:0 by me wouter tullekens." On the back of one of the slips, Tullekens calculated that he had bought from Rosven tulips worth ƒ2,758 and that he had sold him tulips worth ƒ162 in six transactions (all this was saved because of a later lawsuit after Tullekens refused, for a time, to keep his end of the bargain) (see fig. 49).[15]

Such privately arranged sales might require some discussion, and in fact we have a detailed example from a notarial document of such a discussion in late 1634. Jan Jansz Schoft, a cloth merchant in Enkhuizen, went to see Abraham Casteleyn just outside of Amsterdam and discussed with him the purchase of several bulbs called Slechte Juriae (Bad Juriae), for which Casteleyn was asking ƒ3. Schoft said to him, "that is too much, you must give them for less," but Casteleyn said in response, "I can't give them for any less, the Pasty baker Jan van Broeckenhuysen has taken away, bought, and paid for four bulbs just like these for ƒ3 apiece." (This was, incidentally, news that irritated another Enkhuizen resident, Dirck Maes. Maes had sent Van Broeckenhuysen to buy these two bulbs for him and had been cheated by the baker to the tune of a 100 percent markup:

"how a man can be deceived!" he exclaimed on hearing Schoft's tale.) Discussion of a purchase was perhaps even more crucial several years later, when the sums of money involved were much greater. On January 22, 1637, the Haarlem merchant Bartholomeus van Gennep had made a deal in Amsterdam with Abraham Versluys about the purchase of a variety of tulips, including Geel en Root Croonen, Switsers, Centen, Oudenaerden, LeGrands, Gevleugelde Coornarts, Kistemaeckers, and Gevlamde Nieulanten, altogether totaling ƒ3,421. Versluys gave him until the evening to confirm whether or not he wanted to buy the flowers. That night Van Gennep went back to see Versluys in the Marten Rayen Doelen and told him, in the presence of three Mennonite merchants who were also *bloemisten* (Anthony de Man, Jan de Haes, and Michiel Kistgens) that he did indeed want the bulbs. Yet it seems that Versluys, the seller, had changed his mind, or at least about the price. When, six days later, a notary insinuated him, Versluys said that he had indeed said he would sell the bulbs to Van Gennep, but *not at that price*. This kind of problem occurred often in the autumn of 1636 and early winter of 1637. With prices going up, the people causing difficulties were the sellers, who knew that waiting might get them a better deal. Later, once prices had fallen, they were the victims. In the case of Van Gennep, whose *insinuatie* on January 28 includes precise

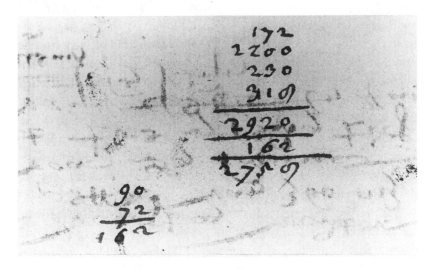

FIGURE 49. Calculations of what Tullekens owed to Rosven.
Regionaal Archief Alkmaar.

details about the price and weight of each type of bulb, we can imagine the negotiation that went into the conclusion of such a deal.[16]

Informal meetings at inns could also produce sales. From the documents available we get a picture of people with bulbs sitting in taverns, ready to mention to likely buyers that they had goods for sale. One such seller, whose behavior also reveals to us the desire to take advantage of the financial climate, is Jan Michielsz, the Haarlem rabbit-seller who was also sometimes called Jan Conijn (Jan Rabbit). Jan Willemsz van den Bosch reported in early February that several weeks earlier he had discussed buying from Matthijs van der Beijten a pound of Switsers that Van der Beijten said he had bought earlier from Jan Conijn. Van den Bosch was not wholly enthusiastic, wanting to make sure before buying anything that Conijn had really sold the bulbs to Van der Beijten, since as it was wintertime the bulbs were not yet in Van der Beijten's possession. When asked, Conijn replied that he could and would deliver them to Van der Beijten when the time came, but only if the *schepenen*—aldermen who enforced justice—required him to do so. Clearly this was not a satisfactory response. Another Haarlemmer, twenty-four-year-old David van der Mersch, confirmed Conijn's sales technique. He said that he had come across Conijn around New Year's Day in the Oude Haentgen (Allert Schatter's inn near the Grote Markt). Conijn said that he had a pound of Switsers to sell "and that they were beginning to go up" in price; he offered them for ƒ120, and when Van der Mersch instead offered ƒ110, he said that if he did not get ƒ120, he would not proceed with the sale. Jan Michielsz, alias Conijn, is a good example not only of someone who relied on casual contacts at inns to make his sales, but of someone who had an eye for the main chance. We have seen how high Switsers were to rise in the following month; Conijn was having none of a lower price than he demanded, since "they were beginning to go up," and, having sold Switsers to Van der Beijten, he was, it appears, prepared to break his contract if the city government would let him get away with it.[17]

Van den Bosch said that Van der Beijten had "auctioned" him the Switsers, although in fact he had not bought them. But this usage suggests the way that tulip sales, wherever they took place, could be conducted like more official auctions. One such sale took place in the garden of the clogmaker Hendrick Lucasz, who was very active among the tulip connoisseurs of Haarlem. A variety of *bloemisten* were present in his garden on May 31, 1636: Jaques Verheus, Jan Goossens, Daniel Messchaert, another Jan Goossens (there were two, one aged thirty-three, the other twenty-four), Stoffel de Way, the baker Henrick Jansz Hal, and the surgeon Jan Gellinckhuysen. Hal "presented for sale, to be delivered by the *aes,* the biggest offset of an Englesche Admirael, which had come out of the garden of Jan van Damme and now was standing in the garden of Jan Govertsz Coopal." Although the sale was taking place in a garden, in other words, that was simply because this was where the *bloemisten* happened to be gathered; the bulb in question was elsewhere and indeed, at the end of May, still in the ground. The sale was clearly one that went from a low to a high bid, with each participant writing his bid down. "[F]inally at the last writings Mr. Jan Gellinckhuijsen Remained Buyer, [at] three guilders per *aes* . . . no one more wishing to write. . . ." In chapter 3 we saw the outcome of this sale: Gellinckhuysen, finding himself the purchaser, wished immediately to extricate himself by paying out money for drink, *wijnkoop,* but this raised objections from his comrades. Even though this sale took place in someone's garden, it was thought necessary to hold to certain rules of good practice.[18]

When more formal sales took place at inns, they seem to have held to a particular set of rules, some of which are described in the longest pamphlet associated with the tulip craze, Adriaen Roman's dialogue between Waermondt and Gaergoedt. One type, described as *de borden* (the boards or plates), was actually essentially a private negotiation, not a public sale. Everyone present had his name inscribed on a board and also was given boards or plates on which they could write their bids. It appears from the pamphlet that people in possession of tulips to sell were not in fact supposed to auction their own bulbs. Instead, if one wished to sell bulbs, it was necessary to discover informally who was interested in buying. Once a prospective buyer was identified, both buyer and seller would choose *seghsmannen* (arbiters helping to arrange the sale) and, through a series of bids and counterbids, come privately to a mutually accepted price, which the *seghsmannen* then announced. It was indicated by small marks on the disks, and if the buyer and seller continued to find it satisfactory during the following, essentially sham, public sale, the marks were left alone. That meant that the sale was completed. As in many kinds of economic transactions, this and other tulip auctions were concluded by the paying of *wijnkoop* (wine money) by the buyer to the seller. According to Roman's pamphlet, this amounted to half a *stuiver* per guilder of the price (in other words, one-fortieth of the total), up to a maximum of ƒ3 per transaction. If one or the other of the pair decided in the end that he did not want to continue with the sale (indicated by wiping out the mark by the price on his board), he would have to pay the small fee known as *rouwkoop* (griev-ing money). *Rouwkoop* was a way of maintaining honor when transac-tions were canceled; if one reneged, one had to indicate that this was not good practice, not thoroughly honorable, through the paying of a fine. *Rouwkoop* restored honorable relations, or it was supposed to.[19]

The other form of sale was called *in 't ootjen* (in the zero) and really was an auction. Here, the main feature was that the seller openly offered his bulbs for sale, with bids written, again, on boards or plates. There was a small reward for the highest bidder, *treckgelt* (pulling money), provided by the seller as an attempt to attract interest and paid whether or not the seller accepted the high bid. The auction was concluded with a familiar call of the person (usually someone chosen from the group, it appears) conducting the auction, of "no one bids? no one? once, no one further, twice, no one? third time, no one? fourth time?" If no one made a higher bid after the fourth call, and the seller was willing to sell at that price, the sale was concluded. Once again, the paying of *wijnkoop* by the buyer indicated that the transaction was indeed complete. This payment was not a mere formality, for the paying of *wijnkoop* was cited in many cases as decisive proof when sellers challenged buyers later attempting to duck out of what they had promised at the time of sale. Once again, the issue was honor: *wijnkoop* displayed the sealing of a promise. The money, as the name indicates, was to be spent by the seller on food and drink: "tobacco, beer, wine, fire, light . . . the poor, also the girls [serving-maids]." An ex-ample of an *ootjen* auction took place on February 6, 1637, at a favorite resort for *bloemisten*, the Menniste Bruyloft (Mennonite Wedding) inn in the Oude Brugsteeg in Amsterdam. Because of a dispute, we learn that Jacques de Poer was the highest bidder. A witness declared later that a pound of Switsers had been auctioned to the highest bidder and "whoever bid the most for the said pound of tulip bulbs would have a shilling as treckgelt. . . ." The price mounted to ƒ1,060 until, in a dramatic climax, "one Jaques de poer . . . standing on a bench, raised the previous bid and, for the said pound of tulip bulbs, bid ƒ1065." The seller, David van der Cruijs, therefore "wished him luck with the purchase, [and] Jaques de poer received and kept the shilling as treckgelt. . . ." For Van der Cruijs, this was proof that De Poer had indeed bought the bulbs.[20]

Transactions like these—private arrangements, auctions in gardens, informal and formal sales at inns—were probably carried out not only by individuals but also by the people buying and selling tulips for tulip companies. As we saw in chapter 3, a number of partnerships and companies were formally set up in the mid-1630s to buy and sell tulips. There are hints in the records of even more, but we can be certain that there were at least six companies. In Amsterdam, Reymont de Smith hired his relative François Heldewier in 1635 to deal in tulips for De Smith's profit, while Nicolaes Block and Jan Minuit in January 1637 set up a (probably short-lived) partnership in which Block would hand over all his dry bulbs to be planted by Minuit, and they would split the proceeds fifty-fifty, a deal also involving the transfer to Minuit of a lease on a house and forty to fifty pounds of poor-quality silk in red, yellow, blue, and green. In 1636 an intercity company was set up with partners Hendrick Jacobsz and Roelant Veruvestraeten of Haarlem and Philips Jansz Rogge and the painter Matthijs Bloem of Amsterdam. Rogge was the last to join the partnership on December 29, 1636. The arrangement was that Veruvestraeten did all the buying and selling of bulbs, while the other three contributed all the capital; each member bore 25 percent of any profit or loss. All sales of tulips by any of the four was supposed to be for the profit of the company. As Veruvestraeten was in Haarlem, one must assume that much of his trading would also have taken place there. In competition with him, among others, would have been a Haarlem company whose beginning date is uncertain but which certainly was settling accounts in 1638, and indeed seems to have continued for several years thereafter. Three of its members, Theunis Davidsz Kop, Leonard Prior, and Pieter Wynants (a different, and slightly younger, man than the Mennonite Pieter Jacobsz Wynants), as noted earlier, were all from the same place in western Germany, a connection no doubt contributing to their involvement with each other in the business of tulips. The complement was made up by Aert Huybertsz and by Ysack Jansz, who made wooden parts for looms. Although we know nothing of the initial arrangements for this company, in February 1638 Jansz gave permission to Huybertsz to settle with disgruntled customers, and in 1645 we learn of a quarrel that took place between these two about the company in 1641, over whether or not Huybertsz actually had the right to tulips he still had in his possession. The implication was that in 1641 the company was still in existence, and still a subject of dispute.[21]

Some of these companies arrived fairly late on the scene, dreaming up the idea of trading in tulips in a more organized fashion only as the whole market for flowers began to heat up around New Year's Day, 1637. More prescient in their judgments were two Haarlem tulip experts, Cornelis Bol den Jongen and Jan Govertsz Coopall. They first went into partnership selling tulips on September 9, 1635, and came together to confirm their contract on November 6, 1636, chiefly, it seems, because Coopall was on his deathbed and wished to protect his family. From their agreement in 1636, we find that Coopall had started the company with a total of ƒ9,644:8 in flowers, and for his sale of flowers in the previous year Bol now paid him ƒ3,923:18 (suggesting, if we assume a fifty-fifty split of profits, a total sale amounting to ƒ7,847:16). In 1636, in an effort to make sure that all financial matters were handled smoothly in case Coopall should die, Bol paid out any money owed to Coopall and they agreed—in fear that their "common things" should become public knowledge—that all garden keys, "books, Registers, memoranda, and notes" concerning the trade should automatically go to the longest lived of the pair (which fairly obviously was going to be Bol). We get the impression here of a well-regulated business, complete with elaborate accounts, which had lasted for more than a year. The drama of the situation in November 1636 is also palpable. The notary, unusually, was called to the house of the dying Coopall on the Groot Heiligland, and the latest company contract was made in the form (as it stated) of a last will and testament. The tulip business was clearly of crucial importance to the two partners and their families.[22]

A similar death had already marred the Enkhuizen tulip company when it met to renegotiate its own contract on December 26, 1636. One of its members, the apothecary Barent ten Broecke, nephew and namesake of the collector Paludanus, had died since the company was set up on February 23, but his fellow apothecaries Jan Jansz Apotheecker and Anthony Jacobsz Apesteijn, the grocer and wine merchant Hendrick Willemsz Vries, and the dyer Cornelis Cornelisz Varwer, remained on board. The initial contract was one in which Varwer did all the work and the others provided all the capital (similar to Veruvestraeten's arrangement in his Haarlem-Amsterdam company); Vries, ten Broecke, and Varwer were each

25 percent shareholders, and the other two apothecaries were in for 12.5 percent each. Varwer was clearly an enterprising man and had prepared the way in January by renting out a garden in the western extension to Enkhuizen in which to grow the tulips, in addition to the garden behind his own house. His vision of profit led him to stipulate that his garden landlord, Jan Maertsz, who was receiving a mere ƒ20 a year for a six-year lease, could claim no ownership of the tulips currently in the garden, or any that might be planted there later, all of which would be for Varwer's sole "profit" (as it was expressed in the lease). Perhaps he already had the company, formed seven weeks later, in mind at this point, as he arranged the necessary infrastructure.[23]

Varwer was the one with the tulips, and in some ways the dynamics of this company were always a matter of Varwer versus the capital partners. In any case the latter were mostly connected to each other, as we learned in chapter 3: the three apothecaries were all *vrunden*, including the brothers-in-law Barent ten Broecke and Anthony Jacobsz Apesteijn, and they were all comrades in the same profession, one that had long been interested in tulips. When the company formed, the others bought from Varwer all the tulips he owned, both in Enkhuizen and elsewhere, for ƒ2,675, and they arranged that Varwer would no longer buy or sell bulbs except for the sake of the company. Any bulbs he had previously sold would go to the profit of the company, and any he had bought but would be paying for in the summer of 1636 would come out of the company's funds. But Varwer was not allowed to lift a bulb of "any Importance" without the knowledge of all the other partners, and the presence of at least one of them. This was, then, not exactly a partnership of trust.[24]

Varwer got an additional ƒ2,700 from the four partners on July 25, 1636, but on August 17 the contract was dissolved, for what reason we do not know. He promised to pay the money back, at 16 percent interest, the following July. But in December Varwer returned with a further proposition for his colleagues, now missing Barent ten Broecke, who had died during the autumn. We have a graphic account of the meeting of the company, at Apotheecker's house, from two witnesses who also acted as *seghsluyden* (arbiters) for the transaction. One can imagine that, with tulips proving so much more clearly profitable than they had been earlier in 1636, by December 26, Vries, Apotheecker, and Apesteijn were more willing to come to terms with Varwer. He presented them with more "capital tulips" to

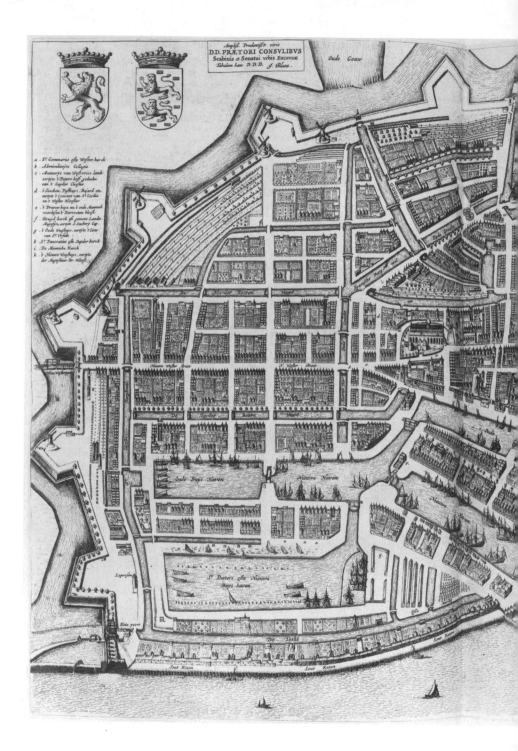

FIGURE 50. Cornelis Biens, map of Enkhuizen, 1649. British Library. The western extension of the town was filled with gardens.

sell to them (a way of their investing in the business by buying up his stock), saying that he wished to "do *vrunt schap*" as he had with them the previous year: in other words to go into trade with him "on the Conditions of last year," that he conducted all the trade and took a quarter of the profit. After some discussion out of the room, Apotheecker and Vries came back in, saying, "Corn[elis] Corn[elisz] Varwer we have resolved with each other to go into business with you and to make a contract with you as we did last year, so that you will have a quarter part, what shall we give as a present for your wife[?]" (Such a present was often a means of sealing a contract.) They freed him from any responsibility for paying the heirs of ten Broecke the interest he owed for the money borrowed in July, and overall they seemed much more conciliatory now that more profits were to be won. Varwer stressed those profits, mentioning "that big money has already been won on the items sold." There was some further discussion of conditions, and an agreement (after an initial demand by Varwer for ƒ600) of a present for his wife of ƒ400, no small sum. The deal concluded with the resolution to hold a "Meal or party where the wives also will be, toward the good success of the said trade." Varwer's wife was then called to the house. Having been told the conditions, she said, "Everything that my husband has done, I am also content with"—suggesting that perhaps she herself was involved in his activities in the trade. She also asked about a particular flower, a small Anvers, which her father had given her ("*Mijn bloemtien*," my little flower); had this been included in the deal? Sadly for her, all the tulips Varwer owned had been included in the new sale of bulbs to the capital partners. So the Enkhuizen company went back into business. On January 28, Varwer bought for ƒ1,250 the offsets of three tulips belonging to his three partners, to be paid over three years beginning in July 1638.[25]

In February 1637, having made all these arrangements, these four men must have got something of a shock. The market for their tulips fell through the floor. Since the tulips Varwer was selling in the winter were only to be delivered and paid for in the summer, it will have been difficult for them to recover their investment. The money Varwer owed his partners from the loan of July 1636, which was to have been paid back in July 1637, could not be repaid until 1646, and then without interest. By then Hendrick Willemsz Vries was also dead. But Apotheecker and Apesteijn, not to mention the heirs of Vries and Ten Broecke, must have been glad to have been paid at all. So many debts from the tulip trade never were.[26]

For people like Varwer and his colleagues, or the partners in other tulip companies, or the individual buyers and sellers of tulips such as Jan Hendricxsz Admirael, Hans Baert, Salomon Seys, and so many others, this was a business fraught with uncertainty. Even if one was interested in tulips for aesthetic reasons or to be in fashion—and as we have already seen, the crossover with the art market suggests that this was indeed a factor for many *bloemisten*—tulips could not be relied on. As a multitude of lawsuits indicates, because of mutation, illness, or even, potentially, fraud, tulips that bloomed in one way in the summer could not necessarily be counted on to look the same the following year: a flower bought in the summer of 1636 by Pieter de Clercq as a Lack van Rijn "now coming into flower appears not to be such" in April 1637. And even if flowers bloomed exactly as they were expected to do, the influence of the seasons added risk to nearly every transaction. Except in the summer, a sale would remain essentially theoretical (despite any written contract) as long as the bulbs were planted in the earth. There would always be a moment of reckoning in the summer when buyers saw their flowers, acknowledged the goods, and paid up, and clearly, before 1637, this usually happened. But when a sale in January was not completed until June, its outcome remained precarious and the tulip trade risky.[27]

Yet this kind of risk, and indeed this kind of trading in commodities for future delivery, was no new thing to Dutch society. It might have been surprising for foreign contemporaries—the converted Sephardic Jew Joseph de la Vega, who wrote about the Amsterdam stock exchange, was still astounded and disgusted by speculators decades later, calling them "double-dealers" and "schemers"—but in the Netherlands it was already becoming standard practice in the previous century. The Baltic grain trade, so important to the development of the Dutch economy, was commonly conducted as a futures market from the mid-sixteenth century, and in the early seventeenth such important commodities as herring or spices were sold before the ships carrying them had come in. The speculative trend also incorporated VOC stock sold *in blanco*, before the seller had actually received it, and although this practice was prohibited by the States-General six times between 1610 and 1636, it continued in a modified form. Although it is not always clear, particularly prior to the final season before the crash, that future delivery of tulip bulbs meant anything more than a necessity imposed by the seasonal nature of their cultivation, by the end of 1636 we certainly find exchange of *coopcedullen*, paper promises about bulbs rather than the bulbs themselves. It does, however, seem evident that the ultimate delivery of these bulbs in the summer was actually intended. It was not the case, as some authors have claimed, that buyers would merely pay or be paid the difference between the purchase price and the current price when the end of the term came. Rather, bulbs were delivered and planted by their new owners, who did not necessarily make a resale. Nevertheless, this was, it seems, a futures market, although without the protections of a modern one. But it was not a novelty in the Netherlands.[28]

The fact that the States-General tried to ban forward selling of VOC shares tells us something about attitudes toward speculation in the Netherlands at this time. Although speculative practices reached into a variety of economic fields—trade, development of land, drainage of polders— there was still a sense that this was not actually productive work, but a form of gambling. One religious text by Johannes Cloppenburgh dated the end of 1636 decried the "foul winning of Money with Money." Gambling—playing cards, playing *triktrak* (a form of backgammon), dicing, making bets—was a matter of some concern for Dutch Reformed preachers and writers, not to mention other Protestant groups and Catholics, although views on the harmfulness of these pastimes were divided. Those who opposed gambling not only referred to the sins associated with it, such as drinking or fighting, but also to its very nature: that it made a mockery of God's providence, calling on it to attend to something excessively trivial. This was said to be a form of taking God's name in vain. Yet despite the disapproval expressed by writers such as Godefridus Cornelisz Udemans or Jean Taffin, the Reformed Church did little to condemn gambling in practice. In fact, lotteries, a common way of raising money for municipal projects such as orphanages and almshouses, confused the issue by being both directed toward charity and toward personal gain ("a pretty trick to turn covetousness into charity," wrote one British observer in around 1625). Although the arrival of a stricter Calvinist public culture after the Synod of Dordrecht in 1618 meant the decline of lotteries, such events, while they were held, were extremely popular. The Haarlem lottery of 1606–1607, held to fund the building of an almshouse for the aged,

FIGURE 51. Willem Duyster, *Game of Trictrac*,
c. 1625–30. National Gallery, London.

sold 308,047 lots of 6 *stuivers* apiece to nearly 25,000 people throughout the region. And when announcing the results, in which every lot, and the little verse the lot-holder wrote when he bought it, was read out in turn, lottery officials arrived in the Grote Markt in Haarlem on April 17, 1607, and proceeded to draw lots day and night for a staggering fifty-two days. The top prize, a gilded silver cup weighing 1.6 kilos plus ƒ600, was won by an Amsterdammer, Jan Jansz Cooninck, on May 3 at three o'clock in the morning.[29]

All-out gambling, without the excuse of charitable intent, indeed remained a central feature of Dutch culture despite the strictures of some Calvinist preachers. It sometimes seemed that the Dutch would make a bet on anything. Rembrandt, for example, was one of 100 people in Leiden in 1631 who bet that they would be alive a year later. In 1624 a man in De Burg bet that he could sail himself from Texel to Wieringen in a trough intended for kneading dough. Frequently purchases would be made in the form of bets, where if the conditions of the bet—often victory in battle—were met by a certain time, the buyer would get his goods for free. In 1641 Philips Castels sold Claes Cornelisz de Lange in Haarlem a roan horse; if Castels was still alive on July 26, 1642, De Lange had to pay the ƒ83 owed, but otherwise he would pay nothing. In 1631

FIGURE 52. Willem Buytewech, *Lottery on the Groenmarkt in The Hague*, c. 1620. Institut Néerlandais, Paris.

the future *bloemist* Franck Pietersz de Jongh made a similar deal with the baker Harman Jansz, selling him a "milk cow" with the condition that if within two years, starting the previous Thursday at noon, there was peace with Spain, Jansz would have to pay ƒ230 for the cow. Since peace did not come for nearly twenty more years, De Jongh was being somewhat over-optimistic. Another *bloemist*, Rogier Alleman, missed the boat by only two weeks, betting on March 19, 1648, the price of a piece of linen (ƒ60) that peace would not be declared before the end of May; the Treaty of Münster, regrettably for him, was signed on May 15.[30]

One could argue that tulipmania was part of this culture of risk. And indeed some bets were themselves intertwined with the sale of tulips.

Some tulip deals were couched in bets about life expectancy. In November 1636, Pieter Pietersz Hazes, a merchant in Hoorn, sold three fellow-merchants a tulip he had bred, the Admirael Hazes, for ƒ1,000, but agreed that if any of five children related to him died in the following year, the bulb was theirs gratis. Later the same day they made similar terms for two offsets of this bulb for ƒ400. This somewhat macabre bet was, at least, a vote of confidence by Hazes in his young relations' health. A similar vote for his own constitution, although perhaps not for the value of tulips, was made by Pieter Dircksz Tjallis, a *regent* of Enkhuizen, on the precarious date of February 7, 1637, when he bet Claes Gerryts and the shipwright Pieter Jansen Hellingman all the tulips in his large garden that he would still be alive on January 17, 1639 (if he was, they would have to pay him ƒ225 for the tulips). Other *bloemisten* bet on the war. We know of at least three bets about the outcome of the siege of Schenckenschans, a fortress in Cleves that had been taken by the Spanish at the end of July 1635 and ultimately recaptured by the Dutch at the end of April 1636. Given the fort's strategic importance for the Netherlands, the siege, conducted by the stadholder Frederik Hendrik, was the drama of the war in the mid-1630s, and, as the bets indicate, all Dutch eyes were fixed on it. On September 17, 1635, Jan Hendricxsz Admirael bet Jeronimus Victory a Generael Gouda worth ƒ650 that the fortress would be captured in the next six months. At the end of March 1636, Jacob Willemsz de Wet made a losing bet with Cornelis Coelembier that Schenckenschans would not have fallen by the end of June. If De Wet had won, Coelembier would have had to give him a tulip called a Lyon, not to mention having to pay for a Dürer print and two prints by Rembrandt that, in the event, Coelembier got for free. Jan Jansz in Haarlem was not so lucky: he won his bet of an Oudenaerde bulb, but his betting partner in the meantime had died. He took the bet seriously enough, however, that he took the widow to court to obtain the bulb.[31]

With bets on tulips so similar to bets on cows, kneading-troughs, or any of the other topics that caught the fancy of gaming Dutchmen, one might be tempted to see the tulip trade as a reckless gamble, another game of chance whose thrill came from the fact that fate presided. Yet one could also see it as simply trade. For trade in this period was itself fraught with risk. Besides the unpredictability of supply, the uncertainty of markets, and the inability to get speedy information about conditions elsewhere, overseas traders had to face the simple problems of transport. Ships of the period were not built to endure some of the conditions they faced, particularly lengthy and hazardous journeys to the Pacific, or heavy seas in the north Atlantic. The risk of shipwreck was always high. Storms, moreover, were not the only danger. Pirates, in particular the Dunkirkers who besieged Dutch ships off the Flemish coast as part of the Spanish war effort, or the Berbers of north Africa, took a heavy toll in sunken or captured ships and sailors held for ransom. Between 1626 and 1646, the value of captured ships alone was ƒ23 million; in 1628 a Dutch or English ship was captured or sunk by Dunkirkers on average every thirty-six hours. If a ship arrived at its destination, merchants often had to trust in the fulfillment of rather vague agreements made with captains about sale and loading of new goods, and the risk of mistreatment by local officialdom, of arrest or seizure of property, was always a concern. Even those not engaged in overseas trade had to worry, along with long-distance merchants, about changeable markets, spoilage, cyclical inter-ruptions to production, and the toll taken on labor or raw materials by flood, disease, or famine.[32]

Yet, despite these problems, Dutch merchants in the seventeenth cen-tury engaged not only in trade, but in more adventurous trade than pre-viously, exploring new markets and new areas, including the East Indies and the Americas. That they were willing to do so was one of the factors that made the Netherlands the most commercially successful country in Europe in the period. The trade was not wholly reckless, however. There were ways to reduce risk, whose existence itself contributed to the will-ingness of people to invest in trade. Sometimes merchants trading to the same part of the world would take concerted action to protect com-munal interests: the formation in 1625 of a directorate in Amsterdam to coordinate the Levant trade, for example, was the result of such efforts. Traveling in convoy was another way of dealing with difficulties far from home, and the Dutch government set up a number of consulates in areas where Dutch ships were likely to run into problems. Financial protec-tions were also available. Frequently Dutch investors would only buy a certain fraction of the cargo of a particular vessel, and although it was perfectly common for large merchants to be the sole investor in a particu-lar voyage, shares as small as $1/_{128}$ were known. If a merchant thus spread his investment among numbers of vessels, shipwreck or capture of any one of these would naturally be less damaging. The reliance on family and *vrunden* for credit was also an important asset for any merchant. As for financial precautions, investors could take out what were known as bottomry loans, which provided both credit and insurance at high interest for long-distance voyages. Most important was marine insurance, which was available very early in the northern Netherlands: the earliest surviving policy in Amsterdam dates from January 20, 1592.[33]

Yet insurance, although appearing to be founded on a desire to reduce risk, only points to risk aversion on the part of the insured. The insurer, on the contrary, was making a gamble on the success of any particular voyage, and indeed yet more of a gamble given that insurance policies at this time were based on no real statistical foundation. To insure a ship was to make a bet, and this was just how the government before the Dutch Revolt had seen it. In 1568 Philip II issued an edict banning life insurance and bets on voyages, and a partial revocation in 1570, while giving some order to the trade, continued to refer to "abuses, frauds, and crimes" associated with insurance. It is easy to imagine that, in a society apparently obsessed with gambling, the risks insurance entailed would have been a positive pleasure. For an ordinary person engaging in trade, risk would at the very least have seemed a normal part of daily existence. That said, however, the riskiness of business would certainly have called on deep reserves of patience, capital, trust in God, and trust in each other. This was the atmosphere in which trade was conducted: trade in spices, trade in wine, trade in cloth, and trade in tulips.[34]

For although we cannot speak of a mass market in tulips—the days of the tulip fields in the area between Haarlem and Leiden were well in the future—and although hardly any of the *bloemisten* were specialist gardeners whose only business was flowers, we can still see tulips as a normal item of trade. The trading in tulips that were not actually on hand for much of the year has been a matter of wonder for some commentators, but, as we have seen, trading in commodities, such as grain or herring, for future delivery had been a feature of Dutch economic life for decades. Tulips were only a sideline for nearly everyone involved in the tulip trade, but most merchants at the time had fingers in a variety of pies and might, like the Amsterdam *bloemist* Liebert van Axele, at one moment be dealing in saltpetre and at another in insurance and in Venetian mirror glass. Tulips were a luxury commodity, it is true, but, except

{ 223 }

for the lack of transport costs, they are perhaps not so easy to differentiate from the "rich trades," the high-value, low-bulk items that gave the Dutch economy such luster in this period: spices, dyestuffs, porcelains, and the like. The apparent normality of tulip-trading is evident from the attitude of the government.[35]

After things went wrong in the tulip trade, some governmental authorities expressed disdain for its emptiness and vanity, but while all was going swimmingly they sang a different tune. In the summer of 1636, the States of Holland, looking for new ways to raise money, weighed up the possibility of new taxes on wood, on the consumption of cheese, and on leather, but rejected all of these for the possibility of a tax on tulips. This was referred back (as was normal for all provincial legislation) for discussion by the towns in the session of the States of mid-September to mid-October 1636. The States' resolution noted the recent springing up "here in this Country of a certain new sort of trade; that is in Flowers, Tulips, and Bulbs of the same, in which a great deal of money is spent daily. . . ." They saw that this "could produce a good sum of money yearly," and thus suggested a tax parallel, perhaps, to other luxury taxes in discussion at this time, such as imposts on servants, gold and silver cloth, tobacco, and card-playing. But the towns were not wholly enthusiastic. While Hoorn's burgemeesters voted to authorize the tax, the *vroedschappen* of Alkmaar and Enkhuizen, for example, decided it was a poor idea, with those of Haarlem and Amsterdam agreeing that it was "impracticable." In the event, their protests proved unnecessary. The session of the States ended on February 7, 1637, just at the time of the crash in tulip prices, and another did not begin until March 6. By the time the subject was raised again on May 3, it was decided that, "considering the change and unfortunate circumstances which have come to exist recently with the said Flowers," the whole idea should be abandoned.[36]

But the fact that the States had found tulips a fit subject for a tax suggests their view of the flower trade not as an aberration, not as a crazy *windhandel*, but simply as a trade of a new product, one of many new products that had been flooding the country for the previous forty and more years. It is true that some prices for some tulips jumped radically over the space of a short period during the time following the planting season of autumn 1636. The rapidity of the change in prices during January 1637 must have led some tulip-watchers to conclude that the price rises were unsustainable. Some of the prices were indeed high. If we compare them to contemporary commodity prices on the Amsterdam exchange, we find that for the ƒ1,000 one might pay in January 1637 for one hypothetical Admirael van der Eyck bulb, one could have bought 4,651 pounds of figs, or 3,448 pounds of almonds, or 5,633 pounds of raisins, or 370 pounds of cinnamon, or 111 tuns of Bordeaux. On a more everyday level for most Dutch people, ƒ1,000 would buy a modest house in Haarlem, or, if we look at consumables, 11,587 kilos of rye bread, or 13.4 vats of butter, or 5,714 pounds of meat. Although we know little about wages in this period, we can establish the income of craftsmen and laborers to place against these figures. For the first half of the century, the figures were fairly static: a master carpenter in Alkmaar at this time made a little more than a guilder a day (24 *stuivers*), meaning that a tulip costing ƒ1,000 would cost him nearly three years' wages. This amount would have the purchasing power of €9,395.36, or around $12,000, in today's money.[37]

But these figures are deceiving. Many tulips were bought and sold by people with far higher incomes than that of a master carpenter, but regrettably we have no way of estimating the yearly income of international merchants or even many skilled craftsmen, some of whom, as we have already mentioned, could possess considerable wealth. Certainly if we look at the kind of people who spent large sums on tulips, we find that they were not, for the most part, at the lower end of society. Although the sources naturally do not provide us with anything like a complete list of tulip buyers, of those I can identify who spent more than ƒ400 on bulbs (a total of only thirty-seven people), nearly all were wealthy merchants, often involved in international trade in Amsterdam or the cloth or brewing trades in Haarlem. Familiar names appear on this list, including the brewer Abraham van Meeckeren and the merchants Batholomeus van Gennep, Abraham van Wachtendonck, Liebert van Axele, Michiel Kistgens, and Jan de Haes. There were several master craftsmen—the master shipwright Pieter Willemsz Groes in Enkhuizen bought ƒ5,000 worth of bulbs; the baker Jan Abrahamsz in Haarlem bought a Viceroy for ƒ1,000, the *sleper* (bargeman) Aert Huybertsz, who in any case was part of a tulip company, spent ƒ710 on bulbs—but on the whole the pattern is fairly uniform. The wealthier *bloemisten* were typically the ones who spent the most on bulbs.[38]

For many international merchants, although ƒ1,000 might represent a sizeable figure, it was hardly outrageous. The accounts at the Wissel-bank (exchange bank) of some of the larger merchants in subsequent years (account books are only extant from 1644 on) give us a picture of constant movements of such sums. On May 9, 1644, for example, the account of the *bloemist* Reymont de Smith had a balance of ƒ162,757:10:8 and recorded in the previous month payments including ƒ2,530 to Guillielmo Bartholotti and ƒ2,400 to Guilliam Momma, not to mention transfers into his account of sums like ƒ5,476:17:8 from Jeremias Calandrini, ƒ2,304:10 from Bartholotti, and ƒ3,000 from the Coymans brothers. Reymont de Smith was clearly on the upper end of the scale of *bloemisten*, but a variety of other familiar names (Casteleyn, Poelenburch, Bessels, Momboir, Kistgens, Halmael, Moens, and Wachtendonck, for example) figure in the registers of the bank, where an account was necessary to take part in international trade. For many, the sum of ƒ1,000 was unlikely to have been a frightening one. The amounts invested in VOC stock in 1602—which could run as high as ƒ85,000 from the biggest investor, Isaac le Maire—tell us that. The nontulip economic activities of *bloemisten* could thus easily involve sums much higher than any amount spent on tulips. To take only one example, at the same time as the Mennonite merchant Jacob Abrahamsz van Halmael was pondering tulip deals with people like Abraham van Meeckeren, on November 22, 1636, he bought a load of goods from a fellow-merchant, Hendrick Onderborch, worth ƒ12,000. A full ƒ6,000 of this he paid up-front. Someone like Halmael was used to moving large sums of money if he thought it would be to his profit.[39]

The traveler Peter Mundy, writing about the Netherlands in 1640, could not refrain from wondering at the payment of "incredible prices For tulip rootes." His words echo the fascination people have had for this event over the centuries. Two aspects struck him: the incredible prices, and the "tulip rootes." However, as we have seen, the prices were not really so incredible. Most were relatively moderate, although, admittedly, considerably higher than for some other luxury goods, in particular paintings, which never approached the prices paid for some bulbs. And, as we have also noted, the people who paid the highest prices were often those most used to making these kinds of investments in trade. But what has made tulipmania such a source of legend was not so much the prices, but the "rootes." The reason people have been astounded by tulipmania is that it seems insane to pay so much for a tulip bulb. This was as true in 1637 as it is today, or at least for some onlookers. Their reactions will be discussed in chapter 5; here, our task is to consider the actual nature of the trade. As I have been stressing, the "mania" of tulipmania is perhaps not so wild as we have been led to believe. Some of the merchants who bought tulips, as we have discussed, were in any case *liefhebbers,* interested in the aesthetic side of the flowers, in the pleasure and sociability of collecting and the culture it entailed. Others—and some of the *liefhebbers* as well—probably had a chiefly financial interest in tulips. But for either group, buying tulips was not insane. For it is no irrational decision to buy what fulfills your needs. For the *liefhebbers*—who in any case have never been much blamed for their interest in tulips, which has from the start been deemed "proper" precisely because it was considered unmercenary—collector's items were naturally likely to be expensive. Indeed, that was partly the point: thus the decision of the owner of all twelve flowers of the Semper Augustus in the 1620s, who chose to keep them to himself to preserve their rarity (and, no doubt, their price). But it was no less rational for calculating merchants to invest their money in tulips. After the fact—as happened in other financial crises in later centuries—it is easy to preach irrationality, but there was nothing intrinsically crazy—nor did most before the crash say there was—about buying a product it was clear one could sell on at a higher price. The unsustainability of the price was not predictable, and if a crash happened, it was not necessarily to be foreseen. The tulip, as we will see, was blamed in pamphlets after the crash as being merely a *nietighe blom:* a "paltry flower." But the value of a tulip was simply the value placed in it by its buyers and sellers. One might just as well say *nietighe goud:* paltry gold. Tulipmania was only irrational after the fact; if the market had held, it would have been supremely sensible to invest one's money in tulip bulbs.[40]

Even the supposed frenzy of the trade seems to have been exaggerated. In an effort to portray the *bloemisten* as irrational, both contemporary and later accounts refer to bulbs being passed from hand to hand in frenetic fashion. A German chronicle published in 1640, *Meteranus Novus,* suggested that the same flower might have been sold a hundred times over— "and in addition it was such a blind business that many a flower was sold to the twentieth person, to the thirtieth, without any of them ever seeing the flower." The historian of Haarlem Theodorus Schrevelius commented in 1648 that "flowers that had just been sold, were sold again . . . and always with profit," and consequently, according to his nineteenth-century successor, Cornelis de Koning, "bulbs that at first were worth one to two guilders, rose within a few days to a hundred, to a thousand guilders, yes even higher in price." (The source from which he mainly plagiarized, dated 1669, mentioned prices rising only "from one or two guilders [to] a hundred, sometimes more"; the temptation to exaggerate, so common to writers on this subject, was too much for De Koning.) We cannot know about every transaction, but from lawsuits when one member of a chain failed to deliver, we can make some estimate of the rapidity of exchange. The longest chain I have found in 1636–1637 is five people, and we know that it must have begun no later than July 1636, because the first member of the chain (in whose garden the bulbs remained) is Volckert Coornhart, who was buried on August 4, 1636. Coornhart had sold a quarter-pound of Oudenaerders to Jacobus Grimmaris, a teacher at the Haarlem Latin School; Grimmaris sold on to Jan Dircksz Ossecoop; Ossecoop sold the tulips to Pieter de Jonckheer, who also had died by the early winter of 1637; and at some time in the autumn Jonckheer had sold the bulbs to Stoffel de Way. Five owners in six months—for the ownership of the bulbs became an issue in late January—certainly does not represent long-term possession of the bulbs, but nor does it reflect the wild-eyed trading portrayed in the literature. Chains were, moroever, not always signs of major profits. Sometimes tulips simply changed hands for the same price as they had been previously bought. For example, in 1636 Colaert Braem sold a bulb called Jan Gerritsz to Pieter Govertsz for ƒ36:10:8, and Govertsz sold it on to Bastiaen van de Rype for exactly the same amount. The same happened when Remeus Francken sold to Jan Pott, who then sold to Barent Arentsz, both times for ƒ24; Pott made no profit whatsoever. Although naturally profits did feature in many transactions—otherwise the prices could not have risen to the degree they did—the picture is not quite as frantic as it has been painted.[41]

Yet no matter how short the chain or how low the profits, such transactions still carried a great potential for problems. On February 3, 1637, with tulipmania at its peak, the ability to deliver a quarter-pound of Oudenaerders was of considerable moment to someone like Jacobus Grimmaris. Because he could not deliver, he had been taken to court by his buyer, Ossecoop, as had Ossecoop by the guardians of Jonckheer's children, and the guardians themselves by De Way. The trouble was that Grimmaris said he "had to get the bulbs from corennaert at Amsterdam." What Grimmaris perhaps did not know was that Volckert Coornhart had died in July, probably of plague, and that even Coornhart's wife, Anneke Braems, could not provide him with the tulips, because she had died immediately after her husband and was buried the same day he was in the Oude Kerk in Amsterdam. No one in this chain, it seems clear, would be seeing any Oudenaerders. Jeuriaen Jansz was just as unlucky when he bought a half-pound of Switsers from Jan Pietersz de Wroo in the summer of 1636: De Wroo admitted that he had sold the bulbs to Jansz but said "that he [himself] was supposed to receive them from another who has gone bankrupt." If Grimmaris or De Wroo could not collect the bulbs they had sold on, they were not out of pocket—they would not have to pay until they received them. But their inability to deliver goods they had promised would (even at this stage, before the crash) have done nothing for their trustworthiness. The situation after the crash was different, but no less problematic. Now, it was buyers who usually failed to complete sales: people who would not pay their debts. There was little that could be worse for a man's reputation.[42]

The atmosphere of the Kleine Bank van Justitie in Haarlem became more agitated in the autumn of 1636 as the usual matters of failure to pay for delivered bread, wine, or clothing were increasingly swamped by cases about tulips. The number of quarrels handled each Tuesday and Friday by the court rose markedly during the months after the tulips had last bloomed; they were almost always about failure to deliver bulbs, as sellers evidently could see a better offer down the line. It clearly did not take a crash to cause disputes about flowers. But there came a time when tulip cases suddenly ceased. From February 10 until April 24, 1637, not a word was said in the Kleine Bank about tulips. The reason was the crash. What we hear in the court records is a stunned silence. With tulips not being sold, and tulips not yet ready to be delivered (not that most ever *would* be delivered), for two months no one knew what to say. And no one knew what to do.

It would be wonderful if we could say what caused tulip prices to fall. Economists say the same about other crashes in history, whose causes are much debated but often remain unexplained. Our problem is a lack of information. We see tulips being bought and sold for increasingly high amounts as we approach the beginning of February—as we will recall, the Wynants family said that on February 1 the tulip trade was "all the rage." On February 5, the Weeskamer in Alkmaar held its auction of the tulips of Wouter Bartholomeusz Winckel, and the prices, if we are to believe the derisive pamphlets about the trade, were at a high point. Yet on February 7, *bloemisten* in Utrecht were already meeting to elect representatives to discuss a crisis with their comrades from other towns. What happened, and when? The only source that addresses these questions is the much-cited pamphlet, *Waermondt ende Gaergoedt,* whose testimony—since it was a work of propaganda—must always be approached with caution. Even its author, Adriaen Roman, admitted bewilderment at the causes of the crash. The character Waermondt (True Mouth), who represented good sense in this series of dialogues between the greedy and the wise, is made to say, "Where it comes from people scarcely know . . . it falls like a downpour in the summertime. . . ." The tale Waermondt tells—and even the character has to admit that it is hearsay—is that on Tuesday, February 3, some *bloemisten* were occupied with tulip deals at a Haarlem inn. One of them attempted to sell a pound of bulbs for ƒ1,250, but repeated attempts only saw the price drop, ultimately to ƒ1,000, without a successful sale. Waermondt says that (according to his cousin) the news of a failure to sell at such a price "was like a running fire through all the *collegiën* in the whole town; the next day everything was at a standstill. . . ."[43]

The stress on news is important: having knowledge was crucial here, as it had been when the trade was in full spate. We can see that, along with the flow of information, the cessation in trade (which in any case was only temporary) clearly reached different places at different times. Indeed, it is curious, if the news of a perceived uncertainty about the continuation of a rise in price shot so rapidly through Haarlem, why Haarlemmers like Jan Quakel, someone who was at the center of the trade, were willing to offer high prices for bulbs at the Alkmaar sale on February 5. Quakel bought three tulips at a price of ƒ3,250 (although, like other buyers at Alkmaar, he later refused to pay). But one wonders how the sale could have taken place if information traveled this quickly. Perhaps Quakel and others who bought at the Winckel sale were already in Alkmaar several days before the auction. Or perhaps these buyers did not believe that tulips would really fall so much in price, as indeed seems to have happened with Pieter Gerritsz van Welsen, who was still willing to hazard ƒ11,400 of his money in mid-March, no matter how much he regretted it afterward. But in any case, despite Waermondt's claim that trade in Haarlem stopped on February 4, we continue to hear of transactions there and in other towns for a number of days. At the sitting of the Kleine Bank van Justitie in Haarlem on Friday, February 6, people were still pressing for delivery of bulbs, and no mention was made about pressing for payment. On February 7, similarly, Pieter Dircksz Tjallis made his bet in Enkhuizen, offering all his bulbs for ƒ225, or for nothing if he was dead by January 17, 1639; this could of course have been an endorsement of the newly low price of bulbs, although it is notable that Pieter Jansz Hellingman and Claes Gerryts were willing to make the bet and risk paying the money. Back on February 6, in the Menniste Bruyloft in Amsterdam, a place that should have been full of the latest news about the tulip trade, Andries de Busscher successfully sold a pound of Switsers to Joost van Cuyck for ƒ1,100, on the condition that each provide security, De Busscher for the delivery and Van Cuyck for the payment. But we can see the doubts beginning to set in. The next day De Busscher appeared with Van Cuyck in the Beurs to ask Alister van de Cruijs to stand as *borg* (guarantor) for the delivery of the bulbs. Van de Cruijs, who was probably a relative of De Busscher, agreed, but Van Cuyck was not satisfied. "I am not content with the guarantor, I want a guarantor of my own choosing," he said. When Van de Cruijs offered to give a pledge for ƒ1,200, Van Cuyck said, "I need to think about it." The fact that on February 11 a witness to the sale, Johannes van Westrenen, appeared at a notary's office to declare what he had seen (including the detail that he himself had shaken hands with Van Cuyck and wished him joy over the purchase) makes it plain what happened next. On the night of February 6, the Menniste Bruyloft had still been full of "various persons and Bloemisten," trading in tulips, but by February 7 the news was out in Amsterdam. Van Cuyck now knew about the crash and was slipping out of the noose.[44]

But the "why" remains unclear. Perhaps certain buyers began to wonder if the steep price rises of the previous few weeks could be sustained; anyone buying high would inevitably lose money if people were unwilling to go even higher. There had been a little criticism of the trade as it was going on. A few pamphlets, such as the *Clare Ontdeckingh der Dwaesheydt der ghener haer tegenwoordich laten noemen Floristen* (Clear Revelation of the Foolishness of Those Who Now Call Themselves Florists) of 1636, had made pointed remarks about this new form of business. But, as we will discuss further in chapter 5, such criticisms were chiefly about the misjudged weight placed on mammon instead of God and worries about social mobility, not that the bottom would soon fall out of the market. This was hardly surprising, given that nothing of this kind had ever happened before. But we cannot take public criticism as a reason for the crash. A more likely reason, which has sometimes been suggested, is excess supply. Schrevelius wrote in 1648 that "a great and overabundant growth of tulips took place," although he did not attribute the crash to it; in 1808 Cornelis de Koning said that "through vigorous cultivation, so many Tulips came on the market that the price began to fall," an interpretation picked up by modern authors, including Wilfrid Blunt, whose odd twist was that "the amateurs grew bored, and flooded the market." It is hard to explain reasons why the crash happened exactly when it did; the trade was circumscribed by the tulip's growing season, so that from around mid-September on, any tulips being sold were sold on paper, for the bulbs themselves were in the ground. Thus the supply in early February was exactly the same as the supply had been in September. However, the culprit may well have been an increase in bulbs over the long term. With the market on the rise, at least some attempt will have been made to grow more tulips. The reason the weight of bulbs and number of offsets were important to buyers was that through offsets (which were evident in a heavy bulb) the number of tulips a buyer owned could be increased. Schrevelius noted in his discussion of the event in 1648 that "one person bought, another rented a Garden . . . they sowed, they bred [tulips]." Certainly the market in gardens was brisk in this period. We can see from the pace of the tulip trade in the late autumn of 1636 and the winter of 1637 that a short-term increase in demand occurred, which both fed on and influenced great increases in prices. But a longer-term increase in numbers of bulbs on the market—or even the knowledge that, through offsets, more would soon be appearing—would eventually have caused prices to decline.[45]

In 1797, Beckmann rather curiously used an opposite argument about supply to suggest that in fact no one valued the bulbs themselves, only the profits springing from them. "Had the object of the purchaser been to get possession of the flowers, the price in such a length of time must have fallen instead of risen"; that is, they would have fallen because if people wanted tulips, the supply of tulips would naturally grow. He assumed that it would be easy to increase the supply of tulips, by agricultural improvements or by importation; this, he picturesquely remarked, "has been sufficiently proved by the price of asparagus at Göttingen." Beckmann ignored the difficulties this would entail: transport costs for importation; greater organization; and, in particular, greater speed, because, as we know, it took years to produce new tulips, seven to ten if grown from seed, one to three if grown from offsets. It was, admittedly, not in most people's long-term interest to increase the supply of rarer bulbs; more tulips would indeed eventually mean lower prices, as Cornelis Double must have calculated when he "viciously" bored holes in the tulips he sold. That does not, of course, mean that the product had no aesthetic value, as Beckmann claimed. Collectors also like to think their collections are rare. It might well have been that some wished to increase the numbers of bulbs, while others hoped to keep them scarce and valuable. In either case, a long-term increase in supply, or the idea that such an increase might be on its way, still might have caused uncertainty among buyers. But however we may argue this, it is difficult to say exactly what caused buyers to hesitate in early February. "People scarcely know where it came from," according to Roman's Waermondt, but people nevertheless feared the consequences.[46]

These consequences were, at first, more imagined than certain. And they must have been much imagined. "What will it be like in the time of delivery?" asks Gaergoedt in Roman's pamphlet. "Everyone is of a different opinion," Waermondt reports, and this must have been of considerable concern to them all. Because of the custom of delivering bulbs and paying for them only during the "dry bulb time" in the summer, in virtually every case no money had been exchanged for tulips since August or September. Financially, not many people were at risk—at least if they chose to take their obligations lightly. Only those actually left with bulbs on their hands would find them unsaleable at the prices they had hoped to get for them—although even then, the figures hoped for during the sharp price rise in January represented only notional losses, as long as sellers had not been buying other goods on credit in expectation of later profits. Others, for example those in the midst of a chain sale, would probably never see a bulb in these circumstances, and certainly not pay for one. For that to happen, those further up the chain would already have had to agree to receive and to pay, and this was unlikely. Thus in the chain running from Coornhart to Grimmaris to Ossecoop to Jonckheer to De Way, only Coornhart was certain to have suffered a loss, and in any case he was dead. But even if many buyers were potentially off the hook financially, they still had to face their neighbors when defaulting on their promises. That was bound to cause problems.[47]

The winter must have been a time of great uncertainty for both buyers and sellers. Several understanding sellers did agree to release potential buyers from their contracts. Thus, for example, the Mennonite Jacob Abrahamsz van Halmael was unwilling to deal too harshly with his coreligionist Abraham van Meeckeren and Van Meeckeren's mother, Maria Vlaminghs. On February 10 he canceled the contract they had made a month earlier for a deal involving ƒ1,800 worth of Scipio and Groot Gepluymaseerde bulbs, which Van Meeckeren was exchanging for thirteen and one-half lasts of Swedish barley. Van Meeckeren simply had to pay ƒ160 for reneging on the contract, clearly an example of *rouwkoop* (grieving money). Most others, however, were not so lucky. Yet there was little way to know what would happen until the summer came and the seller could attempt to deliver the bulbs.[48]

What people wanted was a clear way forward. Well before it was obvious that most buyers would attempt to default, *bloemisten* tried to take matters in their own hands. As we have already seen, as early as February 7, when some hapless folk were still learning about the crash, thirty-six tulip traders met in Utrecht to elect three representatives for a meeting of their colleagues from the Holland towns later in the month (see fig. 53). On February 23, the Utrecht deputies, François Sweerts, Bastiaen Hendricksz van Gheesbergen, and Anthony Verbeeck, joined a group from Amsterdam, Haarlem, Leiden, Delft, Gouda, Alkmaar, Enkhuizen, Medemblik, Hoorn, and De Streek at a meeting in Amsterdam to discuss what to do. Their concern was that the price rises in tulips had led to "misunderstandings"—not to mention to the fear that "damage, yes, utter ruin" might ensue if there was no regulation about defaulters. The deputies decided on a course of action, although clearly with some trepidation: those from Enkhuizen, Medemblik, and Hoorn only signed on condition of approval by those whom they were representing, and, despite a "softening" of the terms, the representatives of Amsterdam refused to sign altogether. This already faulty agreement, lacking

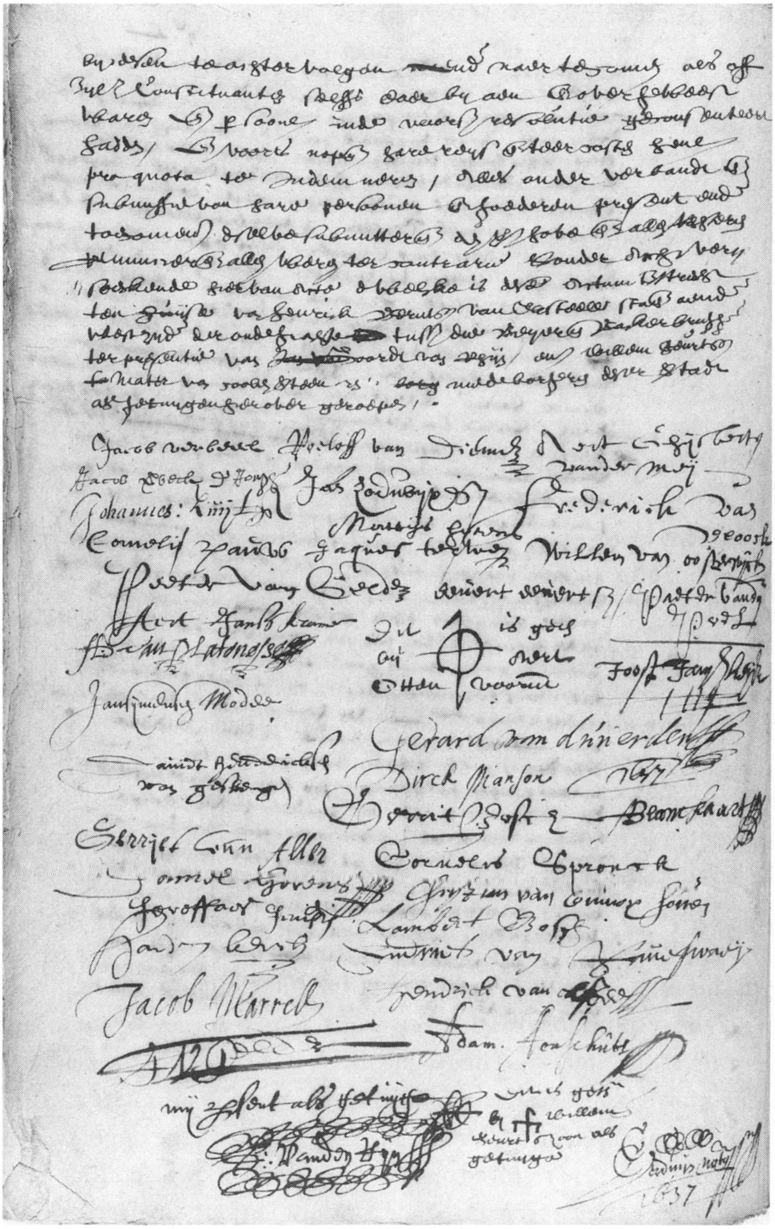

FIGURE 53. Signatories to an agreement electing representatives in Utrecht to the meeting of *bloemisten* to take place in Amsterdam on February 23, 1637. Het Utrechts Archief, Utrecht.

full cooperation from one of the centers of the trade, stipulated that any deals made before the end of November 1636, at which point the prices had begun their sharp rise, would go through, but that any transaction made after that point could be rejected by the buyer if he made his views known in March, ending the torturous uncertainty, and if he paid a fine of 10 percent of the purchase price. But without everyone's agreement this would never work, especially as the authority of this meeting was—akin to that of the *collegiën* from which it sprang—only informal. As March approached and there was apparently little sign of cooperation with this agreement, unhappy *bloemisten* looked for governmental assistance.[49]

At first solutions were sought locally. Buyers and sellers of tulips pressed local officialdom to rule on the situation. A few of the *bloemisten*, after all, were themselves *regents* and used to government, men such as Jan van Clarenbeeck and the unfortunate Cornelis Guldewagen and Johan de Wael in Haarlem, or Pieter Dircksz Tjallis in Enkhuizen. On March 4, one month after the fall in prices, we first hear in Haarlem that "various inhabitants of this city" wished to suggest to the States of Holland and West Friesland that the trade in flowers since the previous planting time should be "nullified and cancelled." This was a more radical proposal than that made on February 23 in Amsterdam, which had allowed a 10 percent return on sales, and in which only transactions since November were to be revoked; the last "planting time" (*planttijt*) would have been over by late September. The *vroedschap* debated on March 4 the question of how the deputies to the States should behave in this circumstance, and it was agreed that they should support their citizens in their attempts to nullify the trade. Three days later the burgemeesters confirmed this in their own meeting. Hoorn's *regents* were of the same opinion, having heard about the resolutions of other towns. On March 11 they wrote to their deputies at the States in The Hague to ask that they help the *bloemisten* in their town to be "freed without damage from their promises and their commitments of debt." Alkmaar, interestingly, took the opposite view. The *vroedschap* there resolved on March 14 that their own deputies in The Hague should "insist" that the trade continue, and, as for Haarlem's proposal that it be annulled, they should ensure, "with all possible zeal," that "the contrary be adopted." This is hardly surprising. Whether the trade was annulled or not, someone was going to lose money, be it buyers or sellers. Who it was depended, apparently, on who had the greatest voice in the city councils.[50]

The States took up the question in April. They were unsure how to proceed, so on April 11 they sent the question to the Hof van Holland, the high court. The court responded on April 25. It, too, was uncertain. Its members suggested further investigation of conditions of the trade in the towns. But in the meantime, the court offered various weak solutions for the unhappy sellers, embodied in a proclamation by the States dated April 27. The entire agreement made by the *bloemisten* on February 23, not to mention the request of Haarlem to cancel the transactions that had taken place since the planting season, was ignored: all the transactions remained in full force. The best course of action, they said, was to get the magistrates of the various towns to persuade the opposing parties to come to an agreement, if they could; if they could not, details of the problems should be sent to the court. In the meantime, however, sellers who could not get their buyers to receive their bulbs and pay should first insinuate them, and if this threat of legal action had no effect, they were authorized to sell their bulbs as they could, with the loss thereby incurred to be suffered by the recalcitrant previous buyers. But the best thing, the States added in a kind of postscript, was to "try the *viam concordiae* and use all possible methods to get the parties to resolve things in a friendly manner"; only if this were not possible should the judicial system become involved.[51]

This was hardly satisfactory. To be told simply to try to get people to smile and come to an agreement did little to solve the problems invoked by the crash. Tulips were becoming a public order problem. The burgemeesters of Haarlem had made sure the Hof van Holland knew it. In a letter of mid-April now attempting to persuade the court to annul previous transactions, they blasted the *bloemisten* (again, rather hypocritically, given the participation of various *regenten*, including one sitting burgemeester, in the trade). The tulip business, which, they said, had mainly taken place in Haarlem, was not only "a rage, practiced by some profit-seeking persons through sly and evil practices" but also was useless, "tending toward the diversion from other necessary trade and industry." If the sales since September were simply canceled, this would not only preserve from "ruin and shame" hundreds of people "of good name" but also tend toward the "great rest and tranquillity" of the town. Alas, they were to be disappointed. Not only did the proclamation of the court not annul the contracts, but it left it up to the sellers to try to recover their money, feebly urging the towns to try to get their inhabitants to settle things amicably. This was not a recipe for calm. In Haarlem, feelings had been stirred up for weeks. Rhymesters and pamphleteers, some of whom came out of the moralizing *rederijkerskamers* (chambers of rhetoric, or drama societies), had been working overtime writing pamphlets and satiric songs. Such songs, generally sung to older tunes, were part of both a widespread nonprofessional singing culture and a means, one among several, of insulting those whose honor was somehow in question. Their singing in the streets was provocative, to say the least, for those being insulted, and on March 17 the Haarlem burgemeesters forbade the sale of "the little songs and verses which are daily sold by the booksellers about the tulip trade," going to the trouble of having copies collected by bailiffs. And the situation was bound to get worse when the tulips had bloomed. It was only then, in May and June, that the bulbs would be dug up and available for delivery. It was only then that the intentions of buyers would really be tested. Then the singing of satiric songs would be the least of anyone's worries.[52]

Take, for example, the case of Hans Baert. Baert, a wealthy Haarlem merchant, was heavily involved in the tulip trade, owning a garden in the Rosenprieel outside the Kleine Houtpoort. He was one of three tulip experts identified in a document about the trade in 1639, and he was frequently asked by the Kleine Bank van Justitie in 1636 to act as arbiter in various disputes about flowers. In 1637, the disputes were his. On Wednesday, June 24, he kept the Amsterdam notary Jan Warnaertsz busy. He had sold tulips to a number of Amsterdam merchants who were all refusing to receive the bulbs and pay. Jan Warnaertsz paid visits to each of them in turn: Matthijs Schouten, who had bought a Hollantschen Admirael and a Petter on January 3 for a total of ƒ1,250; Michiel Kistgens and Jan de Haes, who had bought an Admirael van der Eyck on January 18 for ƒ1,205; Jan Pietersz Neckevelt, who had bought an eighth of a pound of Witte Croonen on January 28 for ƒ325; and François Hendricxsz Coster, who had bought a Laten Blijenberger on December 28, 1636, and a Nieuwenberger on January 6, 1637, totaling ƒ295. The problem was the time of year: the bulbs, for their health, needed to be lifted from the earth, but

FIGURE 54. Jan Jorisz van Vliet, *Liedjeszanger*. Atlas van Stolk,
Rotterdam. Such a figure might have sold tulip songs.

if Schouten and the others did not come to see them dug up, there was no way to prove later on that they were the bulbs in question. Schouten said he had already taken care of the matter through his brother-in-law (which proved not to be true), but others were more brazen in their refusal. As Neckevelt said, "because others have not received from me, I will do as I have been done by."[53]

Neckevelt was in good company. "I will do as another does," said Liebert van Axele when challenged by Abraham de Goyer. "I am not inclined to accept them," said Aert Dircksz Cruidenier to the notary sent by François de Schot. "What another does, it would be needless for me to do [more]," said Cornelis Swaech in Enkhuizen on being insinuated by Simon van Poelenburch. "I will do as others have done," said François Hendricxsz Coster when he was approached again in November, this time by a desperate Willem Schoneus of Haarlem, to whom Coster owed a total of ƒ5,830. As the somewhat ritualized responses suggest, there was a kind of strength in numbers that made it easier for defaulting buyers to stand up to their sellers. This will have been well known by the time of a second series of insinuations in September, now timed because of the need to plant the bulbs again, thereby rendering them unmoveable until the following summer. But as sellers invoked the April 27 edict of the States, they seem, from the language of the insinuations, to have realized quite well even in June that they were going to get nowhere against such a strong and unified refusal to receive and pay. The notary Jan Warnaertsz, for example, was reduced to a repeat of his round of *insinuaties* for Hans Baert in September, with virtually the same results.[54]

This impression is confirmed by the more generalized accounts of what happened provided by experts for lawsuits taking place further away. If payment was made at all, it was at a fraction of the original price. In mid-June 1637, David Clement, Willem Gael, Daniel Olthoff, and Pieter Joosten de Sanger, all from Haarlem, said that they "in the past winter were present at many and various sales of flowers, and they bought and sold various tulips, involving many thousands." But, they said, "the delivery and payment for them did not follow, but by many and various was not done, but by some honorable people was concluded for one two three four yes five per cent at the highest." The group reported that, as they understood it, the same was true in other towns, such as Amsterdam, Gouda, Hoorn, Enkhuizen, and Alkmaar. A similar report came from

Adriaen Jansz, a grocer and spice merchant from Alkmaar, when he was questioned in 1638 in aid of a lawsuit in Leeuwarden. "It is true," Jansz said of himself, "that he, the witness, last year, 1637, trading in tulips in the city of Alkmaar, sold various and many types and sorts of tulips and bulbs, both pound goods and others, involving notable sums of money, to be delivered when the bulbs were suitable to be taken up out of the ground, and to be paid cash: which everyone, in good faith, had promised each other: and also made written contracts and firm bonds to do so, signed by both parties." And yet, Jansz said, "despite all this, no one out of all those with whom he, the witness, made a contract, has completed the sale nor received any bulbs: much less paid anything or given any satisfaction. . . ." You can almost hear the frustration in his words, or the sigh.[55]

In these circumstances, the hope of the States that the towns would be able to bring their citizens to accord was faint. For an individual seller, like Hans Baert, or Jan Hendricxsz Admirastel, or Willem Schoneus, or others distressed in the summer of 1637, it was hard to know how to proceed. The proclamation of April 27 had suggested that the courts should be only the last resort for quarrelling *bloemisten*; the States did not want a sudden burst of lawsuits clogging the judicial systems of either the towns or the province. Haarlem took this recommendation to extremes. On May 1, the burgemeesters ordered that notaries and lawyers were not allowed to take action against those who owed money for tulips, nor were the bailiffs allowed to deliver any orders, protests, or *insinuaties*. This was immediately problematic. Clement, Gael, Olthoff, and De Sanger, reporting on conditions in June, said that "no law is being carried out over this," mentioning the restrictions on legal officials; very unusually, Egbert van Bosvelt, the notary taking down their testimony, intervened: "I, the notary, also declare this to be true, and the prohibition by the lord Burgemeesteren of this city was delivered to me personally by the sworn bailiff." Yet the prohibition did not prevent people from going to the Kleine Bank van Justitie, nor the court from acting—for a while.[56]

Tulips had, after all, been a subject of numerous lawsuits in 1636 and early 1637, as sellers failed to deliver bulbs or the tulips planted proved, the following season, to be something other than what had been promised. Although suits about tulips abruptly disappeared as trade ceased from February 7, in late April, as tulips began to bloom, Haarlemmers began turning up again on Tuesdays and Fridays to protest their treatment by buyers (and sometimes by sellers). The court did continue sometimes to rule on cases such as Salomon Seys' protest at the "bad flowers" sold him by the artist Joost van Haverbeeck (August 9), or some of the "pay it with flowers" suits, when those being sued for payment for other goods (for example, a skirt) claimed they had actually been exchanged for bulbs. But as tulips came more frequently into the deliberations of the court, its four commissioners became less certain how to react. This was no doubt in part encouraged by the attitude of some defendants in civil suits. On May 12, Joost Soene, being sued for ƒ14, railed not only at the charge against him but at the fact that he had been brought to court over tulips at all. "The defendant, present, says that the demand springs from sale of flowers, which are not worth a *stuiver*, And in any case no law is being practised about this"; the case should therefore be scrapped, he said, and he would gladly return the flowers. The wife of Cornelis Jansz Ryp made the same argument the following week when being sued for the price of two silver spoons by Rogier Alleman: since no judicial decisions were being made on flowers, and the spoons were in exchange for tulips, she had no obligation to pay. The hesitation of the court in the face of these remarks is palpable. In response to Soene, the commissioners, "considering that this question is about the sale of flowers, are not minded to go into the business, but order the parties to come to an accord, or, if they cannot, to address themselves to the Burgemeesteren." And by the time Ryp's wife made her argument on May 18, the court had reverted to a standard response: cases to do with the flower trade should wait "until the time that a certain general law shall be devised." Through the summer they gave such an answer repeatedly: to wait "until a certain order has been contrived over the sale of flowers."[57]

So just as disputes in the tulip trade were heating up, as the tulips were becoming ready to come out of the ground, one of the only institutions available to give townspeople any "order" in this matter was abdicating its responsibilities. The burgemeesters of Haarlem grew restive, not least because those among their number were involved. In mid-June they wrote to the Hof van Holland again, pleading with the high court to revoke the order of April 27. To leave all the tulip sales in force, they said, made it impossible for people to come to any legal solutions and led only to confusion. Only the revocation of the edict would make possible the "furthering of calm and the prevention of manifold inconveniences." But the high court did not react to this approach, and the confusion in the minds of *bloemisten* about how to proceed in their disputes continued during the "dry bulb time." Planting season, in September, brought another wave of disputes in all the towns, as the need to put the bulbs in the earth for the next eight months lent urgency to financial claims. Hans Baert, for one, sounded desperate. "He is ready to deliver them to you," the notary Jan Warnaertsz said to Hendrick van Bergom in Amsterdam on September 29, "as he has offered on various occasions and as he offers now, Yes has also offered to come to the cheapest terms possible or to take the case to the Commissioners here in the city . . . which to date has produced no results. . . ." Invoking the proclamation of April 27, Baert said he would plant the tulips, or sell them, at Van Bergom's risk unless he received them and paid within the current month. As that month ended the following day, it is evident Baert was not expecting much. (With good reason: he was still chasing this money in November 1638.) But at the same time, his fellow *bloemisten* were clamoring for resolution. On September 25, Theunis Wolphertsz burst out in the Kleine Bank in Haarlem with yet another protest that he owed nothing on tulips because "neither at the Hof van Holland nor in any of the towns of Holland are any judicial decisions being made over flowers," nor, he added, by the judicial officials of Haarlem, who were forbidden to get involved either legally or indirectly with "all those who daily frequent the town hall." The picture this evokes—of disappointed petitioners crowding on the steps of the Haarlem *stadhuis*, their backs to the Grote Markt and fading hope on their faces—gives us a sense of the months of frustration incited by the authorities' dithering policy.[58]

This situation clearly could not go on. Once again, then, and nearly a year after the crash, it was pressure from below that brought some semblance of a solution. On January 30, 1638, the burgemeesters of Haarlem decided ("at the request and constant persistence of various inhabitants of this City") to set up a commission to deal with the problems stemming from the flower trade, known later as the Commissarissen van de Bloemen Saecken (Commissioners for Flower Affairs, henceforth CBS). A similar panel appears to have been set up in Alkmaar, and perhaps other towns. The Haarlem CBS, consisting of four appointees, was to meet in the Prinsenhof every Wednesday and Saturday from 9 A.M. to 11 A.M. and from

2 P.M. to 4 P.M. Anyone ordered to appear would have to do so, with fines for nonappearance ranging from 30 *stuivers* for the first time to ƒ12 for the third offense. The CBS was intended to soothe the quarrels that had been raging in Haarlem since the crash (and indeed before it occurred). Yet its original incarnation was still as vague as earlier solutions, or non-solutions, to the crisis. The burgemeesters saw it as a means of solving disputes by *accommodatie*—accommodation and compromise. The same was true in Alkmaar: the commission there was appointed to "hear the parties and to unite them." As we saw in quarrels over tulips that came before the Kleine Bank, arbitration and discussion were always a favored method of reestablishing social harmony in seventeenth-century Holland. In this case, however, talking might not be enough.[59]

Although we find cases from the Kleine Bank van Justitie being referred to the CBS as early as late February, it took the commissioners until May to come up with a firm and standard solution for the disputes that faced them. We know from the only extant decision of the commission, over the money owed by Wouter Tullekens of Alkmaar to Pieter Willemsz van Rosven in Haarlem, that in February the CBS was still attempting to enforce the full payment of debts: Tullekens was told to pay the full ƒ2,568 he owed. Given that Rosven had to chase Tullekens through the courts in Alkmaar for a further eighteen months, this solution was not ideal, and the CBS must have come to realize that it would be impossible to get most buyers to accept the tulips and pay. On May 28, 1638, at the request of the commission, the burgemeesters ruled that contracts that came before the panel would be settled with a fee—*rouwkoop*—of 3.5 percent. This is the same fee that was given to compensate a seller in the cancelation of a normal sale of goods. Thus the buyer gained nothing from this settlement, except (and perhaps this was a large "except") being released from his promise to buy; the seller kept his bulbs, now much reduced in value, and received very modest compensation. This was not wholly satisfactory for the seller, and certainly not satisfactory for the buyer, who was worse off than he had been when he had simply refused to pay at all.[60]

The confusion, or dissatisfaction, over institutional solutions to tulip problems remained. The CBS would rule on a transaction and give copies of the decision to the buyer and seller. But that was often not the end of it. A short time later the parties would find themselves back in the Kleine Bank van Justitie, with the seller brandishing his extract from the "bloem rolle" (the register of the CBS) and demanding his 3.5 percent *rouwkoop*, which, though so much less than the sum originally owed, was still not forthcoming from the buyer. This happened for the first time almost immediately, on June 14, 1638, when Salomon Seys sued Gerrit Pietersz for his 3.5 percent. A host of familiar names followed his example, with large transactions, now reduced to small amounts by the size of the *rouwkoop*, appearing for the first time in the Kleine Bank. The schoolmaster Jacobus Grimmaris turned up in court demanding the ƒ9:10 he was owed by Gerrit Jeroensz on an original price of ƒ271:10. Pieter Gerritsz (probably the wealthy Van Welsen) sued the yarn merchant Daniel de Clercq for ƒ42, which meant that the price of the bulbs had been ƒ1,200. Andries de Preyer demanded ƒ25 from Bartholomeus van Gennep, the *rouwkoop* for a transaction of around ƒ714. The Kleine Bank almost always ruled in favor of the decision of the CBS, making these appearances in the small claims court ritualistic at best. And the quarrels were hardly over at this point. When the baker Jan Abrahamsz appeared to demand ƒ19 from the major yarn entrepreneur Cornelis Coelembier, a sum suggesting an original debt of around ƒ543, Coelembier "flatly denied owing the sum, or even being acquainted with the plaintiff."[61]

The fact that CBS cases turned up in the Kleine Bank at all argues for a certain lack of trust in the institutional answers to the crisis. If one ruling did not suit the parties concerned, they would look for another one. Between the CBS, the Kleine Bank, the *schepenen*, private arbitration, and the possibility of appeal to a higher court, a variety of institutions—sometimes overlapping in jurisdiction—could lend authority to any particular solution. Or the disputing parties could make their own. This happened in a quarrel between Jacques Bertens, Salomon Seys, and Aert Huybertsz. Bertens had bought a tulip called a Manassier from Seys for ƒ710, and Huybertsz had then purchased it from Bertens for ƒ850. Bertens and Seys went to the CBS to work out their side of the bargain, and of course the judgment handed down was that Bertens should pay Seys 3.5 percent of ƒ710. However, this left Bertens with no settlement with Huybertsz, and in any case he apparently was not happy with having to pay this fine to Seys. The three met together on July 3, 1638, at the Coninck van Vranckrijck inn to talk it through. They agreed that Seys should settle for a mere 3 percent rather than the 3.5 percent he was owed, and that this money should come not from Bertens but directly from Huybertsz, who was thereby paying Bertens by paying Bertens' debt. Honor, presumably, would then be satisfied. Except that it was not. The fact that Bertens and Huybertsz appeared before a notary on November 29 to protest that "Seys had also been content" with the settlement makes it clear that Seys was in fact far from content and that this dispute was ongoing.[62]

That these discussions took place at all, however, makes manifest the culture of negotiation, of arbitration, that we have noted so often in the tulip craze. Hans Baert's attempts to reason with his debtors—"[he] has offered to come to the cheapest terms with you," the notary reminded Hendrick van Bergom, François Hendricxsz Coster, and Jan Pietersz Neckevelt—reminds us of this culture. So does the attitude of the States and of the towns. In their April 27 proclamation, the States of Holland made it clear that judicial proceedings should be the last resort; towns should "bring the parties into accord and unity." Similarly, the fondness of city institutions like the Kleine Bank van Justitie of using arbitration as a means of solving disputes makes it plain that it was civic harmony, rather than a culture of winners and losers, that was the highest priority. When Haarlem's magistrates wrote to the Hof van Holland pleading that a clearer solution for quarrels over tulips be issued than the vague April 27 *plakkaat*, they did so not for a desire for justice, but for the sake of "general calm." Some debts did get paid: Cornelis Varwer repaid his loan from the other members of the Enkhuizen tulip company, albeit in 1646; Matthijs Schouten in Amsterdam came to an agreement with Willem Schoneus in Haarlem; Wouter Tullekens in Alkmaar fulfilled his obligations to the Haarlemmer Pieter Willemsz van Rosven (although only after a CBS decision, a court case in Alkmaar, and arbitration). Yet negotiation did not always provide the calm the States and the towns were hoping for. In Enkhuizen, Cornelis Cornelisz Swaech, pretending innocence, said in late April 1637 that he was happy to point out an Oudenaerder, as promised, to buyer Ellert van Resum so that he could pay the *f*178 owed. Van Resum responded tartly with what must have been considered a poor offer at best. "I have offered him five *rijksdaalders* [*f*12.5], that is, Two for the flower and Three for the *rouwkoop*, and that's just for today, otherwise not at all, and if he . . . does not take it [now] then he may try his best in the future, the sooner the better, be it through law or outside of it. . . ."[63]

Talking things out was a time-honored solution, but perhaps this situation was just too difficult for calm discussion. The question is, however, what made it so difficult. Was it the large sums of money involved? Naturally this will have played a major role in the anger and frustration felt by sellers, although in almost all cases the tulips had not actually been delivered, so that sellers still had their flowers, if not their money. They still, of course, would have felt unhappy at being left with goods that might have cost them much more than the prices they now could charge for them. (This did not, however, stop people from buying tulips in the following years; the desire to own the flowers was not wiped out with the crash.) But was the buyers' frantic search for solutions just an attempt to shore up their slipping financial position?

One of the things we hear most often about tulipmania is that it bankrupted a sizeable proportion of the population. "Substantial merchants were reduced almost to beggary, and many a representative of a noble line saw the fortunes of his house ruined beyond redemption," wrote Mackay, the source for so many modern accounts of tulipmania, and for so many of their errors. But was this true? Although the bankruptcy records for this period are patchy, it is difficult to find any bankrupts associated with tulipmania. The Vianen tulip dealer Francisco Gomes da Costa, it is true, fell into severe financial difficulties in 1646, but this was nothing new; the whole reason he was living in Vianen during tulipmania was that he had already gone bankrupt in the early 1630s, and Vianen, as a free city outside of normal jurisdiction, was until 1795 a well-known place of refuge for the financially irresponsible. (*Naar Vianen gaan*, to go to Vianen, was a synonym for bankruptcy.) But visible bankrupts from tulipmania are few. The Haarlem silversmith Isaac Alingh was bankrupt by the spring of 1640, when his house was auctioned (and bought by a fellow-*bloemist*, Jan van Clarenbeeck, for *f*2,900; Clarenbeeck's guarantors were two other *bloemisten*, Carel van Wansele and the painter Willem Claesz Heda). Unless there were many more tulip sales than we know about, however, it is hard to believe that Alingh could have been bankrupted through his contact with tulips. In 1638 we learn that Alingh had sold a tulip to the woollen cloth merchant Frans van de Broecke in return for enough cloth to make a suit of clothes; after the fall in prices, Van de Broecke insisted that Alingh pay for the cloth. Such a demand does not ruin a silversmith. Another possible bankrupt is Michiel van Limmen, rather ironically the secretary of the Kleine Bank van Justitie in Haarlem, who had listened to and noted down so many disputes about tulips in his time. In July 1637 a Michiel van Limmen in Amsterdam applied to the Hoge Raad of Holland for *cessio bonorum,* an expedient in Roman law in which someone in financial difficulties ceded his property voluntarily to his creditors while avoiding the opprobrium of bankruptcy and the total deprivation of all necessities of life. But the Haarlem Van Limmen—if this is the same one—was in sufficiently good financial shape in 1642 to act as surety for the purchase of a house costing ƒ950. The baker Theunis Jansz was bankrupt by the beginning of 1639, but it is impossible to know if this was related to tulips or not. Otherwise, I have found no bankruptcies that can be attributed to tulipmania. Although some bankruptcies of poorer people, less likely to turn up in these records, might well have occurred, if there was a rash of financial disasters among artisans, it was never discussed by the magistrates of Haarlem.[64]

The classic case of bankruptcy from tulipmania that is always given, indeed the only name usually mentioned in the literature, is the painter Jan van Goyen. Van Goyen had the misfortune to make several tulip deals on January 27 and February 4, 1637, just at the time of the crash. He both sold tulips and bought others from a burgemeester of The Hague, Allert Claesz van Ravesteijn. On Ravesteijn's death in 1641, Van Goyen still owed him ƒ897 for tulips, plus a painting of Judas worth ƒ36 that had been part of the January 27 transaction. The fact that Van Goyen died bankrupt is usually mentioned as a sign of the fatal consequences of tulip-dealing. But Van Goyen's debts at his death on April 27, 1656, were at least ƒ18,000, many of them incurred in his active speculation in land well after the fall in tulip prices. Van Goyen bought, sold, and developed property from the 1620s through the 1640s, and although this, no less than flowers, turned out ill for him, it does show that it was not tulips, or at least not tulips alone, that caused Van Goyen to die in penury twenty years after the crash.[65]

Indeed, when we look at *bloemisten* after the fall in tulip prices, the general impression is of relative financial health. Rather than having their houses sold at bankruptcy auctions, instead, like Clarenbeeck, they bought the property of other bankrupts: in Haarlem, Reynier Tulckens, Carel van Wansele, Pleun Jansz van Doorn (for ƒ4,310!), Pieter Willemsz van Rosven, David Clements, Johan Cortoor, Hans Baert, Andries van den Broecke, and Cornelis Pietersz Emaus all did so, while numerous others made bids at bankruptcy sales. Except for Isaac Alingh, no known *bloem-ist* had his house and property auctioned in Haarlem between October 1637 and the end of 1648. We see many signs of prosperity among those who had been dealing in tulips: in April of 1637 Hans Bailly felt confident enough to buy a house for ƒ1,585, for which he paid one-third in cash; around the same time Pieter Gerritsz van Welsen bought a house for ƒ810, despite the ƒ11,500 he owed to Dirck Boortens for tulips. Hans Baert, despite his unhappy experiences with Amsterdam buyers, felt no compunction about buying a garden in 1642 for ƒ580. In Amsterdam, the events of February seem not to have put off *liefhebbers* such as Lambert Massa, Adam Bessels, or Jan Hendricxsz Admirael when it came to bidding at the great art sale of Jan Basse from March 9–30, 1637. The inventories and wills of *liefhebbers* and *floristen* like Paulus van Mackelenberch and Abraham de Goyer indicate enviable wealth and interior decor. In 1640, three Mennonite *bloemisten*, the brothers Jacques and Pieter de Clercq and their nephew Abraham Ampe, started a potash company in which each invested ƒ6,000. Although all these details are just that—details—an overall look at the conditions of tulip buyers and sellers gives little indication that they were in major financial difficulties.[66]

Nor was the country. Another myth about tulipmania was that it destroyed the Dutch economy. "[T]he final chapter of this bizarre story is that the shock generated by the boom and collapse led to a prolonged depression in Holland. No one was spared," writes the economist Burton Malkiel in a classic example. Although there is disagreement among economic historians of the Netherlands about when the economy was depressed in the seventeenth century, neither camp suggests that a decline occurred in the late 1630s and early 1640s, either as a result of tulipmania or for other reasons. It is persuasively argued by several historians that, with some periodic downturns, the Dutch economy continued to grow until the mid-seventeenth century in nearly every area, including industry, overseas trade, and the living standards of the population. Real wages, the balance of prices against incomes, continued to rise until well after this period. Although there were periods of hardship, the worst years of the era were the early 1620s and 1626–1631, not after 1637. If tulipmania affected this situation at all, economic historians appear to acknowledge, it would have been in only a minor way. In fact, it is difficult to pinpoint any major economic effects of the crash. This makes sense when we consider the relatively small group of those involved in tulip trading and, among those, the even smaller group—buyers currently holding bulbs—who will have lost money in the crash. As we have discovered that, among known transactions, those involved with bulbs of high value were for the most part well-off merchants who appear not to have gone bankrupt after the fall in prices, a lack of major effects on the economy will also be relatively unsurprising. It seems that, amazing as some prices will have been to some contemporaries, it was for the most part not "utter ruin" that prompted the clamoring for lawsuits in the Haarlem town hall in 1637.[67]

If most people were not ruined by tulipmania, if the country was not thrown into economic difficulties because of its consequences, what caused the sense of crisis that clearly enveloped the towns in the months after February 1637? What caused the pursual through the courts of settlements of what ultimately proved to be only a few guilders, once the CBS had ruled that only a payment of 3.5 percent would be awarded to sellers? The kinds of sums being chased by people like the linen merchant Andries de Preyer, who pursued his fellow-merchant Bartholomeus van Gennep from the CBS to the Kleine Bank for a mere f25, seem less than lavish. True, this f25 was something like three weeks' wages for a master craftsman, but the loss of a figure of this size was hardly going to break a wealthy man like De Preyer, especially as he had already had to give up on the idea of receiving the f714 or so that he should have been paid by Van Gennep for flowers.[68]

We must remember that the f25 was *rouwkoop*. It was not payment for tulips, which De Preyer would have kept in any case. *Rouwkoop* was a payment from one honorable man to another to excuse himself from backing out of a contract. Abraham van Meeckeren paid it to Jacob Abrahamsz van Halmael when he withdrew from his purchase of bulbs after the crash, to keep his relations with his fellow-Mennonite and commercial associate civilized. It would not matter financially to Andries de Preyer or his fellow merchants, denied their hundreds of guilders for tulips, whether or not they received another f10 or f15 or f20. But it would matter in another way. It would touch their honor.[69]

When the Kleine Bank van Justitie threw up its hands in the summer of 1637, declaring that it did not know what to do about tulip disputes, it referred to the need to establish "a certain order" in the handling of the flower trade. The burgemeesters feared a disturbance of the peace. This fear, the fear of disorder, was justified, because when the question was one of honor—of the repayment of debts, of the breaking of obligations—the consequences for the community could be dire. David Clement and the other *bloemisten* who reported on conditions after the crash said that "some honorable people" at least tried to pay a few percent on their debts, but most did not. If people did not keep their promises, where, then, was honor to be found? Tulipmania did have a profound effect on society, even if it was not a financial one. It fractured social relations by reminding burghers how fragile their connections were. If a debt of honor—the payment of *rouwkoop*—could only be extracted by the invocation of multiple legal authorities, a culture of negotiation and arbitration was in peril. It is no wonder that the magistrates of Haarlem—some of whom had themselves had their fingers burned—wished to deride the trade.[70]

Dirck Boortens and Pieter Gerritsz van Welsen tried to keep things civil in the spring of 1637. They tried hard. The fact that Van Welsen had promised Boortens ƒ11,700 of his money was not, they said, going to damage their relationship, despite the increasing signs that this money (not yet paid) had been thrown away. The pair strove to behave as gentlemen, and they did this by talking, coming to an agreement longer than any other contract about tulips I have seen. It is true, they said, that the States-General, the States of Holland and West Friesland, the Gecommitteerde Raden, the Hof van Holland, or the burgemeesters of Haarlem or other towns might come out with a *plakkaat* or ordinance to regulate the trade: "be it that all sales of tulips should be annulled or that certain costs should be given as *rouwkoop* or *uitkoop* [a fee for buying someone out], or that no law or decision about the sales of tulips should be made, or that people ought not to deliver or receive and pay, or something of that kind." But, they said, whatever kind of ordinances, orders, or commands might be given by government, whatever benefits or remedies of law might be provided by the authorities, that meant nothing to them. They, as "persons of honor," did not need such expedients. They promised not to exploit these governmental remedies, but to abide by the promises they had given each other. The implication was that a civil society, a proper society, did not need the orders of government, but only the ability to discuss and come to an agreement. Only that way, through personal good faith, not government action, could social bonds be maintained. And "as a sign that this is sincerely meant and in good faith," they declared themselves ready to say so before any court you might choose.[71]

Too good to be true? Of course it was. All the more reason to be upset. All the more reason to grieve.

FIVE

Bad Faith

"THE FLOWER TRADE IS A WONDER FOR US, AND beyond our understanding," wrote an anonymous songster just before the crash in 1637. In the weeks just before and particularly just after the drop in price, short pamphlets and broadsides with *spotdichten,* satiric songs, were printed and sold in the towns where the tulip trade had been flourishing—until, in Haarlem at least, the burgemeesters outlawed their sale on March 17. Perhaps presciently, the thirteen-stanza song in question, like several others about the tulip trade, was intended to be sung to the tune of yet another song, "Hoe legh ick hier in dees ellende" (roughly, "what a mess I'm in," or even "how did I get myself into this mess?"). The mess referred to in this earlier song was about as bad as it could get: the grave. The dead protagonist of "Hoe legh ick hier in dees ellende" has been robbed of his five senses and lies cold under the ground. His body, which he had previously spent so much time adorning, is now *spijs,* food for the hungry worms, and his head, once crowned with beautiful curly hair, now rolls in the churchyard for all to see. The sight should, he feels, be instructive, and he warns all those hearing his song that the same fate awaits them soon enough.[1]

It was no doubt its conveniently lugubrious tune that connected this particular song to some of those about the tulip trade. But the question of "how did I get myself into

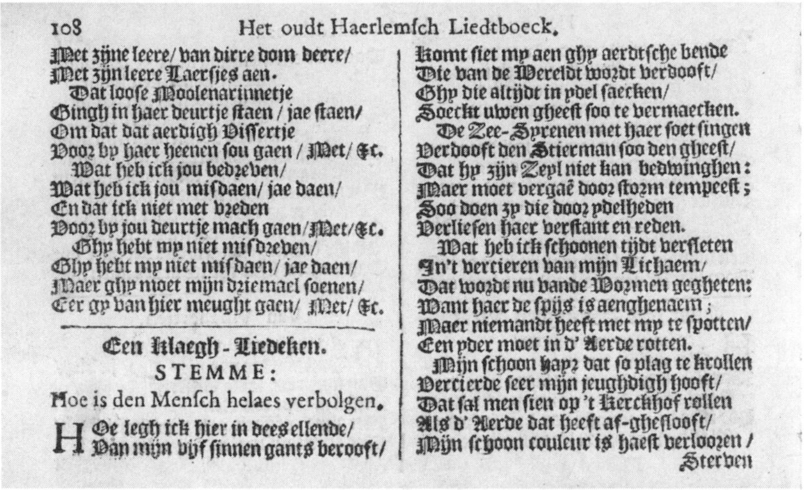

108   Het oudt Haerlemfch Liedtboeck.

Met zijne leere/ van dirre dom deere/
Met zijn leere Laerfjes aen.
    Dat loofe Moolenarinnetje
Gingh in haer deurtje ftaen / jae ftaen/
Om dat dat aerdigh Viffertje
Door by haer heenen fou gaen / Met/ &c.
    Wat heb ick jou bedzeven/
Wat heb ick jou mifdaen/ jae daen/
En dat ick niet met bzeden
Door by jou deurtje mach gaen/Met/&c.
    Ghy hebt my niet mifdzeven/
Ghy hebt my niet mifdaen/ jae daen/
Maer ghy moet mijn dziemael foenen/
Eer gy van hier meught gaen/ Met/ &c.

Een klaegh - Liedeken.
S T E M M E :
Hoe is den Menfch helaes verbolgen.

H Oe legh ick hier in dees ellende/
   Van mijn vijf finnen gantz berooft/

Komt fiet my aen ghy aerdtfche bende
Die van de Werelot wordt verdooft/
Ghy die altijot in ydel faecken/
Soeckt uwen gheeft foo te vermaecken.
    De Zee-Sprenen met haer foet fingen
Verdooft den Stierman foo den gheeft/
Dat hy zijn Zepl niet kan bedwinghen/
Maer moet vergaê door ftozm tempeeft ;
Soo doen zp die door pdelheden
Verliefen haer verftant en reden.
    Wat heb ick fchoonen tijot verfleten
In't vercieren van mijn Lichaem/
Dat wozot nu vande Wozmen gegheten:
Want haer de fpijs is aenghenaem ;
Maer niemandt heeft met my te fpotten/
Een pder moet in d' Aerde rotten.
    Mijn fchoon hapz dat fo plag te krollen
Vercierde feer mijn jeughdigh hooft/
Dat fal men fien op 't Kerckhof rollen
Als d' Aerde dat heeft af-ghslooft/
Mijn fchoon couleur is haeft verloozen /
            Sterven

FIGURE 55. The song beginning "Hoe legh ick hier in dees ellende," in *Het Oudt Haerlemsch Liedtboeck*, c. 1630. Koninklijke Bibliotheek, The Hague.

this mess?" dominates the contemporary rhetoric about the tulip trade. Tulipmania and the events surrounding it set off a round of questioning about a host of social and cultural issues. How do we know what is real? How do we know what is valuable? What use is money? What use is art? How should our society work? Whom can we trust? These issues, and many others, are revealed in the verses and texts written both for and against the trade, not to mention in the actions of the *bloemisten* themselves. They reveal a profound sense of social disorder, of a disruption to the fragile bonds of honor and trust that ultimately held society together.

The themes of "Hoe legh ick hier in dees ellende" were familiar to Dutch society. *Vanitas* still lifes with skulls, butterflies, and, eventually, bubbles, clocks, coins, and smoking candles reminded viewers of the transitory nature of human existence and the need to focus on heaven. Tulips, whose brief period of blooming was a metaphor for the comparable brevity of life, featured in some of them, and of course contemporaries would have been familiar with the biblical message that man "cometh forth like a flower, and is cut down" (Job 14:2). Both religious and secular culture was full of warnings of the falseness of confidence in this-worldly happiness. A rather uncheerful verse in a songbook of around 1620, the

Nieuwen Jeucht-Spieghel (New Mirror of Youth), pointed out presciently that the false world was not to be trusted: "Her Flower is beautiful, her Fruit stinks,/Her certainty is betrayal, Her Medicine is poison. . . ." This message was unlikely to escape people in the winter of 1636–1637. Death was surely on people's minds at the time that "Hoe legh ick hier in dees ellende"—so clearly popular—was being sung of an evening in the front rooms of Dutch town houses. This was a time of plague.[2]

It started in the summer of 1635, according to one account in Leiden. Between July 14 and the end of the year 14,281 people in the town were buried, with the highest death toll coming in the week of October 6, when 1,278 died in seven days. This was in a town of 54,000. The students at the university left, and other towns closed their doors to Leiden's wares, but it proved impossible to keep the plague from spreading. Dordrecht, Delft, Rotterdam, Enkhuizen, and many other Holland towns found themselves in the thick of the plague; in Amsterdam it was said that 8,177 died in 1635; Enkhuizen, a town of 19,000, lost 2,640 in the second half of 1636. In Haarlem we hear of it first in September 1635. On September 10, in an attempt to prevent the contagion reaching the town, the burgemeesters ordered the old clothes sellers, who normally held a market every six weeks, not to do so. But this was no use. In October, 107 died of the plague; in November, 189. And that was only the beginning.[3]

The authorities tried to control the "hot sickness," as it was often known. In April 1636 they put in force regulations similar to quarantine, forcing houses where someone had the illness to keep doors and windows closed for six weeks after the last death in the house (although no quarantine was actually in place), forbidding occupants to carry on trade for the same period and preventing them from entering other buildings to buy provisions, from going to funerals of other people, from going to the marketplace. They also appointed a series of officials to take care of the afflicted, such as the consolers of the sick (*sieckentroosters*) and midwives for pregnant women with plague, who repeatedly died and had to be replaced. The midwife Maeycken Oliviers, appointed in mid-October 1635, only lasted until February; the *sieckentrooster* Lieven Lourens began his work on May 6, 1636 and was already ill by the end of June. In the same month, the burgemeesters ordered the opening of a new cemetery; and in July, a general day of prayer to try to rid Haarlem of its sickness, which took place on August 5. Nevertheless, according to the contemporary historian Schrevelius, "every day many, yes, countless Bodies were dragged out of houses and put in the earth, occasioning sighs and lamenting, crying and weeping in the Alleys and the Streets." In the worst plague months for Haarlem, August through November 1636, it was said that 5,723 people died; in Amsterdam, the figure for 1636 was 17,193.[4]

Profit from tulips did not protect one from the plague. Think of Jan Govertsz Coopall. As we have previously heard, when he and Cornelis Bol den Jongen called a notary to his house on the Groot Heiligland on November 6, 1636, to renew the contract for their tulip company, they went through every detail of the finances: how much money each had expended, how their company should be continued, and, most importantly, what should happen if one of them died. This was a euphemism: it must have been obvious that that one was Coopall. He was on his deathbed, and the contract was made "by form of last will." In time of plague, property was in many ways central. For a number of young families, tulips formed the bulk of the estate. This was surely the case for the children of Wouter Bartholomeusz Winckel in Alkmaar, with tulips worth ƒ90,000 on February 5, 1637, and it must have also been true of others dying at this time, such as Pieter de Jonckheer, whose tulips were sold to benefit his orphaned son Joost, or the baker Ysack Schot, who made the mistake in 1636 of entrusting on his deathbed Huybert Claesz de Bruyn with ƒ1,000 and all the tulip bulbs planted behind his house on the Kraaienhorstergracht. (De Bruyn, despite being captain of the Night Watch, was later accused of secretly replanting Schot's bulbs for his own benefit rather than selling them, as promised, for the support of Schot's widow, Abigael Verschuyll, and her children.) For Jan Govertsz Coopall, one of the most important matters for his last days on earth was putting his tulip business in order. He had little time for anything else: he was buried on November 15, nine days after renegotiating his contract with Bol. And not only Coopall himself. His father was buried on November 29, and children of Coopall's were buried on November 29, December 13, December 20, and January 10. As disease was striking their household, Coopall's widow, Aeltgen Jansdr, now sick with plague herself, was (perhaps not surprisingly) still concerned with tulips. She called in the notary Jacob Schoudt on November 22 to make new arrangements to continue the tulip company with Bol for the benefit of her family. One of her *vrunden*, the master tailor Jan van der Linde, contracted to trade on her family's behalf, selflessly agreeing taking only a salary of ƒ700 per year from Bol and none of the profits from the flowers.[5]

"These dangerous times," as the *vroedschap* of Enkhuizen called them, provoked considerable unease in florists and nonflorists alike. A formula used in most wills at this time acknowledged that nothing was so certain as death. This was not a comfort in plague time, nor was the uncertainty entailed in this very certainty. The will of the Haarlem notary Wouter Crousen de Jonge, the same one who had been doodling tulips on the back of his notarial acts in 1635, amplifies on this theme. We learn that Crousen was making his will while "considering in this tainted plague time the quickness of death and its uncertain hour. . . ." There was, in fact, a rush of will-writing; one notary in Rotterdam wrote more wills in fourteen months than he had done in the previous four years. Most later writers describing tulipmania have made reference to the plague, usually suggesting that the fear of death was a reason for a gambling mentality: there was simply nothing left to lose. On the other hand, it is difficult to see desperation in the actions of the *bloemisten*; they met together in inns and gardens, discussed, over years, the minutiae of tulips and the network of those growing the flowers, organized themselves in a semi-guildlike structure, and appear to have recognized a set of experts and authorities over the trade. It has been argued about England in the same period that plague had become so usual that people were not as frightened of it as they previously had been, and one English observer reported in the later seventeenth century that the Dutch "are nott att all afraid of yᵉ plague: they have nott a care to preserve themselves from itt: they fly nott att all: they shut nott up their houses. . . ." This was, as we have seen, not entirely true, yet in some ways life and trade continued much as normal.[6]

Yet with such major and protracted mortality there will have been many repercussions. One of these was certainly financial. Death meant inheritance, and with so many people dying, estates, which were often divided up among many members of families, would have been quickly providing unexpected capital to potential buyers of tulips. One example is Geertruyt Schoudt, who was persuaded at that Sunday dinner at Pieter Wynants' house to buy a pound of Switsers precisely because she was expecting to receive part of the estate of her late brother-in-law, Jacob van der Hulst. Extra money in one's pockets and, perhaps, the euphoria of survival—the top prices were paid for tulips just as the plague was abating and the burgemeesters were considering holding public prayers of thanks—may well have contributed to the flower trade. Yet even with more capital in different hands, even with a sense of having made it through a dark time in January 1637, there was still plenty of cause for worry. Large-scale mortality from plague caused social upheaval; the redistribution of wealth did the same. Plague was unpredictable; the world was uncertain. A healthy young man could be dead two days later. And it was not only florists who died, but also flowers.[7]

In this case, it was not tulips that died. They were planted in the ground in the winter of 1637, and if they happened to die, that would not be evident until the spring. Instead, it was Flora, the goddess who in this culture personified the flower trade. In good times, Flora smiled on the land, adorning it with beautiful blossoms. A song from a Haarlem songbook of 1636 has Phoebus praising her as a goddess "in her beautiful Flower-dales" where "each little Flower smells sweetly"; since she cannot do without Phoebus nor he without her blossoms, Phoebus chooses her as his bride. This positive image reflected to some degree on the flower trade. One professional florist in Amsterdam, Marcus Cornelisz, adopted Flora as his surname as early as the 1620s and lived in a house called Flora on the Keizersgracht. Yet the unpredictability of the world, the whims of fate, indeed the idea of pride coming before a fall all were visible in what happened in February 1637—the death of Flora and the fall of the flower trade.[8]

In the pamphlets and songs of February and early March, the crash is constantly portrayed as a death. Perhaps it was predictable, perhaps it was a result of the whims of fate, whims that were just as evident in the plight of victims of the tulip trade as in the bodies being carried out of the *pesthuis* outside of Haarlem. Flora was said to be ill, with consumption, with the pox, with childbed fever; or she was in fact dead, with her followers in mourning around her grave. The titles of pamphlets and songs said it all: *Flora's Fainting Sobs, Haarlem's Neighborhood-Chat about Flora's Sickbed in the Gateway of the Hospital, New Mourning Cloak Song for the Florists, Death-Roll and Wake of Floortie-Floraas, Consolation for the Torn Brotherhood of Mourning-clad Cap-brothers, Consolation for all the Grieving Florists who mourn the Death of Flora, Goddess of the Florists;* even *The Open-*

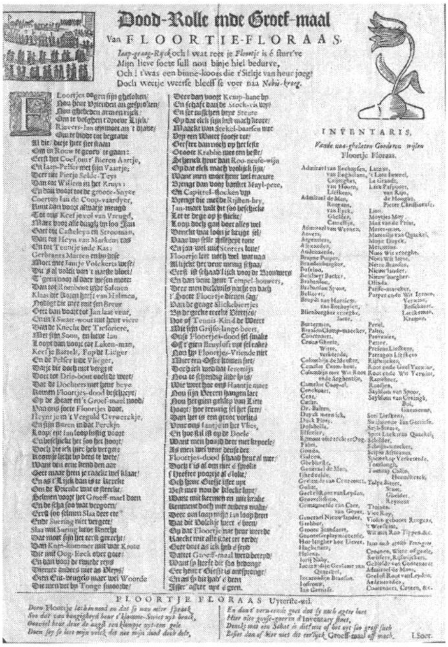

Dood-Rolle ende Groef-maal

Van FLOORTIE-FLORAAS.

Laap-graag-Ryck och! wat reet je *Floortje* is ĕ sturr've
Mijn lieve soete sull nou binje hiel bedurve,
Och! t'was een binne-koors die t'Sieltje van heur joeg!
Doch weetje weerse bleeff se voor naa *Nebis-kroeg.*

INVENTARIS,

Vande naa-ghelaten Goederen wijlen Floortje Floraas.

FIGURE 56. Jan Soet, broadside, *Dood-rolle ende Groef-maal van Floortie Floraas*, 1637. Wageningen UR Library. The theme of death (image of a funeral procession, inventory of tulips, will) runs throughout, with knowing references to *bloemisten* such as Cornelis Coelembier, Kees Bartels, and others

ing of the Will and the Division of Property by the Relatives and Heirs of the late Floortje Floraas. These productions, many of which were by Jan Soet, an Amsterdam innkeeper, or Steven van der Lust, both connected to the Wijngaertrancken, a Haarlem chamber of rhetoric, were intended to ridicule the false expectations of the *bloemisten*, dashed, as so many hopes must have been in the last months, by the death of a goddess so beloved. It was intended as humor, but the humor was dark. Among other things, it would have been salt in the wounds of the anxious tulip traders, as indeed it was intended to be. A marginal note in one pamphlet reports that a piece of satirical street theater was enacted in Haarlem, where one sour jokester wandered the streets in broad daylight holding a lantern with six candles, searching for enough cloth to make mourning cloaks for all the weeping *bloemisten*.[9]

One man grieved for his wife in February 1637, another for his money. The contrast, drawn in the satirical pamphlets, was intended to strike the reader forcefully. Yet a link was also drawn. What connection was there between the two? In the period of the plague, so severe in the summer and autumn of 1636, writers pondering the reasons for this trauma for Dutch society reflected frequently on one of its names, *de gave Gods*, the gift of God. Even medical writers such as Johan van Beverwijck, the city physician in Dordrecht, felt compelled to argue that (despite the fact that the plague was a punishment from God) the disease actually was contagious and it was therefore worth taking some precautions against it. The question was what was being punished. One writer on the plague, Van Godewijck, said that we deserved the plague because, from our earliest youth, "the world was our darling, and our greatest joy." Another, Viverius, warned in 1636 that elegant, courtly clothing, the wearing of a rapier, not only was no help against the plague but a positive cause of it. If we love our earthly pleasures too much, these authors suggested, then we forget about heaven. It was the message of *vanitas*, and God was making sure the Dutch learned it.[10]

Critics of the tulip trade were more specific in their identification of the worldliness that had earned the wrath of God. Even in the days before tulips fell in price, a few of these writers were critical of the way *floristen* seemed to put worldly concerns above those of the soul. Flowers, they insisted, were not loved for themselves, but for the money that could be made from their sale. These are not florists but goldists, one pamphlet insisted, even if the gold they worship is green. How can they be real lovers of flowers if they want them to be rare? How can they be real lovers of flowers if their favorites change with the fashions? How can they be real lovers of flowers if they want them to be weak and changeable? This must, indeed, be nothing like the adoration of God's creation that is demanded of us all. Instead it was contrary to God. There was, they said, a better flower than the tulip: the rose of Sharon, a metaphor for Christ in the Song of Solomon. This holy rose should get more attention than "the tullipa or Irias." "A flower at S[h]aron, that's what Christ was named . . . and this is the right tulip which men should plant in the garden of the heart . . . of which all other flowers are a lesson and an instruction." But, these authors complained, "the tullipa stands planted in their heart and has the upper hand." This concentration on the earthly rather than the heavenly flower could have dire consequences. One song, produced by Steven van der Lust of the Wijngaertrancken, and predating the crash, reports God's punishment of a supposedly flower-mad medieval Greek town, Verdiza, in which thirty thousand florists were said to have died in one week. In a later song, Van der Lust reminds his hearers of their own analogous situation: "Remember how we stood in September, when 508 were buried in seven days. . . ." He suggested that those still alive should think of God's plagues before honoring the tulip above God. Tulips would not help you *in extremis*, another writer pointed out: "If the voice comes from God tonight, o flower fool, your poor soul will be yanked away, and you will be plucked like a flower; who will have your tulip bulbs then? . . . and will the priceless tulip come to your aid?" Only Christ could do that; the earthly wealth of tulip bulbs would in any case be lost forever.[11]

The theme of Dutch unease with their own wealth, of discomfort, particularly within Protestant culture, with the prosperity brought by decades of growth and commercial expansion, has been well explored by a number of authors, most famously Simon Schama in his *Embarrassment of Riches*. The pleas for moderation during the plague epidemic—wear no rapiers, buy no tulips—echo a wider concern, particularly in religious circles, that wealth allowed one to grow away from God. Pamphlets like Van der Lust's *Nieu-Iaers Pest-Spieghel* (New Year's Plague-Mirror) (fig. 57) invited Haarlemmers to draw lessons from the plague in much the same way as Schama's burghers frightened themselves with omens such as beached whales or, a hundred years later, with the collapse of the sea dikes and subsequent floods. These were not natural phenomena, they felt, but warnings or punishments from God. Yet the questions raised by the reactions to the tulip trade seem to go beyond these themes. Although we find in the tulip songs a commentary on the proper relationship of God to mammon, the events of 1636–1637 evoked a series of deep concerns about how one should live in a material society, or indeed a society at all.[12]

The commentaries on the tulip trade, however, were not a wholesale criticism of luxury or of worldliness. Many pamphlets and songs made little reference to these themes and frequently dwelt more on stupidity than on sin. The most prominent strain in the pamphlet literature

FIGURE 57. Title page, Steven Theunisz van der Lust,
Nieu-Jaers Pest-Spieghel, 1637. Koninklijke Bibliotheek, The Hague.
The identification of the Wijngaertrancken, whose motto
is "Liefd' Boven Al," is prominent.

comes out as an overwhelming confusion, as if, at times, truth itself was
called into question. The question was one of value: what was worthy,
what was valuable, what was real. The tulip trade seemed to put any cer-
tainties into disarray.

It was not necessarily a bad thing, for example, to own valuable objects. But tulipmania seemed, for some observers, to negate any previously held standards of value. Pamphleteers and songsters were incredulous about the tulip trade in part because they could not conceive why a tulip should be so valued. (Of course, this view is behind most of the fascination with tulipmania today.) Not only was it not better than the Rose of Sharon, it was not noticeably better than any other flower and considerably less tangibly valuable than most standard commodities or treasures. Stories about the accidental consumption of tulip bulbs as food—apocryphal versions appear in most modern accounts of tulipmania, but they date back to Clusius at least—must owe themselves largely to these views. The initial point of such stories is the tragedy of an expensive bulb being eaten as an onion by an ignorant stranger (thus emphasizing the lack of judgment of the untutored): John Evelyn, reporting such an occurrence in Pierre Morin's house in Paris, said "one may imagine what rage *Morine* was in, at the losse. . . ." But underneath these comedies of errors lie real doubts about value. Is something actually valuable if it is essentially interchangeable with an onion? And if it is, how would you know?[13]

Another running theme questioning tulips' value, a complaint at the infiltration of the tulip among more traditional flowers—surely a discourse, at some level, on the questionable foundation of novelty or fashion—similarly dates back much earlier than the 1630s. An exchange of Haarlem *rederijkers'* poems in 1611 took the form of a complaint by the white lily that its place as top flower was being usurped by the tulip, with a robust response by the tulip defending its usefulness and pointing out that there was room for all flowers. (This has recently been shown to be part of a quarrel about immigration, with most of the flowers the names of chambers of rhetoric.) Similar statements, with real flowers (as well as *rederijkers*) in mind, were frequently made in 1636 and 1637. One of the earliest tulip songs, the *Clare Ontdeckingh der Dwaesheydt der ghener die haer tegenwoordigh laten noemen Floristen,* contains a dialogue between the flowers and Flora in which traditionally valued blooms like roses, lilies, carnations, and daisies complained that they were being "thrown away and disdained" in favor of the "newly found tulip." From what did the tulip gain her precedence? the other flowers asked. "Is it antiquity? no, what then? Is it sweetness of smell? Far from that, this fame has always been lacking to her. What does she have as a virtue, is she medicinal? Not at all: what then? She is beautiful, that's all." Another song reiterated that "She is without fragrance, odor, taste, useless for medicine"; indeed she was positively harmful: "poisonous venom." "Although I am beautiful," the tulip confessed in a third pamphlet, "my powers are small."[14]

Part of this was of course a resistance to the slow infiltration of exotic plants valued for their beauty rather than their usefulness. But it also reflects a questioning of the assignment of value to any object. A constant epithet against the tulip is *nietighe blom*, paltry flower, and it was surely a question in the minds of many during the 1636–1637 planting season how the tulip could vary so greatly in price. Flora will triumph, according to one disapproving song, "as long as her merchants give four thousand guilders for a flower which in the judgment of truth actually is worth half a *stuiver*"—that is, practically nothing. But how was this value determined—either the four thousand guilders or the half *stuiver*? There was little sense, at least among those critical of the tulip trade, that this in fact was simply determined by the market price, and that tulips, like virtually anything, have no intrinsic value. The author of the *Clare Ontdeckingh* did suggest in a note that "so long as those are found who are willing to give more, they will receive more," but the only lesson drawn from this story of supply and demand was that "greed has neither limit nor end." Clearly something was wrong with the values of part of the merchant class if, in comparison with tulips, gold and diamonds were seen as "shit."[15]

If tulips were worthless, their popularity, not to mention their expense, raised eyebrows among those with clear ideas about how money should be spent. Here the question is less about whether it is appropriate to indulge in luxuries—which the religious argument, and indeed the argument about medicinal plants, clearly implies—but rather simply whether this particular luxury was in fact worth the money. This was surely a problem in a society like the Netherlands in the early seventeenth century, where the expansion of trade to the East and West Indies brought many new products into the Dutch ports. With the material culture of the country changing, and with more money in many people's pockets to buy new products, who was to say what they should cost, especially if they were in demand? The same questions must have gripped those engaged in the art market and in the market for natural curiosities, a group that, in any case, overlapped significantly with the buyers and sellers of tulips. Even a verse defending the tulip invited derision to be cast on those for whom collecting shells and "the skin of dead bodies of bird or fish" was a pleasure, who placed "little plants and leaves in curious little drawers in the best room in the house" and "keep them like a treasure." How do you know that something is actually valuable if someone values it but you do not? Paintings themselves apparently had to be excused as useful to those casting aspersions on the tulip. There are plenty of other things made for the "pleasure of the eye," the author of the *Clare Ontdeckingh* wrote, such as paintings, engravings, costly buildings and clothing; but these give employment to their makers, and in the case of paintings "have great use as depictions of stories and memorable histories." The tulip had none of these but was "an empty plant," which would provide the same pleasure as—that is, no more pleasure than—a cheaper lily or a rose. Beauty is no measure of value, in other words, and any esteem to be bestowed on paintings results from an ability to set moral examples or to put food on the table. Yet even with this narrow conception of usefulness it must have been hard to set, or to justify, their price.[16]

By valuing tulips over God, or indeed by valuing tulips over gold, *floristen* were showing a deplorable laxity of judgment. The tulip would not save you; the tulip would not buy your bread (or if it did, it would not for long). For the tulip was not only overvalued, the pamphlets claimed, but it was also unreliable. Flowers were of course longstanding *vanitas* symbols, but the comparison between the fragility of earthly wealth and flowers had a special poignancy in these circumstances. While writers made the usual comparisons, they also pointed out that tulips really *were* transitory. "Know that it is a plant," urged one author. "Where is there anything weaker than the most beautiful flowers? A mole, a mouse, a cat, a worm, a mite, a frost" will destroy the best tulip in an instant. This uncertainty had its moral dimension, which was connected to the confusion we have just noted over proper standards of value. The tulip was no object in which to place one's trust, particularly when the trust involved money and credit. "All those who build their hope on this build on sick foundations," advised one song. Another, perhaps reflecting on the fact that tulips grow best in the sandy dune soil of North Holland, drew the appropriate moral. "A flower which is planted standing on the seaside on sand is no pleasure"; with its "insecure roots," it would be killed by the first whirlwind.[17]

Of course, it was no exaggeration to say that the tulip was unreliable.

Any *bloemist* could have told you that. The inability to tell whether a bulb or offset planted in the autumn would indeed look as it had done in the blooming season made the concept of value for money particularly problematic. Even brilliantly colored tulips that were sold in good faith (a phrase much used at the time) might well turn out to be dull or plain in a subsequent season. This did not inspire confidence. In the pamphlets and tulip songs, the unreliability of the flower was partly intended to be a contrast with the reliability of God. God, not tulips, would save you; to build your life on tulips was to build on a "sick foundation." But to have poor judgment in this matter was also to have poor judgment about people. The tulip, like Flora, is in some ways a metaphor here for its own sellers; to rely on them was also to build on sand. When pamphleteers criticized the inability of *bloemisten* to judge value, some made a connection between this kind of monetary confusion and a fundamental social confusion about trust. When the tulip trade crashed, some authors suspected that it was not through any economic mechanisms that they in any case would have been ill-equipped to explain. It was rather the fault of certain deceitful practices carried out by a cabal of essentially criminal florists. One manuscript pamphlet, never published, makes dark comments about the way that a small group of twenty or thirty *bloemisten* seemed to be pulling the strings in the trade. These, the author said, were Mennonites—"are they not mostly Mennonites, fine brothers, who most of the time in their trade are false and artful, too much so for many people to be able to trade with them?" If you deal with them, you are already "half deceived." And as for the rest, "are they not Jews and bankrupts or nothing better . . . ?" Adriaen Roman made similar accusations, without pinning them on a particular group. He claimed in *Waermondt ende Gaergoedt* that "deceitful (not to say false) practices" had ruined the trade, practices such as forcing the prices up through creating apparent demand by buying up what was offered in the *collegiën* and selling on a falsely created rising market. Whether such practices actually occurred is impossible to say; certainly almost no references are made to them, only a vague charge of "deceit," which could just as likely mean simply charging ƒ1,000 for a "worthless" bulb. However, the poet Gerrit Jansz Kooch did write decades later, admittedly after a set of verses that sounds straight out of a tulip pamphlet, that Abraham de Goyer had confessed "that he himself had given twelve hundred guilders for a tulip bulb but . . . in order to animate another bad head" to do the same. It was because people did not really know the value of tulips that they could be so deceived, said the pamphleteers; and it was also because they did not really know the value of their fellow man.[18]

It was this social anxiety, this sense of not having the measure of others, that was most frightening for contemporaries. It was crucial in this society, a society anxious for order, to know just who was who. This became relevant to the tulip trade when commentators thought about luxury and consumption. Although the more religious pamphlets and songs denounce the search for profit, most seem to make finer distinctions about who was actually benefiting from the trade in tulips. For most, it was social mobility, not raw profit, that was the problem. Some of the songs specify that it is "the great" (*de grooten*), such as lords, merchants, rentiers, as well as doctors, apothecaries, and even ministers and elders of the church, who were chiefly involved in trading in tulip futures. But—as we explored in chapter 3—many made a point of widening the social spectrum to artisans, particularly weavers, who were said to have left their trades to join in the race for quick wealth. Since cloth (both linen and wool) was, next to brewing, the most important industry in Haarlem, as well as in Leiden and other towns affected by the tulip craze, the idea that the textile trade was being abandoned wholesale by most of its workers was a suggestion of real crisis. "It is indeed no small thing," stated one early pamphlet, "that people value the beautiful, necessary crafts with which God has so richly nourished the human race less than the unreliable tulips." A repeated image depicts weavers leaving or even destroying their looms in hope of something better. One song consists of the lament of a supposed Joost van Kortrijcke (from Kortrijk or Courtrai in the southern Netherlands, the origin of many immigrants to Haarlem, but perhaps also a pun on *kort rijk*, quickly rich). Joost, a weaver, recounts that, seeing his comrades Pieter, Jan, and Gillen getting money and beer in taverns as they pursued the tulip trade, "I too sprang from the loom. Tanne, I said to my wife: Break the loom in a thousand pieces. Now one can quickly become a rich man, without working." Tanne, "as willing as I was," threw her spinning wheel away, and they both hastened to the tavern.[19]

Such behavior was regarded by some pamphleteers as damaging to the economy, as well as trivializing the great advances in overseas trade

FIGURE 58. Gillis Salomonsz Rombouts, *Weaver's workplace*, c. 1656.
Frans Hals Museum, Haarlem.

for which Holland had become so famous in the past forty years. But more important in these texts than the economic effects of weavers trading in tulips is the sense that the rapid social advancement this implied was, to say the least, inappropriate. Even before the crash, *spotdichten* made much of the apparent new social circumstances of weavers made rich by tulips. "People can now live in another way," one pamphlet notes disapprovingly. Modes of transport seemed particularly to obsess these writers: weavers and tailors now apparently rode about on horses or in wagons or *calessen*, small open coaches, and even, in the winter, a sleigh. One author vented his disgust that the florists, who had themselves sprouted from the "shit wagon," had come to be able to ride around on "knightly horses." In similar fashion the fancy clothing and superior food and drink apparently enjoyed by tulip traders was criticized. "I don't know if enough velvet and satin has been made" to take care of the eventual demand, said Gaergoedt in Adriaen Roman's first dialogue. The trade, which in part took place at inns, meant that "the belly-god," Bacchus, was being worshipped, as one song put it, "with pastry, snipe and wild fowl, a glass of wine la la, roasted capons . . . Zandvoort fish, the best on the stall . . ." Beer was no longer good enough for such people; even wine was nearly beneath them, and we hear tell of banquets with tobacco, brandy, and sugared wine. In short, everyone lived like princes and counts. Or so we are told.[20]

Of course, as we learned in chapter 3, this picture of the tulip trade as overwhelmed by the lower orders, by weavers doing piecework in their homes, is not substantiated by the evidence. As we discovered, if we look at the known *bloemisten*, thinking about factors such as marriage, property ownership, church membership, and trade relations, we find that those taking part formed a relatively small and fairly homogeneous group, consisting mainly of middle-level merchants, professional men, painters, and people mainly on the higher level of the skilled craftsmen. Although many of those interested in tulips were involved in craft trades such as textiles or brewing, they were at the very least among the petty bourgeoisie. Even in some of the pamphlet literature, we discover that we are not talking about the dregs of society. In Adriaen Roman's dialogues, Gaergoedt, the spokesman for the deluded craftsmen seduced by profit, was indeed a weaver, but he was a master who clearly had some store of wealth. After the crash, he laments the fact that he had spent his money on flowers rather than buying more looms; and his problem in February 1637 was that, despite the textile trade being in such good condition, he could not find the journeymen he needed for his work. Elsewhere, we read that craftsmen were lured by the trade because they thought, "I can't earn as much in a year with all my journeymen as I can in a week in this trade, and pleasantly, too, in good company in the *comparatie*" (another word for *collegie*). Here we can perhaps recognize the middle-level craftsmen, bakers, coopers, and blacksmiths we find in the archives. In Pieter Jansz van Campen's *P.I.C. Biggel-Tranen* (Trickling Tears), a dialogue between "Rich" and "Poor" sees "Rich" collecting flowers, but not for profit, with "Poor" declaring his satisfaction that he had avoided the losses of his wealthier neighbors ("I thank my God who gives me my senses"). But these hints are few in the literature, and even Van Campen reports that "there are many poor people"; mainly, despite what we learn from archival sources, we are told in the pamphlets that tulips were traded by a "foul rabble" who thought that they could "deck themselves out as princes."[21]

One might also judge the reliability of the songs and pamphlets by looking at economic data to see if, in fact, the Joost van Kortrijckes of Haarlem or Leiden really sold up or broke the tools of their trade in their enthusiasm for the riches tulips would bring. This is harder to judge, as guild records are very incomplete for Haarlem. But if we rely on the substantial data that the economic historian N. W. Posthumus provides in his massive study of the Leiden cloth industry, we can see that no noticeable disruption in manufacturing occurred at this point that could be attributed to the wholesale abandonment of looms. Although there was a dip in production in the 1630s, it began in 1634, too early to owe anything to the tulip trade, and numbers of workers remained constant; indeed in the case of one group, producers of says, they showed a substantial increase. In Haarlem, I have found no archival comment, for example in the records of the city government or the church, that might indicate a concern about the health of industry or a drain on resources of charity because of the tulip trade and its results.[22]

It seems, then, that in fact the pamphlet literature's dramatic invocation of the whole artisanal class dropping tools in favor of tulip-trading is substantially a fantasy. Those who criticized the trade imagined the kind of world in which the ultimate consequences of quick and enormous speculative profits were played out. Yet although the pamphlets and songs cannot serve as accurate portraits of tulipmania, they do give us a window into the kind of traumas this experience will have inflicted on Dutch urban society. If the tulip trade evoked not a financial crisis but a cultural one, we can learn here, as well as in the experiences of *bloemisten*, what was so troubling about a spectacle of wholesale social change.

It is worth thinking for a moment about the texts themselves. Who was writing these songs, songs that, we can assume from the ban on their sale in Haarlem, were proving so popular that they themselves were socially destructive? Most of the pamphlets are anonymous, but we can make some judgments about their social origins in their assumption of and claim to literacy, their frequently complicated language and rhyme schemes, their occasional use of Latin and reference to ancient history, and their evident identification of honor and decency with burghers, and rich burghers at that. But we do have a few more concrete clues. As I have hinted earlier, there is a telling identification of some of the pamphlets with members of the *rederijkerskamers*, the chambers of rhetoric. These

DEN
SPIEGHEL

der Schoonheden,

Waer in verthoont worden de wonderlyke ende Schoone Wercken Godts / elck Mensche nut ende opzbaerlyck te ondersoecken / vervatet in negenthien Referepnen op de Vzage :

VVat is het alderschoonst, dat yemant kan versinnen !
Dat tusschen 'tgroot Gewelff hier is gesloten binnen.

Midsgaders / noch negentien Referepnen op den Regel :

In dese Schoonheyt elck verlustight Hert en Ooghen.

Item / noch negenthien Liedekens op desen Zin :

Ziet hier Gods wonder werck : in dese Schoone dingen.

Voor gestelt by de Vlaemsche Kamer :
De Wit Angieren,
Binnen Haerlem 1635.

Tot Haerlem :
Gedruckt by Jan Pietersz de Does inde Voor-School-steeghe / inde Witte Passer / 1636.

FIGURE 59. Title page of *Den Spieghel der Schoonheden*, 1636.
Stadsbibliotheek, Haarlem. The proceedings of a rhetorical contest
held in Haarlem around the time of the tulipmania.

chambers were amateur dramatic societies, already well established in the sixteenth century, whose members wrote songs, sometimes published in songbooks, and wrote and performed plays. Periodically the societies would sponsor rhetorical contests between chambers in different towns, sometimes associated with church festivals and, in the seventeenth century, increasingly with political events or the activities of city governments. Towns, sometimes rather grudgingly, gave financial support to the chambers, at times in return for the requirement that their members be involved in charitable activities, such as performing during the fifty-two days it took to draw the lots for the 1606 Haarlem lottery.[23]

Experts on *rederijkerskamers* have mainly reserved judgment on the social location of their members. They seem, however, to have come chiefly from the lesser bourgeoisie, and in 1591, for example, one Haarlem chamber represented its members in a document addressed to the burgemeesters as "good simple burgers and craftsmen." But although the majority came from the middle sectors of society, or even below, a significant number came from the upper and upper middling groups. One *rederijkerskamer* whose fingerprints are on some of the tulip pamphlets is the Wijngaertrancken in Haarlem, whose members included various famous artists, including Frans Hals and Salomon Bray. Its motto, *Liefd' boven al* (Love above all) appears on a number of songs, not to mention the name or the motto (*Lust na Rust,* Desire for Tranquillity) of one of its long-standing officers, Steven Theunisz van der Lust (see fig. 57 above). Van der Lust, a painter, wrote a number of plays, not to mention regularly writing for songbooks such as *Sparens Vreughden-Bron,* a Haarlem book from 1614 that contains seven of his songs. The "rethorijckers of Haarlem" (a spelling that itself reveals a *rederijker* origin) were, according to one pamphlet, central to the project of criticizing the trade. When we think about the messages being broadcast by such works, then, we have to think about their origins; although we cannot be as concrete as we would like to be about the social location of the *rederijkers'* songs, we can at least say that they represented a middle to lower-middle level viewpoint.[24]

If these writers were worried about potential social change, it is not surprising. The Dutch had seen considerable alteration in the make-up of their society in the previous forty years. With the rapid expansion of Dutch commerce, living standards were on the rise; Marcus Boxhorn, describing the towns of Holland in 1634, remarked that "many rich and

FIGURE 60. Job Berkheyde, *Rehearsal of the Wijngaertrancken Chamber of Rhetoric, Haarlem*, second half of seventeenth century. Stiftung Preußische Schlösser und Gärten, Berlin-Brandenburg.

powerful inhabitants of Holland have increased their means not a little and increase them daily through their navigations in faraway lands." Although most of those who have written about social mobility in the Netherlands in the seventeenth century have dated the real "aristocratization" of the richer burghers to the period after 1650, it is clear that, from the late sixteenth century on, wealthy men like Adriaan Pauw or Johan

Huydecoper were aping aristocratic lifestyles, even sometimes acquiring (or faking) noble titles and coats of arms. Both Marten Jan Bok and S. A. C. Dudok van Heel have found examples from this period of wealthy merchants attempting to display their descent from at the very least the oldest urban patrician families; Gerard Schaep, a regent of the Burgersweeshuis in Amsterdam, for example, had "fifteenth-century" portraits of his family made to order. Real social mobility was the background to this change, so that someone with the name of Joan Huydecoper—the name means "hide-seller"—became one of the most powerful *regents* of Amsterdam and the lord of Maarsseveen. The fashion for collecting, and indeed for gardens and for *buitenplaatsen,* weekend retreats in the countryside, was part of this movement. Huydecoper's house in Amsterdam had "a very elegant big Garden, with a Fountain, and moreover several statues in it," according to his architect, Philips Vingboons, and the explosion of the market for gardens to the north and especially the south of Haarlem's city center is also important evidence of a new vision of gardens as part of a culture of leisure. This kind of aristocratic association was obviously of central importance to the creation of a market for exotic bulbs and flowers. But rapid social advancement could also lead, both at higher and lower levels of society, to a host of other problems.[25]

In the vision of social critics, the kind of social mobility thought to result from tulipmania led to an inversion of the proper order of things. This was, of course, true of the social structure itself. An unbridled and rapid acquisition of wealth by the poorest would, if true, completely reverse the structure of wealth in society. "To whom is Flora to be compared?" asked one pamphlet: "For she now makes rich people out of the poor." This was not necessarily a good thing. Certainly it was not if the previously poor came to "dominate" society, a word used in several songs. In the pointedly named "Transformatie," a section of *Floraas Swijmel-Snicken,* we read of "Flora who made weavers and tailors and other foul rabble into coach and horse-riders, whom people saw constantly in the inn, with wine and delicious beer, dominating, almost like little lords." Jan Soet's words here were echoed in a song about weavers and tulips that appeared in a general songbook published in 1643. Mary Smul, a weaver's wife, exclaims to her neighbor, Grietje, "Away now with Weaving . . . Let us Dominate . . . I mean to wear a Lady's clothing within half a year. . . ."[26]

Underpinning such a wholesale social change, pamphleteers thought, was a series of other disturbing inversions. In the first place, it was not just that artisans were supposedly living like counts, but that they had got to this state through gambling rather than through honest toil. Although merchants were forever gambling themselves, betting on virtually everything they could think of, not to mention pursuing trade that was ultimately one big gamble, there was a difference between making a living through careful calculation and investment and a quick profit apparently based on nothing but air. In the sixteenth century, Ilja Veldman has recently pointed out, a popular theme of the visual culture of Dutch burghers was the importance of labor. Alongside the new vilification of poverty in this period was a new work ethic, reflected in such prints as Maarten van Heemskerck's series *Reward of Labor and Diligence* of 1572. Although after 1600 these themes cease to be prominent in books and prints, this is attributable, according to Veldman, to the thorough inculcation of these values into burgher culture; there was no need to reiterate what was obvious to everyone. Certainly the consistories of the reformed churches in the seventeenth century were hard on those demonstrating manifest idleness. In the pamphlet literature of 1636–37, much was made of the desertion of traditional industries for the tulip trade. In part the problem was, again, social advancement; a story told by Waermondt suggested that it was better (for artisans or farmers) to work than to become merchants.[27]

But idleness was only to be expected in a trade carried out (in point of fact, like many others) partly in taverns. The inversion of good labor to sinful drink—made worse by the availability of *wijnkoop*, which was cashed in on beer and wine after auctions—was obvious in pamphlets decrying not only the luxury of successful tulip buyers but the activities of those still on the make. The flight from labor involved the worshipping of the wrong god—usually Flora, but in many cases Bacchus, the god of revelry, whose "church" was the tavern. "A Christian flees from Bacchus' churches," but the *bloemisten*, on the contrary, were guilty of "continually sitting in drinking houses," wasting time and money, sinning in myriad ways. Such songs raised a series of oppositional images for the reader or listener: drinking preferred to work, idleness to labor, the tavern to the church or the workplace. And the consequences of these choices raised the specter of another inversion: the tulip preferred to the family.[28]

In this upside-down world, tulip buyers and sellers were portrayed as possessing inverted social values. Rather than working, they lived it up in taverns. But as this was simply a sign that transactions in a futures market were taking place, rather than real profit being gained, it also, writers claimed, meant that families were starving at home. A man's honor at this time was predicated on his ability to maintain his family. One *bloemist*, for example, the bookbinder Theunis Jansz, got in trouble years after the tulip craze for "daily sitting from Morning to Night on the brandy in taverns" and for treating his wife badly into the bargain; in telling him to mend his ways, the burgemeesters of Haarlem said he should behave "as a man of Honor ought to do." Yet during tulipmania, the pamphlets claimed, men ignored such invocations of honor. "People were leaving wife and child neither money nor bread at home," reported one song, and the fancy meal including Zandvoort fish of which we heard earlier was supposedly eaten while "the children were at home, with the grieving women, sitting gnawing poor rye bread from their hand." To pay their *wijnkoop* florists were said to have to sell their beds in addition to their looms, a potent image for the destruction of the family as well as its support. Although a few songs pointed out that speculation in tulips could occur through the desire to support one's family—to see one's wife wear pretty clothes and live in a beautiful house—or that women were also participating in the trade, on the whole the image that predominates is the inverted spectacle of the wise wife, grieving with the rye bread, and the foolish husband, temporarily drinking sugared wine. The eventual losses, pamphlets suggested, could lead to further family breakdown, as the disappointed florist returns home to give his "beloved wife a kiss . . . [so that she] for a time had two black eyes. . . ." But in the world of inversion, this violence could be turned around as well, and in typical carnival fashion it is sometimes the wife who is in charge. One verse paints the picture of a wife (who has already emasculated her husband by teaching him to spin) beating the man on his bare buttocks for buying such tulips as Switsers and Geele Croonen. The moral, made explicit in the song, was that if other men did not stop their tulip trading they could expect the same treatment.[29]

The world of the tulip, then, was portrayed as a world of inversion. Even the seasons were turned upside down, with a spring flower gripping the attention of society in December and January; "Let Flora sleep in the winter cold," urged Pieter de Clopper in one song. This was a world in which work and family alike were to be sacrificed for nothing. The wider point was, once again, one about judgment. Those deeming tulips to be more important than their social responsibilities had no proper sense of judgment. In this society, what was important was to have knowledge: of the proper order of things, of the way the world worked. The tulip turned this upside down, because in this new society, pamphleteers implied, there was no way really to know.[30]

This, in fact, was the true problem with social mobility. It was not just that the poor became rich. The supposed new prosperity of artisans would also have the unfortunate consequence of causing unaccountable social mixing. The weaver Gaergoedt in the dialogue *Samen-Spraeck tusschen Waermondt ende Gaergoedt* made his aspirations for the upcoming summer of 1637 clear. "I intend to have a brewery. . . . We will buy a country house, or one of the best houses in the city, and live as rentiers. . . ." He even suggested he might try to buy the office of *baljuw* "or some other great office." As these employments and this style of living would make him indistinguishable from the richest of his fellow townsmen, his speedy social rise would naturally have been of some concern for those already well established on the urban hierarchy. The idea that those of different ranks might be dealing with each other, and indeed end up on similar social levels, was a matter for serious reflection. Gaergoedt's interlocutor Waermondt, the wiser of the two in Roman's pamphlet dialogues, painted a picture of a situation that, if true, would be profoundly disturbing. "Many thought: how foolish I've been, what idiocy I've committed; here I've been walking with a gardener, there I've stood with a weaver, there I've spoken with a baker's boy, here a weaver of fashioned goods, there a letter-carrier, here a goods-carrier, there a driver, here a woman, there a girl, whom I would, before this, have scarcely thought [it right] to nod to in order to keep my honor. . . ." Such social integration or, more properly, social confusion, was unconscionable. The later songs thus comment in satisfaction on the way that after the crash weavers supposedly had to leave their fine horses to return to the "wooden horse"—that is, to the loom. The tulip trade was fine, some writers claimed, as long as it was limited to the rich, but for "Jan Alleman"—the common man—or "for those of bad blood," it was a mistake. Someone raised to riches from poverty was just a *schijn-heer*, a "seeming-gentleman"; and (as the proverb went) shoemakers should stick to their lasts.[31]

The problem of a *schijn-heer* was that you did not know if he was a *heer* or not. As we have seen, social mobility in the Netherlands had transformed, over a period of decades, craftsmen into merchants, and merchants, sometimes, into *regenten*. The social confusion that might result if this happened too quickly, as was predicted in 1637, betrays, perhaps, some discomfort with what had happened so far. How would one know how to behave in society if one was unsure precisely with whom one was dealing? This problem of confusion was exacerbated in both Amsterdam and Haarlem by the great immigration from the Spanish Netherlands which had transformed the economy and society of the western United Provinces since the late sixteenth century. Haarlem, for example, had more than doubled in population from 1572 to 1622, and this was due almost entirely to southern immigration; Amsterdam similarly grew from 30,000 in 1585 to 104,932 in 1622, and at the end of this period around 25 percent of its population consisted of immigrants from the south. Although such immigrants were often wealthy and in command of much of the investment in the main towns in the province of Holland, in fact they found it difficult to break into circles of social and political influence. This was no doubt at least in part because of the suspicion engendered, even over a long period, by the infiltration of newcomers into an established and oligarchical society. Gerbrand Adriaensz Bredero's famous play *De Spaanschen Brabander* (1617) makes this suspicion of southerners plain. The main character, Jerolimo, is an elegant bankrupt who has fled from Antwerp to Amsterdam. While ridiculing his new home in his own laughable southern accent, he plans an ultimately successful fleecing of a variety of trusting Amsterdammers taken in by his deliberately fine clothes and lordly bearing. Although directed in this case at the southerner Jerolimo, the message delivered at the end of the play is more universal: "Although you can see people, that doesn't mean you know them."[32]

The pamphlet literature about the tulip trade echoes these sentiments, resonating with a general confusion over the proper ordering of society in which middle-class authors reflected on their own position. The claims of extreme social mobility naturally fall within this category. But, as I have suggested, the problem was not just that someone who did not deserve to be rich might suddenly gain wealth, but that, through his clothing, horse, and carriage, he would become indistinguishable from those who had previously had status in the towns. In short, he would become a *schijn-heer*. Jan Soet, the Amsterdam innkeeper, poet, and at one time, like Van der Lust, member of the Wijngaertrancken, who wrote several tulip songs, made a similar point in one of his earlier works, a long poem from 1636, unconnected with tulips, called the *Hedensdaagh-sche Mantel-Eer* (Present-day Coat-Honor). In this poem Soet attacked the dominance of the search for wealth in his era; every trade, he complained, from printer to blacksmith, was obsessed with money. But the main concern for him was not so much the triumph of luxury, but rather the social confusion money brought through its blurring of the social order. Soet's preoccupations reflected a common theme of Renaissance literature, the ability, indeed the propensity, to mask one's true reality and the inability to know the truth about one's neighbor. Soet deplored a society in which "it is money that brings the honor" and "money washes off filth." Clothes make the man, and therefore "coat-honor," *mantel-eer*, might be paid to those who in fact deserved no honor at all. Soet described prostitutes who, because of their elegant clothing, were honored as ladies, declaring that "beautiful clothes hide shame." In a time of social change, nothing is set, appearances can deceive, and nothing can be relied upon. This is a problem of social status, but it is also a problem of truth. Who is telling the truth and who telling lies?[33]

As we have seen, this was a major concern for the writers of songs and pamphlets about the tulip trade. Weavers, if enriched, might end up with exactly the same exterior as merchants, and therefore the same *mantel-eer*. A verse appearing in pamphlets both before and after the crash reported that "Flora is great in these matters, that she can make the great folk so small, and the small so great, that they have much in common, and they bounce up and down together, on wagons, carts, and carriages." Everyone, according to a verse printed on a cartoon against the tulip trade, "was practically a count, people held a princely state . . . it was away with weaving now, the loom thrown on the fire, people could live in another way, a fair gelding in the stable, and every day one two three hours out in the carriage. . . ." In this situation, how was one to tell the difference between the real counts, or even the real honorable merchants, and those to whom, before this, one would scarcely have nodded?[34]

The goddess Flora, standing in for the tulip trade, was herself an example of this problem. Although her godly qualities were often positively

FIGURE 61. Rembrandt, *Saskia van Uylenburgh as Flora*,
1635. National Gallery, London.

presented in contemporary culture (see fig. 61)—the several portrayals
by Rembrandt are only one example—unsurprisingly she was less well
treated in the literature surrounding tulipmania. This was true even before the crash. In that period, the tulip was constantly personified as the
goddess, and it was her godlike qualities that made her of particular con-

cern to pamphleteers and songsters. To worship Flora, a pagan goddess, was idolatrous; Flora was compared to the Golden Calf, to Baal, to Diana of Ephesus, as the florists were portrayed as turning away from God to paganism and material gain. It was not she who had made the flowers, but God, and consequently all flowers, not just the multicolored tulips, should as godly creations be given exactly the same attention. One pamphlet noted that "every flower serves him, be it grey to the eye, yellow, white, or purple, striped flamed, stippled, the one flower makes the other beautiful. . . . But this deluded florist chooses, with his idiotic behavior, only the striped tulip." After the crash, however, we learn that Flora was not what she had seemed. To believe in the promises of Flora was to believe in lies. The problem—as we saw with Soet's prostitutes dressed as ladies—was that it was so hard to tell the difference.[35]

Like Soet's supposed ladies, Flora, the goddess, was actually a whore. In a tradition of writings about her since Boccaccio, Flora was identified here as a prostitute, the "Bloem-hoertje," or little flower whore. She promised her lovers everything, but when it came to the point it was just "a big nothing." Her beautiful appearance—her combed hair, "like a slippery mermaid," her tulip-like clothing, bordered, varied, and flamed—hid a false "knave-goddess," seductive yet, beneath it all, suffering from the pox. That Flora should turn out so different from what she had seemed was not just a failure of insight on the part of tulip buyers. The usual image of prostitutes in the Netherlands at this time was that of active seductresses, shameless in their efforts to gain a clientele (see fig. 62). Thus Flora the whore did not simply disappoint her clients; she deceived them, promising them gifts when in fact all she had to offer was wind. In one pamphlet she prepared a banquet and then, instead of allowing her guests to eat, proceeded to beat them with the spit on which the dinner had been cooked.[36]

This vision of deceit raised in its turn multiple questions about trust. Buyers' trust in their own judgment was of course called into question by the seductive lure of Flora. The goddess, the bride—and the comparison with marriage is made in several of the songs—turns out to be a whore. These events must have inspired reflections on the precarious nature of speculative trade and of the expansion into new commodities so important to Dutch commerce in the first half of the seventeenth century. But trade involves not only trust in one's own capacities, but also in the

FIGURE 62. Jan Steen, *Mauvaise Compagnie*, c. 1675.
Louvre. A prostitute steals from a client.

word of others. Flora is doubly indicted here. As deceiver, and indeed as
whore, Flora violated the codes of honor of Dutch society. Nor was it an
accident that the metaphor of whoredom should be invoked in a case of
financial disaster. Particularly for women in early modern society, sexual
accusation could imply a variety of failings, especially economic ones,
and Dutch popular literature of the period often suggested the equation
of a woman turning whore with a man going bankrupt. Either was a betrayal of social norms and a disturbance to communities, and it is im-

portant for us to note how crucial the notion of financial responsibility, including solvency, was to a definition of honor in the Netherlands at this time. In Holland, unlike in southern Europe, "bankrupt" was a common insult, equivalent to "rogue"; as scholars have noted about England and France as well, one of the worst insults that could be flung at a man was that of cheating in business. (When Christoffel van Beringen called out in public, in the Bastaert-Pijp in Haarlem in 1644, that in 1637 Pieter and Hendrick Jacob Wynants had cheated him and were "untrustworthy," he could not have touched their honor more keenly.) The tulip, in the midst of this nexus of interlocking values, was not to be trusted. Flora was a whore; she was also a swindler.[37]

But the question of potential dishonor, of lack of trust, had to extend from Flora to her acolytes. The invocations of fate, of which Flora is in some sense a representative, certainly give a sense of the invevitability of the crash: "The higher they climb, the greater they fall; so it went here, but it was all foolishness," wrote Pieter Jansz van Campen. Yet in the end it was not Flora, but individuals, who could be named, who refused to pay for tulips they had promised to buy. Jan Soet's *Dood-Rolle* ("Death-Roll") consisted of a list of mourners at the grave of Flora, with many familiar names in the funeral procession (Bol, Schoneus, De Bruyn, Coelembier, Ketelaer, Casteleyn, Bartelsz, Neckevelt, Sweerts, to name a few) and others identified by knowing hints to a clearly informed audience (see fig. 56 above). Similarly, his *Testaments Openinghe* ("Opening of the Will") mentions the signatories to the agreement coming out of the meeting on February 23 in Amsterdam, which had been published as a broadside, in the exact order in which their names had happened to appear in print. This listing of merchants implicated in the trade underlined the way that the tulip crash struck at the heart of a commercial society that by necessity relied on reputation and mutual credit. A futures trade obviously depends on trust—deals made in October did not come to fruition until June—but so did all other commercial and social transactions. As Craig Muldrew has recently shown in detail in an English study, all of social relations in the early modern period was based on a series of calculations about credit. The crucial thing for individuals was to understand fully the credit relations in which they were bound up. This period saw an increasing concern over the interconnections between the credit of households linked by reciprocal debt; if one household defaulted on its debts, this

FIGURE 63. Anon., *Allegory on Tulipmania*. Frans Hals Museum, Haarlem.

would have ramifications that would shudder through the whole of the community. This possibility was precisely what worried those prescient enough to predict a crash of the tulip trade in advance, and shocked everyone involved after the beginning of February. The author of a manuscript pamphlet from before the crash pictured the chains of credit built up around tulips as the workings of a clock. "You know well that if inside a clock a cog has just one uneven tooth, the whole thing stops." This was just what would happen if the first buyer in a chain could not pay for his tulips and pass them on (and, presumably, this also applies if it happened anywhere along the chain). And if one could not pay, and therefore none could deliver, what would happen to any individual buyer or seller? "Will he be able to maintain his credit?" Such a person would have to go to Vianen, the refuge for bankrupts, another verse advised, "for you have no chance of regaining credit here."[38]

Without honor there was no credit, and without credit no honor. The two concepts, crucial to functioning in early modern society, were mutually inextricable. Although the pamphlets and songs that burst into print in the winter of 1637 conjured up a complex of images about the social consequences of the tulip trade, some fanciful and many exaggerated, and although their tone was usually satirical and derisive, behind the scoffing were real concerns and fears for the future. It seems, from our examination of the *bloemisten*, that the wholesale social revolution imagined by pamphleteers was not in fact taking place, but rather that middle-level merchants and well-off craftsmen were taking their chances in a new and temporarily profitable trade. Yet the destruction of credit relations, and, alongside it, the destruction of trust, were not dreamed up by the fevered brains of *rederijker* songsters moralizing about a potentially disordered society. That was not imagined. That was real.

In the summer of 1637, strange scenes were enacted in various gardens in Amsterdam. On June 12, Abraham de Goyer stood in his garden by the Walepad outside of town, accompanied by the notary Barent Jansen Verbeeck and two witnesses. He was locating tulips. Verbeeck took notes. In the fourth bed, in the middle row, the fourth flower was dug up from the earth and declared to be a Purper en Wit van Quakel. Then, in the fifth bed, in the middle row, the fourth flower was dug up and identified as a Bruyne Purper. In the same bed, in the same row, the eleventh flower was lifted and found to be a Beste Juri with two offsets. They also dug up three Laten Blijenburghers. Nor was this the end of their ritual. On the same day, De Goyer and Verbeeck then went to the nearby garden of Willem Willemsz, near the Reguliershof, and found in the third bed, the middle row, the eighth flower, an Admirael Lieffgens. Now De Goyer was finished, but not Verbeeck. Five days later Jan Hendricxsz Admirael called him to his gardens in the Rozenstraat and behind his own house on the Prinsengracht, where the notary went through the process again: a Paragon Lieffgens with two offsets, a Somerschoon with three, a Latour, a Scipio, a Gouda, all put in a little box, marked and officially sealed before witnesses. Adam Bessels had done the same on May 14 with his notary, Philip Venturin, noting that the tulips were marked with little sticks with words on them: "Mombours Croonen," "Mombours gebiesde." And it happened elsewhere, too: the wine-seller Gerrit Leendertsz Bosch dug up three bulbs before a notary and witnesses in his garden on the Singel in Alkmaar on July 23, and a minutely detailed description of their location was inscribed for posterity in the notarial protocols of Baert Jansz Harenkarspel.[39]

What was going on here? What was this precision for? These scenes were the result of a culture of proof and promises, a culture that enveloped the tulip trade. Tulips were perhaps particularly susceptible to problems over trust. The nature of the flower made this so. There were perhaps two weeks in the year in which the flower's blossom—the reason for its price, high in the case of beautifully marked multicolored varieties such as the Viceroy, lower for the single- or double-coloreds less prized by connoisseurs—was actually visible to buyers. For the rest of the year, buyers had to take the promises of sellers on trust. And for sellers, unless bulbs were handed over and payment made immediately, as happened during the "dry bulb time" of June to September, it was exactly the same. Buyers could promise that they would accept the bulbs in May or June, when they were ready to be lifted, but how could sellers be sure? Precisely because of the way the bulbs were sold, the tulip trade was surely one of anxiety for both sides of any transaction.

A further difficulty was the nature of tulips themselves. One of their attractions was that they were changeable, that, suddenly, through reasons inexplicable in that era, a plain tulip could one year emerge from the bud as flamed or striped. But the process did not always work in this advantageous way. A tulip that displayed itself beautifully one year could, in the next, be plain and dull, or one of its offsets could look quite different from the original bulb. Variety was the tulip's charm, but it had a dark side: unpredictability when owners were anxious to inspire trust. This naturally caused disquiet among buyers. If someone had bought a particular variety in bulb form he wanted it to bloom just as it was promised to do. We find a variety of lawsuits such as Pieter de Clercq's against Elsgen Gysberts or her husband Huybert Jansz over a bulb bought in the summer of 1636 as a Lack van Rijn and, in the spring of 1637, "now coming up is discovered not to be such." This was such a recognized possibility that a form of usual practice developed, expounded by three tulip experts, Hans Baert, Johan Quakel, and Salomon Seys, in 1639: "here in

Town [Haarlem] the custom is, and always has been, that when someone sells a tulip bulb when growing, whether as a Gouda, or otherwise, and the tulip bulb does not bring forth such a flower, as the Seller has sold to the Buyer, that the Buyer is not obliged to receive it." But such custom was unenforceable without a court ruling, and it did not help those worrying about whether the bulbs they had would turn out as expected. Some people sought guarantees: Remeus Francken, for example, refused to pay for tulips he had bought in the summer of 1636, telling the Kleine Bank van Justitie that he "acknowledged the purchase" but "desires assurance that they are swittsers." The court refused to accept Francken's conditions, but in another case around the same time, Salomon Seys was indeed forced to declare the identity of an offset and hand over ƒ15 after Franck Pietersz de Jongh demanded, before paying for it, a financial pledge "that the flower in question must be a blijen burger."[40]

An experienced *bloemist*, though uncertain of the biological mechanisms that led to possible variation, would at least know that such variation was natural and conceivable. But even when change could be natural, there was always the possibility of deceit. How was anyone to know, when a bulb was either buried in the ground in January, or in the form of a dry bulb, dirt brushed off and wrapped in paper in July, that this bulb was in fact a Switser or a Blijenburger? Or how could one know what offsets might or might not appear on these bulbs when they were in the ground? When the cloth merchant Heyndrick Jacobsz Coninck had tried to buy the offsets of some of Andries Mahieu's bulbs in 1611, Mahieu replied, apparently amused, "Why would you want to have anything to do with my bulbs? Do you want to buy a cat in a sack[?]" (This did not prevent him from selling, nor from becoming engaged in a later quarrel over the sale.) The apparent interchangeability of bulbs was always going to lead to accusations of deception. This sometimes happened when a bulb came up otherwise than expected; Cornelis van Breugel, having bought an offset of a Bruyne Purper in Alkmaar and found that it did not in fact resemble a Bruyne Purper, asserted that the mother bulb was "a false flower" and the three offsets resulting were "false bulbs." He might as well have been accusing Flora of being a whore.[41]

It was bad enough to receive a bulb less beautiful, and therefore less valuable, than the one apparently bought. But there was always the chance you would not receive one at all. As prices rose in 1636, the main arguments over tulips involved the failure of sellers to deliver. Despite any promises previously made, the lure of a better price a few weeks down the line was apparently too much for some sellers, as we saw earlier in the case of the rabbit-seller Jan Michielsz or Jan Conijn. The Kleine Bank van Justitie in Haarlem saw a string of such cases in the summer and autumn of 1636: Teunis Jansz failed to deliver to Jan Gellinckhuysen; Jacques de Clercq failed to deliver to Cornelis Pietersz Emaus; Jan Verwer to Bartholomeus van Rijn; Andries de Preyer to Colaert Braem; and so it continued, every Tuesday and Friday, through the whole season. The desperation of Bartholomeus van Gennep, whose seller, Abraham Versluys, changed his mind about the tulips he had planned to sell Van Gennep in the course of January 22, 1636, is palpable in Van Gennep's *insinuatie* six days later. He sent a notary and witnesses to tell Versluys "that he still wished to go through with the said Sale," but if Versluys refused, he would take him to court. In the event, of course, given what happened in the following weeks, Van Gennep was better off as he was.[42]

Because of these problems inherent in buying tulips, those engaged in the trade formulated practices to try to increase the certainty that they were not, in fact, buying a cat in a sack. For example, as Franck Pietersz de Jongh asked, they could ask for some sort of financial guarantee that the tulips delivered would be the right ones, or indeed that they would be delivered at all. When Cornelis de Vogel acted as broker between some buyers in Haarlem and the Enkhuizen tobacco merchant Zacharias Lepij, he asked for security from Lepij for the eventual delivery at the same time as he offered it for his masters' later payment. It was also for this reason that Adriaen de Busscher, in the company of his buyer, Joost van Cuyck, sought out Alister van de Cruijs in the Beurs in Amsterdam on February 7. De Busscher wanted to make it crystal clear to Van Cuyck that, with Van de Cruijs as *borg*, the bulbs would indeed be delivered. Indeed, if such security was not offered, it might damage future transactions involving the same flowers. One reason Abraham van Wachtendonck protested in May 1637 against the requests for him to receive and pay ƒ550 for a pound of Centen and a pound of Switsers was that his sellers, Cornelis and Abraham de Bruyn, had refused to offer any security for the delivery. Without this, he could not prove to anyone to whom he might have sold the bulbs that he would actually have them to deliver himself when the summer came. He commented to the notary delivering Abraham de

Bruyn's *insinuatie*, "he has not been willing to put my mind at rest and in-sure the delivery at the time when I could have sold [the bulbs] with great profit. . . ." Because of this, Wachtendonck saw no reason to keep to the contract they had made. (If he had been able to sell the tulips on, Wach-tendonck would now have been facing the same problems of delivery as the De Bruyns, but this was conveniently forgotten.)[43]

Buyers also protected themselves by insisting that they see the bulbs they had bought in flower before the bulbs were lifted. That way it was easy to see that the blossom on which so much money had been spent was in fact what had been promised, neither completely different nor, in some way, lesser: poorly colored or marked, or clearly diseased. If the buyer had no chance to see his tulips, the complete anonymity of the small brown bulbs could arouse serious suspicion. Such bulbs could be absolutely anything. Jacques de Clercq of Haarlem faced such suspicions when dealing with a buyer in Enkhuizen, Barent Ferreres, inconveniently a lawyer as well as a *bloemist*. Ferreres (and perhaps partners) had failed to collect a Gouda bulb that had earlier been planted in a garden in Haarlem but now, in late September 1636, was dry and out of the ground. But Fer-reres said that he was not obliged to receive the bulb. The problem was that De Clercq "had lifted it without their knowledge and cognizance, without warning them; that he should have lifted it with their knowl-edge or at least with witnesses that they had appointed; and as this is not proper, it is not without suspicion of fraud." Without proof, De Clercq was learning, without knowledge, there could be no trust.[44]

But obviously De Clercq was equally a victim of broken promises. It was not just buyers who needed tokens of trustworthiness, but sellers as well. The well-established system of *borgen*, guarantors of payment, was much used in the tulip trade as it was in so many others, to give the seller certainty that he would receive his due. If the buyer himself could not, in the end, afford the tulips, or backed out of the transaction, the seller had the right to turn to any *borg* previously agreeing to back the buyer and re-quire the money of him. Friends and relatives, confident of the financial security of their principal, regularly stood as *borgen*, usually in expecta-tion that their services would not be required. But their availability gave not only credit to the buyer, but assurance to the seller as well.

Even buyers' visitations of tulips, which gave them assurance of the goods they had purchased, protected the seller too. If tulips could be seen in bloom, and in particular if the bulb were immediately lifted, sellers could demonstrate a commendable openness in their business affairs. No one could quarrel with such a transaction, in which both money was exchanged and the wares actually on display for the purchaser. It might, for that brief quarter-hour, not even have been a sale of futures; despite the fact that a contract had been made months earlier, this exchange could have taken place on an open market stall. It was thus not merely a convenience for buyers or a way of ensuring a smooth sale. For sellers to maintain their honor and reputation, they had to demonstrate manifest transparency in their business dealings. And someone had to witness that the seller was behaving as an honorable man.

For this reason, refusal by buyers to follow the informal rules would, for sellers, have been frustrating, even (after the crash) traumatic. Take Jan Hendricxsz Admirael's problems with Wilhelmus Tiberius. Tiberius, sometimes known as Puteanus, was rector of the Latin School in Alkmaar. He bought tulips from Admirael in 1636 but for some reason, after they had bloomed in the summer of that year, refused to collect them and pay. Admirael wrote him "various missives" urging completion of the contract, and in early July Tiberius promised to come and receive them within eight days; predictably, he did not. Admirael was beside himself. He could not dig up the bulbs without Tiberius coming to see them first, because otherwise his buyer could accuse him of passing off any old tulip bulbs, not the ones specified by their contract. Yet, since the bulbs were supposed to be out of the earth for the whole summer, while waiting for Tiberius to turn up in Amsterdam they were probably coming to harm. "The tulips [are] standing in the earth, to their great damage and ruin, and through the rain which falls daily could end up perishing and rotting," Admirael's *insinuatie* of July 16 ominously intoned. Tiberius must come within twenty-four hours or a lawsuit would result. Saying this was naturally useless, but it was crucial for Admirael, both financially and socially, for his buyer, or some credible witness, to see the tulips lifted.[45]

Here we find the explanation of the strange scenes in Amsterdam in the summer of 1637. Abraham de Goyer, Adam Bessels, and Jan Hendricxsz Admirael counted, located, dug up, and named bulbs in order to maintain their honor after the crash. If the buyers refused to come and watch—and Abraham de Goyer, for example, had been trying for weeks to get Abraham van Wachtendonck to collect his Laten Blijenburgers and

Liebert van Axele to take his Bruyne Purper, Beste Juri, and Purper en Wit van Quakel—then a notary would have to do so. If the bulbs remained in the ground, they would perish. For a seller like De Goyer, it was a difficult choice, between ruining his stock and ruining his honor. The notary might allow the saving of both.[46]

This was a decision about reputation, but it was of course also about credit. For someone like Abraham de Goyer, Adam Bessels, Jan Hendricxsz Admirael, or, for that matter, their debtors, credit and honor were intimately bound together. And intertwined with both were questions of judgment, transparency, and trust. If one could not judge properly the reputation of others—their creditworthiness, their reliability, their unlikeliness to bring other households into debt—then one's ability to function in commercial society (or society at all) would be severely impaired. And if one could not demonstrate, on a daily basis, one's own trustworthiness and identity as a man of honor, then one was equally lost.

For this reason it was important to identify and isolate bankrupts. According to Ripa's *Iconologia*, a much-translated emblem book, in some early modern societies bankrupts were forced to wear green hats; in France, Italy, and Spain they were put on display and in Italy sometimes forced to wear special clothing. In Augsburg bankrupts were identified with women, forced to sit with them at weddings. In the Netherlands, the reformed consistory censured men who failed to pay their debts or defaulted on their rent, and a bankrupt would not only have trouble maintaining his family but would feel substantially unable to take part in society. Such a person would be worthy of no credit, either in terms of money or of trust. We read in the Haarlem city records for 1639 that one man was a bankrupt and therefore "merited no belief." These questions of credit would help to explain the fears of social mixing in seventeenth-century Holland; they led to the suspicion of southern immigrants, not to mention someone who until two weeks ago was a linen weaver. Bredero's Jerolimo, after all, fled Antwerp as a bankrupt; and the same was true of the real-life Francisco Gomes da Costa, a tulip dealer living in Vianen precisely because there he could not be punished for the debts he had left in Amsterdam. But Da Costa was unusual. For honorable men, in the center of their community, reputation was everything. One had to know who was who, and one had to be known.[47]

The fact that mechanisms existed to protect *bloemisten* from the uncertainties of both the tulip and its conditions of trade might appear to indicate that the sale of tulips had always operated in an atmosphere of distrust. Although in some ways this is true, the underlying emphasis was instead still on trust: trust that parties to both sides of a transaction would indeed follow through. If a buyer could not find the cash for his purchase, at least his *borgen* would be able to do so (for if they did not, their own honor would be in question). The assumption of trust was what made trade possible at all. Sometimes, naturally, people failed to pay for the things they bought; the existence of courts like the Kleine Bank van Justitie, or, for that matter, of security for purchases testifies to that. And indeed the fact that buyers and sellers were willing to find guarantors for their payment and their delivery, or to submit to the inconveniences of arranging to see the lifting of bulbs, suggests again that to do so was to prove one's sincerity and honor.

But even these protections could fail. In August 1637, the Hoge Raad of Holland and Zeeland heard the plea of two Middelburgers who had stood as *borgen* for a purchase of tulips on February 2 for *f*3,500. The buyers, Jan Joosten Plavier of Haarlem and Jacob Jansz de Ridder of Leiden, defaulted on their payment to the seller, Anthony Beliaert, who took them to court in Middelburg. Since this court ordered them to pay, they appealed to the Hoge Raad. But their *borgen*, one of whom was Plavier's uncle, appealed themselves to the same court, saying that, despite their promises, they should not have to back up the buyers. "Neither they nor the said buyers had any knowledge of the worth of the said flowers," they claimed. The claim of ignorance is telling, and says much about why the breaking of contracts must have proved so shocking for sellers. Although it could well have been true that neither the buyers nor their guarantors knew much about flowers, to say so was an attempt to gain sympathy, because here, too, was a question of trust. Ignorance was no excuse for nonpayment, and to have guarantors as well as principals default was shocking. The far greater shattering of honor was this refusal to pay for the flowers, not only by buyers but also their *borgen*; yet in this case somehow it now became the fault of the seller, who was obliquely accused of charging far more than the tulips were worth. Susanna Sprangers, widow of Outger Cluyt (and daughter-in-law of Clusius' assistant Dirck Cluyt) was more pointed when withdrawing from a sale before the crash. Cluyt, a well-connected *liefhebber* who had written a short treatise on tulips, must not have talked much to his wife about tulips. In November 1636, soon after her husband's death, Sprangers sold a "notable party" of tulips to Lambert Massa for only *ƒ*100, far less than they were worth, and, more to the point, far less than they would have been worth a month later, when she attempted to cancel the sale. But for Sprangers this became Massa's fault. She had, as an *insinuatie* of Massa pointed out, "no knowledge of the flowers and not knowing the value of them, allowed herself to trust in your sincere dealing since you have good knowledge of this trade." The invocation of trust would have made it difficult to refuse such a request. But this was little help for Massa, who, if he accepted, would lose considerable opportunity for profit. And for Anthony Beliaert, who had sold the tulips in Middelburg, a plea of ignorance was no help at all. Not only did the system of *borgen* prove unreliable, not only did he stand to lose *ƒ*3,500, but now, despite the fact that it was his buyers who were defaulting, suddenly it was *his* honor that was in question. Given the manifest dishonor of *buyers* after the crash of 1637, for Beliaert and many other sellers such an accusation, frequently made in the pamphlets, must have seemed a heavy blow.[48]

Even for those sellers who were not explicitly accused of dishonor, the tulip crash proved a tremendous shock to notions of trust. Because of the apparent feeling of safety in numbers—"I shall do as another has done"—buyer after buyer refused either to collect bulbs or to pay what was due. As the lifting season and the following planting season came and went, sellers were placed in the position of having first to lift bulbs without the buyers present, then to have to plant them again with no resolution to their quarrels, effectively trapping them in the ground for another eight or nine months. It was the brazenness of the refusals—"I am not minded to receive them"—that seemed to gall. The frustration of sellers is only too evident in the reaction of Jacob van der Meer and Jacob van der Gheest to Willem Lourisz of Heemskerck. Van der Meer and Van der Gheest occupied the unhappy role of guardians to the children of Wouter Bartholomeusz Winckel in Alkmaar. It was his tulips that had been auctioned for *ƒ*90,000 on February 5, 1637, just as the crash was in the process of taking place. Recovering any of that vast sum would prove nearly impossible. In one lawsuit that has survived, they spent several years trying to get *ƒ*510 out of Willem Lourisz, who had bought an Anvers Festus bulb for that amount at the auction. He and his *borgen* were told to come and visit the flower in the spring of 1637 so that they could collect the bulb. The defense of the buyers, when taken to court, was that indeed they had been present at eleven o'clock on the day appointed, but no one had been there to open the gate of the garden, so, sad to say, they had to go away again. They would not be willing to take the bulb without seeing it, because (echoing the old proverb) that would be "as if one were buying a cat in a sack." The guardians were furious: of course Van der Meer had been at the garden, and even if he had not, the buyers knew well enough where he lived and could have come to find him. In any case, they said, why would the sellers fail to show the bulb and allow the completion of the transaction? There was nothing they would like more. It was impossible to believe that the buyers had actually shown up at all, and if they had really wanted the bulb they would not have allowed a small hitch to get in the way of their purchase. "The defendants are simply making do with Impertinent, unfounded, and haphazard devices, such as are used by those who do not feel like paying their debts." The tulip "had stood in bloom so beautifully at the time that the accused should have come to see it, collect it, and pay for it." Yet despite this the buyers were making "frivolous" claims. Their "blue and absurd excuses" drove Van der Meer and Van der Gheest to distraction until at least 1639. What did this behavior have to do with a culture of honor? "The defendants," they said, "ought to be ashamed."[49]

It was not, then, that no one had previously broken faith in his business dealings, whether about tulips or anything else. But what proved so upsetting for *bloemisten*, and for those observing them, was the sheer volume of broken contracts and the feeling that contracts could indeed be broken with impunity. "I hear that the *briefgens* [sales contracts] binding people are going to be torn up, and the promises will go awry, which will grieve many who still have honor," Pieter Jansz van Campen declared in one pamphlet. Without proper control, this could be not only disappointing but dangerous. Such danger had already been seen in the tulip trade, where passions could run high. In July 1636, for example, Huybert Fransz was said to have slandered Pieter Willemsz van Acht in a dispute over flowers, saying "You rogue, thief . . . deceiver," and threatening to strike him. The painter Joost van Haverbeeck went even further. In a quarrel at the end of 1635 over bulbs he was selling, which weighed less than expected, he became so overwrought at discussions about a possible compromise that he became violent, threatening to teach his buyer a lesson. This was not his first offense. Six months earlier the professional gardener David de Milt had also quarreled with Haverbeeck over tulips, and the result was that, entering his garden, De Milt had "found that almost all his flowers were destroyed, some of them pulled out of the ground, others cut off and thrown along the edges of the garden. . . ." The reasons for violence were far greater after the crash. The scene in Van Campen's pamphlet *P.I.C. Biggel-Tranen* of a pair fighting—"You shall (I swear to you) pay me in full,/Or I will get it from you with my knife or my fists"—demonstrates the kind of social breakdown pamphleteers feared might result from buyers' disregard of their obligations. Nor was this entirely fanciful. It was said that the yarn seller Jan Pietersz Geldorp, quarreling over tulips with his fellow Haarlemmer Reynier Tulckens in an Amsterdam tavern in February 1637, had not only struck him but stabbed him as well, and that he had threatened him with a knife again in Haarlem in the summer of 1638. Geldorp had to call in witnesses (the arbiters in their quarrel) to deny the charge in front of a notary. This is what happened when people acted, as some put it, "in bad faith." The solution, according to one pro-tulip song, was to make sure that only the honorable had the enjoyment of the tulip. Those more bitter about the trade drew a darker moral.[50]

"What confusion and riots, trials, quarrels, yes fights will come out of this," predicted one author just before the crash. Another provided a prophecy: that all sorts of Christians, all sorts of *floristen,* would "still dispute, yes fight, quarrel, and rage, about bulb, flower, pound good, and *asen,* like fools." It was foolish to fight over a *nietighe blom,* and that foolishness was constantly stressed in all the pamphlet literature. But in tulipmania it was the quarrels that constituted the true crisis. Such discord was antithetical to burghers adhering to a set of beliefs about the proper management of social relations in urban Dutch society. As in most early modern communities, it was considered crucial to preserve harmonious relations among members of local society, both for the maintenance of public order and the smoothing of the path for economic transactions that might otherwise go irrevocably awry. Dutch culture at this time was one of compromises, designed to keep the social order functioning. The whole existence of institutions like the Kleine Bank van Justitie in Haarlem, set up in a variety of Dutch towns in the early seventeenth century, was based on the need to mediate in order to neutralize disputes that would otherwise bring destruction to a pluralistic community. It is telling how often disputes, even those brought to courts like the Kleine Bank, were solved by sending them to arbitration by third parties. The point was to give all parties the chance to come to an amicable resolution in the company of those who understood the dispute. Without this, social chaos was just around the corner.[51]

Yet the cultural consequences of a wholesale breaking of faith were difficult for anyone to contain. It was clear that those involved in the trade were searching for order and direction; as tulips became an established feature of local society, customs evolved, experts were consulted on normal practice, and a panel of *bloemisten*, the *collegie*, exercised informal authority over the trade. Yet, lacking a guild, the trade was essentially unregulated, and those frowning on its effects found this problematic: "it is the duty and function of the political authorities to make sure that all good order in the Republic is maintained," wrote the author of the *Waerschouwinghe* in January 1637, and this duty included "creating order in this abuse of flowers. . . ." When the crash took place, the yearning for order became more acute. "Everyone feared the summer," reported the wife of Gaergoedt in the dialogue between him and Waermondt, and "I wish there had never been flowers in this country." How were these fears to be answered? The government did not in fact step in quickly to ease the concerns of the *bloemisten*. First one solution was found—the florists' meeting of February 23—then another—the Hof van Holland's pronouncements of April 27. But even they provided no real resolution to conflicts, asking towns only to urge their citizens to "try the *viam concordiae* and all possible methods to bring parties into friendly accord." By leaving the peacemaking largely to individuals, this provided no real solution. After months of dithering by local courts, the commission on tulips set up a year later in Haarlem went some way toward resolving disputes, but, as we saw in chapter 4, it hardly ended them. Just when order was needed, there was no one to create it.[52]

The quarrels engendered by broken promises would have been quite enough to incite a shock to the culture of social harmony in Dutch urban society. But a tradition of ridicule made it worse. "Wear your mourning, heathen Florists: But laugh, upright Christians," wrote one songster. Not everyone was crying in February 1637, and the laughter was for that reason doubly painful. Alongside the trauma of a wholesale breaking of promises and a disturbing vacuum of solutions was an extra division in local society, between the sufferers and the scoffers. The *rederijkers*, or one group among them, seemed ready-made to ridicule this new spectacle of foolishness in their society. "Let us call up the Wijngaerdenier and pray that he will curse the tullipano, For she has seduced so many men," urged another verse, calling on Steven van der Lust's own chamber of rhetoric to broadcast the blame. The publishing of *spotdichten* and pamphlets, the singing of satirical songs in the narrow streets of Haarlem, the acting out of street theater deriding the foolish florists: all were salt in the wounds for suffering *bloemisten*. More than that, they caused further conflicts. "What has followed has been a source of quarrels: For as one laughs and jeers at the Floristen, the other brings everything to light in verse . . . Just the thing to clear away revenge and anger!"one songster ironically intoned.[53]

The fall in prices occurred in early February: carnival time. In the tradition of early modern carnival, those watching the tulip trade invoked a host of inversions in a society almost crying out for ridicule. In the vision of the pamphleteers, the world was indeed turned upside down, with women beating their husbands and a summer flower the focus of attention just at the time when it was not in bloom. Tulipmania also invited an apparent inversion of values: Flora worshipped instead of God, drink preferred to labor, and an apparently worthless flower prized above all the riches of the earth. And no greater inversion could have taken place than the mass advancement of the weavers and tailors of north Holland to the status of carriage-riders and eaters of the best Zandvoort fish. We can see the carnivalesque element to the rhetoric in the prints and paintings inspired by the crash. Jan Brueghel's painted allegory on the tulip trade, for example, which pictures scenes of *bloemisten* discussing flowers, weighing bulbs, and paying, all under the escutcheon of a red and white striped tulip, uses the stock image of apes as fools (see plate 12). Even "Floraes Mallewagen," painted by Hendrik Pot and subsequently issued as a print, owes its theme in part to carnival (see plate 13 and fig. 64). The wagon with sails, powered by the wind, derives in part from the wind chariot of mathematician Simon Stevin, intended to use wind power to sail up and down the beaches of the North Sea coast. But equally it echoes a longstanding tradition of boats of wheels, with their implied reference to Sebastian Brant's *Ship of Fools,* as centerpieces of carnival processions

De Mallewagen
aliäs
het valete der Bloemisten

FLORA

Pottebackers hoff

Generael Bol
Semper Augustus
Admirael va Horn

Liefhebberi

Wy wissen me vaeren

Hooghwagen

Gray ryck

Legaturen

Doellen

Witte Wambis

Baftart Fyy

Wstboom

Passemacker

Croehof

Ceraldt

Brabanson Voor

Andevaerde

D. Viceroy

Preunier

Spinnecop verbetert

Groote geplumiceerde

Comparity der Bloemisten
tot Harlem

FIGURE 64. Crispijn van de Passe,
Floraes Mallewagen, 1637.
Atlas van Stolk, Rotterdam.
Comparatively wealthy burghers,
with Haarlem in the background,
follow Flora's fool's chariot, saying
"we want to ride with you."

FIGURE 65. Ship of fools from Sebastian Brant,
Dat Narren schyp, 1497. British Library.

(see figs. 65 and 66). Such ships appeared in the Nuremberg Schembart carnivals of 1506 and 1539 and had a long tradition in the Germanic lands; we find them in Leiden, Nijmegen, and Bergen-op-Zoom, and in Utrecht a guild of the Blue Ship organized carnival processions in the sixteenth century. Their reappearance in these visual commentaries on tulipmania draws the obvious comparisons to carnival, as did the many references to foolishness and the fool's cap. If pamphleteers and painters wanted to criticize, they had an ample stock of images on which to draw. But were these images true? And what were the consequences of their use?[54]

In fact, pamphleteers like Jan Soet and Steven van der Lust, railing

Anno. 1539, ist ein Faßnacht erlaubt worden, die Haubtleuts zu
Schembart warn, Jacob Müffel, Martin von Plauen vnd Jochaim Tetzel,
Liesen von der Trinck stuben auß __ warn 150. Jm weiß atlaß beklai-
det mit gelb vnd Praunen Schirben auß, allso geprenet die Höll
war ein groß Schiff darin ein Pfaff __ ein Doctor, Narx vnd
Teuffel, Dasselbe ist nach __ mals von Jnen
auff dem Marckt ge. __ sturmet worden,

FIGURE 67. Title page, Cornelis van der Woude, *Tooneel van Flora*, 1637. Koninklijke Bibliotheek, The Hague. This pamphlet argued in favor of the tulip trade.

against Flora and laughing at her acolytes, were only one side of the story. Other works defended the trade, and they make it clear that the images of the tulip business put forward in the pamphlets were not necessarily to be believed. Some of these pamphlets, like the *Tooneel van Flora* (Theater of Flora), were direct criticisms of the anti-tulip literature (see fig. 67). The *Tooneel*, by the Alkmaar schoolmaster and *rederijker* Cornelis van der Woude, makes plain the social dislocation caused, not by artisanal advancement or economic collapse, but by social and cultural breakdown. When some members of the middling ranks succeeded where others had failed, when some defaulted on substantial debts to others, and when meddling pamphleteers chose to stir up trouble, this caused anger and resentment in no small measure. The title page of this late pamphlet broadcasts a sense of weariness in the face of the earlier productions, commenting that "Een voorsichtich eerlijck man; sal altijt meer ghedulden, dan straffen" (loosely, "a careful honorable man will always opt for patience rather than punishment") and "Uyt haat: spruyt smaad" ("out of hate springs slander"). In this long work, Van der Woude argued that those attacking the trade were simply jealous of the prosperity of others. There was nothing intrinisically wrong with the tulip trade, he said, because it was simply a trade like any other; and it was not only unfair but disruptive to the social order to denounce it. Another song, *De Rechte Bloem-Prijs* (The Just Price of Flowers), which specifically attacked the *Dood-Rolle* of Jan Soet and other pamphlets, argued that everyone had the right to enrich his own house. The debate still touched, then, on questions of value, on worries about capitalism, on the problem of balancing God and Mammon. But, said authors like Van der Woude, could not these questions be asked of trade in tobacco or cloth? How were tulips any different? As for the craziness of valuing tulips, if it was madness to admire the works of God, then the world was full of madmen; and if it was madness to trade in tulips, it was madness to trade *tout court*. As it would have been clear to all that no one in this society would hold that position, most of the attacks, such authors implied, were actually based on either Schadenfreude or envy.[55]

What we should believe, however, in the anti-tulip pamphlets is the picture they give of social disharmony and cultural disarray. The truth of this is clear from the archives; Van der Woude's concern, for all its concentration on the pamphlets, mirrors it too. Prominent in works like the *Tooneel van Flora* is the message that one must preserve the peace. If social harmony was the key to a happy society, tulipmania gave Dutch society an unhappy shock. Trust, honor, truth, civility, restraint: all were sacrificed when people broke their promises and could not agree. Nor did the reaction help the situation; the songs were slander and they sprang from hate. To enshrine disagreements in mocking songs and verses was, according to one author, more damaging than the tulip trade itself. Van der Woude argued that those attacking the trade should mind their own business, or, as he charmingly put it, "weed their own garden." If he was writing, he said, it was to keep the peace, "to maintain a civic modest quietness among ourselves."[56]

The world may have been turned upside down in 1636 and 1637. But as these voices from the other side of the argument suggest, this was not because in the tulip trade the poor temporarily became rich, nor, or at least not entirely, because the wise turned out to be fools. The pamphlets both for and against the tulip—not to mention many actual tales of broken promises and bad faith—make plain that the disorder of society was more serious, and perhaps more long-lasting, than that implied by carnival ridicule. But the damage was, for the most part, not financial. It was the confusion of values, the breakdown of honor, and the destruction of trust bound up in the events of the 1630s that caused this damage to Dutch society. These led, at the very least, to bitter disputes and anger, and even, it seems, to a questioning of truth and of reality itself. "What is worse than cheating or being false?" Pieter de Clopper wrote. "Let us know ourselves as liars all." What was wrong with the tulip trade was not riches, not commerce, but the setting aside of an ordered society based on trust: seeking "inconstant wealth before honor." That was a message from the middling ranks. But it was not a message to the poor, but a warning to themselves.[57]

Cabbage Fever

NINETY YEARS LATER, THEY WERE TALKING about cabbage.

It was 1720, the time of the South Sea Bubble. European capitals were awash with schemes to make money. First in Paris, then in London, governments attempted to deal with (or if possible wipe out) the mounting deficits resulting from the War of the Spanish Succession by converting their debt into more short-term financial obligations. The South Sea Company in London, for example, undertook to fund the public debt by offering to exchange its own shares, which were rising, for the more long-term and sometimes nonconvertible annuities owned by public creditors. The intense interest such schemes provoked generated a large number of other projects; companies were created to promote investment in commerce and industry of various kinds and especially to sell insurance against the vagaries of commercial life. Some of these companies were based on little more than the paper their project was printed on; others had a solid financial basis. But their abrupt appearance and large number prompted an excitement in the investment world that spread rapidly across Europe.[1]

The Dutch were not exempt. Investors from the Netherlands, driven in part by the low return they were getting at home, were keen to put their money into foreign speculative projects. They invested in John Law's Mississippi scheme in Paris in 1719 and the South Sea Company in 1720, and from June until October 1720, a spectacle similar to that in France and England played itself out on Dutch soil. Some forty-odd companies were advertised there, which, although focusing less on the public debt than those based elsewhere, also tended to specialize in insurance and lending as well as products such as cloth, sugar, and tobacco. Like some of the companies set up in England, some of these schemes were perfectly serious in intent. Local insurance companies were proposed in a variety of Dutch cities, such as Utrecht, Delft, Gouda, and The Hague, and the trend in Dutch speculation in foreign schemes was reversed to some degree in the summer of 1720, as a variety of English speculators chose to invest in the Netherlands. With trade moving beyond the Beurs, the Kalverstraat in Amsterdam—the narrow street running between the Regulierspoort and the Dam—became, for a few months, a fashionable scene of concentrated discussion of investment opportunities and the making of money. But, as in London and Paris, these schemes came to nothing. Fears of a crash in Paris started circulating as early as March 1720, and a series of financial moves, including an attempt in May to cut the price of Mississippi Company stock, led to a collapse in the Mississippi scheme in June. South Sea stock in London started to lose its value from August 18, 1720. In October, the Dutch followed suit. Shares in the Dutch companies, as well as the long-established West India Company, suddenly fell.[2]

Like tulipmania, the crashes of 1720 led, among other things, to satire. The *spotliedjes*, prints, and paintings of 1637 became the poems, prints, plays, and playing cards of 1720 and 1721. Such items were widespread in England, but even some of the English prints had their origins in the Netherlands, which in any case by this time had something of a corner on the European market for satiric cartoons. The Dutch were loud in their ridicule of the *windhandel*—trade in wind, a term that occasionally cropped up in 1637—producing plays like *Nederland in Gekheid, wegens de Wind Negotie* (Netherlands in Craziness, because of the Wind Trade) or songs like "De Actionisten in 't Dolhuis, of de Verydelde Wind Negotie" (The Stock-Jobbers in the Madhouse, or the Defeated Wind Trade). A collection of plays, prints, and songs was produced called *Het Groote Tafereel der Dwaasheid* (The Great Tableau of Folly), some of whose prints were also made into decks of playing cards for the amused delectation of the unaffected.[3]

Many of the satirical prints contained cabbage (see fig. 68). In one, Aesop pointed out a group of monkeys (a symbol of foolishness) eating cabbage while wolves chased innocent sheep. The title page of one play showed a satyr drawing back a curtain on a scene crowned with a banner that read, "De Wareld vol Cool" ("the world full of cabbage"). Beneath the banner is a crowd clamoring for pieces of paper on which were written the names of types of cabbage, including worthless cabbage, cowardly cabbage, and crazy cabbage. Another play referred to "the Company of Cabbage" as an emblem for all the ridiculous companies supposedly set up in the craze, and a third made reference to "Carrot shares" and "Cabbage selling." This medley of vegetables symbolized the mistakes of the speculation. The carrots referred to the Hoorn Company: the growing of carrots was important to the region around Hoorn, so bunches of carrots were often scattered around prints to indicate the company's particular idiocies. As for cabbage, its significance was wider. *Kool* could mean simply nonsense, craziness, and it also referred to a proverb, *koop je geen kool*: don't buy any cabbage, don't be sold a bill of goods. Don't be so stupid as to get involved in speculation.[4]

Don't buy cabbage; don't buy a cat in a sack. The apparent lessons of tulipmania were still relevant in 1720. And the Dutch knew it. Carrots and cabbage were not the only plant life to appear in the *Groote Tafereel*. Observers of the speculative mania of 1720 were clearly expected to know about tulips as well. The famous print from 1637 by Pieter Nolpe, *Floraes Gecks-kap*, showing tulips being sold in a tent in the form of a fool's cap in a scene replete with the symbolism of folly, was reprinted without comment in the *Tafereel* (see fig. 69). References to the imagery of tulipmania appeared in other Dutch cartoons of 1720, such as a print whose title referred to the fool's cap and whose image included a wind car, similar to the one depicted in the painting and print of *Floraes Mallewagen* in the 1630s (see fig. 70). Another print included a verse comparing the events of 1720 to tulipmania, which, it said, ended up sending "Flora's darlings" into poverty. Indeed, in one play tulipmania—in which "a tulip, a hyacinth, was worth sometimes a thousand pounds, When one found them to be snow white and beautifully striped"—was said to be surpassed by the bubble of 1720. The same view was expressed in verses depicting a

FIGURE 68. *Arelquyn Actionist*, cartoon from *De Groote Tafereel der Dwaasheid*, 1720. British Library. The scene of made speculators collecting shares in the form of wind (farts) is displayed by harlequins on a stage decked with carrots and cabbage. A shop sign says "Kool te Koop," cabbage for sale.

meeting of the gods on Olympus, in which Flora is invited to speak by Jupiter. She deplores the slander on her name, although she leaves the final opinion up to the listener. But certainly it made more sense, in her view, to spend a thousand guilders on "flowers beautiful in color, or scent, than for a piece of paper," a South Sea share certificate. Momus (no doubt thinking about the current price for hyacinths) responds that if the wind (trade) falls, Flora herself will end up rising. The judgment of Jupiter, king of the gods, is that both kinds of "Foolishness" should be wiped away.[5]

The appearance of tulipmania in the flood of satires in 1720 tells us several things. The first is that the tulip craze was well known to an educated eighteenth-century public. The briefest reference to tulips— including the simple reprinting of the Nolpe cartoon—was evidently enough to call forth a host of images about crazed investment in an empty product. Tulipmania also clearly served for the satirists as a warning. That was also, in part, the function of their own productions. On the title page of the *Tafereel*, in the place where the publisher's name would normally stand, we read only that the work was printed "for the warning of descendants." The same language of warning appeared not only in the propaganda of 1637, but in the supposedly more historical accounts that followed. Abraham Munting, for example, a favorite source for many later accounts, deviated from his usual matter of fact style in his practical botanical manual of 1671, *Waare Oeffening der Planten*, when it came to the tulip. Instead of only explaining tulips' cultivation and properties, as he did with other plants, Munting included a long discussion of tulipmania, mainly drawing picturesque (but unattributed) examples of prices from the third of the *Waermondt ende Gaergoedt* pamphlets. For Munting, the tulip craze was extraordinary, but it was also frightening. If this "Tulipish or crazy trade" had continued, he said, the economy of all of Holland would have been ruined. So he could not be silent on the subject, because "our Descendants should consider this as a Mirror, and as a warning" so that they will not "descend again into such improper trade."[6]

Many Dutch historians, particularly in earlier eras, have perceived their role in the same way (if they have been willing to mention tulipmania at all). For Jacob van Lennep in 1856, the tulip trade was "ridiculous," "foolish," "crazy"; P. J. Blok in 1913 reported that many households were ruined, many lives laid waste, more than figures can convey. Clearly this could occur again if similar attitudes toward capitalism should re-emerge. In 1936 J. C. H. de Pater saw tulipmania as the "dark side" of the Golden Age, an example of what can happen when enthusiastic growth goes too far. But the timing of the interest in tulipmania through the centuries shows just how often this event has been seen through the lens of

FLORAES GE
of
Afbeeldinge van't wonderlijcke Iaer van *1637* doer
de Luy Rijck ſonder goet, en Wijs ſo

De Compagnie

d'ander uytbroeyde,
waeren.

Flora

FIGURE 69.
Cornelis Danckerts,
Floraes Gecks-Kap,
cartoon from 1637
reprinted in *De Groote
Tafereel der Dwaasheid*,
1720. British Library.
The fool's cap, *compari-
tie* (*collegie*), and Flora
are all prominent.

Deez' Schets vertoond het vreemd gewest
Van Gekskop, 't geen men op het lest
Door Missispse en Bubbel-winden,
En Zuidzé stormen kwam te vinden.
Maar menig die van 't vaste land
Zyn heil ging zoeken op dat strand
Vind zig te dérelyk bedrógen,
Eerst blonk het alles schoon voor oogen:
Nu is 't vol gistig ongediert.
't Geen door de scherpe Distels zwierd
En doorns, die dat land omvangen.
Vol Schorpioenen, Spinnen, Slangen,
Waar by de Kat en Nagtuil voegt,
Die 't list verágten, om vernoegt
In duisterheid van roof te léven.
Wat vrugten kan dat land tog géven
't Geen 't allermeest bestaat in schyn.
Als Valsheid, Droefheid, en Fenyn!
Terwyl de Gekheid daar als Koning
In Quinquenpoix houd hof en woning,

Regerende door kwaá Praktyk.
Zyn nieuw gebakke Koninghryk.
Maar ach! waar zal die Vorst belanden?
Het eiland beefd. en op de stranden
Bruld een verwoede zuide-wind,
Waar door zig elk verlégen vind;
En roept het eiland krygt de stuipen.
Zo dat hy die niet wil verzuipen
Moet denken op een snelle vlugt.
Fluks maakt men op dit droef gerugt
Veel wagens naar de nieuwste moden.
Daar de Acties zyn tot 't zeil van nóden,
Om dus van Gekskops malle strand
Te ráken in een ander land.
Van Wanhoop, Droefheid, Armoed', Schanden,
Of liever naar de Néderlanden,
In Kuilenburg, of Ysselstyn,
Of in Vianen, zo 't kon zyn.
Om daar als Uilen 't hoofd te buigen;
Wyl Quinquenpoix tog leid in duigen.

FIGURE 70. *Afbeeldinge van 't zeer vermaarde Eiland Geks-Kop,* cartoon from *De Groote Tafereel der Dwaasheid,* 1720. British Library. Here the fool's head is presented as the map of an island, surrounded by smaller islands named Poverty, Sorrow, and Despair. A *mallewagen* is another echo of 1637; its flag says "na Vianen," to Vianen, where one could escape creditors.

the present. Tulipmania has always been more a warning than a historical event.[7]

Sometimes the warning was specifically about flowers. Momus was right to be concerned in the Olympian council of the gods about the potential resurrection of Flora. A hundred years after tulipmania, in the 1730s, the hyacinth was in the ascendant. Prices similar to those paid in the 1630s were being paid in the eighteenth century for these fragrant flowers, valued for their early blooming, their scent, the variety within one flower, their durability, and of course their rarity. In 1713 one British traveler, Robert Hale, brother of the dean of Bristol, visited the nursery of "the famous Flowerist of Harlem," George Voorhelm, but came away disappointed: the hyacinths were "so mighty deer y^t I did not venture to buy any." But in this situation the Dutch could easily remember the example of the tulip. A long and comparatively impenetrable satire on certain *liefhebbers* of hyacinths, *Flora's Bloem-Warande in Holland,* noted pointedly that if Flora was great in 1634–1637, she was even greater in 1720–1730, not to mention in 1731–1734, which the authors had just experienced. The satiric journalist Justus van Effen made similar remarks in his *Hollandsche Spectator*; in the guise of a worried weaver in Haarlem, he reminded his audience in dialect of the problems with the tulips a hundred years earlier—and "now we are experiencing the same times all over again." The bulb grower E. H. Krelage was in a comparable mood when he denounced an apparent gladiolimania in 1913, although his fear was more for the reputation of his own industry than for the health of the economy or the sanity of investors.[8]

But the usual time for a burst of comments about tulipmania is when authors become nervous about finance. 1720 was only the beginning. Many of the main commentators on the tulip craze had their eye firmly on their own concerns. Johann Beckmann, writing in the 1780s, noted that the price of tulips suddenly fell, "as the Lotto now falls," saying that just as people now laugh at tulipmania, their descendants would ridicule the "Lottomania" of his own times. Speculation on the stock market was also subject to his frowning gaze, and he commented that it was worth talking about tulipmania if only to give his readers a better understanding of his own era's craze for stock-jobbing. In 1808, a historian of Haarlem, Cornelis de Koning, said the trade in bulbs was similar to forward selling of shares in his era, and a similar point was made in 1830 by the Graf zu

Solms-Laubach, who plagiarized Beckmann's chapter on tulipmania in a pamphlet introduced by a worried passage about the contemporary trade in government bonds and followed by a table of prices of such bonds in Europe between 1815 and 1829. And when Beckmann was translated into English in the mid-nineteenth century, an editor commented in a footnote, "How well the author's remarks apply to the recent mania in railway scrip!"[9]

More recent times have hardly been immune to this presentism. It may not have been the case that N. W. Posthumus wrote about tulipmania in the late 1920s because of the rising stock market—he certainly never made the comparison—but the repercussions of twentieth-century crashes haunt the accounts of tulipmania thereafter. Economists instructing students and the public about speculative manias have been quick to leap on the fragile tulip, ignoring the lack of applicability to their own era. Burton Malkiel's famous *A Random Walk down Wall Street* of 1973 assumed (without actually investigating the matter) that tulip traders used "call options" rather than actually buying bulbs, which was not the case; using call options broadened the market, Malkiel opined, and "the same is true today." John Kenneth Galbraith, who published *A Short History of Financial Euphoria* in 1990, soon after the 1987 stock market crash, did not go quite so far as Malkiel in his invention of dramatic details—he preferred to rely on Mackay's propagandistic account—but he was frank enough about his intention to teach a financial lesson, remarking (ironically enough) that "there can be few fields of human endeavor in which history counts for so little as in the world of finance." Still, Galbraith intended tulipmania to teach a lesson, post-1987, about what we can do about "recurrent descent into insanity" on the markets. The same kind of tulip-studded warnings were made in innumerable newspaper articles, financial newsletters, and Web sites during the Internet stock boom of the late 1990s (see fig. 71).[10]

By adapting the tulip to contemporary concerns, authors from the very beginning have only seen what they wanted to see. Yet, ironically, this presentist vision was based on seventeenth-century fears and dreams. The story of tulipmania as a threat to social order and rational capitalism was as frightening then as it is today, and as skewed. Part of that story required the crash to be devastating, required the chastened speculators

FIGURE 71. Frame from *This Modern World, by Tom Tomorrow,*
published on www.salon.com on February 22, 1999.
Tulipmania was referred to often during the
Internet stock boom. Permission of Daniel Perkins.

to return to their proper station in life, and required tulips to become an object of loathing for the Dutch. Despite the large number of paintings of tulips after 1637, including some of the most beautiful tulip portraits, we still hear from such sources that floral still lifes would simply serve to remind Dutch viewers of their folly and shame.[11]

But this did not happen. The simple fact that the Dutch tulip industry laid its real foundations after 1637 shows that the flowers remained popular with the Dutch. The courts continued to be full of cases about tulips in 1639, but some of those cases were about tulips bought after the crash. Inventories and wills in the subsequent decades still cited tulips as precious items. As we recall, Abraham Casteleyn's collection of tulip bulbs was catalogued meticulously in 1644. And the silk merchant Abraham de Goyer, who had sold tulips in the 1630s from his garden outside the Regulierspoort, made sure in his will of 1652 to specify proudly that his wife, Elysabeth Suenis, would get to keep the "fourteen Tulpaes . . . be they planted or unplanted, for which she herself keeps the register," and which, having started with one small bulb, she "bought, sold, and bred for herself." These tulips were clearly still valuable. They were clearly still valued.[12]

~~~~~~

VALUE, OF COURSE, IS RELATIVE, AND THIS IS ONE OF THE lessons the historian, as opposed to the financial analyst, should take away from a study of tulipmania. When we ponder the legend of the tulip craze, we come away not only with the sense that the story told for nearly four hundred years is propagandistic, but also of how that propaganda both had later resonance and was specific to its own times. From Adriaen Roman to John Kenneth Galbraith to Tom Tomorrow, we are enjoined to learn from the past. The question is what lessons we should learn.

All the commentators have had things in common. They suggest that one should have knowledge, in this case sufficient knowledge not to buy cabbage or cats in sacks. They also have made clear that there is only one proper standard of value. Tulip bulbs, it is strongly implied, are not intrinsically worth a lot of money. To think they are is to be greedy and to deserve punishment, or at least to be foolish, and therefore to deserve punishment as well. The possibility of avoiding punishment is apparently not considered. Comments on tulipmania have been comments on capitalism, and they never speak of it with approval.

I am not writing to defend capitalism, but to defend a more historical sensibility. Barthes' image of the early modern Dutch as crass, passionless materialists is not worth much consideration; clearly this is a caricature. But it is worth considering the way tulipmania can indicate the complexity of what materialism we see in the early modern period. Tulips, precisely because of their novelty and their importance in a culture of collecting and self-fashioning—which not everyone shared—raised questions about knowledge and value. How do we know what is valuable? What if we cannot agree on that value? Supply and demand cannot always answer this question, especially when value is related not only to objects but to people and their relationships with each other. Tulipmania touched on both.

To understand value, one must have knowledge, and how that knowledge is acquired is crucial for the spread of taste and, potentially, the spread of conflict. The overlap between the communities of *liefhebbers* and the communities of tulip traders is evident here. Not only did similar values, including an overlap of intellectual and commercial concerns, pervade these groups, but, as we have noted, similar interests, such as an enthusiasm for art as well as nature, continued to occupy those interested in the flowers. In various ways, a culture of self-fashioning pervaded all these groups, including the craftsmen of Haarlem, and this self-fashioning was itself related both to knowledge and to commerce. In both worlds—the commercial and the intellectual—structures of authority are based in part on the display of expertise. As both art-loving and natural historical communities also necessarily involved themselves with commerce—the most obvious example being the art market—the ability to demonstrate such expertise had consequences both for status and for commercial success. To show that you were knowledgeable was to show that you were of high status, at least in a community valuing that knowledge; it would also assist you by making sure no one sold you a cat in a sack.

Problems arose, however, when people differed on standards of value. We see many instances of that in the case of tulipmania. For some, capitalism was incompatible with good religion; for others, cultural interests were incompatible with good capitalism. Elizabeth Honig writes in her wonderful essay, "Making Sense of Things," that Dutch still life paintings "do not, or at least do not obviously, ask us to judge the relative values of the things they contain."[13] For her, to ask such a question is to misconstrue seventeenth-century visions of capitalism. I would argue that such questions of value were in fact alive and well in the seventeenth century, although they did not necessarily throw up a wholesale questioning of capitalism. The propagandistic pamphlets and songs of 1637 asked many questions about relative value. God might be more important to some than Mammon, but more crucial was whether tulips were better than gold. For some the answer was tulips and for others gold, but few people said that nothing was valuable other than higher things. Some pamphlets also dealt more with the matter of who should take part in a circle of tulip experts (in other words, who was valuable rather than what was valuable) than whether tulips should in fact be an object of value. Here the question was access to knowledge, to the status that knowledge might bring, and, in particular, to the commercial success for which knowledge was so important. All these issues might be important to the same people.

To operate successfully within either an intellectual community or a commercial one—or one which, as in tulipmania, was both—one had to have knowledge, but one also had to have honor. Honor was, moreover, bound up intimately with witnessing. To be able to deal successfully in tulips, one had to know one's bulbs, but one had as well to be able to demonstrate one's probity. One of the main technical crises of tulipmania was the frustration of being unable to prove one's own honesty. If a bulb was buried in the ground, it was difficult as a seller to show that one's own knowledge was matched by one's honor. And if a buyer took the decision not to witness the lifting of a bulb, the seller was actually being denied a chance to show his honor. This, just as much as the refusal to pay for tulips, helped to cause the social and cultural disturbance of 1637. One way of ducking commercial and social responsibility in this crisis was to claim a lack of knowledge, indeed to turn your back on knowledge. If you said you did not know anything about tulips, as Susanna Sprangers and others did, the knowledge that otherwise gave both *liefhebbers* and *bloemisten* the status of expertise suddenly turned them into suspected swindlers. The con artist always knows more, is always cleverer than the victim. No wonder pamphlets suggested that the trade was being run by Mennonites, Jews, or bankrupts, or that the crash was caused by manipulation of the markets. These tropes crystallized the rejection of the knowledge on which tulip experts prided themselves.

This was, then, if not a financial crisis, or even a crisis specifically about capitalism, a crisis over a culture of value. Tulipmania shows us the way that a society in flux questioned both its social structure and its cultural tropes. Knowledge and expertise were always going to be important, but what kind of knowledge? About trade? About art? About people? About God? And if you were an expert on something someone else did not value, did that make you a fool, or even a swindler? Knowledge and expertise were ways of assigning value, and that value was, here, up for grabs. This was particularly problematic in a society that structured itself to avoid conflict. The Dutch culture of discussion and arbitration was largely successful, but it was at the very least sorely tested here. To find the *viam concordiae*, as the Hof van Holland suggested, was to assume a shared system of values. What was shared by all, however, was an understanding of the normal meaning of honor, and it was this, not bankruptcy, that worried tulip sellers in 1637.

~~~~~~

IT IS 1645. TWO MEN ARE QUARRELING. THEY CALL IN ARBITERS to make a judgment. They hire lawyers. Decisions are made based on the quality of the goods, but the parties fail to listen. One man decides to take his case to the Hof van Holland. He obtains an order from the high court that the other party may not gain judgment from any other authority, yet his opponent has already approached the *schepenen* in Haarlem. The dispute goes on.

What is the reason for this quarrel? A tulip. Not a tulip sold during tulipmania, but a Nonpareille, a bulb and several offsets clearly exchanged no earlier than 1644. The value of this tulip, its preciousness, was still so great that lawyers were paid, arbiters approached, and the bulb planted over the winter in the garden of a neutral party. The Hof van Holland, the appeals court of the province, was thought no inappropriate place for such a discussion. In 1645, tulips were still at the center of things.[14]

And who were these parties? We know their names. The seller of the Nonpareille was Abraham van Meeckeren, the Mennonite Haarlem brewer who in February 1637 backed out of a deal to exchange Swedish barley worth ƒ1,800 for an equivalent value in tulip bulbs. The scare he had had in 1637, and the ƒ160 in *rouwkoop* he had been forced to pay, seems not to have taken his mind off of tulips. And who was the unhappy buyer, the man who insisted that the offsets were too paltry and withered to go through with the sale? That was Hans Baert. We remember him, too. Hans Baert, the Haarlemmer who sold tulips to so many Amsterdam merchants in early 1637, had notaries running around Amsterdam in June and September trying, with little success, to get his money back. Even the arbiters in the Nonpareille case are familiar: Cornelis Coninck, Hans Bailly, Abraham Huijgen van Adrichem, Jan Abrahamsz, all familiar from 1636 to 1637, all still involved in tulips. The painter Willem Claesz Heda, a frequent arbiter in the 1630s and accused in 1654 of planting someone else's tulip in his own garden, was hanging around the periphery of the Nonpareille case as well. All of these took the Nonpareille very seriously indeed. When Heda and another veteran of 1637, Andries van den Broecke, asked to see the bulb in March 1637, the sugar refiner Van Adrichem, who as a neutral party had it in his care, solemnly replied that "I do not know if I am allowed to let you see it . . . it is forbidden to me." The fact that Heda and Van den Broecke—not directly involved—not only wished to see the bulb but swore this before a notary in June makes the weightiness of this affair palpable.[15]

What does the Nonpareille case tell us? Why should we care that in 1645 Baert and Van Meeckeren found themselves standing in the Toelast, the inn of Teunis Dircksz Mes on the Jansstraat, and watching the Nonpareille being weighed in front of witnesses?

Why should we care? Because for these men interest in tulips was not finished. Nothing ended in 1637. For them, tulips were not suddenly loathsome. For them, lost money did not lead to chastened acceptance and a return to old ways. For them, the quarrels were not over, and the lessons were not learned. For these men the tulip trade was not a moral tableau. It was part of life, and life was not over yet in 1645.

Nor, it should be said, was the breaking of trust. That was the shock of 1637, and, for Hans Baert and Abraham van Meeckeren, that was the shock of 1645. Like the lure of the tulip, the shattered promises also remained. If they had not, tulipmania would have remained a wonder, but it would not have seemed a peril. If they had not, all those later writers would have had little to say.

GLOSSARY

aes, pl. *asen*: measure of weight, equal to 0.048 grams

beurs: stock exchange

bloemist: contemporary term for person interested in/trading in tulips

borg: financial guarantor for someone making a purchase or borrowing money

burgemeester: one of a small panel of ruling officials at the top of local government

collegie, pl. *collegiën*: a place of auction or sale, and a panel of authorities ruling over the sale

coopcedulle: document proving that a sale had taken place

curieux: a person interested in curiosities, a connoisseur

florist: contemporary term for person interested in/trading in tulips

guilder: unit of money (see "A Note on Money" below)

heer: gentleman, lord

Hof van Holland: superior court of the province of Holland

insinuatie: notarial document in which a notary records visiting someone on behalf of a client to make a demand or threat

Kleine Bank van Justitie: court of petty sessions, small claims court

Kunstkammer: collection of artifacts and rarities

liedje: song

liefhebber: connoisseur

offset: growth on a tulip bulb that eventually becomes a new bulb

rederijker: member of a chamber of rhetoric

rederijkerskamer: chamber of rhetoric: local dramatic and poetic society

regent: a member of the ruling class, holding governmental office and/or running an institution such as an orphanage

rijksdaalder: unit of money (see "A Note on Money" below)

rouwkoop: literally "grieving money": a fee to be paid by someone reneging on a commercial transaction to the other party in that transaction

schepen: alderman, also possessing legal powers

seghsman: arbiter assisting in arranging a sale

spotliedje: satiric song

spotdichten: satiric poems or songs

stuiver: unit of money (see "A Note on Money" below)

treckgelt: money paid by the seller to the highest bidder in one type of tulip auction

vinder: guild official appointed to assure the quality of the goods produced

vrienden, vrunden: close relatives/friends who formed a conscious network

vroedschap: city council

Weeskamer: Orphans' Chamber, institution managing the finances of children of whom one or both parents had died

windhandel: literally "wind trade": derogatory term for an essentially empty trade (used of tulipmania and also in 1720)

wijnkoop: a fee paid by the purchaser in a commercial transaction for entertainment, with payment indicating the sealing of the transaction

A NOTE ON MONEY

1 pond Vlaams = 6 guilders
1 rijksdaalder = 2.5 guilders
1 guilder or Carolus gulden ($f1$) = 20 stuivers
1 stuiver = 12 penningen

Prices were often written thus: f15:12:8 (= 15 guilders, 12 stuivers, 8 penningen).

In 1636, one guilder ($f1$) had the purchasing power of €10.28, or f22.65 in 2002. In 1637, one guilder had the purchasing power of €9.40, or f20.70 in 2002.

Source of figures on purchasing power: Historical currency calculator at the website of the International Institute of Social History, www2.iisg.nl/hpw/calculate2 .html.

ABBREVIATIONS

AVDGH: Archief van de Doopsgezinde Gemeente, Haarlem

AN: Archives Nationales, Paris

AWG: Archiefdienst Westfriese Gemeenten, Hoorn

BL: British Library, London

CBG: Centraal Bureau voor Genealogie, The Hague

DTB: Dopen, Trouwen, en Begraven (archival records on baptisms, marriages, and burials)

ex. cat.: exhibition catalogue

ƒ: guilder

f.: folio

GAA: Gemeentearchief Amsterdam

GAD: Gemeentearchief Delft

HGA: Haags Gemeentearchief, The Hague

GAL: Gemeentearchief Leiden

HUA: Het Utrechts Archief (formerly Gemeentearchief and Rijksarchief Utrecht)

KB: Koninklijke Bibliotheek, The Hague

KBJ: Kleine Bank van Justititie (small claims court, Haarlem)

KP: E. H. Krelage, ed., *De Pamfletten van den Tulpenwindhandel 1636–1637* (The Hague: Martinus Nijhoff, 1942)

Nat. Arch.: Nationaal Archief, The Hague (formerly ARA, Algemeen Rijksarchief)

NA: Notariëel Archief

NHA: Het Noord-Hollands Archief, Haarlem (merger of the former Archiefdienst voor Kennemerland and the Rijksarchief Noord-Holland)

not.: notary

OAE: Oud-archief Enkhuizen

ONA: Oud-notariëel Archief

ORA: Oud-rechterlijk Archief

Posthumus: N. W. Posthumus, "De Speculatie in Tulpen in de Jaren 1636 en 1637 (II)." *Economisch-Historisch Jaarboek* 13 (1927): 3–85

Posthumus 1934: N. W. Posthumus, "De Speculatie in Tulpen in de Jaren 1636 en
   1637 (III)." *Economisch-Historisch Jaarboek* 18 (1934): 229–40
PRO: Public Record Office, London
RA: Rechterlijk Archief
RAA: Regionaal Archief Alkmaar
RKD: Rijksbureau Kunsthistorische Documentatie
SP: State Papers
Tp.: Transport (records of land and house sales)
UBA: University Library, University of Amsterdam
UBL: University Library, University of Leiden
UB Gent: University Library, University of Ghent
VOC: Verenigde Oost-Indische Compagnie (United East India Company)
WIC: West-Indische Compagnie (West India Company)
WK: Weeskamer (Orphan's Chamber)

NOTES

Introduction

1. NHA ONA Haarlem 173/480v–481, not. Salomon Coesaert, April 12, 1645.
2. Figures on the Dutch flower trade from Kees de Vré, "Bloemenhandel/Bollen-kweker ziet weinig in biologische teelt," *Trouw* (May 18, 2002); John Parkinson, *Paradisi in Sole Paradisus Terrestris* ([London]: no publisher, 1629), "Epistle to the Reader." The tulip book *Tot lof der eedele tulpa* is now in a private collection. I am grateful to Sam Segal for permitting me to look at his photographs of it.
3. UB Gent, Meul. 2424, "Waerschouwinghe aen alle goede Inghesetenen van ons Lieve Vaderlant, teghen de Betoverende Bedriegerie der Genen die haer laten noe-men Blomisten oft Floristen," manuscript published in E. H. Krelage, "Het Manu-script over den Tulpenwindhandel uit de Verzameling Meulman," *Economisch-Historisch Jaarboek* XXII (1943): 38.
4. William Crowne, *A True Relation of all the Remakable Places and Passages Observed in the Travels of the right honourable Thomas Lord Howard, Earle of Arundell and Surrey, primer Earle, and Earle Marshall of England, Ambassadour Extraordinary to his sacred Majesty Ferdinand the second, Emperour of Germany, Anno Domini 1636* (London: for Henry Seile, 1637), 8, 20, 67; Laurens van Zanten, *Spiegel der Gedenkweerdighste Gheschiedenissen Onses Tijts, Meestendeel voorgevallen in Europa Zedert het Jaar 1600 tot 'et Jaar 1660* (Amsterdam: Joannes van den Bergh, 1661).
5. GAA Archief 520/120/1–3, Particulier Archief Museum Amstelkring. For Cats, see HUA, Archief van de Oud-Bisschoppelijke Clerezij, invoice number 207, Johan de Roy (pseudonym for Jodocus Cats) to Boudewijn Cats, February 5, 1637. I am very grateful to Christine Kooi, who kindly sent me the quotation from Cats.
6. Theodorus Schrevelius, *Harlemias, ofte, om beter te seggen, De eerste stichtinghe der Stadt Haerlem* (Haarlem: Thomas Fonteyn, 1648), 212, 216.
7. E. H. Krelage, "Windhandel," *De Tuinbouw* I, no. 1 (January 4, 1913), 9. Krelage's of-ficial position is mentioned in *De Tuinbouw* I, no. 4 (January 13, 1913). On Krelage, see his obituary in *Haerlem Jaarboek* (1956): 14–16. His works on tulipmania (which also include a number of articles) are *Bloemenspeculatie in Nederland* (Amster-dam: P. N. van Kampen & Zoon, 1942); *Drie Eeuwen Bloembollenexport* (The Hague: Rijksuitgeverij, 1946); and *De Pamfletten van den Tulpenwindhandel 1636–1637* (The Hague: Martinus Nijhoff, 1942). Miles Kington's comments, in his article "Foot-ball hooligans stole my Tuscan church!" (*The Independent*, July 13, 2000), were placed in the mouth of a director of a fictitious center, Subject Matters, founded

to aid authors who discovered that someone else was working on the same topic on which they had spent years. The books that appeared around the time of Kington's article were Anna Pavord, *The Tulip* (London: Bloomsbury, 1999), Mike Dash, *Tulipomania: The Story of the World's Most Coveted Flower and the Extraordinary Passions it Aroused* (London: Gollancz, 1999), and Peter M. Garber, *Famous First Bubbles: The Fundamentals of Early Manias* (Cambridge, MA: MIT Press, 2000).

8. Jacques Normand, *L'Amiral* (Paris: Calmann-Lévy, 1895, but first published in three acts in 1880). The list of goods appears in many sources, but one of the earliest, following the publications of 1637, is Tobias van Domselaer, *Beschryvinge van Amsterdam* (Amsterdam: Marcus Willemsz Doornick, 1665), VI, 340; the original is in *Clare ontdeckingh der dwaesheydt der ghener die haer tegenwoordigh laten noemen Floristen* (Hoorn: Zacharias Cornelisz, 1636), but neither of these sources, unlike some later ones, takes the list as anything other than a comparison of the value of a bulb, rather than an actual sum paid for one; Charles Mackay, in his influential *Extraordinary Popular Delusions and the Madness of Crowds* (London: Richard Bentley, 1841), however, does, as do some of his followers, such as Burton G. Malkiel, *A Random Walk Down Wall Street* (New York: W. W. Norton, 1973), 31–32, not to mention a variety of historians. The comment about bulbs being thrown on the *Mesthoop* appear, among other places, in Lieuwe van Aitzema, *Saken van Staet en Oorlogh, In, ende omtrent de Vereenigde Nederlanden* (The Hague: Johann Veely, Johan Tongerloo, and Jasper Doll, 1669), II, book 17, 503–4; Abraham Munting, *Nauwkeurige Beschryving der Aard-Gewassen* (Utrecht and Leiden: François Halma and Pieter van der Aa, 1696): 910–11; Domselaer, *Beschryvinge van Amsterdam* VI, 340. Beckmann's comments are in *A History of Inventions, Discoveries and Origins*, trans. William Johnston and enlarged by William Francis and J. W. Griffith, 4th ed. (London: Henry G. Bohn, 1846), I, 27.

9. Johann Beckmann, *Beyträge zur Geschichte der Erfindungen* (Leipzig: Paul Gotthelf Kummer, 1782), 3 vols., translated as *A History of Inventions* (see n. 7 above). Abraham Munting's first work to discuss tulipmania is *Waare Oeffening der Planten* (Amsterdam: Jan Rieuwertsz, 1672), although he reproduces this account essentially verbatim in his later *Nauwkeurige Beschryving der Aard-Gewassen* (see note 7). The pamphlet that has always served as the main source for writers on this subject is Adriaen Roman, *Samen-spraeck tusschen Waermondt ende Gaergoedt, Nopende de opkomste ende ondergangh van Flora* (Haarlem: Adriaen Roman, 1637), which has been reprinted, along with its two companion pieces, in an edition by N. W. Posthumus in the *Economisch-Historisch Jaarboek* 12 (1926): 21–43. Posthumus' articles on this subject, including published documents, are "De Speculatie in Tulpen in de Jaren 1636 en 1637," *Economisch-Historisch Jaarboek* 12 (1926): 3–99; 13 (1927): 3–85; and 18 (1934): 229–40; and "The Tulip Mania in Holland in the Years 1636 and 1637," *Journal of Economic and Business History* I, no. 3 (May 1929): 434–66. Summaries of some of the documents figure as illustrations in Dash's *Tulipomania*, but no questions are asked of them. Simon Schama's account in *The Embarrassment of Riches: An Interpretation of Dutch Culture in the Golden Age* (New York: Alfred A. Knopf,

1987), 350–65, although mainly following traditional lines, is placed in a useful context of discussion about attitudes toward capitalism in the period. I should note here in the strongest terms that the documents printed by Posthumus in his 1927 and 1934 articles are not to be trusted. Posthumus not only was extremely sloppy about his transcriptions (there are errors in nearly every word), changing punctuation and spelling, pretending to transcribe when in fact he was summarizing, and leaving out sometimes important passages or information and occasionally getting citations wrong, but he or those doing the research for him also made some crucial errors, either of transcription (for example, transcribing viᵉ as 9ᵉ in one document, causing him to get the date of a transaction wrong: see Posthumus' 1927 article, henceforth cited simply as Posthumus, 46), or through his silent "translation" into either more modern or more archaic forms. Several of these "translations" of written-out numerals into Arabic ones resulted in mistakes in figures, figures on which others (e.g., Peter Garber) based price series. Thus, for example, in Posthumus, 71, he transcribed "hondertvijffentseventich" (175) as 125; even more seriously for any price series, for one document he changes "vier hondert" (400) to 4,000 guilders. I have collated all of Posthumus' documents against the originals (unless I was not allowed to, in the case of one document in the Nationaal Archief, or the document was not locatable, as in one in Hoorn) and indicate in my notes when the problems are particularly egregious. I urge anyone wishing to do further research on this subject to consult the originals rather than Posthumus' transcriptions.

10. Deborah Moggach, *Tulip Fever* (London: Vintage, 2d ed., 2000), 153. Other novels that have recently appeared incorporating tulipmania include Gregory Maguire, *Confessions of an Ugly Stepsister* (New York: ReganBooks, 1999), and Gijs IJlander, *Twee Harten op een Schotel* (Amsterdam: L. J. Veen, 1998).

11. For a general account of the Dutch economy in this period, see Jan de Vries and Ad van der Woude, *The First Modern Economy: Success, Failure, and Perseverance of the Dutch Economy, 1500–1815* (Cambridge: Cambridge University Press, 1997); a comparison with other nations can be found in Jan de Vries, *The European Economy in an Age of Crisis 1600–1750* (Cambridge: Cambridge University Press, 1976). De Vries and Van der Woude note (p. 59) that more than 60 percent of the population of the province of Holland was urban. For an overview of Dutch trade, see especially Jonathan Israel, *Dutch Primacy in World Trade 1585–1740* (Oxford: Clarendon Press, 1989). Among the general treatments of Dutch society in the period, see Jonathan Israel, *The Dutch Republic: Its Rise, Greatness, and Fall 1477–1806* (Oxford: Oxford University Press, 1995); J. L. Price, *Dutch Society 1588–1713* (London: Longman, 2000); and the cultural histories by Simon Schama, *The Embarrassment of Riches*, and Willem Frijhoff and Marijke Spies, *1650: Bevochten Eendracht* (The Hague: Sdu Uitgevers, 1999). On the "general crisis" theory, see Trevor Aston, ed., *Crisis in Europe, 1560–1660* (London: Routledge and Kegan Paul, 1965) and Geoffrey Parker and Lesley M. Smith, eds., *The General Crisis of the Seventeenth Century* (London: Routledge and Kegan Paul, 1978).

12. PRO SP 84/74/15, Dudley Carleton to John Chamberlain, The Hague, October 4/14, 1616, printed in Maurice Lee, Jr., ed. *Dudley Carleton to John Chamberlain 1603-1624: Jacobean Letters* (New Brunswick, NJ: Rutgers University Press, 1972), 218. On Quellinus' sculpture on the western tympanum of the Amsterdam town hall, see Katherine Fremantle, *The Baroque Town Hall of Amsterdam* (Utrecht: Haentjens Dekker & Gumbert, 1959), 176–78.

13. Roland Barthes, "The World as Object," in Norman Bryson, ed., *Calligram: Essays in New Art History from France* (Cambridge: Cambridge University Press, 1988), 112, 113.

14. Hal Foster, "The Art of Fetishism: Notes on Dutch Still Life," *Princeton Architectural Journal* 4 (1992): 6–19.

15. Foster, 11, 17.

16. Norman Bryson, *Looking at the Overlooked: Four Essays on Still Life Painting* (Cambridge, MA: Harvard University Press, 1990): 100.

17. Schama, *The Embarrassment of Riches*. For an excellent summary and critique of other visions of the relationship of the Dutch to capitalism, especially in the realm of still-life painting, see Elizabeth Alice Honig, "Making Sense of Things: On the Motives of Dutch Still Life," *Res* 34 (Autumn 1998): 166–83.

18. De Vries and Van der Woude, *The First Modern Economy*; see also especially Israel, *Dutch Primacy in World Trade*.

19. On this see chapter 5.

20. Bryson, *Looking at the Overlooked*, 100.

21. For recent reflections on the role of microhistory in the history of science, see Paula Findlen, "The Two Cultures of Scholarship?" *Isis* 96 (2005): 230–37, and Florike Egmond and Peter Mason, *The Mammoth and the Mouse: Microhistory and Morphology* (Baltimore and London: The Johns Hopkins University Press, 1997).

22. David Freedberg, "Science, Commerce, and Art: Neglected Topics at the Junction of History and Art History," in David Freedberg and Jan de Vries, eds., *Art in History/History in Art* (Santa Monica, CA: The Getty Center for the History of Art and the Humanities, 1991), 337–428.

23. Pamela Smith and Paula Findlen, "Commerce and the Representation of Nature," the introduction to their edited collection of essays, *Merchants and Marvels: Commerce, Science, and Art in Early Modern Europe* (New York: Routledge, 2002), 1–25, gives an excellent entrée into this literature. Smith and Findlen have also been responsible for some of the most interesting work in the field. See, for example, Paula Findlen, *Possessing Nature: Museums, Collecting and Scientific Culture in Early Modern Italy* (Berkeley: University of California Press, 1994), and, on the relationship of the epistemology of craft to the history of science, Pamela Smith, *The Body of the Artisan: Art and Experience in the Scientific Revolution* (Chicago: University of Chicago Press, 2004). Many of the other works falling within the remit of Freedberg's call to action are cited in notes below, but it is worth mentioning here such recent books as Lorraine Daston and Katharine Park, *Wonders and the Order of Nature 1150-1750* (New York: Zone Books, 1998); works on the art market such as the

whole *oeuvre* of John Michael Montias and Marten Jan Bok's *Vraag en aanbod op de Nederlandse kunstmarkt* (proefschrift, Universiteit van Utrecht, 1994); books on collecting such as the influential exhibition catalogue edited by Ellinoor Bergvelt and Renée Kistemaker, *De Wereld binnen handbereik: Nederlandse kunst- en rariteitenverzamelingen 1585-1735* (ex. cat. Amsterdam, Amsterdams Historisch Museum, 1992), 2 vols., or Antoine Schnapper's *Le géant, la licorne, la tulipe: Collections et collectionneurs dans la France du XVIIe siècle* (Paris: Flammarion, 1988); on the art and science of botanical representation, Claudia Swan, *Art, Science, and Witchcraft in Early Modern Holland: Jacques de Gheyn II (1565-1629)* (Cambridge: Cambridge University Press, 2005), and Brian Ogilvie's expansive *The Science of Describing: Natural History in Renaissance Europe, 1490-1620* (Chicago: University of Chicago Press, 2006); on botanical communities and knowledge, Deborah Harkness, *The Jewel House of Art and Nature: Elizabethan London and the Social Foundations of the Scientific Revolution* (New Haven, CT: Yale University Press, forthcoming 2007); on the sale and collection of French flowers and their role in courtly society, Elizabeth Hyde, *Cultivated Power: Flowers, Culture, and Politics in the Reign of Louis XIV* (Philadelphia: University of Pennsylvania Press, 2005); on the relationship of market concepts to the art market and to representation, Elizabeth Alice Honig, *Painting and the Market in Early Modern Antwerp* (New Haven, CT: Yale University Press, 1999). My own work has been on the relationship of scholarly interaction, knowledge, and the press; see my *Impolite Learning: Conduct and Community in the Republic of Letters, 1680-1750* (New Haven, CT: Yale University Press, 1995) and, also on some of these themes, *White Lies* (forthcoming).

24. Florike Egmond and Peter Mason, eds., *The Whale Book: Whales and other Marine Animals as described by Adriaen Coenen in 1585* (London: Reaktion Books, 2003), 110.

25. Egmond and Mason note Coenen's social mixing in their introduction to *The Whale Book* (see, e.g., ix-x), and Egmond discusses the particular nature of this further in her article "Clusius, Cluyt, Saint Omer: The Origins of the Sixteenth-Century Botanical and Zoological Watercolours in *Libri Picturati* A. 16-30," *Nuncius* 20 no. 1 (2005): 67.

26. This question of the relationship between commerce and scholarship is one I have discussed in *Impolite Learning* (e.g., see chap. 1) and will also be one of the dominant themes of my forthcoming book on Jacques Saurin, *White Lies*. The theme is naturally important to the present work, both in relation to botanical communities and to collectors and tulip traders; on the natural history community, see also Ogilvie, *The Science of Describing*, 13-14.

27. On the communication of economic knowledge, see in particular the work of Clé Lesger, who attributes the economic prominence of seventeenth-century Amsterdam in part to its status as a center of the exchange of commercial information. See Clé Lesger, *Handel in Amsterdam ten tijde van de Opstand: Kooplieden, commerciële expansie en verandering in de ruimtelijke economie van de Nederlanden, ca. 1550-ca. 1630*, Amsterdamse Historische Reeks, Grote Serie 29 (Hilversum: Verloren, 2001).

28. Most famously, Steven Shapin and Simon Schaffer, *Leviathan and the Air-Pump: Hobbes, Boyle, and the Experimental Life* (Princeton, NJ: Princeton University Press, 1986), and Steven Shapin, *A Social History of Truth: Civility and Science in Seventeenth-Century England* (Chicago: University of Chicago Press, 1994).

29. See, for example, Elizabeth Honig, "The Beholder as a work of art: A study in the location of value in seventeenth-century Flemish painting," *Nederlands Kunst-historisch Jaarboek* 46 (1995): 253–97. Findlen, *Possessing Nature*, discusses the way such displays of knowledge about *naturalia* affected status in the context of seventeenth-century Italian cabinets of curiosities.

30. Willem Frijhoff and Marijke Spies, *1650: Hard-Won Unity* (London: Palgrave Macmillan, 2005); originally published in Dutch as *1650: Bevochten Eendracht* (The Hague: Sdu Uitgevers, 1999). See also, on the construction of an identity of harmony in diversity in Haarlem through the mythology of the Damiate, Willem Frijhoff, "Damiette appropriée: La mémoire de croisade, instrument de concorde civique (Haarlem XVIe–XVIIIe siècle)," *Revue du nord* (2006). I am very grateful to Willem Frijhoff for allowing me to read this article before its publication.

31. Fernand Braudel, *The Mediterranean and the Mediterranean World in the Age of Philip II*, trans. Siân Reynolds (New York: Harper and Row, 1972), I, 21–22 (preface to the first edition, 1946).

Chapter One

1. Jan Somer, *Beschrijvinge van een Zee ende Landt Reyse Naer de Levante*, 2nd ed. (Amsterdam: Joost Hargers, 1649), 4, 8v, 11–12v. Somer is identified as the son of the *baljuw* of Middelburg and described as "cort van persoene ende cruepel, gaende met een crijcke" (short of stature and crippled, walking with a crutch), in UBL Vulc. 101, Willem Jasperduyn (also known as Willem Jaspersz Parduyn) to Carolus Clusius, letter 2, Middelburg, December 16, 1593. This letter is also printed in F. W. T. Hunger, *Acht Brieven van Middelburgers aan Carolus Clusius* (Middelburg: J. C. & W. Altorffer, 1925), 6–8. Jasperduyn is the way Parduyn signed his name on these letters and the name under which they are catalogued at UBL.

2. Somer, *Beschrijvinge*, 11–12.

3. Somer, 11–12v.

4. Somer, 3, 13.

5. Somer, 4–4v, 10, 11, 29.

6. UBL Vulc. 101, Willem Jasperduyn (Parduyn) to Clusius, letter 2, Middelburg, December 16, 1593; printed in Hunger, *Acht Brieven*, 7–8.

7. UBL Vulc. 101, Jehan Somer to Clusius, Middelburg, May 8, 1597. Also printed in Hunger, *Acht Brieven*, 18–19. Clusius acknowledged the receipt of the portrait of the yellow fritillary with a citation to Somer in his *Rariorum plantarum historia* (Antwerp: Christoffel Plantijn, 1601), II, cap. xi, 153.

8. Jonathan Israel, *The Dutch Republic* (Oxford: Clarendon Press, 1995), 113, 117, 309; Jonathan Israel, *Dutch Primacy in World Trade, 1585–1740* (Oxford: Clarendon Press,

1989), 64, 159; Clé Lesger, *Handel in Amsterdam ten tijde van de Opstand* (Hilversum: Verloren, 2001), 40; Jan de Vries and Ad van der Woude, *The First Modern Economy* (Cambridge: Cambridge University Press, 1997), 354–55, 366, 383; J. G. van Dillen, *Van Rijkdom en Regenten* (The Hague: Martinus Nijhoff, 1970), 11, 117. See also W. S. Unger, "Middleburg als handelstad," *Archief* (1935): 1–177. It is regrettably difficult to conduct detailed research on early modern Middelburg because of the destruction of the municipal archive in May 1940.

9. F. W. T. Hunger, *Charles de l'Ecluse: Carolus Clusius: Nederlandse Kruidkundige 1526–1609* I (The Hague: Martinus Nijhoff, 1927), 212; Jan Briels, *Vlaamse Schilders in de Noordelijke Nederlanden in het begin van de Gouden Eeuw, 1585–1630* (Haarlem: H. J. W. Becht, 1987), 236.

10. UBL Vulc. 101, Willem Jasperduyn (Parduyn) to Clusius, letter 3, November 1, 1596, also printed in Hunger, *Acht Brieven*, 14; UBL Vulc. 101, Parduyn to Clusius, letter 4, September 8, 1599, also printed in Hunger, 17; UBL Vulc. 101, Peeter Garet to Clusius, letter 4, Amsterdam, January 30, 1602; Onno Wijnands, "Commercium Botanicum: The Diffusion of Plants in the 16th Century," in Leslie Tjon Sie Fat and Erik de Jong, eds., *The Authentic Garden* (n.p.: Clusius Foundation, 1991), 81; Brian Ogilvie, *The Science of Describing: Natural History in Renaissance Europe, 1490–1620* (Chicago: University of Chicago Press, 2006). Clusius' memorandum is printed in Hunger, *Charles de l'Ecluse* I, 267. Clusius reported on Drake's voyage in *Aliquot notae in Garciae aromatum historiam* (Antwerp: Christoffel Plantijn, 1582). The importance of VOC towns for collecting is mentioned by Rudolf van Gelder, "De wereld binnen handbereik," in Ellinoor Bergvelt and Renée Kistemaker, eds., *De Wereld binnen handbereik* (ex. cat. Amsterdam, Amsterdams Historisch Museum, 1992), 25. A good example of the effect on collectors of living in a VOC port is Loet Schledorn, "De Kamer Delft van de VOC: een rijke bron," in Ellinoor Bergvelt et al., eds., *Schatten in Delft: Burgers verzamelen 1600–1750* (ex. cat. Delft, Het Prinsenhof, 2002), 31–41.

11. Beatrijs Brenninkmeijer-De Rooij, "For Love of Flora: A Brief Look at Seventeenth-Century Flower Painters," in *Boeketten uit de Gouden Eeuw* (ex. cat. The Hague, Mauritshuis, 1992), 44, n. 31; on Pelletier, see Adélaïde L. Stork, "Four hundred years of tulip-growing in the Netherlands," *Text of the Clusius Lectures, 1994* (Leiden: Clusiusstichting, 1994), 10; UBL Vulc. 101, Willem Jasperduyn (Parduyn), November 1, 1596, also printed in Hunger, *Acht Brieven*, 12; Jacob Cats quoted in Laurens J. Bol, *'Goede Onbekenden': Hedendaagse herkenning en waardering van verscholen, voorbijgezien en onderschat talent* (Utrecht: Tableau, 1982), 49.

12. Laurens J. Bol, *The Bosschaert Dynasty: Painters of Flowers and Fruit* (Leigh-on-Sea: F. Lewis, 1960), 17–18; Abraham Bredius, "De Bloemschilders Bosschaert," *Oud-Holland* 31 (1913): 140; Brenninkmeijer-De Rooij, "For Love of Flora," 18–19. The suggestion that Bosschaert painted Somer's fritillary is made by Bol, *The Bosschaert Dynasty*, 18.

13. A. L. J. Vandewiele, "Wat groeide er in de tuin van Pieter van Coudenberghe," in *De Botanica in de Zuidelijke Nederlanden (einde 15e eeuw-ca.1650)* (ex. cat. Antwerp,

Museum Plantin-Moretus, 1993), 23; Ogilvie, *The Science of Describing*, 151 ff.; Henk
Zantkuyl, "Stedelijke erven en tuinen tot omstreeks 1850," in *Erf en tuin in Oud-
Amsterdam: De ontwikkeling van het omsloten erf en de stadstuinen in de oude binnen-
stad* (ex. cat. Amsterdam, Amsterdams Historisch Museum, 1982), 9–10; A. G.
Morton, *History of Botanical Science* (London: Academic Press, 1981), 120–21; Karel
Davids, "Amsterdam as a Centre of Learning in the Dutch Golden Age, c. 1580–
1700," in Patrick O'Brien et al., eds., *Urban Achievement in Early Modern Europe:
Golden Ages in Antwerp, Amsterdam and London* (Cambridge: Cambridge University
Press, 2001), 324; B. Elliott, "Le Rôle des fleurs dans les Jardins d'agrément de la
Renaissance au XIXe siècle," in Sabine van Sprang, ed., *L'Empire de Flore* (Brussels: La Renaissance du Livre, 1996), 155. On the culture of the botanical garden
in Leiden and art surrounding it, see Claudia Swan, *Art, Science, and Witchcraft in
Early Modern Holland*, and Claudia Swan, "Medical Culture at Leiden University
ca. 1600: A Social History in Prints," *Nederlands Kunsthistorisch Jaarboek* 52 (2002):
216–39. On botanical gardens in universities, see Karen Reeds, *Botany in Medieval
and Renaissance Universities* (New York and London: Garland, 1991).

14. F. W. T. Hunger, "Bernardus Paludanus (Berent ten Broecke) 1550–1633: Zijn Ver-
zamelingen en zijn Werk," in C. P. Burger and F. W. T. Hunger, eds., *Itinerario: Voyage ofte Schipvaert van Jan Huygen van Linschoten* III, 260; Roelof van Gelder, "De
wereld binnen handbereik," 25; Roelof van Gelder, "Paradijsvogels in Enkhuizen:
De relatie tussen Van Linschoten en Bernardus Paludanus," in Roelof van Gelder,
Jan Parmentier, and Vibeke Roeper, eds., *Souffrir pour parvenir: De wereld van Jan
Huygen van Linschoten* (Haarlem: Uitgeverij Arcadia, 1998), 33–34; Leslie Tjon Sie
Fat, "Clusius' Garden: A Reconstruction," in Tjon Sie Fat and De Jong, *The Authen-
tic Garden*, 3–4; Florence Hopper, "Clusius' World: The Meeting of Science and
Art," in Tjon Sie Fat and De Jong, 15; Penelope Hobhouse, *Plants in Garden History*
(London: Pavilion Books, 1992), 118.

15. Morton, *History of Botanical Science*, 118–19, 145; Hobhouse, *Plants in Garden History*, 100; Keith Thomas, *Man and the Natural World: Changing Attitudes in England
1500–1800* (London: Allen Lane, 1983), 226; Wijnands, "Commercium botanicum,"
75, 79–81; W. T. Stearn, "Préliminaires: Les fleurs et l'art, une affinité elective," in
Van Sprang, *L'Empire de Flore*, 18–19; John Parkinson, *Paradisi in Sole Paradisus Terrestris*, "Epistle to the Reader." Parkinson is referring to John Gerard, *The Herball or
Generall Historie of Plantes* (London: John Norton, 1597). On empirical observation
and botany, see especially Ogilvie, *The Science of Describing*, especially chap. 4.

16. *De Tulp: 400 jaar bron van inspiratie* (ex. cat. Lisse, Museum voor de Bloembol-
lenstreek, 1994), 3; Sam Segal, "Tulips Portrayed. The Tulip Trade in Holland in
the 17th Century," in Michiel Roding and Hans Theunissen, *The Tulip: A Symbol of
Two Nations* (Utrecht/Istanbul: M. Th. Houtsma Stichting/Turco-Dutch Friendship Association, 1993), 9–10; Turhan Baytop, "The Tulip in Istanbul during the
Ottoman Period," in Roding and Theunissen, 51; Wijnands, "Commercium botanicum," 77; Nevzat Ilhan, "The Culture of Gardens and Flowers in the Ottoman
Empire," in Tjon Sie Fat and De Jong, *The Authentic Garden*, 133; Arthur Baker, "The

Cult of the Tulip in Turkey," *Journal of the Royal Horticultural Society* LVI (1931): 238; Somer, *Beschrijvinge*, 26–26v.

17. "The Painted Garden: Turning the Pages of the Book of Tulips," *Cornucopia* 3, no. 13 (1997): 81–82; Wijnands, "Commercium botanicum," 78; Baytop, "The Tulip in Istanbul," 54; E. H. Krelage, *Drie Eeuwen Bloembollenexport* (The Hague: Rijks-uitgeverij, 1946), 454–55; Ariel Salzmann, "The Age of Tulips: Confluence and Conflict in Early Modern Consumer Culture (1550–1730)," in Donald Quataert, ed., *Consumption Studies and the History of the Ottoman Empire, 1550–1922* (Albany: State University of New York Press, 2000), 83, 94; Nicolaas de Roever, "Een Vorstelijk Ge-schenk: Een Blik op de Vaderlandsche Nijverheid in den Aanvang der Zeventiende Eeuw," *Oud-Holland* 1 (1883): 171–72; K. Heeringa, ed., *Bronnen tot de Geschiedenis van de Levantschen Handel*, RGP Grote Serie 9 (The Hague: Martinus Nijhoff, 1910), I, 270.

18. Krelage, *Drie Eeuwen*, 451–52; Ogier Ghiselin de Busbecq, *The Turkish Letters of Ogier Ghiselin de Busbecq*, trans. Edward Seymour Foster from 1633 ed. (Oxford: Clarendon Press, 1927), 24–25, Vienna, September 1, 1555; Conrad Gesner, *De Hortis Germaniae* in Valerius Cordus, *Simesusii Annotationes in Pedacii Dioscordis Anazar-bei Medica materia libros V* (n.p.: 1561), 265; Conrad Gesner to Adolph Occo, 1565, quoted in H. Graf zu Solms-Laubach, *Weizen und Tulpe und deren Geschichte* (Leip-zig: Arthur Felix, 1899), 55.

19. Baker, "Cult of the Tulip," 240; Baytop, "The Tulip in Istanbul," 52, 53; Matthias de L'Obel, *Kruydtboeck oft Beschrijvinghe van allerleye Ghewassen, Kruyderen, Hesteren, ende Gheboomten* (Antwerp: Christoffel Plantijn, 1581), 161; Petrus Hondius, *Dapes inemptae, Of de Moufe-schans/dat is, De soeticheydt Des Buyten-Levens, Vergheselschapt met de Boucken*, new ed. (Leiden: Daniel Goels, 1621), 89–94.

20. Carolus Clusius, *Rariorum aliquot Stirpium, per Pannoniam, Austriam, & vicinas quasdam Provincias observatum Historia* (Antwerp: Christoffel Plantijn, 1583), 169; Krelage, *Drie Eeuwen*, 452–53; on Syvertsz, D. A. Wittop Koning, *Compendium voor de Geschiedenis van de Pharmacie van Nederland* (Lochem/Gent: De Tijdstroom, 1986), 189; D. A. Wittop Koning, *De Handel in Geneesmiddelen te Amsterdam tot om-streeks 1637*, PhD thesis, University of Amsterdam (Purmerend: J. Muuses, 1942), 122. Claims have been made for Pieter van Coudenberghe in Antwerp as the first possessor of a tulip in the Netherlands (in 1558) by J. De Koning, *Tulipa 'Rood & Wit': 400 Jaar Tulpen in Beeld* (Leiden: Rijksherbarium/Hortus Botanicus, 1994), 9, and by Francine de Nave, "Van Hulpwetenschap tot zelfstandige discipline: De botanica in de Zuidelijke Nederlanden tijdens de 16de eeuw," in *De Botanica in de Zuidelijke Nederlanden (einde 15e eeuw–ca. 1650)* (ex. cat. Antwerp, Museum Plantin-Moretus, 1993), 14. However, this appears to spring from a misreading of Gesner's *De Hortis Germaniae*.

21. The best biography of Clusius is Hunger, *Charles de l'Ecluse*, although his extra-ordinary correspondence in the UBL still awaits comprehensive treatment. Fortu-nately a major project at the Scaliger Institute at the University of Leiden, headed by Florike Egmond, is currently investigating and digitizing this body of manu-

scripts. Details of Rudolph II's changes appear in UBL, BPL 1526-26, Clusius to Joachim Camerarius, Vienna, August 20, 1577 and Vienna, October 7, 1577. His attempts to get paid are mentioned frequently in letters up to July 1578.

22. Lipsius quoted ("jay bien entendu par mons' lipsius") by Marie de Brimeu in UBL Vulc. 101, Marie de Brimeu to Clusius, letter 2, Leiden, September 18, 1591; UBL Vulc. 101, Jan Mouton to Clusius, letter 1, Tournai, October 18, 1570; UBL Vulc. 101, Jean de Brancion to Clusius, letter 1, Malines, July 26, 1571. Brancion's "jolites turquesq[ues]," sent to him from Constantinople, are mentioned in UBL Vulc. 101, J. de Croix to Brancion, Posome, Hungary, October 5, 1572.

23. Clusius discusses his experiments with tulips in *Rariorum plantarum historia* II, cap. vii, 142–43 and, for example, UBL BPL 2596-26, Clusius to Camerarius, Vienna, April 23, 1577; these are also discussed by Hunger, *Charles de l'Ecluse* I, 352–53. Seed from Turkey is mentioned in UBL BPL 2596-26, Clusius to Camerarius, March 14, 1576, and UBL BPL 2596-26, same to same, August 12, 1584; the noblewoman's bulb is in UBL BPL 2596-26, same to same, August 24, 1576.

24. UBL Vulc. 101, De Saint-Maurice de Bellefontaine, Besançon, May 15, 1588; UBL BPL 2596-26, Clusius to Camerarius, Frankfurt, November 18, 1589; UBL BPL 2596-26, same to same, Frankfurt, August 15, 1592 O.S.

25. Justus Lipsius, *De Constantia*, trans. as *Two Bookes of Constancie* by John Stradling (London: Richard Johnes, 1595), II, 63–64; Lipsius to Clusius, June 3, 1587, quoted in Mark Morford, "The Stoic Garden," *Journal of Garden History* 7, no. 2 (1987): 168.

26. UBL Vulc. 101, Somer to Clusius, Middelburg, May 8, 1597 and Hunger, *Acht Brieven*, 19; Rembertus Dodonaeus [Rembert Dodoens], *Cruydt-Boeck* (Leiden: François van Ravelingen, 1608), pt. 2, chap. xxvii, 387; Jean Franeau, *Iardin d'Hyver ou Cabinet des Fleurs* (Douai: Pierre Borremans, 1616), 130, note (r); Parkinson, *Paradisi in Sole Paradisus Terrestris*, 8; Lipsius, *Two Bookes of Constancie*, II, 60.

27. On the transition from utility to beauty, see Helena Wille, "De Botanische Werken van R. Dodoens, C. Clusius en M. Lobelius," in *De Botanica in de Zuidelijke Nederlanden*, 33, and I. G. de Buysscher and W. de Backer, "Renaissance Tuinkunst in de Lage Landen in het Licht van de Botanische Activiteiten van de Officina Plantiniana," in Wille, 61. Examples from Thomas Hill, *The Arte of Gardening* (London: Edward Allde, 1608), 97–98; Dodonaeus, *Cruydt-Boeck* (1608 ed.), pt. 2, chap. xxvii, 391; Parkinson, *Paradisi*, 66–67; Gerard, *Herball*, 120; D. H. Cause, *De Koninglycke Hovenier* (Amsterdam: Marcus Doornick, 1676), 73. As Brian Ogilvie (*The Science of Describing*, 186) points out, despite published statements to the contrary, aesthetics was already important in naturalists' everyday work in the sixteenth century and proved a major organizing principle for Clusius in his botanical work. On the Van Ravelingens' editions of Dodonaeus, see M. Sabbe, "Een en ander over Dodoens' Cruyd-Boeck-Uitgeven van 1608 en 1618 en de Van Ravelingen's," *De Gulden Passer* n.s. 15 (1937): 89–106; Léon Voet, "Het Plantijnse Huis te Leiden," *Bijdragen en Mededelingen van het Historisch Genootschap* 75 (1961): 10–36; Léon Voet, "Christopher Plantin as a Promoter of the Science of Botany," in F. de Nave and D. Imhof, eds., *Botany in the Low Countries (end of the 15th century-ca. 1650)* (ex. cat. Antwerp,

Museum Plantin-Moretus, 1993), 39–45; Léon Voet, *The Golden Compasses* (Amsterdam: Vangendt & Co., 1969) I, 173–74; P. G. Hoftijzer, "De 'belabbering' van het boekbedrijf. De Leidse Officina Raphelengiana, 1586–1619," *De Boekenwereld* 7, no. 1 (September 1990): 8–19.

28. Parkinson, *Paradisi in Sole Paradisus Terrestris*, 9; Scudéry, "A Monsieur, de la Chesnée Monstereul, sur son Traité des Tulipes," in the Sieur de La Chesnée Monstereul, *Le Floriste François, Traittant de l'origine des Tulipes* (Caen: Eleazar Mangeant, 1654), n.p.; Pierre Morin, *Remarques necessaires pour la culture des fleurs* (Paris: Charles de Sercy, 1658), 79–80.

29. Gerard, *Herball*, 117; Clusius, *Rariorum plantarum historia* II, cap. vii, 139–40; Krelage, *Drie Eeuwen*, 458, 460. On changes in tulips in this period, see Sam Segal, *Tulips by Anthony Claesz* (Maastricht: Noortman, 1987), 1.

30. Dodonaeus, *Cruydt-Boeck* (1608 ed.), 389; Dodonaeus, *Cruydt-Boeck* (1618 ed.), 365; Dodonaeus (1608 ed.), 389.

31. NHA ONA Haarlem 133/434, not. Jacob Schoudt, June 14, 1635 (also inaccurately/incompletely printed in Posthumus, 16–17).

32. Emmanuel Sweerts, *Florilegium* (Frankfurt am Main: Anthonius Kempner, 1612); Crispijn van de Passe, *Hortus Floridus in quo rariorum & minus vulgarium florum Icones ad vivam veramq[ue] formam accuratissime delineatae* (Arnhem: Joannes Janssonius, 1614); UBL Vulc. 101, Jan Mouton to Clusius, Tournai, May 6, 1585; Mark Laird, "Parterre, Grove, and Flower Garden: European Horticulture and Planting Design in John Evelyn's Time," in Therese O'Malley and Joachim Wolschke-Bulmahn, eds., *John Evelyn's 'Elysium Britannicum' and European Gardening* (Washington, DC: Dumbarton Oaks, 1998), 205; Géza Hajós, "Renaissance Gardens in Austria," in Tjon Sie Fat and De Jong, *The Authentic Garden*, 91; John Dixon Hunt, "'But who does not know what a Dutch garden is?' The Dutch Garden in the English Imagination," in John Dixon Hunt, ed., *The Dutch Garden in the Seventeenth Century* (Washington, DC: Dumbarton Oaks, 1990), 179, 182, 187–88; De Buysscher and De Backer, "Renaissance Tuinkunst," 62.

33. S. A. C. Dudok van Heel, "Regent Families and Urban Development in Amsterdam," in Peter van Kessel and Elisja Schulte, eds., *Rome-Amsterdam: Two Growing Cities in Seventeenth-Century Europe* (Amsterdam: Amsterdam University Press, 1997), 133; S. A. C. Dudok van Heel, "Tulpen uit Amsterdam," *Maandblad Amstelodamum* 79 (January–February 1992): 2; Zantkuyl, "Stedelijke erven," 10. Abraham Casteleyn is listed as a *liefhebber* in the first edition of Crispijn van de Passe, *Den Blom-hof, inhoudende de rare oft ongemeene Blommen die op den tegenwoordighen tijdt by de Lief-hebbers in estimatie gehouden werden* (Utrecht: for Crispijn van de Passe, 1614), Abraham de Goyer in the expanded list of *liefhebbers* in the tulip appendix of later editions of Van de Passe's *Hortus Floridus* (copy used, Bodleian Vet.B2.c.1, is a made-up copy of texts from 1614–1617, but the tulip appendix is clearly later than 1614). Their property on the Walepad (De Goyer) and St. Pieterspad (Casteleyn) is taxed in 1631: J. G. and P. J. Frederiks, eds., *Kohier van den Tweehonderdsten Penning voor Amsterdam en Onderhoorige Plaatsen over 1631* (Amsterdam: Koninklijk Oud-

heidkundig Genootschap te Amsterdam, 1890), 72. De Goyer's purchases of gardens in the *paden* are detailed in GAA Arch. 5062 (Archief van Schepenen, kwijtscheldingen) no. 13, f. 234v, September 1603; Arch. 5062 no. 16, ff. 289–90, August 8, 1606; Arch. 5062 no. 18, ff. 297v–298v, May 7, 1609; Arch. 5062 no. 17, f. 163v–164, May 12, 1608; Arch. 5062, no. 20, ff. 4v–5, April 3, 1610; Arch. 5062, no. 20, ff. 227–227v, May 12, 1610; Arch. 5062, no. 29, ff. 131–131v, June 1, 1622; Arch. 5062, no. 37, ff. 86v–87, March 23, 1639. On Haarlem, see Bert Sliggers, "Buitenplaatsen aan het Zuider buiten Spaarne," in J. J. Temminck et al., *Haarlemmerhout 400 Jaar: mooier is de wereld nergens* (ex. cat. Haarlem, Frans Halsmuseum, 1984), 98. Grietgen Hendricxsdr's sale is NHA ORA Tp. 76-59/133, April 15, 1639.

34. UBL Vulc. 101, Jan Mouton to Clusius, letter 2, Tournai, December 21, 1584; UBL BPL 2724d, Christiaen Porret to Matteo Caccini, Leiden, January 6, 1610; Hondius, *De Moufe-schans* (1614 ed.), 91. Hondius is mentioned as a breeder of tulips in Dodonaeus, *Cruydt-Boeck* (1618 ed.), 1491.

35. Dodonaeus, *Cruydt-Boeck* (1608 ed.), pt. II, book VII, chap. XXVII, 388. On sociability and botany, see also Ogilvie, *The Science of Describing*, and Harkness, *The Jewel House of Art and Nature: Elizabethan London and the Social Foundations of the Scientific Revolution* (New Haven, CT: Yale University Press, forthcoming, 2007).

36. UBL Vulc. 101, Jean de Maes to Clusius, letter 11, Brussels, October 7, 1602.

37. UBL Vulc. 101, Jean de Maes to Clusius, letter 11, Brussels, October 7, 1602. L'Amoral's move to Prague is mentioned in UBL Vulc. 101, Jean de Maes to Clusius, letter 14, Brussels, February 15, 1604. Clusius refers to Boisot as an old friend in UBL BPL 2596-26, Clusius to Camerarius, London, April 21, 1581; Boisot mentions his sister's flowers and the fact that his niece is married to the postmaster in UBL Pap. 1 a, Jan Boisot to Clusius, Brussels, May 7, 1582; Jean de Maes discusses du May in UBL Vulc. 101, Jean de Maes to Clusius, letter 10, Brussels, August 16, 1602.

38. UBL BPL 2724 d, Christiaen Porret to Matteo Caccini, January 15, 1611; UBL Vulc. 101, Jan Mouton to Clusius, letter 7, Tournai, February 15, 1589; UBL Pap. 1 a, Jan Boisot to Clusius, Brussels, May 7, 1582; UBL Vulc. 101, Jacques Plateau to Clusius, letter 12, Tournai, February 8, 1602; Dodonaeus, *Cruydt-Boeck* (1618 ed.), 1491.

39. Crispijn van de Passe, *Den Blom-Hof* (1614) and *Hortus Floridus* (Bodleian copy, 1614–1617), tulip appendices; L'Obel, *Kruydtboeck*, 162; Franeau, *Iardin d'Hyver*, 126–27. Paula Findlen points out that despite social mixing, the field of study of natural history was defined by those who had been humanistically educated; she also notes the dependence of the naturalist on those much further down the social scale, and on commerce, since naturalists had to talk to tradespeople to learn about natural products. See Paula Findlen, *Possessing Nature: Museums, Collecting, and Scientific Culture in Early Modern Italy* (Berkeley: University of California Press, 1994), 157, 171.

40. Crispijn van de Passe, *Den Blom-Hof* (1614) and *Hortus Floridus* (Bodleian copy, 1614–1617), tulip appendices. Outger Cluyt is mistakenly listed as "Carolus Clutius," but because he is said to be a doctor and to live in Amsterdam, it is clearly

Outger who is intended. On Cluyt, see H. A. Bosman-Jelgersma, "Augerius Clutius (1578–1636), Apotheker, Botanicus en Geneeskundige," *Farmaceutisch Tijdschrift voor België* 59, no. 2 (March–April 1982): 167–74. [Nicolas de Valnay], *Connoissance et Culture Parfaite des Tulippes rares, des Anemones extraordinaires, des Oeillets fins, Et des belles Oreilles d'Ours panachées* (Paris: Laurent d'Houry, 1688), "Avertissement"; La Chesnée Monstereul, *Floriste françois*, 180–81.

41. Lipsius, *Two Books of Constancie* II, chap. 3, 64.

42. UBL Vulc. 101, Johannes de Jonghe to Clusius, Middelburg, May 14, 1596, also printed in Hunger, *Acht Brieven*, 3; Bibliothèque Royale, Brussels, Ms. Côte III 893, f. 146, cited in Georgina Masson, "Italian Flower Collectors' Gardens in Seventeenth Century Italy," in David R. Coffin, ed., *The Italian Garden* (Washington, DC: Dumbarton Oaks, 1972), 79; [Valnay], *Connoissance et culture parfaite*, 4–8.

43. Hunger, *L'Ecluse* I, 354; UBL BPL 2526-26, Clusius to Camerarius, Antwerp, August 19, 1581; UBL BPL 2526-26, same to same, Vienna, May 15, 1582; UBL BPL 2526-26, same to same, Leiden, July 21, 1596; UBL Vulc. 101, Marie de Brimeu to Clusius, letter 12, The Hague, August 18, 1596; UBL Vulc. 101, same to same, letter 13, The Hague, September 7, 1596; UBL Vulc. 101, same to same, Liège, September 9, 1602; UBL Vulc. 101, same to same, letter 22, Liège, July 3, 1603; UBL Vulc. 101, Jan van Hoghelande to Clusius, Leiden, June 5, 1591; UBL Vulc. 101, Jan Mouton to Clusius, letter 4, Tournai, May 6, 1585; UBL Vulc. 101, Matthias de l'Obel to Clusius, letter 1, June 18, 1601.

44. Brian Ogilvie (*The Science of Describing*, 13–14) claims that the values of the natural history community in the sixteenth century displayed "a sharp contrast with the capitalist organization of bulb-selling" in the seventeenth century. But as we can see here, the contrast was more a subtle shading from one ethos into another. For sales of hellebore, see UBL BPL 2596-26, Clusius to Camerarius, Vienna, August 14, 1576; for sales in Brussels, see UBL Vulc. 101, Jacques Plateau to Clusius, letter 3, Brussels, August 6, 1586; on Nicolas, see UBL Vulc. 101, Jean de Maes to Clusius, letter 13, Brussels, March 31, 1603; on Baltin, see UBL Vulc. 101, same to same, letter 8, Brussels, November 11, 1601; on Clusius' purchase through Camerarius, see UBL BPL 2596-26, Clusius to Camerarius, Vienna, November 27, 1574; on martagons, UBL Vulc. 101, Jean de Maes to Clusius, letter 11, Brussels, October 7, 1602.

45. UBL Vulc. 101, Jacques Plateau to Clusius, letter 3, Brussels, August 6, 1586; UBL Vulc. 101, Jean de Maes to Clusius, letter 12, Brussels, December 7, 1602; UBL Lips. 4, Clusius to Lipsius, Leiden, October 21, 1594. I am grateful to Randall McNeill for his assistance with the letter to Lipsius.

46. UBL Vulc. 101, Jean de Maes to Clusius, letter 11, Brussels, October 7, 1602.

47. UBL Vulc. 101, Marie de Brimeu to Clusius, letter 18, Liège, March 26, 1601. Volckert Coornhart follows up on floral business of his late father Dirck in GAA NA 341/155–56, not. Willem Cluyt, September 26, 1611. For Boisot's views, UBL Vulc. 101, Jean Boisot to Clusius, letter 9, Brussels, June 25, 1592; UBL Vulc. 101, Jean de Maes to Clusius, letter 5, Brussels, April 8, 1599.

48. Dodonaeus, *Cruydt-Boeck* (1618 ed.), 365.

Chapter Two

1. GAA NA 1184/129–129v, not. Jan de Vos, August 17, 1635. Also printed inaccurately in Posthumus, 17–18.

2. On collectors of Lucas van Leyden, see Bart Cornelis and Jan Piet Filedt Kok, "The Taste for Lucas van Leyden Prints," *Simiolus* 26, nos. 1–2 (1998): 18–86.

3. I. H. van Eeghen, "De Restauratie van Prinsengracht 509, 515 of de Kalkvaars-gang," *Maandblad Amstelodamum* 68 (1981): 92–93; GAA DTB 432/291, August 6, 1627; the eight houses mentioned are in GAA NA 918/38, not. Barent Jansen Verbeeck, February 15, 1636; Admirael's father is called "vader van de kalckmeeters" in the record of his purchase of land on the Prinsengracht, GAA Arch. 5062/28, ff. 157–157v, June 3, 1621; notice of Admirael's death by his daughter-in-law is in GAA NA 1140/56, not. Jan van de Ven, January 17, 1662.

4. Gardens mentioned in GAA NA 919/201–201v, not. Barent Jansen Verbeeck, June 15, 1637 (also inaccurately printed in Posthumus, 69–70); Cornelis van Breugel and Victory in GAA NA 918/179v–180, not. Verbeeck, June 12, 1636; Verwer in GAA NA 917/310, not. Verbeeck, December 1, 1635; Poelenburch in GAA NA 889, not. Jacob van Swieten, April 24, 1636 (inaccurately printed in Posthumus, 21–22) and NA 919/145v–146, not. Verbeeck, May 19, 1636; De Hooge in NA 919/195–195v, not. Verbeeck, June 13, 1637; on Winckel, GAA NA 920/334–35, not. Verbeeck, December 2, 1638. On Tiberius, GAA NA 918/228–29, not. Verbeeck, July 16, 1636; GAA NA 995/534, not. Gerrit Coren, August 23, 1636; GAA NA 918/228–29, not. Verbeeck, July 16, 1636; GAA NA 918/519v, not. Verbeeck, December 8, 1636; RAA ONA Alkmaar 107, not. Cornelis de Haes, January 2, 1637; GAA NA 919/64–64v, not. Verbeeck, February 13, 1637 (very incompletely/inaccurately printed in Posthumus, 46–47); GAA NA 1009/106, not. Coren, April 6, 1638. Admirael's bet with Victory is in GAA NA 917/272v–273, not. Verbeeck, October 16, 1635.

5. Poelenburch was from Haarlem, the son of Willem Dircksz Poelenburch, teacher at the Latin School there. On the father, see Hans van de Venne, *Cornelius Schonaeus (1540-1611): Leven en werk van de Christelijke Terentius*, thesis (Leuven: Katholieke Universiteit Leuven, 2001), I, 210, 421; on Poelenburch's relation to Matham, see, among other places, GAA NA 583/275, not. Laurens Lamberti, July 16, 1642, will of Dirck Matham; on his engravings, see Ludwig Burchard, *Die Holländischen Radierer vor Rembrandt* (Berlin: Paul Cassirer, 1917), 45. Poelenburch's sale of tulips to René Morin in Paris is in AN, Minutier Central, ET/CV/329, October 5, 1617, and May 25, 1618; I am very grateful to Beth Hyde for sending me this document. On Admirael's connection with Hans van Conincxloo, see John Michael Montias, *Art at Auction in 17th Century Amsterdam* (Amsterdam: Amsterdam University Press, 2002), 75–76. Admirael's purchases at the Basse sale on March 25, 1637, are in GAA WK 5073/962, Weeskamer auctions, March 9–30, 1637. On Admirael's art in the 1660s, see GAA NA 2487/2, not. Jacob Hellerus, March 22, 1660, summarized in Irene van Thiel-Stroman, "The Frans Hals Documents," in Seymour Slive, ed., *Frans Hals* (ex. cat. Washington/London/Haarlem, 1989–1990), 408, and GAA NA

1056/267v–268, not. Justus van de Ven, printed in Walter J. Strauss and Marjon van der Meulen, eds., *The Rembrandt Documents* (New York: Abaris Books, 1979), 196.

6. Kretser's *ondertrouw* (official bethrothal) to Sara van Loon at the age of 28 is at GAA DTB 431/439, October 24, 1626. Other tulip transactions involving Kretser or bulbs in his garden are at NHA ONA Haarlem 165/271–271v, not. Jacob van Bosvelt, August 1, 1636, also printed in Posthumus, 27–28, and NHA ONA Haarlem 158/164, not. Wouter Crousen den Jonge, July 6, 1636, also printed in Posthumus, 25. For the Barend van Someren sale, GAA WK 1078, Weeskamer auctions, February 22, 1635, extracted in Strauss and Van der Meulen, *Rembrandt Documents*, 116. His role as gentleman-dealer is discussed in Gary Schwartz, "The Shape, Size and Destiny of the Dutch Market for Paintings at the End of the Eighty Years' War," in Klaus Bussmann and Heinz Schilling, eds., *1648: War and Peace in Europe*, Essay Vol. II: Art and Culture (ex. cat. Münster/Osnabrück, 1997–1998), 237; Seymour Slive, *Rembrandt and His Critics* (The Hague: Martinus Nijhoff, 1953), 44. On the contract with Pieter van den Bosch, see John Michael Montias, "Art dealers in the seventeenth-century Netherlands," *Simiolus* 18, no. 4 (1988): 246. Kretser's role as appraiser is described in A. Bredius, *Künstler-Inventare* I (The Hague: Martinus Nijhoff, 1915), 230, and GAA NA 1915/67009, not. Frans Uyttenbogaert, June 27, 1657. His collection is most comprehensively described by Lambert van den Bos, *Konst Kabinet van Marten Kretzer* (Amsterdam: Nicolaes van Ravesteyn, 1650). On the society, J. H. W. Unger, "Vondeliana. II. Vondel's Handschriften," *Oud-Holland* 2 (1884): 113–19; Hugo Postma, "Rembrandt en de Broederschap der Schilderkunst; een nieuwe hypothese voor de Pallas Athene in Museu Calouste Gulbenkian," *Oud-Holland* 109, no. 1–2 (1995): 89–93; Jan Vos, *Strydt tusschen de Doodt en Natuur, of Zeege der Schilderkunst* (Amsterdam: Jacob Lescaille, 1654), 206; Thomas Asselyn and Joost van den Vondel, *Broederschap der Schilderkunst* (Amsterdam: Jakob Vinkel, 1654). The godfathers of his daughters are in GAA DTB 41/373, April 3, 1635, and DTB 6/365, April 24, 1633.

7. The literature on early modern collecting is vast. Some fundamental sources are Oliver Impey and Arthur MacGregor, eds., *The Origins of Museums: The Cabinet of Curiosities in Sixteenth- and Seventeenth-Century Europe* (Oxford: Clarendon Press, 1985); Krzysztof Pomian, *Collectors and Curiosities: Paris and Venice 1500–1800*, trans. Elizabeth Wiles-Portier (Cambridge: Polity Press, 1990); Antoine Schnapper, *Le Géant, la licorne, la tulipe: Collections et collectionneurs dans la France du XVIIe siècle* (Paris: Flammarion, 1988), and *Curieux du Grand Siècle* (Paris: Flammarion, 1994); and Paula Findlen, *Possessing Nature: Museums, Collecting, and Scientific Culture in Early Modern Italy* (Berkeley: University of California Press, 1994). For the Netherlands, see especially Ellinoor Bergvelt and Renée Kistemaker, eds., *De wereld binnen handbereik: Nederlandse kunst- en rariteitenverzamelingen 1585–1735* (ex. cat. Amsterdam, Amsterdams Historisch Museum, 1992), and Ellinoor Bergvelt, Debora J. Meijers, and Mieke Rijnders, eds., *Verzamelen: Van rariteitenkabinet tot kunstmuseum* (Heerlen: Open Universiteit/Gaade, 1993). On merchants and collecting, see Mark A. Meadow, "Merchants and Marvels: Hans Jacob Fugger and the Origins

of the Wunderkammer," in Paula Findlen and Pamela Smith, eds., *Merchants and Marvels: Commerce, Science, and Art in Early Modern Europe* (New York: Routledge, 2002), 182–200. Buckingham is quoted in Lorraine Daston, "The Factual Sensibility," *Isis* 79, no. 3 (1988): 456. On foreign purchases of rarities in the Netherlands, see Roelof van Gelder, "De Wereld binnen handbereik," in Bergvelt and Kistemaker, *De Wereld binnen handbereik*, 15–16; Roelof van Gelder, "Noordnederlandse verzamelingen in de zeventiende eeuw," in Bergvelt, Meijers, and Rijnders, *Verzamelen*, 140; and S. Muller Fz., "Nederland als markt van zeldzaamheden," *Oud-Holland* 31 (1913): 207–8. On shops, David Beck, *Spiegel van mijn leven: een Haags dagboek uit 1624*, ed. Sv. E. Veldhuijzen (Hilversum: Verloren, 1993), 133; and Philip Skippon, "An Account of a Journey Made Thro' Part of the Low-Countries, Germany, Italy, and France," in [A. and J. Churchill], *A Collection of Voyages and Travels* (London: A. and J. Churchill, 1732), VI, 389.

8. BL Add. Ms. 20,001, f. 17v, travel diary of Jacob Wurmsser von Vendenheym, June 22–24, 1610; John Evelyn, *The Diary of John Evelyn*, ed. E. S. de Beer (Oxford: Clarendon Press, 1955), II, 39, August 1641; for attacks on the idea of ownership of paintings throughout the social spectrum (an idea advanced by, e.g., Hanns Floerke), see John Michael Montias, "Socio-Economic Aspects of Netherlandish Art from the Fifteenth to the Seventeenth Century," *Art Bulletin* 72, no. 3 (September 1990): 361–62, and Marten Jan Bok, "Art-Lovers and their Paintings: Van Mander's Schilder-boeck as a Source for the History of the Art Market in the Northern Netherlands," in Ger Luijten et al., *Dawn of the Golden Age: Northern Netherlandish Art 1580–1620* (ex. cat. Amsterdam, Rijksmuseum, 1993–1994), 144–47. The argument about increased purchasing power is made by Marten Jan Bok in "The Rise of Amsterdam as a cultural centre: the market for paintings, 1580–1680," in Patrick O'Brien et al., eds., *Urban Achievement in Early Modern Europe: Golden Ages in Antwerp, Amsterdam and London* (Cambridge: Cambridge University Press, 2001), 190–99. On average numbers of paintings owned, see John Michael Montias, *Artists and Artisans in Delft: A Socio-Economic Study of the Seventeenth Century* (Princeton, NJ: Princeton University Press, 1982), 220; Eric Jan Sluijter, "'All striving to adorn their houses with costly peeces': Two Case Studies of Paintings in Wealthy Interiors," in Mariët Westermann, ed., *Art and Home: Dutch Interiors in the Age of Rembrandt* (ex. cat. Denver, Denver Art Museum, 2001), 104; and Jaap van der Veen, "De Verzamelaar in zijn kamer: Zeventiende-eeuwse privé-collecties in de Republiek," in Huub de Jonge, ed., *Ons Soort Mensen: Levensstijlen in Nederland* (Nijmegen: SUN, 1997), 132.

9. On Antwerp *liefhebbers* of art and *Kunstkammer* paintings, see Julius S. Held, "Ars Pictoriae Amator: An Antwerp Art Patron and his Collection," republished with postscript in Anne W. Lowenthal, David Rosand, and John Walsh, Jr., eds., *Rubens and his Circle: Studies by Julius S. Held* (Princeton, NJ: Princeton University Press, 1982), 59 n. 3; Zirka Zaremba Filipczak, *Picturing Art in Antwerp 1550–1700* (Princeton, NJ: Princeton University Press, 1987), esp. 51–54; and Elizabeth Honig,

"The Beholder as Work of Art: A Study in the Location of Value in Seventeenth-Century Flemish Painting," *Nederlands Kunsthistorisch Jaarboek* 46 (1995): 253–97. On southerners and art in the north, Thera Wijsenbeek-Olthuis, "Vreemd en eigen: Ontwikkelingen in de woon- en leefcultuur binnen de Hollandse steden van de zestiende tot de negentiende eeuw," in Peter te Boekhorst et al., *Cultuur en maatschappij in Nederland 1500–1800: Een historisch-antropologisch perspectief* (Heerlen: Open Universiteit, 1992), 100; Sluijter, "'All Striving,'" 103–4; Jaap van der Veen, "Galerij en kabinet, vorst en burger: Schilderijencollecties in de Neder-landen," in Bergvelt et al., *Verzamelen*, 157; Marten Jan Bok points out the continu-ing influence of northerners in "Art-Lovers," 144. The argument that Rembrandt's collection was an avenue to social status is from R. W. Scheller, "Rembrandt en de encyclopedische kunstkamer," *Oud-Holland* 84 (1969): 128–31. Scheller's inter-pretation was attacked by Egbert Haverkamp Begemann, "The Present State of Rembrandt Studies," *Art Bulletin* 53, no. 1 (1971): 88–104. Haverkamp Begemann points to Rembrandt's sincere interest in the *naturalia* and *artificialia* he collected, but of course the reality of his interest does not preclude the social consequences it might have incurred. Roelof van Gelder and Jaap van der Veen note the excep-tionality of a painter owning such an elaborate collection, but they argue that if Rembrandt was aiming for social advancement, his conduct was insufficiently civil to achieve it, and that he probably had no such aim. See Van Gelder and Van der Veen, "A Collector's Cabinet in the Breestraat: Rembrandt as a Lover of Art and Curiosities," in Bob van den Boogert, ed., *Rembrandt's Treasures* (ex. cat. Amster-dam, Rembrandthuis, 1999), 61, 84–89. On the Reynsts, Anne-Marie S. Logan, *The 'Cabinet' of the Brothers Gerard and Jan Reynst* (Amsterdam: North-Holland Publish-ing Company, 1979), 9, 11–12.

10. On some qualities entailed by the early modern idea of the marvelous, see Joy Kenseth, "The Age of the Marvelous: An Introduction," in Kenseth, ed., *The Age of the Marvelous* (ex. cat. Hanover, NH, Hood Museum of Art, Dartmouth College, 1991), 40–51. On the bird of paradise, UBL Vulc. 101, Jan van Wely to Clusius, Am-sterdam, June 13, 1605.

11. On Porret, GAL, Kohier van gedwongen lening 100e penning, 1600, f. 29v; and Penning Leyden en Rijnland ("Ruytergeld") 1602, f. 31. His collection catalogue is *Catalogus Oft Register Vande Sonderling-Heden oft Rariteyten Ende Wtgelesen Sin-nelickheden Van Indiaensche ende ander wtheemsche Zee-Horens/Schelpen/Eerd ende Zeegewassen/Mineralen/ende oock vreemde Gedierten; mitsgaders eenighe constichlijck ghemaecte handwercken ende schilderijen Die Christiaen Porrett, wijlen Apoteker/in zijn Cunstcamer vergadert had* (Leiden: Jan Claesz van Dorp, 1628). The only copy of this I know of is in the RKD. Jaap van der Veen gives an explanation of the frequently used term "sinnelickheden" in Van der Veen, "De Verzamelaar in zijn Kamer," 140: it can mean things greatly desired as well as things that give pleasure to the senses.

12. Aristotle, *Physics* 199a; Pliny, *Natural History* XXXV.xxxvi.64–66. The following material is adapted from an article published previously, Anne Goldgar, "Nature

as Art: The Case of the Tulip," in Smith and Findlen, eds., *Merchants and Marvels*, 324–46.

13. These ideas are discussed in many different sources, but see, among others, Erwin Panofsky, *Idea: A Concept in Art Theory*, trans. Joseph J.S. Peake (New York: Harper & Row, 1968; orig. publ. 1924), 48; Ernst Kantorowicz, "The Sovereignty of the Artist: A Note on Legal Maxims and Renaissance Theories of Art," in Millard Meiss, ed., *De Artibus Opuscula XL: Essays in Honor of Erwin Panofsky* (New York: New York University Press, 1961) I, 268, 271; Walter S. Melion, *Shaping the Netherlandish Canon: Karel van Mander's Schilder-Boeck* (Chicago: University of Chicago Press, 1991), 20–21; Desiderius Erasmus, *Colloquies*, quoted in Brenninkmeijer-De Rooij, "For the Love of Flora," 38; on floral still life, Paul Taylor, *Dutch Flower Painting 1600–1720* (New Haven, CT: Yale University Press, 1995), 82–83; Constantijn Huygens, "In praestantissimi pictoris Dan. Segheri rosas," in *A Selection of the the Poems of Sir Constantijn Huygens (1596-1687)*, ed. and trans. Peter Davidson and Adriaan van der Weel (Amsterdam: Amsterdam University Press, 1996), 129; Jan Vos, "Op de geschilderde Bloemen van PATER ZEEGERS. Aan de Lent," in *Strydt tusschen de Doodt en Natuur*, 28.

14. John Rea, "Flora, To the Ladies," in Rea, *Flora, seu, De Florum Cultura* (London: for Richard Marriott, 1665). Samuel Gilbert similarly wrote in *The Florists Vade-Mecum* (London: for Thomas Simmons, 1682), 87, "Presuming Painters find their skil outdone/At Sight of these, so Pensil'd by the Sun, That *Paterzeger*, doth himself confess/He colours wants their glories to express." *De Rechte Bloem-Prijs*, a pro-tulip broadside, is reprinted (with changes to the text) in E. H. Krelage, ed., *De pamfletten van den Tulpenwindhandel 1636-1637* (The Hague: Martinus Nijhoff, 1942), 269.

15. On Bernard de Palissy, Lorraine Daston and Katharine Park, *Wonders and the Order of Nature 1150-1750* (New York: Zone Books, 1998), 285–86, and Martin Kemp, "'Wrought by No Artist's Hand': The Natural, the Artificial, the Exotic, and the Scientific in Some Artifacts from the Renaissance," in Claire Farago, ed., *Reframing the Renaissance: Visual Culture in Europe and Latin America 1450-1650* (New Haven, CT: Yale University Press, 1995), 191–93; on naturalistic automata at Aldobrandini, see John Dixon Hunt, "'Curiosities to adorn Cabinets and Gardens,'" in Impey and MacGregor, eds., *The Origins of Museums*, 198–200; on Pratolino, Roy Strong, *The Renaissance Garden in England* (London: Thames and Hudson, 1998), 78–83, and Somer, *Beschrijvinge*, 4–4v.

16. The best account of items that are half art, half nature, is Kemp, "'Wrought by No Artist's Hand.'" On coconuts, see Rolf Fritz, *Die Gefässe aus Kokosnuss in Mitteleuropa 1250-1800* (Mainz am Rhein: Verlag Philipp von Zabern, 1983); Fritz' analysis of the scenes on coconuts is on p. 55. On ostrich eggs, Isa Ragusa, "The Egg Reopened," *Art Bulletin* 53 (1971): 435–43, and Creighton Gilbert, "'The Egg Reopened' Again," *Art Bulletin* 56 (1974): 252–58. Skippon's visit to Cliver's collection is in Skippon, "An Account of a Journey," 385. Many such objects are pictured in *Prag um 1600: Kunst und Kultur am Hofe Rudolfs II.* (ex. cat. Essen, 1988).

17. [Nicolas de Valnay], *Connoissance et Culture Parfaite des Tulippes rares, Des Anemones*

extraordinaires, Des Oeillets fins, Et des belles Oreilles d'Ours panachées (Paris: Laurent d'Houry, 1688), "Avertissement." This book was attributed to Valnay by Krelage in *Drie Eeuwen Bloembollenexport*, 538; Krelage mentions a first edition of 1669, but I have so far not found such an edition. On the gardens of Louis XIV and floral sales and collecting in seventeenth-century Paris, see Elizabeth Hyde, *Cultivated Power;* on Louis XIV's gardens and political power, see both Hyde and Chandra Mukerji, *Territorial Ambitions and the Gardens of Versailles* (Cambridge: Cambridge University Press, 1997).

18. The idea of a pairing of gardens and collections is often mentioned by scholars. See, for example, Findlen, *Possessing Nature*, 259; Masson, "Italian Flower Collectors' Gardens," 68, and Erik de Jong, "Nature and Art: The Leiden Hortus as 'Musaeum,'" in Tjon Sie Fat and De Jong, eds., *The Authentic Garden*, 37–70. Clusius' request for fish is in his request to the VOC, printed in Hunger, *Clusius*, I, 267; his sending medals to Jean de Brancion in return for plants is mentioned in UBL Vulc. 101, Jean de Brancion to Clusius, letter 2, Malines, August 3, 1571. Porret's garden is called a collection by Van der Veen, "Verzamelaar," 141; the same remark is made of Paludanus' garden in Van Gelder, "Noordnederlandse Verzamelingen," 125. Paludanus' *album amicorum*, which functioned both as a guest book for the collection and a book of friends and acquaintances from his travels, is KB ms. 133 M 63; it contains many aristocrats as well as a variety of well-known foreign scholars. On the Leiden *hortus* and collection, see De Jong, "Nature and Art," esp. 38–40; Klaas van Berkel, "Institutionele verzamelingen in de tijd van de wetenschappelijke revolutie (1600–1750)," in Bergvelt et al., eds., *Verzamelen*, 192; and Claudia Swan, *Art, Science, and Witchcraft in Early Modern Holland*, 51 ff.

19. Casteleyn was dead by August 28, 1644, when his inventory begins; he was buried on September 1, 1644, in the French Reformed Church: GAA DTB 1130/105. His will is GAA NA 939A/173–74, not. Barent Jansen Verbeeck, August 9, 1644. The inventory of the money, tulips, and rarities (which was separate from the inventory of his other goods) is GAA NA 939A/186–238, not. Verbeeck, August 28–October 6, 1644. The money is listed on ff. 186–92; the fourteen volumes describing the tulip bulbs on f. 233. The tulips are inventoried on ff. 192–230. The final balance of Casteleyn's account at the Wisselbank (for August 1644) is in GAA Arch. 5077, Rekeningboek Wisselbank, February–August 1644, f. 927. This Abraham Casteleyn was different from and, as far as I know, unrelated to the Haarlem city printer of the same name, who was, however, the son of the printer Vincent Casteleyn and brother of the painter Vincent Casteleyn, one of whom (it is impossible to tell which) was involved in the tulip trade. The Haarlem Casteleyns were Mennonites; Abraham and Isaac Casteleyn in Amsterdam were not.

20. The *artificialia* are in GAA NA 939A/237–38, and the collection of shells and other objects on ff. 234–38. The codicil to Casteleyn's will is GAA NA 939A/176, not. Barent Jansen Verbeeck, August 11, 1644.

21. H. E. Coomans, "Schelpenverzamelingen," in Bergvelt and Kistemaker, eds., *De wereld binnen handbereik*, 194, 196; Hendrik Engel, *Hendrik Engel's Alphabetical List*

of Dutch Zoological Cabinets and Menageries, ed. Pieter Smit, 2nd ed. (Amsterdam: Nieuwe Nederlandse Bijdragen tot de Geschiedenis der Geneeskunde en der Natuurwetenschappen no. 19, 1986), 6; Georg Everhard Rumphius, *D'Amboinsche Rariteitkamer* (Amsterdam: François Halma, 1705); on De Gheyn and Sichem, see Roelof van Gelder and Jaap van der Veen, "A Collector's Cabinet in the Breestraat," 68, 61, n. 64; on Volkersen, see Filips von Zesen, *Beschreibung der Stadt Amsterdam* (Amsterdam: Joachim Noschen, 1664); [Philibert van Borsselen], *Strande, oft Gedichte van de Schelpen, Kinckhornen, ende andere Wonderlicke Zee-schelpselen, Tot Lof van de Schepper aller dinghen* (Amsterdam: Dirck Pietersz, 1614; 1st ed. was 1611). Sam Segal has been able to identify precisely the species of shells in various shell still lifes and notes that they were almost never European; see Sam Segal, *A Prosperous Past: The Sumptuous Still Life in the Netherlands 1600–1700* (The Hague: SDU, 1989), 85, 88.

22. Van Borsselen, *Strande*, 8–9; on Parduyn, Coomans, "Schelpenverzamelingen,"199; on Gaston d'Orléans, Schnapper, *Géant*, 189–90, and S. Peter Dance, *Shell Collecting: An Illustrated History* (London: Faber and Faber, 1966), 37; Marrell's inventory is printed in Bredius, *Künstler-Inventare* I, 112–19; on Tradescant's portrait, Prudence Leith-Ross, *The John Tradescants: Gardeners to the Rose and Lily Queen* (London: Peter Owen, 1984), 161; the 1656 catalogue is John Tradescant, *Musaeum Tradescantianum: Or, a Collection of Rarities. Preserved at South-Lambeth neer London by John Tradescant* (London: for Nathanael Brooke, 1656), shells on pp. 10–14. Evelyn's comments are from his "De Vita Propria," in De Beer, ed., *Diary* I, 85–86 (about 1644), and *Diary* III, 33, May 23, 1651.

23. Balthasar Gerbier to the Earl of Arundel, Brussels, January 30/February 9, 1633, printed in W. Noel Sainsbury, *Original Unpublished Papers Illustrative of the Life of Sir Peter Paul Rubens, As an Artist and a Diplomatist* (London: Bradbury & Evans, 1859), 296; on the southern Netherlandish interest in tulips, see Ursula Härting, "Rubens' Garten in Antwerpen," in Ursula Härting, ed., *Gärten und Höfe der Rubenszeit im Spiegel der Malerfilie Brueghel und der Künstler um Peter Paul Rubens* (ex. cat. Hamm/Mainz, 2000), 59–66; the tulip song is *Een Nieuw Liedeken, Tegen de verachters der Floristen* (Hoorn: Zacharias Cornelisz, 1637), reprinted in Krelage, *Pamfletten* (henceforth *KP*), 114, and also in *Floraes Sotte-Bollen: Afghemaelt in Dichten en Sanghen* (n.p., n.d.: Amsterdam? 1643?), 35; on the shell "Speculation-goods," Bol, *The Bosschaert Dynasty*, 39; Roemer Visscher, *Zinne-Poppen*, ed. Anna Roemers (Amsterdam: Johannes van Ravesteyn, 1669; orig. ed. Amsterdam: Willem Jansz, 1614), 4, 5. Visscher was presumably not entirely averse to speculation, as he invested ƒ1,800 in the first sale of shares of the VOC in 1602: J. G. van Dillen, *Het oudste aandeelhoudersregister van de Kamer Amsterdam der Oost-Indische Compagnie* (The Hague: Martinus Nijhoff, 1958), 133.

24. Benjamin Daydon Jackson, ed., *A Catalogue of Plants cultivated in the Garden of John Gerard, in the years 1596–1599* (London: privately printed, 1876), 53; Gerard, *Herball*, 117.

25. *Catalogus . . . vande Sonderling-Heden oft Rariteyten . . . [van] Christiaen Porret.* On

NOTES TO PAGES 87–89

Paludanus' collection in 1592, Jacob Rathgeben, *Warhafte Beschreibung Zweyer Raisen* ... (Tübingen: In der Gellischen Truckeren, 1603), insert between pp. 44 and 45; for a full inventory of his collection, UBL BPL 2596–99, Collectie Hunger, transcription of catalogue of cabinet of Paludanus from ms. original in KB Copenhagen, ff. 190–203 (in original ms., ff. 130–40). Antoine Agard's catalogue is *Discours et roole des medailles & autres antiquitez ... à present rangees dans le Cabinet du Sieur Antoine Agard* ... (Paris: no publisher, 1611), see 14–17, 26, 27, 31. On collections of agates, see Schnapper, *Géant*, 191–92. On *pietra dura* furniture, see C. Willemijn Fock, "Pietre Dure work at the court of Prague and Florence: Some Relations," in *Prag um 1600*, 51–59; J. F. M. Sterck, "Dirck van Rijswijck. Een Amsterdamsch Goudsmid en Mozaïekwerker," *Jaarverslag Koninklijk Oudheidkundig Genootschap* (1908–1909), 35–54. The assumption that marble floors were standard features of Dutch households is challenged in C. Willemijn Fock, "Werkelijkheid of schijn: Het beeld van het Hollandse interieur in de zeventiende-eeuwse genre-schilderkunst," *Oud-Holland* 112, no. 4 (1998): 187–246; she states that they were a status symbol on p. 208.

26. Thomas Nicols, *A Lapidary: Or, the History of Pretious Stones* (Cambridge: Thomas Buck, 1652), 133; *Catalogus ... [van] Christiaen Porret*; Evelyn, *Diary* II, 133, April 1–6, 1644; Thomas Moufet, *Insectorum sive Minimorum Animalium Theatrum* (London: for Benjamin Allen, 1634), 107; Van Borsselen, *Strande*, 10, 11, 8.

27. Rea, *Flora* (2nd ed., 1676), 47; [Antoine-Joseph Dezallier d'Argenville], *La Théorie et Pratique du Jardinage*, ed. and augmented by Alexandre le Blond (Paris: Jean Mariette, 1722), 249; La Chesnée Monstereul, *Le floriste françois*, 208–13; Dossier Tulpen, private collection of Sam Segal, typescript list of tulip names from twenty-four tulip books. My thanks to Dr. Segal for allowing me to consult this.

28. On the introduction of marbled paper to Europe, Phoebe Jane Easton, *Marbling: A History and a Bibliography* (Los Angeles: Dawson's Book Shop, 1983), 33 ff.; Rosamond B. Loring, *Decorated Book Papers* (Cambridge, MA: Harvard College Library, 1942), 12–13; Richard J. Wolfe, *Marbled Paper: Its History, Techniques, and Patterns* (Philadelphia: University of Pennsylvania Press, 1990), 3–14; Graham Pollard, "Changes in the Style of Bookbinding, 1550–1830," *The Library* 5th ser. 11, no. 12 (June 1956): 79. On the role of the Netherlands, Easton, *Marbling*, 63–66, and J. F. Heijebroek and T. C. Greven, *Sierpapier: marmer-, brocaat- en sitspapier in Nederland* (Amsterdam: De Buitenkant, 1994), 15–17. On Paludanus and marbled paper, Heijebroek and Greven, *Sierpapier*, 14; on marbled paper in Porret's collection, *Catalogus ... [van] Christiaen Porret*; on the term "Turkish paper," Easton, *Marbling*, 56. Sir Thomas Herbert's *Travels in Persia 1627–1629* quoted in Charles M. Adams, *Some Notes on the Art of Marbling Paper in the Seventeenth Century* (New York: New York Public Library, 1947), 4; on the Agate pattern, Easton, 111. Evelyn's "An Exact Account of the Making of Marbled Paper" is quoted in Adams, *Some Notes*, 11. Anna Maria von Heusenstain demanded the tulip "das tirckhish papir" in UBL Vulc. 101, Von Heusenstain to Clusius, Vienna, May 7, 1591. (In another letter to Clusius mention is made of a "plante ... du papier Persien et Turquesque" that Clu-

sius had sent, but it is not clear if this was actually a tulip. UBL Vulc. 101, Jacques Plateau to Clusius, letter 9, Tournai, September 8, 1592.) The tulip Coquille marbrée is listed in La Chesnée Monstereul, *Le floriste françois*, 221.

29. On Blijenburgh, Th. H. Lunsingh Scheurleer, "Early Dutch Cabinets of Curiosities," in Impey and MacGregor, eds., *Origins of Museums*, 117; on shell collecting and Jan Govertsz van der Aer, Bergvelt and Kistemaker, eds., *De wereld binnen handbereik*, catalogue volume, 46; Ger Luijten, ed., *Dawn of the Golden Age*, 588; Coomans, "Schelpenverzamelingen," 198; Lunsingh Scheurleer, 116; Dance, *Shell Collecting*, 34; Segal, *A Prosperous Past*, 79.

30. Evelyn, "De Vita Propria," in De Beer, ed., *Diary I*, 86; Franeau, *Iardin d'hyver*, 4 of Elégie XXVI; Emmanuel Sweerts, *Florilegium* (Frankfurt am Main: Anthonius Kempner, 1612), "Au lecteur"; Parkinson, *Paradisi in Sole Paradisus Terrestris*, "To the Courteous Reader"; *Den Spieghel der Schoonheden, Waer in verthoont worden de wonderlyke ende Schoone Wercken Godts ... Voor gestelt by de Vlaemsche kamer: De wit Angieren Binnen Haerlem 1635* (Haarlem: Jan Pietersz de Does, 1636), entry of Matthijs JonckHeer; Norman Bryson, *Looking at the Overlooked: Four Essays on Still Life Painting* (London: Reaktion Books, 1990), 8.

31. For the iconological approach, see especially Ingvar Bergström, *Dutch Still-Life Painting in the Seventeenth Century*, trans. Christina Hedström and Gerald Taylor (London: Faber and Faber, 1956), and Bergström, "Disguised Symbolism in 'Madonna' Pictures and Still Life," *The Burlington Magazine* 97 (1955): 303–8, 342–49. The exhibition catalogue *Stilleben in Europa* (ex. cat. Münster, Westfälisches Landesmuseum für Kunst und Kulturgeschichte, 1979–1980) is often cited as taking this approach too far. Sam Segal's work on tulips and art generally supports an allegorical interpretation of pictures of tulips; see, for example, Segal, "De symboliek van de tulp," in Sam Segal and Michiel Roding, *De Tulp en de Kunst* (ex. cat. Amsterdam, Nieuwe Kerk, 1994), 8–23. Eddy de Jongh supports a middle way in this discussion, endorsing the idea of allegory in some still life, but saying that it is not easy to tell what either the intentions of the artist or the reception of the spectator would have been: see De Jongh, "The Interpretation of Still-Life Paintings: Possibilities and Limits," in De Jongh, ed., *Still-Life in the Age of Rembrandt* (ex. cat. Auckland, Auckland City Art Gallery, 1982), 27–37. Those interested in the contextual approach to still life are inspired by Roland Barthes, "The World as Object," in Norman Bryson, ed., *Calligram*, 106–115; they include Bryson, *Looking at the Overlooked*, chap. 3, and Hal Foster, "The Art of Fetishism: Notes on Dutch Still Life," *Princeton Architectural Journal* 4 (1992): 6–19. The founding work in the school stressing representation is Svetlana Alpers, *The Art of Describing: Dutch Art in the Seventeenth Century* (Chicago: University of Chicago Press, 1983). On artifice, see Celeste Brusati, "Natural Artifice and Material Values in Dutch Still Life," in Wayne Franits, ed., *Looking at Seventeenth-Century Dutch Art: Realism Reconsidered* (Cambridge: Cambridge University Press, 1997), 144–57.

32. The idea that floral still life sprang from natural history illustration by people like Hoefnagel is associated particularly with Laurens J. Bol, *'Goede Onbekenden'*: see

especially p. 37; on Hoefnagel's relations to science and to artifice and on floral still life's debts to him and to sixteenth-century ornamentation, see Marjorie L. Hendrix, "Joris Hoefnagel and the Four Elements: A Study in Sixteenth-Century Nature Painting" (PhD thesis, Princeton University, 1984). On the idea of still lifes as collections, see, for example, Bryson, *Looking at the Overlooked*, 107–8, 128–29, and Brusati, "Natural Artifice," 151. Svetlana Alpers is among those who have suggested that floral still lifes were "pictures of collectibles": Alpers, "The Studio, the Laboratory, and the Vexations of Art," in Caroline A. Jones and Peter Galison, *Picturing Science, Producing Art* (New York: Routledge, 1998), 407–8. Elizabeth Honig argues that the logic of still lifes is the logic of collections: Honig, "Making Sense of Things: On the Motives of Dutch Still Life," *Res* 34 (Autumn 1998): 176 ff.

33. On Antwerp *Kunstkammer* paintings, see especially Filipczak, *Picturing Art in Antwerp*. De Goyer's eight floral still lifes are listed in his inventory, GAA NA 968, not. Benedict Baddel, March 18, 1653; Essings and Meyers' in Meyers' inventory, RAA ONA Alkmaar 106, not. Cornelis de Haes, May 7, 1640. Plateau's "pourtraicts" of items in his cabinet appear in, among other places, UBL Vulc. 101, Plateau to Clusius, letter 3, Brussels, August 6, 1586; UBL Vulc. 101, same to same, letter 13, Tournai, November 4, 1602; UBL Vulc. 101, same to same, letter 14, December 4, 1602; UBL Vulc. 101, same to same, Tournai, April 20, 1605. Hoghelande's "painctresse" (who had died) is mentioned in UBL Vulc.101, Jan van Hoghelande to Clusius, letter 9, Leiden, August 12, 1592. On Morin's miniatures, Evelyn, *Diary* II, 132, April 1–6, 1644; J. Laurent quoted in Schnapper, *Géant*, 55. On pictures of objects in collections, see Swan, *Art and Science, and Witchcraft*, 71–72.

34. The fixative purpose of still life is discussed by, among others, Bol, *The Bosschaert Dynasty*, 17; Taylor, *Dutch Flower Painting*, 115–16; and Celeste Brusati, "Stilled Lives: Self-Portraiture and Self-Reflection in Seventeenth-Century Netherlandish Still-Life Painting," *Simiolus* 20, no. 2/3 (1990/1991): 180. Laurent quoted in Schnapper, *Géant*, 55.

35. The argument that tulip books were sales catalogues has been made most often by Sam Segal, who, however, at least once has qualified this by saying they were "usually" (*meestal*) intended for this purpose: Sam Segal, "Exotische bollen als statussymbolen," *Kunstschrift* 31, no. 3 (1987): 93–94. The potential of other uses (including the discovery by Pieter Biesboer of an inventory with framed tulip drawings) is mentioned by Cynthia Kortenhorst-Von Borgendorf Rupprath in a catalogue entry in James A. Welu and Pieter Biesboer, eds., *Judith Leyster: A Dutch Master and her Work* (ex. cat. Haarlem, Frans Halsmuseum, 1993), 217. Dr. Segal mentioned that the prices were those of Alkmaar in conversation with me on April 10, 2001. The broadside containing the prices at Alkmaar is *Lijstje van Eenighe Tulpaen verkocht aan de meest-biedende op den 5 Februarij 1637*, which is reprinted in *KP*, 140–43.

36. Norbert Schneider, *The Art of the Portrait* (Cologne: Benedikt Taschen Verlag, 1994), 6, 9; on individualism, see Richard Brilliant, *Portraiture* (London: Reaktion Books, 1991), 9, 14; and for a general discussion of this literature, see Joanna Woodall, *Por-*

traiture: Facing the Subject (Manchester: Manchester University of Press, 1997), introduction, and Shearer West, Portraiture (Oxford: Oxford University Press, 2004), chaps. 1–2. On Dutch portraiture, Woodall, "Sovereign Bodies: The Reality of Status in Seventeenth-Century Dutch Portraiture," in Woodall, Portraiture, 75; on schutter portraits and individualism, see Brilliant, Portraiture, 50, 53. Maler's picture of Schwarz appears, with the inscription translated, in Lorne Campbell, Renaissance Portraits: European Portrait-Painting in the 14th, 15th and 16th Centuries (New Haven, CT: Yale University Press, 1990), plate 152; drinking pictures discussed on p. 209. Campbell discusses portraits' function of showing sitters' appearance at a particular time on p. 214, and Da Vinci is cited on p. 193. Hortensia Borromeo, Countess of Hohenems, quoted in Campbell, 193. On the subject of substitution for the absent, see also Woodall, 8–9, Campbell, 220, and Brilliant, 40.

37. Brilliant, Portraiture, 8–9; Schneider, Art of the Portrait, 101; for a discussion of this issue, see Woodall, Portraiture, 16–17. Examples of contrafeytsel or pourtraict occur in, among others, UBL Vulc. 101, Jehan Somer to Clusius, Middelburg, May 8, 1597; UBL Vulc. 101, Jacques Plateau to Clusius, August 6, 1586, and November 4, 1602; UBL Vulc. 101, Jacques Garet le jeune to Clusius, letter 4, September 9, 1589. Claudia Swan has also published a volume of botanical watercolors in Kraków, which she believes were Cluyt's: Claudia Swan, ed., The Clutius Botanical Watercolors: Plants and Flowers of the Renaissance (New York: Harry N. Abrams, 1998). The attribution is persuasively disputed by Florike Egmond in "Clusius, Cluyt, Saint Omer: The Origins of the Sixteenth-Century Botanical and Zoological Watercolours in Libri Picturati A. 16–30," Nuncius 20, no. 1 (2005): 11–67. Swan writes about the substitutive function of images in "Ad vivum, naer het leven, from the life: defining a mode of representation," Word and Image 11, no. 4 (October–December 1995): 369–70. On Guy de la Brosse's collection of plant portraits, see Schnapper, Géant, 57.

38. On portraits of dwarves, see Schneider, Art of the Portrait, 67. On dogs in the seventeenth century, see Thomas, Man and the Natural World, 110, 117, and Karel Davids, Dieren en Nederlanders: Zeven Eeuwen Lief en Leed (Utrecht: Matrijs, 1989), 38–41; Thomas makes the point about dogs as luxury objects on p. 110. Bondt's funeral procession is described in Davids, 38; the anonymous English traveler's comments appear in BL Sloane ms. 1293, f. 26, "Costumhes de Hollanda" (1670s). On dog portraits in the seventeenth century, see William Secord, Dog Painting 1840-1940 (Woodbridge, Suffolk: Antique Collector's Club, 1992), 37–39. John Caius, Of Englishe Dogges, the diversities, the names, the natures, and the properties, trans. Abraham Fleming (London: Rychard Johnes, 1576), 42, 20–21. On Hoefnagel, Bol, 'Goede onbekenden', 37; on Desportes and Oudry, Secord, 41–42; on Wootton, Arline Meyer, "Household Mock-Heroics: The Dog Portraits of John Wootton (1682-1764)," Country Life 175, no. 4512 (February 9, 1984): 340–42, 384. On Lipsius and his dogs, Mark Morford, Stoics and Neostoics: Rubens and the Circle of Lipsius (Princeton, NJ: Princeton University Press, 1991), 4; Wolfram Prinz, "The Four Philosophers by Rubens and the Pseudo-Seneca in Seventeenth-Century Painting,"

Art Bulletin LV, no. 3 (September 1973): 420; and Simon Schama, *Rembrandt's Eyes* (London: Penguin, 1999), 146–50. On naming, John Algeo, *On Defining the Proper Name* (Gainesville, FL: University of Florida Press, 1973), 81–83; Elsdon C. Smith, "The Significance of Name Study," in D. P. Blok, ed., *Proceedings of the Eighth International Congress of Onomastic Sciences* (The Hague and Paris: Mouton, 1966), 492.

39. Algeo, *On Defining the Proper Name*, 50. The number of tulip names is estimated by Sam Segal, *Tulips by Anthony Claesz* (Maastricht: Noortman, 1987), 3–4.

40. Report on the Fortuyn tulip in *Het Parool*, May 6, 2003; William Turner, *The Names of Herbes 1548*, facsimile ed. James Britten, B. Daydon Jackson, and W. T. Stearn (London: The Ray Society, 1965); G. M. [Gervase Markham], *The Second Booke of the English Husbandman* (London: for John Browne, 1615), 31; Parkinson, *Paradisi*, 82, 48; Gerard, *Herball*, 108–9; Hunger, *L'Ecluse* I, 351.

41. La Chesnée Monstereul, *Le floriste françois*, 33–37, 35.

42. For eighteenth-century hyacinth names, George Voorhelm, *Traité sur la Jacinte*, 3rd ed. (Haarlem: N. Beets, 1773; 1st publ. 1752), 51. President and Superintendent were listed by Rea, *Flora* (1665 ed.), 55, 61; Duc, Duchesse, Comte, and Contesse by Christiaen Porret in UBL BPL 2724d, Porret to Matteo Caccini, Leiden, August 22, 1610.

43. On Varia Brakel: UBL Pap. 1 a, Jan Boisot to Clusius, May 7, 1582; on Drap d'or: UBL Vulc. 101, Jan van Hoghelande to Clusius, letter 7, May 20, 1592; Sweerts, *Florilegium*, "Catalogus den ersten Boeck tracterende van de Bloemen met bollen" and "Catalogue du premier livre des fleurs a bulbes"; on Caperonia, UBL Vulc. 101, De Vulcob to Clusius, Paris, November 6, 1584; Van de Passe, "Register over de gheslacten der Tulipaenen, ende die sonderlick gheestimeert worden," in "Cort Verhael," *Hortus Floridus* (here Bodleian copy 1614–1617).

44. A. M. van der Woude, "Het gebruik van de familienaam in Holland in de zeventiende eeuw," *Holland* 5, no. 3 (June 1973): 109–31; for figures on Alkmade, 115, 117; P. J. Meertens, *De Betekenis van de Nederlandse Familienamen* (Naarden: Mij A. Rutgers, 1944), 13.

45. Jan Conijn appears on NHA NA 149/75v–76, not. Jacob Schoudt, February 2, 1637 (inaccurately printed in Posthumus 42); "bolletgen dirck" in NHA ORA 87-1/34, Desolate Boedels, Executieboek, July 22, 1648; Gerritgen in NHA Stadsarchief Haarlem, Rood 218/93 and 96, Burgemeestersresoluties, November 6 and 17, 1639; for Tulp, S. A. C. Dudok van Heel, "Tulpen uit Amsterdam," *Maandblad Amstelodamum* 79 (January–February 1992), 3–4, and Dudok van Heel, "Dr. Nicolaes Tulp alias Claes Pietersz: Deftigheid tussen eenvoud en grandeur," in T. Beijer et al., eds., *Nicolaes Tulp: Leven en Werk van een Amsterdams Geneesheer en Magistraat* (Amsterdam: Six Art Promotion, 1991), 49–51. For Guldewagen, G. H. Kurtz, "Het Huis dat Jacob van Campen Bouwde," *Jaarboek Haerlem* 1957, 52–53; on Olycan, Slive, ed., *Frans Hals*, 181; on Indischeraven and Spaerpott, Van Dillen, *Oudste Aandeelhoudersregister*, 172, 208; on Alderwerelt, Mary Susan Sprunger, "Rich Mennonites, Poor Mennonites: Economics and Theology in the Amsterdam Waterlander Congregation during the Golden Age" (PhD thesis, University of Illinois, Urbana-

Champaign, 1993), 116. On Anthony Jacobsz' family's names, AWG ONA Enkhuizen 970/act 180, not. J. J. Coppen, February 15, 1636.

46. Theodorus Schrevelius, *Harlemias, Ofte, om beter te seggen, De eerste stichtinghe der Stadt Haerlem* (Haarlem: Thomas Fonteyn, 1648), 213; on naming and collecting, see Findlen, *Possessing Nature*, 172–75; Symon LeFebure's statement is reported in NHA ONA Haarlem 133/434, not. Jacob Schoudt, June 14, 1635, also inaccurately/ incompletely published in Posthumus 16–17; La Chesnée Monstereul, *Le floriste françois*, 32.

47. Gilbert, *Florists Vade-Mecum*, 12; Parkinson, *Paradisi in Sole Paradisus Terrestris*, 63, a passage probably taken from Dodonaeus, *Cruydt-Boeck* (1618 ed.), 367.

48. Nicolas van Kampen, *Traité des Fleurs à Oignons* (Haarlem: C. Bohn, 1760), 71.

49. Rea, *Flora* (2nd ed. 1676), 66; for discussions of methods of changing flowers, see Sir Thomas Hanmer, The *Garden Book of Sir Thomas Hanmer Bart*, ed. Ivy Elstob (London: Gerald Howe, 1933), 17; Van Kampen, *Traité des Fleurs à Oignons*, 58–59; La Chesnée Monstereul, *Le floriste françois*, 175–76.

50. Parkinson, *Paradisi in Sole Paradisus Terrestris*, 22–23; Giovanni Battista Ferrari, *Flora, seu de florum cultura* (Rome, 1633), 457–503, cited in Elisabeth Blair MacDougall, "A Cardinal's Bulb Garden: A *Giardino Segreto* at the Palazzo Barberini in Rome," in MacDougall, *Fountains, Statues, and Flowers: Studies in Italian Gardens of the Sixteenth and Seventeenth Century* (Washington: Dumbarton Oaks Research Library and Collection, 1994), 241; La Chesnée Monstereul, *Le floriste françois*, 170, 172.

51. Mark Laird, "Parterre, Grove, and Flower Garden," 184, n. 44; Masson, "Italian Flower Collectors' Gardens," 71; UBL Vulc. 101, Marie de Brimeu to Clusius, letter 2, Leiden, September 18, 1591 (both quotations); Parkinson, *Paradisi*, 14; Pierre Vallet, *Le Iardin du Roy tres Chrestien Henry IV Roy de France et de Navare* (Paris: no publisher, 1608). Vallet is described on the title pages as "brodeur ordinaire." On Vallet, see also Hobhouse, *Plants in Garden History*, 108. For the comparison with carpets, see also Erik de Jong and Marleen Dominicus-Van Soet, *Aardse Paradijzen: De tuin in de Nederlandse kunst, 15de tot 18de eeuw* (ex. cat. Haarlem, Frans Halsmuseum, 1996), 103.

52. Early references to gold cloth are UBL Vulc. 101, Jan van Hoghelande to Clusius, letter 7, May 20, 1592; Sweerts, *Florilegium*, "Catalogus den ersten Boeck"; in English, "Cloth of golde" and "of sylver" were catalogued in the garden of Walter Stonehouse in 1640: "The Garden of the Rev. Walter Stonehouse at Darfield Rectory in Yorkshire," *The Gardeners' Chronicle* (May 20, 1920): 268. La Chesnée Monstereul's catalogue of tulips in 1654 contained four kinds of "Drap d'argent": *Le floriste françois*, 224; we saw earlier a comparison with gold and silver cloth in Dodonaeus, *Cruydt-Boeck* (1618 ed.), 365. On Sjery naeby and silk, Krelage, *Bloemenspeculatie*, 39. Clusius compared tulips to silk in *Rariorum plantarum historia* II cap. ix, sec. iii, pt. 2, p. 146, and cap. vii, sec. vii, pt. 8, p. 142. On elite use of gold and silver cloth, Valerie Cumming, "'Great vanity and excess in Apparell': Some Clothing

and Furs of Tudor and Stuart Royalty," in Arthur MacGregor, ed., *The Late King's Goods: Collections, Possessions and Patronage of Charles I in the Light of the Commonwealth Sale Inventories* (London: Alistair McAlpine/Oxford University Press, 1989), 326; on gold and silver cloth at the Dutch court, Irene Groeneweg, "Court and City: Dress in the Age of Frederik Hendrik and Amalia," in Marika Keblusek and Jori Zijlmans, eds., *Princely Display: The Court of Frederik Hendrik of Orange and Amalia van Solms in The Hague* (ex. cat. The Hague, Haags Historisch Museum, 1997), 201–3. Some of the many references to clothing in Franeau, *Iardin d'hyver*, are pp. 97, 100, 106; his reference to "les grans" is on p. 125. On collecting and cloth, Lorenz Seelig, "The Munich *Kunstkammer* 1565–1807," in Impey and MacGregor, eds., *The Origins of Museums*, 84–85; Porret, *Catalogus*.

53. Satin-like: *De Nederlandsen Bloem-Hof, of de Nauwkeurige Bloemist* (copy used has no title page; publication attributed by University of Amsterdam Library to Amsterdam: Harmen Machielsz and Nicolaas ten Hoorn, 1699), 7.

54. Seymour Slive, *Rembrandt and His Critics*, 1. For the views of Karel van Mander, see his *Den grondt der edel vry schilder-const*, the first section of his *Het Schilder-Boeck* (Haarlem: Passchier van Wesbuch, 1604). The *Grondt*, or *Groundwork*, has been edited in a separate modern version by Hessel Miedema (Utrecht: Haentjens Dekker & Gumbert, 1973), two vols. On the aesthetic terms used in Van Mander, see Miedema, *Fraey en Aerdigh, Schoon en Moy in Karel van Manders Schilder-Boeck* (Amsterdam: Kunsthistorisch Instituut, 1984), and Miedema, *Kunst, Kunstenaar en Kunstwerk bij Karel van Mander* (Alphen aan den Rijn: Canaletto, 1981), esp. 146–52, 156–59. See also Walter S. Melion, *Shaping the Netherlandish Canon*. On *netticheyt*, Van Mander, *Grondt*, chap. 12, stanza 21, and Dodonaeus, *Cruydt-Boeck* (1618 ed.), 365; see also Melion, 60–63. This is a concept also applied to flower painting: see Taylor, *Dutch Flower Painting*, 96–99. For Pliny on variety, see, for example, Pliny, *Natural History* IX.lii. On variety in Renaissance culture, John Shearman, *Mannerism* (Harmondsworth: Penguin, 1967), 75, 86, 92, 100–101, 105, 139, 140–51. For Van Mander on nature and variety, *Grondt*, chap. 5, stanza 20; on this verse, Melion, 8–9, 21. For Parkinson on variety, *Paradisi in Sole Paradisus Terrestris*, 45; for Dodonaeus on tulips' variety, *Cruydt-Boeck* (1608 ed.), 389.

55. On the development of discussion of art and its relationship to collecting in Antwerp, see Elizabeth Honig, "The Beholder as Work of Art," 280–81; on merchants' art lessons, Jaap van der Veen, "Liefhebbers, handelaren en kunstenaars: Het verzamelen van schilderijen en papierkunst," in Bergvelt and Kistemaker, eds., *De Wereld binnen handbereik*, 125.

56. UBL Vulc. 101, Jan Boisot to Clusius, letter 3, Brussels, August 4, 1588, postscript; Parkinson, *Paradisi in Sole Paradisus Terrestris*, "Epistle to the Reader"; Bosse's book is cited by Honig, "The Beholder as a Work of Art," 273, as a key text for connoisseurs; La Chesnée Monstereul, *Le floriste françois*, chap. 5; J. B. Reyntkens, *Den Sorghvuldighen Hovenier*, 2nd ed. (Gent: Hendrick Saetreuver, 1695); [Valnay], *Connoissance et culture parfaite*, 12–13; UBL BPL 1886, Jan Boisot to Clusius, Brussels, May 17,

1590; Rea, *Flora* (1665), "To the Reader"; Gilbert, *The Florists Vade-Mecum* (1682), "To the Reader"; on the *"Pas Oudinard,"* Rea, *Flora*, 56. On florists' flowers, see Ruth Duthie, *Florists' Flowers and Societies* (Haverfordwest: C. I. Thomas & Sons, 1988).

57. The Seys/Alleman case is NHA ORA Haarlem 116/19, roll, KBJ, August 18, 1637; on Sprangers and Massa, GAA NA 1158/144–144v, not. Joost van de Ven, December 27, 1636; the testimony of Fabricius is in NHA ONA Haarlem 149/95, not. Jacob Schoudt, May 18, 1637 (inaccurately/incompletely printed with incorrect citation in Posthumus, 63–64).

58. See, for example, the chief article on this subject in English, N. W. Posthumus, "The Tulip Mania in Holland in the Years 1636 and 1637," *Journal of Economic and Business History* 1, no. 3 (1929): 441–42; Simon Schama, *The Embarrassment of Riches: An Interpretation of Dutch Culture in the Golden Age* (New York: Alfred A. Knopf, 1987), 360; Taylor, *Dutch Flower Painting*, 14.

59. *Traitté Compendieux et Abregé des Tulippes et de leurs diverses sortes et especes* (Paris: Melchior Tavernier, 1617), 8; GAA NA 341/155–56, not. Willem Cluyt, September 26, 1611; the sale of Pieter Pietersz Tuynman is GAA WK 5073/952, September 25, 1626; Schoft conversation is AWG ONA Enkhuizen 970/154, not. J. J. Coppen, December 6, 1635.

60. Art auctions as a social activity: John Michael Montias, "A Group of Related Buyers at Orphan Chamber Auctions," in Marten Jan Bok et al., *Liber Amicorum W.A. Wijburg* (The Hague: Koninklijk Nederlandsch Genootschap voor Geslacht- en Wapenkunde, 2001), 188. John Michael Montias deals more generally with art buyers who were tulip traders in Montias, *Art at Auction in 17th-Century Amsterdam* (Amsterdam: Amsterdam University Press, 1999), 70–76. In September 1999 John Michael Montias and I had occasion to compare notes about our work, mine on tulips and his on art at auction. I alerted him to the existence of documents about a group of tulip traders in Amsterdam, and at the same time our joint consultation of his database of buyers of art at auction from 1600 to 1640, the Montias/ RKD Databank, confirmed my own previous impressions about the relationship between art buyers and tulip traders in the period. On Bessels, CBG Dossier Bessels, transcription of diary of Adam Bessels (original now lost); GAA DTB 423/234 April 24, 1619 (betrothal to Margaretha Reynst); Logan, *The 'Cabinet' of the Brothers Gerard and Jan Reynst*, chart facing p. 36; on Nicquet, Marten Jan Bok, "Art-Lovers," 158. Abraham de Goyer's inventory is GAA NA 968, not. Benedict Baddel, March 18, 1653; on his pamphlet collection, F. C. Wieder, "De Pamfletten-verzameling van den Amsterdammer Abraham de Goyer van 1616," *Het Boek* 5 (1917): 65–71; on Barent de Goyer, Abraham Bredius, "Rembrandtiana,"*Oud-Holland* XXVIII (1910): 11.

61. On the Spranger and Basse sales, see I. H. van Eeghen, "Rembrandt en de Veilingen," *Maandblad Amstelodamum* 77 (1985), and Montias, *Art at Auction in 17th-Century Amsterdam*. On the conflict over public sales of art in Haarlem, as well as an overall analysis of the art market, see Neil de Marchi and Hans J. van Migroet, "Art, Value, and Market Practices in the Netherlands in the Seventeenth

Century," *Art Bulletin* 76, no. 3 (1994): 458; on the lack of collections of rarities, Pieter Biesboer, *Collections of Paintings in Haarlem, 1572-1745*, ed. Carol Togneri (Los Angeles: The Provenance Index of the Getty Research Institute, 2001), 29, 257. On Nicolaes Suycker de Jonge, Biesboer, *Collections*, 27, 29, 81; his inventory is NHA ONA Haarlem 64 (no folio), not. Egbert van Bosvelt, June 21, 1641. On Paulus van Beresteyn, Biesboer, *Collections*, 30; Pieter Biesboer, "The Burghers of Haarlem and their Portrait Painters," in Seymour Slive, ed., *Frans Hals* (ex. cat. Washington, 1989), 27; Beresteyn's Heemskerck and Goltzius are mentioned in Schrevelius, *Harlemias*, 370; Aernoudt van Beresteyn is mentioned as an art-lover in Van Mander, *Schilder-Boeck*, 208v. Documents connecting tulip buyers with art sales include NHA ORA Haarlem 116/20 (unfoliated), KBJ, roll, June 22, 1638; NHA ORA Haarlem 116/20/111v, KBJ, roll, May 4, 1638; NHA ONA Haarlem 168/70, not. Jacob van Bosvelt, June 22, 1638. On De Grebber's sale, see De Marchi and Van Migroet, "Art, Value, and Market Practices," 458, n. 55. De Grebber's tulip book is the subject of NHA ORA Haarlem 116 / 22 (unfoliated), KBJ, November 29, 1639, where Cornelis Double sued him for restitution of "een boeck met tulpaden," which De Grebber had bought.

62. Heda acted as arbiter for a series of interconnected tulip sales in NHA ORA Haarlem 116/19 (unfoliated), KBJ, roll, February 3, 1637; his 1654 dispute is NHA ORA Haarlem 116/33 (unfoliated), KBJ, roll, May 19, 1654. On Poelenburch, see n. 4 above; Willem de Poorter is identified as a painter in NHA ONA Haarlem 162/289, not. Jacob Steyn, June 12, 1638; Haverbeeck held two tulip auctions mentioned in NHA ONA Haarlem 149/2v-3, not. Jacob Schoudt, December 18, 1635 (inaccurately/ incompletely printed in Posthumus, 19-20). Marrell's participation in the Utrecht meeting is recorded at HUA U4009a019 ff. 250-250v, not. Claes Verduyn, February 7, 1637, also printed in Posthumus, 44. On Jan van Goyen, see chap. 4 below. On Cornelis de Bruyn's cheating of Roelandt Saverij, see Marten Jan Bok, "Roelandt Saverij," in Ger Luijten et al., *Dawn of the Golden Age*, 316. On Jan Serange, see Montias, *Artists and Artisans in Delft*, 207. On Abraham de Cooge, see Jaap van der Veen, "De Delftse kunstmarkt in de tijd van Vermeer," in Donald Haks and Marie Christine vander Sman, eds., *De Hollandse Samenleving in de tijd van Vermeer* (ex. cat. The Hague, Haags Historisch Museum, 1996), 129-30; on a quarrel over whether a painting De Cooge had sold was forged, in which Marten Kretser wrote a testimonial for him, see Erik Duverger, "Een betwist schilderij van Paulus Bril bij een Gents Kanunnik," *Belgisch Tijdschrift voor Oudheidkunde en Kunstgeschiedenis* 35, no. 3-4 (1965): 191-200. Tulip transactions involving De Cooge include GA Delft not. W. van Assendelft, August 28, 1637; GA Delft not. W. van Assendelft, September 8, 1637; GA Delft not. A. van de Block, April 30, 1642, and GA Delft not. A.C. Bogaert, February 18, 1635 (all citations gleaned from RKD Archief A. Bredius, Dossier Abraham de Cooge). On David Jorisz, NHA ONA Haarlem 165/162, not. Jacob van Bosvelt, May 26, 1636.

63. The dossier for this case is HUA Stadsarchief II-2401 and -2402. I am very grateful to Marten Jan Bok for bringing its existence to my attention.

64. On Paludanus' sales, Roelof van Gelder, "Paradijsvogels in Enkhuizen," 34. On specialization and the art market, see especially J. Michael Montias, "Cost and Value in Seventeenth-Century Dutch Art," *Art History* 10, no. 4 (December 1987): 455–66, and De Marchi and Van Migroet, "Art, Value," 452. On the failure of paintings to rise in price during the seventeenth century, see Bok, "Rise of Amsterdam," 200–201; the argument that this was a result of product innovation is, again, from Montias, "Cost and Value." On setting the price for paintings (and thus relevant to concepts of value), see Marten Jan Bok, "Pricing the Unpriced: How Dutch Seventeenth-Century Painters Determined the Selling Price of their Work," in Michael North and David Ormrod, *Art Markets in Europe, 1400–1800* (Aldershot: Ashgate, 1998), 103–11.

65. *Clare Ontdeckingh der dwaesheydt der ghener die haer tegenwoordigh laten noemen Floristen* (Hoorn: Zacharias Cornelisz, 1636); also printed in *KP* 74.

Chapter Three

1. The document about this meal is NHA ONA Haarlem 149/78v–79, not. Jacob Schoudt, February 20, 1637, inaccurately and incompletely printed in Posthumus 47–49. For Pieter Wynants' marriage, see his wills cited below, and Pieter Biesboer, "The Burghers of Haarlem and their Portrait Painters," in Seymour Slive, ed., *Frans Hals* (ex. cat. Haarlem/Washington, 1989), 37; Barbara Jacobs Wynants' marriage contract to Laurens Reael is NHA ONA Haarlem 120/84, not. Jacob Schoudt, January 17, 1633, and Johan E. Elias, *De Vroedschap van Amsterdam 1578–1795* (Amsterdam: N. Israel, 1963) I, 136–37. The codicil to Pieter Wynants' will is NHA ONA Haarlem 137/18v, not. Jacob Schoudt, August 29, 1641, correcting a will of December 23, 1638, also before Schoudt. Geertruyt Schoudt, Jacob de Block, and De Block's wife, Trijntgen Lamberts (Catharina Lamberts Schouten), were related through their connection to the Mennonite Rogier van der Hulst (who was also connected to many of the other Haarlem Mennonites). Van der Hulst was Schoudt's father-in-law through her marriage to Abraham van der Hulst. Trijntgen Lamberts' connection was rather more distant (her first cousin Cornelia Laurens Schouten's husband, Pieter Adriaensz Block, was nephew of Rogier van der Hulst's wife, Elisabeth Jacobs Blocx, and thus her cousin's husband's cousin was Geertruyt Schoudt's late husband). Still, Jacob de Block seemed *au fait* with events in the Van der Hulst family when he remarked to Geertruyt Schoudt that she would be getting money from her late brother-in-law Jacob van der Hulst's estate. Rogier van der Hulst's identification as a Mennonite is from H. A. van Gelder, "Het Menniste Haarlem" (typescript available in the Zaal Mennonitica, UBA, and in the NHA), 15. I am very grateful to Daan de Clercq and Agnes Dunselman for their help in identifying the precise connections among members of this family.

2. On the religious makeup of Haarlem, see Joke Spaans, *Haarlem na de Reformatie: Stedelijke cultuur en kerkelijk leven, 1577–1620* (The Hague: Stichting Hollandse Historische Reeks, 1989), 104, and Joke Spaans, "Levensbeschouwelijke groeper-

ingen," in *Deugd boven geweld: Een geschiedenis van Haarlem, 1245–1995* (Hilversum: Verloren, 1995), 209; Gabrielle Dorren, *Eenheid en verscheidenheid: De burgers van Haarlem in de Gouden Eeuw* (Amsterdam: Prometheus/Bert Bakker, 2001), chap. 5. On Mennonites, see, among others, S. Zijlstra, *Om de ware gemeente en de oude gronden: Geschiedenis van de dopersen in de Nederlanden 1531–1675* (Hilversum: Verloren, 2000); S. Groenveld, J. P. Jacobszoon, and S. L. Verheus, eds., *Wederdopers, menisten, doopsgezinden in Nederland 1530–1980* (Zutphen: Walburg Pers, 1993); Alistair Hamilton, Sjouke Voolstra, and Piet Visser, eds., *From Martyr to Muppy: A Historical Introduction to Cultural Assimilation Processes of a Religious Minority in the Netherlands: The Mennonites* (Amsterdam: Amsterdam University Press, 1994). For Mennonites in Haarlem, see Van Gelder, "Het Menniste Haarlem."

3. Marvell wrote of "the Switzers of our guard" in his "Upon Appleton House, to my Lord Fairfax." Switsers and their "gorgeous Coats of red and yellow" were also celebrated in the pastoral performed for the Norwich Society of Florists on May 3, 1631, [Ralph Knevet], *Rhodon and Iris* (London: for Michael Sparke, 1631), V.vi., and by Jean Franeau ("les Suisses soldats") in *Iardin d'hyver ou cabinet des fleurs* (Douai: Pierre Borremans, 1616), 121.

4. NHA ONA Haarlem 149/78v–79, not. Jacob Schoudt, February 20, 1637.

5. Jean de Parival, *Les Délices de la Hollande* (Paris: la Compagnie des Libraires du Palais, 1665), 88.

6. [Steven van der Lust], "Troost voor de Ghescheurde Broederschap der Rouw-Dragende Kap-Broertjes, ofte Floraes Straet-Ionckers," reprinted in *Floraes Sotte-Bollen: Afghemaelt in Dichten en Sanghen* (no publication details: Amsterdam? 1643?), 62, and also in *KP* 184–85.

7. Lieuwe van Aitzema, *Saken van Staet en Oorlogh, In, ende omtrent de Vereenigde Nederlanden* (The Hague: Johan Veely, Johan Tongerloo, and Jasper Doll, 1669), II, 503; very similar wording is to be found in Abraham Munting, *Waare Oeffening der Planten* (Amsterdam: Jan Rieuwertsz, 1672), 634. Johann Beckmann, *Beyträge zur Geschichte der Erfindungen* (Leipzig: Paul Gotthelf Kummer, 1782), 3 vols; John Beckmann, *A History of Inventions, Discoveries and Origins*, trans. William Johnston and enlarged by William Francis and J. W. Griffith, 4th ed. (London: Henry G. Bohn, ed. 1846), I, 27–29; Charles Mackay, *Extraordinary Popular Delusions and the Madness of Crowds* (London: Richard Bentley, 1841). Mackay's debt to Beckmann is uncredited, as is Beckmann's to Aitzema. More authoritative accounts that still fail to use the manuscript evidence to investigate the social background to tulipmania include E. H. Krelage, *Bloemenspeculatie in Nederland: De Tulpomanie van 1636-'37 en de Hyacintenhandel 1720-'36* (Amsterdam: Patria, 1942); N. W. Posthumus, "De Speculatie in Tulpen in de Jaren 1636 en 1637," *Economisch-Historisch Jaarboek* 12 (1926): 3–99; 13 (1927): 3–85; 18 (1934): 229–40; N. W. Posthumus, "The Tulip Mania in Holland in the Years 1636 and 1637," *Journal of Economic and Business History* 1, no. 3 (May 1929): 434–66.

8. Beckmann, *History of Inventions* I, 27–28.

9. Anna Pavord's suggestion that it is professional nurserymen who operated this

trade, not to mention her postulation that there were "tulip fields" and a large export trade, paints a picture that is far too late for this period. She also takes any person involved seriously in the trade to be a nurseryman, such as Outger Cluyt (actually a doctor), Claes Verwer (actually a bleacher, and in any case not a recorded *bloemist*), and Hendrick Swalmius (actually one of the four ministers of the Grote Kerk in Haarlem, something she does note on p. 169, although at that point she states oddly that his name was "more usually written" as Walmius). Swalmius owned several gardens, but there is no evidence that he was a nurseryman; we do not even have any records of sales by him, although a tulip owned by Wouter Tullekens in Alkmaar is recorded as being planted in his garden on the Kleine Houtweg, suggesting that Swalmius might have sold it to Tullekens. See Anna Pavord, *The Tulip*, 153, 169.

10. GAA NA 1269/28–28v, not. P. Barman, February 24, 1637, also inaccurately printed in Posthumus, 49–50; the record of the Utrecht meeting is HUA NA Utrecht 4009 a 019/250, not. Claes Verduyn, February 7, 1637, also printed in Posthumus, 44–45. Population figures for Amsterdam and Haarlem from Jonathan Israel, *The Dutch Republic: Its Rise, Greatness, and Fall 1477–1806* (Oxford: Clarendon Press, 1995), 621. The officially surveyed population of Haarlem in 1622 was 39,455, according to Samuel Ampzing, *Beschryvinge ende Lof der Stad Haerlem in Holland* (Haarlem: Adriaen Roman, 1628), 38. Official counts for Amsterdam, according to Ed Taverne, were 105,000 in 1622 and 115,000 in 1630 (Ed Taverne, *In 't land van belofte: in de nieue stadt. Ideaal en werkelijkheid van de stadsuitleg in de Republiek* [Maarssen: Gary Schwartz, 1978], 143–44), but, as Taverne points out, these figures are not totally trustworthy. Taverne also cites the following figures for Amsterdam from P. Schraa, "Onderzoekingen naar de bevolkingsomvang van Amsterdam tussen 1550 en 1650," *Jaarboek Amstelodamum* 46 (1954): 1–33: from 1631 to 1640, a population of 126,000 to 139,000. For Enkhuizen, Gusta Reichwein, "Enkhuizen in de zeventiende eeuw," in Rudolf E. O. Ekkart, *Portret van Enkhuizen in de Gouden Eeuw* (ex. cat. Enkhuizen, Zuiderzeemuseum, 1990), 9. The identification of Haarlem as the place where the trade mainly took place ("voornementlijck alhier ter steede heeft in swangh gegaen") was in a letter from the burgemeesters of Haarlem to the Hof van Holland, April 15, 1637: Nat. Arch. 3.03.01.01, inv. 388, ff. 115v–116v, also inaccurately printed in Posthumus, 57.

11. The case of Jan Pietersz v. Pieter Jansz is NHA ORA 116/18/221v and 223, KBJ, September 16 and 19, 1636. It is notable, though perhaps, as it is a piece of propaganda, not particularly significant, that the author of a manuscript pamphlet of January 1637 claimed that there were only twenty to thirty main *bloemisten*. See UB Gent Meul. 2424, *Waerschouwinghe aen alle Goede Inghesetenen van ons lieve Vaderlant, teghen de Betoverende Bedriegerie der genen die haer laten noemen Blomisten oft Floristen*, printed in E. H. Krelage, "Het Manuscript over den Tulpenwindhandel uit de Verzameling-Meulman," *Economisch-Historisch Jaarboek* XXII (1943): 39.

12. Among the influential literature on *verzuiling* are Jakob Pieter Kruijt and Jan Blokker, *Verzuiling* (Saandijl: Heijnis, 1959); Jakob Peter Kruijt and W. Goddijn,

"Verzuiling en ontzuiling als sociologisch proces," in A. N. J. Hollander et al., eds., *Drift en Koers: Een halve eeuw sociale verandering in Nederland* (Assen: Van Gorcum, 1962), 227–63; A. J. Lijphart, *The Politics of Accommodation: Pluralism and Democracy in the Netherlands* (Berkeley: University of California Press, 1968). Simon Groenveld has expressed his ideas on *verzuiling* in the Republic in Groenveld, *Was de Nederlandse Republiek verzuild?* (inaugural address, University of Leiden, January 20, 1995), and Groenveld, *Huisgenoten des geloofs: Was de samenleving der Verenigde Nederlanden verzuild?* (Hilversum: Verloren, 1995). For a critical review of the latter, see José de Kruif in *Tijdschrift voor Sociale Geschiedenis* 22 (1996): 501–2.

13. The sale in Velsen is recorded at NHA ONA Haarlem 149/71–71v, not. Jacob Schoudt, January 12, 1637; Reynier Hindlopen from Hoogwoude is sued in Hoorn by both Jan Jansz Dentel and Jacob Jansz Spangiaert of Hoorn in AWG ORA Hoorn 4430, Rol van Commissarissen van de Kleine Zaken, December 22, 1637. On aristocrats in the Netherlands, see H. F. K. van Nierop, *The Nobility of Holland: From Knights to Regents, 1500–1650*, trans. Maarten Ultee (Cambridge: Cambridge University Press, 1993; Dutch version, *Van Ridders tot Regenten*, was published 1984), and J. Aalbers and M. Prak, *De Bloem der Natie: Adel en Patriciaat in de Noordelijke Nederlanden* (Amsterdam: Boom Meppel, 1987). John Michael Montias informed me that he also found no noblemen in records of the purchase of paintings for this period (private communication, September 6, 2003).

14. See the song "Mary Smuls vreught" in *Tweede Deel van 't Haerlems Liedt-Boeck, Anders ghenaemt den Laurier krans der Amoureusen*, 7th printing (Haarlem: Vincent Casteleyn, 1643), 5–6; *Samen-spraeck tusschen Waermondt ende Gaergoedt, Nopende de opkomste ende ondergangh van Flora* (Haarlem: Adriaen Roman, 1637); and *Tweede T'Samen-spraeck Tusschen Waermondt ende Gaergoedt, zijnde het vervolgh Van den op ende ondergangh van Flora*, 2nd ed. (Amsterdam: Cornelis Danckaertsz, 1643), which are also reprinted in *Economisch-Historisch Jaarboek* 12 (1926): 20–99. On the Kleine Bank van Justitie, see Gabrielle Dorren, *Eenheid en verscheidenheid*, 29. Although the Kleine Bank would not have been the only court to have dealt with cases about tulips, we are forced to rely on it as the only civil court in Haarlem with records surviving; in Amsterdam, the civil court records also no longer exist. Hoorn and Enkhuizen still have extant records for some civil cases, but there are only one or two clearly identifiable cases about tulips in their rolls. Because those lower-status figures we do find for Haarlem are in the Kleine Bank, it is at least possible that, if such records still existed for Amsterdam, we would find more of these figures there than we do at present, when our only source is the notarial record.

15. A tulip tax was first mooted by the States of Holland in July 1636 (*Resolutiën 1636*, Staten van Holland, printed, p. 150, July 10, 1636), proposed in the September 17–October 15, 1636, session (*Resolutiën 1636*, p. 183), and rejected on May 3, 1637 (*Resolutiën 1637*, p. 84). The importance of southerners to northern Dutch society is now a commonplace, but see especially J. G. C. A. Briels, *Zuid-Nederlandse Immigratie 1572–1630* (Haarlem: Fibula-Van Dishoeck, 1978), and Erika Kuijpers,

Migrantenstad: Immigratie en Sociale Verhoudingen in 17e-eeuws Amsterdam (Hilversum: Verloren, 2005). On this subject, and on the comparative exclusion of southern immigrants from government office, see Oscar Gelderblom, "De Deelname van Zuid-Nederlandse Kooplieden aan het Openbare Leven van Amsterdam (1578–1650)," in Clé Lesger and Leo Noordegraaf, eds., *Ondernemers en Bestuurders: Economie en Politiek in de Noordelijke Nederlanden in de late Middeleeuwen en Vroegmoderne Tijd* (Amsterdam: NEHA, 1999), 237–58, and Oscar Gelderblom, *Zuid-Nederlandse Kooplieden en de Opkomst van de Amsterdamse stapelmarkt (1578–1630)* (Hilversum: Verloren, 2000).

16. Jan or Joan Munter, born 1611, became a schepen in Amsterdam in 1653 and was burgemeester seven times between 1673 and 1674; just after tulipmania, in 1638, he was one of the directors (*bewindhebbers*) of the VOC. See Johan E. Elias, *De Vroedschap van Amsterdam 1578-1795* (Amsterdam: N. Israel, 1963), II, 625–26. The contract of his and Pieter Dircks' tulip purchase is GAA NA 866/169v–170, not. Jacob van Swieten, September 16, 1636, printed inaccurately in Posthumus 1934, 232–33. The regents in Enkhuizen involved in tulips were Barent ten Broecke, Pieter Dircksz Tjallis, and Pieter Jansz Uyl, who had all been schepenen. In Haarlem, besides Johan de Wael and Cornelis Guldewagen, we find Jan van Clarenbeeck (schepen, vroedschap), Cornelis Coning (schepen), and Jacob Steyn (secretary of Haarlem, raad, and eventually burgemeester). On De Wael and Guldewagen's offices, see the Haarlem *Herenboek* (Stadsarchief Haarlem Kast 30-500, *Naam-Register van de Heeren van de Regeering der Stad Haarlem* [Haarlem: G. van Kessel, 1733]). On De Wael and Guldewagen's floral difficulties, see NHA ONA Haarlem 149, ff. 95, 97, 104–104v, 111v, 115–115v, 144–144v, 188v, not. Jacob Schoudt, May 17 and 18, June 20, August 26, September 10, 1637; June 12, 1638; and April 12, 1639; and GA Den Haag NA 150/64v, not. Hiob de Vos, June 3/10, 1637. The letter of June 16, 1637, from the burgemeesters of Haarlem to the Hof van Holland, signed by the city secretary, Jacob van Bosvelt, is probably located at Nat. Arch. 3.03.01.01, inv. 4605, incoming and outgoing letters of the Hof van Holland 1636–1639, but as these documents are damaged I was not permitted to consult them. Posthumus prints it (having himself taken it not from the original but from H. Graf zu Solms-Laubach, *Weizen und Tulpe und deren Geschichte* [Leipzig: Arthur Felix, 1899], 115) on pp. 68–69.

17. For Abraham de Schilder, Kohier van de 200e penning, 1631 [henceforth 1631 Kohier], published as J. G. Frederiks and P. J. Frederiks, eds., *Kohier van den Tweehonderdsten Penning voor Amsterdam en Onderhoorige Plaatsen over 1631* (Amsterdam: Koninklijk Oudheidkundig Genootschap te Amsterdam, 1890), f. 94; for De Smith, f. 293v; for Bessels, f. 91; for Coornhart, f. 14v; for Bartholotti, f. 305; for Coymans, f. 302v. The calculations about how many people had fortunes of a particular size comes from Walter J. Strauss and Marjon van der Meulen, eds., *The Rembrandt Documents* (New York: Abaris Books, 1979), 81. An affidavit about Jasper Coymans'

theft of tulip bulbs on two occasions from Paulus du Prijs appears at GAA NA 355/28–28v, not. Willem Cluyt, April 2, 1631.

18. Data on ages come from Amsterdam's DTB, especially the betrothal registers (*ondertrouw*).

19. The tax records for Haarlem are the Verpondingskohier 1628, NHA Stadsarchief Kast 15-232; the Verpondingskohier 1650, NHA Stadsarchief Kast 15-234; and the Kohier van de 200e penning 1653, NHA Stadsarchief restant Enschedé doos 16, EII-901. In the 1628 Kohier, for Pieter Vrients see B-11v; for Nicolaes Suycker (and note that some properties might have belonged to his father of the same name) see C-1v, C-4, M-1, TT-18 (two entries), D-5, I-13, TT-18v, H-5v, R-13, R-13v. The neighborhood analysis by wealth appears in René Smits, "De Plaats waar ik woon: Een onderzoek naar de verspreiding van rijk en arm in Haarlem rond 1628" (doctoraal scriptie, Universiteit van Amsterdam, 1989). On neighborhoods in Haarlem, see also Gabrielle Dorren, *Eenheid en verscheidenheid*, chap. 3.

20. In Amsterdam, of those whose trade could be identified, thirty-three were merchants, two were wine sellers (and thus also probably involved in international trade), two were involved in insurance as well (and thus probably, again, taking part in international trade), three were grocers (again, probably international traders), four were professional florists (one formerly an international merchant and insurer), one was an art dealer, one was possibly an artist (Simon van Poelenburch had been an engraver, but it is unclear what he was doing in the 1630s), and one was a furrier. In Haarlem, we find forty-three merchants, ten merchants concerned with bleaching or bleachers, one dyer, three clothworkers including two identified as weavers, eighteen bakers, ten brewers, eleven innkeepers or owners of inns, five shopkeepers, two wine sellers, two notaries, three lawyers, five surgeons, one doctor, five tailors, three *uitdragers* (people who removed and sold property from the houses of the dead), four artists, five gold- and silversmiths, one glassmaker, eleven gardeners, four smiths, two shoemakers, one clogmaker, one stockingmaker, two bargemen (*slepers*), one cheesemaker, one cooper, one carpenter, one rabbit seller, two printers, one bookseller, three locksmiths, one teacher, one turf carrier, one bedmaker, one sugar refiner, one grocer (probably again meaning international trade in this particular case), one servant, and the precentor of the Grote Kerk. In Enkhuizen (where some of those investing in trade and counted as merchants also had other professions) we find seven merchants (four if one subtracts those also employed in other trades), five apothecaries, two master shipwrights, two bakers, one artist, one carpenter, one master nailmaker, one lawyer, one wheelwright, and one grocer/wine seller (involved in international trade). On the estate of Abraham Anthonisz de Milt, see NHA ONA Haarlem 136/166v–68, not. Jacob Schoudt, November 28, 1640; it should be noted that the person who sold a Coornhart to Jan van de Knier is identified only as Abraham de Milt (NHA ORA 116/18/157v, 158, KBJ, July 11 and 15, 1636). On the amount of the estate of Jan van Damme, see NHA WK 147/26v. The

point that the designation of craftsman might merely indicate the occupation in which someone was trained I owe to John Michael Montias (private communication, September 6, 2003).

21. On the *vrunden* and the relationship of family and friends with business, see Luuc Kooijmans, *Vriendschap en de Kunst van het Overleven in de Zeventiende en Achttiende Eeuw* (Amsterdam: Bert Bakker, 1997), 14–18; also Luuc Kooijmans, "Risk and Reputation: On the Mentality of Merchants in the Early Modern Period," in Clé Lesger and Leo Noordegraaf, eds., *Entrepreneurs and Entrepreneurship in Early Modern Times: Merchants and Industrialists within the Orbit of the Dutch Staple Market* (The Hague: Stichting Hollandse Historische Reeks, 1995), 31–32. Among the evidence for Lambert Massa's business with his brother Isaac is a contract of 1616, GAA NA 530/79–79v, not. Jacob Westfrisius, January 6, 1616; he joined his brother Christiaen in freighting ships in GAA NA 741/131v, not. Hendrick Bruijningh, June 6, 1624, and GAA NA 826/19, not. J. Bruijningh, June 19, 1626. The contract forming the De Clercq–Ampe potash company is NHA ONA Haarlem 169/16–16v, not. Jacob van Bosvelt, November 20, 1649. On Abraham de Schilder and Andries Rijckaert's sugar refinery, see J. J. Reesse, *De Suikerhandel van Amsterdam van het begin der 17de eeuw tot 1813* (Haarlem: J. L. E. I. Kleynenberg, 1908), 274. De Schilder's tulip auction, on May 17, 1633, is referred to in GAA NA 863/405v, not. Jacob van Swieten, December 19, 1634, also printed in Posthumus 1934, 231–32.

22. The author of an anonymous manuscript pamphlet about the tulip trade in January 1637, *Waerschouwinghe*, claimed in fact that most of the *bloemisten* were in fact Mennonites ("sijnt niet meestendeel Mijnisten"), although, since he wished to point out that this was a deceitful trade and said that the rest were Jews and bankrupts, this was more a term of abuse than a statement of fact. See Krelage, "Het Manuscript over den Tulpenwindhandel," 40–41.

23. NHA ONA Haarlem 168/204, not. Jacob van Bosvelt, February 12, 1639. Pieter Moens' statement about De Clercq was recounted by Jacob Symonsz in NHA ONA Haarlem 168/191v, not. Jacob van Bosvelt, January 23, 1639. Details on the quarrel over Anthoni Moens' estate are in NHA ONA Haarlem 168/122–122v, not. Jacob van Bosvelt, September 17, 1638.

24. GAA NA 674/193v–194, not. Jacob Warnaertsz, May 9, 1637. De Man's wife was Josina van der Cooghen, whose will is NHA ONA Haarlem 120/126, not. Jacob Schoudt, May 21, 1633. He appears in the records of the Amsterdam Mennonite community "Bij het Lam," for example in GAA Arch. 1120 no. 11, Doopboek, f. 11, October 28, 1635. Neckevelt's transaction with Bosch is GAA NA 674/186v, not. Jan Warnaertsz, May 6, 1637; his identity as a Mennonite is mentioned in I. H. van Eeghen, "De Restauratie van Keizersgracht 62 en 64," *Maandblad Amstelodamum* 62 (1975): 25. The transaction between Halmael and Van Meeckeren is GAA NA 919/20v–21, not. Barent Jansen Verbeeck, January 12, 1637, and it is canceled in GAA NA 919/61–61v, not. Barent Jansen Verbeeck, February 10, 1637. These are printed in Posthumus, 36–37 and 45–46, but particularly inaccurately; Posthumus, for example, simply omits the participation of Maria Vlaminghs in this deal. It should

be noted that Abraham van Meeckeren may well have converted to the Reformed Church, as his wife, Magdalena Bon, seems not to have been Mennonite.

25. Pieter Biesboer writes of the close family ties connecting different southern Mennonite families and providing them with social and economic support, citing particularly the relationships of the De Clercqs and their relatives and mentioning other similar families that also, as we know, had connections with tulips, such as the Wynants, de Neufville, and Bon families: Pieter Biesboer, "De Vlaamse immigranten in Haarlem 1578–1630 en hun nakomelingen," in Pieter Biesboer et al., *Vlamingen in Haarlem* (Haarlem: De Vrieseborch 1996), 47.

26. On the new canal ring, see Ed Taverne, *In 't land van belofte,* chap. 4, and Koen Ottenheym, "The Amsterdam Ring of Canals: City Planning and Architecture," in Peter van Kessel and Elisja Schulte, eds., *Rome-Amsterdam: Two Growing Cities in Seventeenth-Century Europe* (Amsterdam: Amsterdam University Press, 1997), 33–34; on the prestigiousness of this location, S. A. C. Dudok van Heel, "Regent Families and Urban Development in Amsterdam," in Van Kessel and Schulte, 140. The addresses I give for *bloemisten* in Amsterdam and Haarlem in the following paragraphs are gleaned from a variety of sources, including notarial records, tax records, DTB, and *kwijtscheldingen* and other records of land transport. (Listing these here would be excessively lengthy, but I am happy to provide the information to any interested party.) On the importance of neighborhoods in this society, see Herman Roodenburg, "Naar een etnografie van de vroegmoderne stad: De 'gebuyrten' in Leiden en Den Haag," in Peter te Boekhorst, Peter Burke, and Willem Frijhoff, eds., *Cultuur en Maatschappij in Nederland 1500–1850* (Meppel and Amsterdam/Heerlen: Boom/Open Universiteit, 1992), 219–43, and Gabrielle Dorren, "Communities Within the Community: Aspects of Neighbourhood in Seventeenth-Century Haarlem," *Urban History* 25, no. 2 (1998): 173–88.

27. Victory's inventory is GAA NA 1914/486–495, not. F. Uyttenbogaert, December 20, 1647; all three gardens are listed on f. 492. The suggestion that De Goyer had made ƒ20,000 in one year appears in GAA Arch. 520/120, Particulier Archief Museum Amstelkring, f. 4, a book of poems by Gerrit Jansz Kooch. The poem on tulipmania that precedes this statement on De Goyer, "Op het Wonderlijck Jaer der bloemisten Anno 1637," is indistinguishable from the usual propagandistic tulip songs. Judging by the other poems in the volume, this was unlikely to have been written before 1670.

28. Jeuriaen Jansz's dealings with Heindrick Bartelsz are recorded in NHA ONA Haarlem 165/271–271v, not. Jacob van Bosvelt, August 1, 1636 (also inaccurately printed in Posthumus, 27–28). His estate was inventoried in NHA ONA Haarlem 64 (no folio), not. Egbert van Bosvelt, April 30, 1643. The Weeskamer sale, in which the sale of Jansz's flowers was recorded separately from the auction of other household goods, is NHA WK 160/5v, estate of Jeuriaen Jansz, baker, and his wife, Sara de la Chambre. On f. 9v is recorded the salary of the officials present at the sale of the plants and flowers, as well as the payment for the assistance of Barent Cardoes (professional gardener and *bloemist*) in the auction. The fact that Jansz lived next

door to Alleman is clear from the 1628 tax records: NHA Stadsarchief Haarlem Kast 15-232, C-2, Verpondingskohier 1628.

29. NHA ONA Haarlem 158/185, not. Wouter Crousen de Jonge, August 29, 1636; NHA ONA Haarlem 158/194, not. Wouter Crousen de Jonge, September 5, 1636. Acts also inaccurately and incompletely printed in Posthumus, 29–30.

30. On the social and economic history of Haarlem, see Dorren, *Eenheid en verscheidenheid*; and the chapter by H. A. Diederiks and P. C. Spierenburg, "Economische en sociale ontwikkelingen," in *Deugd boven geweld*, 168–97. For the cloth trade in Haarlem, see Freek Baars, Herman Kaptein, and Floris Mulder, *Haarlem ging op wollen zolen: Opkomst, bloei en ondergang van de textielnijverheid aan het Spaarne* (Haarlem: Historisch Museum Zuid-Kennemerland, 1995). Jan van Clarenbeeck's election to *vinder* of the *twijnders'* guild is recorded at NHA Stadsarchief Haarlem, Rood 217/58v, burgemeestersresoluties October 29, 1635. The election of the inspectors of the Lange Garen for 1640 (when all those mentioned here were elected) is at NHA Stadsarchief Haarlem, Rood 218/164, burgemeestersresoluties, March 16, 1640. The cloth merchants in Utrecht were Gerrig Bosch and Hendrick Hardenberch, plus silk merchants Roeloff van Diemen, Daniel Hoorns, Willem Gerritsz van Oosterwijck, and Jacob Verbeeck den Jonge. The Enkhuizen tulip company consisted of apothecaries Jan Jansz Apotheecker, Barent ten Broecke, Anthony Jacobsz [Apesteijn], plus the *kruidenier* and wine-seller Heyndrick Willemsz Vries and the dyer Cornelis Cornelisz Varwer. On weavers, it should be noted that even the most famous weaver supposedly involved, Waermondt in Adriaen Roman's *Samen-spraeck tusschen Waermondt ende Gaergoedt*, had journeymen and owned looms. See the second dialogue printed by Posthumus in *Economisch-Historisch Jaarboek* 12 (1926): 47.

31. On Kistgens' and De Haes' purchase from Baert, GAA NA 676/5v-6, not. Jan Warnaertsz, June 24, 1637. The purchase by Munter and Dircksz is GAA NA 866/169v-70, not. Jacob van Swieten, September 16, 1636 (crossed out, because the contract was withdrawn); its revocation is GAA NA 866/170, not. Jacob van Swieten, June 20, 1637; both are printed inaccurately in Posthumus 1934, 232–33 and 237. Posthumus comments that this is an example of the inexperienced lower classes being fleeced by the wealthy (Posthumus 1934, 229), but since the number of tulips Munter and Dircksz actually bought for *f*84 is not clear, it is not possible to ascertain this. In September 1636 some tulips were still fairly cheap, so what they paid is not necessarily an unreasonable figure. That said, the wording of the contract does suggest a fair number of tulips.

32. The origins of the members of this Haarlem tulip company are derived from the registers of betrothals: NHA DTB 151/141, March 23, 1631 (Kops); NHA DTB 151/48, February 28, 1632 (Wynants); and NHA DTB 151/197, May 9, 1638 (Prior). None of these three was married in the Reformed Church. The other members of the company were Aert Huybertsz, Ysack Jansz rietmaecker, and Pieter Marcusz. Pieter Wynants is clearly different from Pieter Jacobsz Wynants because he was eleven years younger and was still alive in 1645, which Pieter Jacobsz Wynants was not.

The contract between Heldewier and De Smith is GAA NA 670, unfoliated, not. Jan Warnaertsz, March 21, 1635. On the relationships in the Enkhuizen tulip company, see, for example, AWG ONA Enkhuizen 978/act 50, not. Reijer Sampson, May 16, 1642; the company is first set up in AWG ONA Enkhuizen 931/act 72, not. Cornelis Antonisz Stant, February 23, 1636.

33. See Anne Goldgar, "Poelenburch's Garden: Art, Flowers, Networks, and Knowledge in Seventeenth-Century Holland," in Amy Golahny, Mia Mochizuki, and Lisa Vergara, eds., *In His Milieu: Essays in Memory of John Michael Montias* (Amsterdam: Amsterdam University Press, 2007).

34. NHA WK 179/13, Weeskamer accounts for the estate of David de Milt; NHA WK 147/15v–16, Weeskamer accounts for the estate of Jan van Damme. An example of a Haarlemmer buying at the Winckel sale in Alkmaar is Jan Quakel: see NHA ONA Haarlem 149/210, not. Jacob Schoudt, September 1, 1639. The claim by Robert Shiller that newspapers would give "detailed news of the speculation as it was then unfolding" dates this type of newspaper report much too early; there is nothing in the periodical press about tulipmania (besides the monthly reports in 1623–1624 by Wassenaer), and the pamphlet literature was not only not a form of news but was issued almost entirely after the crash. For his comments, see Robert J. Shiller, *Irrational Exuberance* (Princeton, NJ: Princeton University Press, 2000), 246, n. 2. After publication of his book, Professor Shiller initiated a correspondence with me to discuss this subject.

35. Abraham de Schilder's auction is mentioned in GAA NA 863/405v, not. Jacob van Swieten, December 19, 1634, also printed in Posthumus 1934, 231–32. On the *collegie* for birds in Joost Joostensz Plavier's inn, NHA ONA Haarlem 172/39v–40v, not. Salomon Coesaert, May 9, 1639; Plavier's tulip purchase is recorded in an appeal on their behalf to the Hoge Raad of Holland by his co-purchaser, Jacob Jansz de Ridder of Leiden, over their debt of ƒ5,000 to Antony Beliaert of Middelburg (Nat. Arch. 3.03.02/inv.41, Rekesten Hoge Raad, July 29, 1637) and an appeal by their guarantors (one of whom was Plavier's uncle) to the Hoge Raad to be absolved of responsibility for this debt: Nat. Arch. 3.03.020/inv. 41, Rekesten Hoge Raad, August 26, 1637.

36. Schrevelius, *Harlemias*, 214.

37. La Chesnée Monstereul, *Le floriste françois*, 181; Hanmer, *Garden Book*, 24.

38. NHA ONA Haarlem 165/162, not. Jacob van Bosvelt, May 26, 1636; NHA ONA Haarlem 149/47v–48, not. Jacob Schoudt, July 27, 1636, also inaccurately/incompletely printed and with a now incorrect citation in Posthumus, 26–27; NHA ONA Haarlem 133/434, not. Jacob Schoudt, June 14, 1635, also inaccurately/incompletely printed in Posthumus, 16–17.

39. *Samen-spraeck tusschen Waermondt ende Gaergoedt*, reprinted in *Economisch-Historisch Jaarboek* 12 (1926): 22; the pamphlet is attributed to Adriaen Roman by E. H. Krelage, *Pamfletten*, 13.

40. NHA ONA Haarlem 165/271–271v, August 1, 1636, inaccurately printed in Posthumus, 27–28.

41. Documents about David de Milt's estate are in NHA WK 179; about Jan van Damme's, in NHA WK 147. Cornelis Bol was a linen and yarn merchant—he was regularly among the electors of the inspectors of the Lanckgaren in this period (NHA Stadsarchief Haarlem, Rood 217/12, burgemeestersresoluties, November 26, 1634; 217/60v, November 14, 1635; 217/126v, November 10, 1636), but he also owned expensive gardens, such as a garden outside the Kleine Houtpoort bought in 1633 for ƒ3,600, mentioned in NHA ONA Haarlem 133/392v–393, not. Jacob Schoudt, September 21, 1634, and in a transport document of 1638 he is referred to as a gardener ("Thuynier"): NHA Tp. 76-58/129–129v, May 20, 1638. He set up a tulip company with Jan Govertsz Coopall on September 9, 1635 (the original document is missing but its terms are mentioned in the renewal of the contract at NHA ONA Haarlem 120/387, not. Jacob Schoudt, November 6, 1636; another copy is at ONA Haarlem 134/261). Barent Cardoes, who was one of the representatives of Haarlem at the meeting of bloemisten in Amsterdam on February 24, 1637, gave as evidence of his expertise on May 17, 1637, that he had worked "long years" ("lange jaeren") for Pieter Bol: NHA ONA Haarlem 149/97, not. Jacob Schoudt, May 17, 1637 (inaccurately printed and with incorrect citation in Posthumus, 61–62). Gillis de Milt is identified as a gardener in NHA ONA Haarlem 183/142 not. Barent Jansz Deteringh, June 3, 1640. Pieter Jansz van de Winckel appears to have been working as a gardener (in this case, for Nicolaes Anthony and alongside Abraham Rogiersz) in NHA ONA Haarlem 174/151v, not. Salomon Coesaert, November 3, 1646. Rogier Rogiersz is referred to as a gardener in a document about tulips (NHA ONA Haarlem 165/162, not. Jacob van Bosvelt, May 26,1636) in which he indeed was standing about in a garden with other bloemisten; his brother Abraham Rogiersz was a vinder of the Warmoesiersgilde, the market gardeners' guild, in Haarlem: NHA Stadsarchief Haarlem, Rood 218/4, April 7, 1639.

42. The transaction between Cortoor and Smuyser is described in NHA ONA 149/76–76v, not. Jacob Schoudt, February 4, 1637, also inaccurately/incompletely printed with an incorrect citation by Posthumus, 43–44. Rogier Alleman, who was 23 in 1637, was involved in numerous tulip sales and purchases, including a sale in Enkhuizen to the apothecary Jan Schouten (NHA ONA Haarlem 158/211, not. Wouter Crousen de Jonge, September 31, 1636) and various others that ended up in the Kleine Bank van Justitie, such as the sale of bulbs to Salomon Seys (NHA ORA 116/19, unfoliated, KBJ, August 18, 1637). Alleman's wife, Maeycken Verschuyll, who also worked at De Druyff, bought tulips from Cornelis van Baelen: NHA ONA Haarlem 166/53v, not. Jacob van Bosvelt, January 31, 1637. Allert Schatter's identity as innkeeper of Den Ouden Haen is mentioned in NHA ONA Haarlem 158/125v, not. Wouter Crousen de Jonge, March 9, 1636; he claimed to have traded tulips for cloth in a KBJ case, NHA ORA 116/20/36, KBJ, December 18, 1637. Jan Wynants is identified as an innkeeper in a document about a tulip purchase from Symon Le Febure (NHA ONA Haarlem 133/434, not. Jacob Schoudt, June 14, 1635, also printed inaccurately/incompletely in Posthumus, 17). Pleun Jansz van

Doorn, often known simply as Pleun Jansz, was involved in a number of transactions to do with tulips, including a claim that he had bought tobacco with flowers: NHA ORA 116/19, unfoliated, KBJ, April 21, 1637. Huybert Fransz sued Pieter Willemsz van Acht unsuccessfully over flowers he claimed to have sold to Van Acht: NHA ORA 116/118/141, KBJ, June 17, 1636. The Quakel family's ownership of Den Vergulden Druyff is mentioned in G. H. Kurtz, "Twee Oude Patriciërshuizen in de Kruisstraat: Kruisstraat 45 en 51," *Jaarboek Haerlem* (1961): 120. The purchase of an inn by Seys and Van Breugel is recorded in NHA ORA Tp. 76-56/185v, May 21, 1636. Joost Plavier's identity as innkeeper in the Syde Specxs is frequently mentioned in the archives, for example in NHA ONA Haarlem 57/137v, not. Egbert van Bosvelt, January 3, 1639; his son Joost's inn on the Schagchelstraat appears in NHA ONA Haarlem 172/39v–40v, not. Salomon Coesaert, May 9, 1639; Jan Joosten Plavier's tulip purchase is described in Nat. Arch. 3.03.02/inv.41, rekesten Hoge Raad, July 29, 1637.

43. Wilhelmus Tiberius ultimately passed on the debt Cornelis de Haese owed him to Jan Hendricxsz Admirael to collect: GAA NA 1009/106, not. Gerrit Coren, April 16, 1638. The purchase by "den Secretaris Steyn" of flowers for ƒ42:10 is recorded in the Weeskamer documents for David de Milt, NHA WK 179/3v. Gerrit Tielemansz's suit against Egbert van Bosvelt is NHA ORA 116/18/80v, KBJ, March 28, 1636. Wouter Crousen's doodled tulips are to be found at NHA ONA Haarlem 158/50v, not. Wouter Crousen de Jonge, July 1635.

44. NHA ONA Haarlem 158/125, not. Wouter Crousen de Jonge, March 9, 1636. Interestingly, a tale of deception similar to the Double case is recounted in the anonymous manuscript pamphlet of January 1637, *Waerschouwinghe aen alle goede Inghesetenen*, printed in E. H. Krelage, "Het Manuscript over den Tulpenwindhandel," 46.

45. NHA ONA Haarlem 158/125v–6, not. Wouter Crousen de Jonge, March 9, 1636. It should be noted that the spelling of the name of Witvelt is not certain from my reading of the manuscript. Witvelt's name could in fact be Vleytvelt (however, I have found no other mention of such a person in the archives, while Dirck Witvelt is in fact involved in a KBJ case concerning tulips). The fine paid by Double was known as *in 't gelach*.

46. NHA ONA Haarlem 158/126, not. Wouter Crousen de Jonge, March 9, 1636.

47. For "den tuijn van poelenburch tot Amsterdam," NHA ORA 116/19/30v, KBJ, December 2, 1636; for "corennaert tot amsterdam," NHA ORA 116/19, unfoliated, February 3, 1637. Michiel van Limmen, then secretary of the KBJ, sued Tymon Maertsz over tulips he had bought on December 2, 1637 (NHA ORA 116/19/31, KBJ, December 2, 1636). The suit and countersuit of Stoffel de Way and Bastiaen van de Rype is at NHA ORA 116/18/221, KBJ, September 16, 1636. De Way wanted delivery of a quarter-pound of Oudenaerden from Van de Rype. Van de Rype countersued for ƒ40 for a Jan Gerritsz bulb he had sold to De Way and that De Way had sold on, but not yet delivered, to Pieter Willemsz. In addition Van de Rype wanted ƒ13

profit from a "turlongh" (Terlon). De Way said that Pieter Willemsz would pay Van de Rype directly all that De Way himself was owed. Van de Rype was let off of the original suit concerning the Oudenaerden.

48. Hendrick Woutersz referred to "syne mede Compagnons" in NHA ORA 116/19/27v, KBJ, November 28, 1636, and to "syn cameraett" in NHA ORA 116/19/44, KBJ, January 9, 1637. Contracts setting up or organizing tulip companies are NHA ONA Haarlem 134/270–270v, not. Jacob Schoudt, December 29, 1636 (inaccurately printed with now incorrect citation in Posthumus, 35–36); NHA ONA Haarlem 120/387, not. Jacob Schoudt, November 6, 1636, with another copy at 134/261 (the latter is printed with now incorrect citation in Posthumus, 33–35; this is the revision of a contract originally made on September 9, 1635, but that document is now missing); AWG ONA Enkhuizen 931/act 72, not. Cornelis Antonisz Stant, February 23, 1636; GAA NA 670, unfoliated, not. Jan Warnaertsz, March 21, 1635; GAA NA 866/19–20, not. Jacob van Swieten, January 3, 1637. The existence of another tulip company in Haarlem is referred to in NHA ONA Haarlem 150/143–143v, not. Jacob Schoudt, September 27, 1645. Tetrode sued Schouten over brokerage fees in NHA ORA 116/19/42, KBJ, January 6, 1637. Cornelis de Vogel, a professional broker, represented unnamed buyers in Haarlem in a purchase of bulbs from Zacharias Lepij in Enkhuizen, a deal referred to in GAA NA 544A/1637/12–12v, not. Jacob Westfrisius, May 19, 1637. Pieter de Ketelaer, factor, represented the Haarlem brewer Abraham van Meeckeren and his mother, Maria Vlaminghs, in the scrapping of a contract between them and Jacob van Halmael in Amsterdam: GAA NA 919/61–61v, not. Barent Jansen Verbeeck, February 10, 1637 (also published very inaccurately and incompletely in Posthumus, 45–46). Jan Govertsz Coopall was referred to as "de pryns van de tulpaen" in the burial register, NHA DTB 70/253, November 15, 1636.

49. For Admirael, see chap. 2. For Kooch on De Goyer, see GAA Arch. 520/120, Particulier Archief Museum Amstelkring, f.4. Jan Jansz Schoft of Enkhuizen reports buying tulips from Abraham Casteleyn in Amsterdam in AWG ONA Enkhuizen 970/154, not. J. J. Coppen, December 6, 1635, and at the time Casteleyn made reference to a purchase by a Jan van Broeckenhuysen, also apparently from Enkhuizen. For Van Breugel's activities, see especially GAA NA 918/179v–180, not. Barent Jansz Verbeeck, June 12, 1636. Rogier Alleman sold in Enkhuizen to Jan Schouten: see NHA ONA Haarlem 158/211, not. Wouter Crousen den Jonge, September 14, 1636, also printed inaccurately and incompletely in Posthumus, 30. Jacques de Clercq sold to Barnaert Ferreres of Enkhuizen: AWG ONA Enkhuizen 946/act 99, not. Jan van Conincxvelt, September 20, 1636. Hans Baert sold in Amsterdam to François Hendricxsz Coster, Jan Pietersz Neckevelt, Michiel Kistgens, Jan de Haes, Matthijs Schouten, Hendrick van Bergom: see GAA NA 675/87, not. Jan Warnaertsz, June 25, 1637, inaccurately and incompletely printed in Posthumus, 71–72; GAA NA 676/4–6, not. Jan Warnaertsz, June 24, 1637; GAA NA 676/76v–77, not. Jan Warnaertsz, September 29, 1637. Salomon Seys' dealings with Alleman and Woutersz come up in NHA ORA 116/119, unfoliated, KBJ, August 21, 1637; with Haverbeeck

in NHA ORA 116/19, unfoliated, KBJ, August 9, 1637; his dealings in Groningen with Romijn Jacobsz appear in NHA ORA 116/22, unfoliated, KBJ, July 20, 1640; his sale to Bertens is NHA ONA Haarlem 149/126, not. Jacob Schoudt, November 29, 1638 (also printed in Posthumus, 83–84); to De Jongh, NHA ORA 116/18/206, KBJ, August 20 and 28, 1636, and 116/19/32–32v, KBJ, December 2, 1636; to Pietersz, NHA ORA 116/20, unfoliated, June 14, 1638; to Ryck, NHA ORA 116/20, unfoliated, KBJ, July 6, 1638; his dealings with Baerckensz and Huybertsz are in NHA ORA 116/21, unfoliated, KBJ, September 2, 1639. He is arbiter in NHA ORA 116/18/127, KBJ, May 27, 1636, and in NHA ORA 116/19, unfoliated, KBJ, February 3, 1637. He was proxy for Hans Lailepel in NHA ORA 116/20, unfoliated, June 16 and 22, 1638. He commented on Le Febure's tulips in NHA ONA Haarlem 165/162, not. Jacob van Bosvelt, May 26, 1636. His inn was purchased in NHA Tp. 76-56/185v, May 21, 1636.

50. NHA ONA Haarlem 172/144v, not. Salomon Coesaert, September 16, 1639, also inaccurately printed in Posthumus, 85; NHA ONA Haarlem 57/89, not. Egbert van Bosvelt, June 20, 1637, also printed in Posthumus, 70–71; GAA NA 730B/78 not. P. Carelsz, February 23, 1638 (in Amsterdam, but discussing Alkmaar); AWG ONA Enkhuizen 973/act 142, not. Reyer Sampson, May 7, 1638.

51. The statement about *garen* (yarn) is in NHA ONA Haarlem 150/130v, not. Jacob Schoudt, May 26, 1645. The agreement of the meeting of florists, written and signed the following day, is GAA NA 1269/28–28v, not. P. Barman, February 24, 1637, also printed inaccurately in Posthumus, 49–50. The meeting in Utrecht is HUA NA Utrecht 4009 a 019/250, not. Claes Verduyn, February 7, 1637, also printed in Posthumus, 44–45.

52. Montias, *Art at Auction*, 105–6, 109; Donald Posner, "Concerning the 'Mechanical' Parts of Painting and the Artistic Culture of Seventeenth-Century France," *Art Bulletin* 75 (1993): 583–98.

53. NHA ONA Haarlem 158/185, not. Wouter Crousen den Jonge, August 29, 1636, also printed in Posthumus, 29.

54. The Double case is at NHA ONA Haarlem 158/125–126v, not. Wouter Crousen den Jonge, March 9, 1636.

55. NHA ONA Haarlem 162/173, not. Jacob Steyn, June 10, 1636; NHA ONA Haarlem 162/175–175v, not. Jacob Steyn, June 17, 1636. These documents are also printed inaccurately and incompletely in Posthumus, 23–24.

Chapter Four

1. The agreement between Boortens and Van Welsen is NHA ONA Haarlem 166/130–31, not. Jacob van Bosvelt, April 14, 1637, also incompletely and inaccurately printed in Posthumus, 53–57. Boortens' age is in NHA ONA Haarlem 166/412, not. Jacob van Bosvelt, October 1, 1637. His ownership of a bleachery is mentioned in NHA ONA Haarlem 168/217, not. Jacob van Bosvelt, March 16, 1639. His son's betrothal to Josina Bols is NHA DTB 50/276, February 5, 1635. Pieter Ger-

ritsz van Welsen (sometimes just Pieter Gerritsz or Gerretsen, as on the February 24, 1637, document, where the Gerretsen signature is clearly that of Van Welsen) can be found in a variety of tulip documents, including NHA ONA Haarlem 63, not. Egbert van Bosvelt, November 14, 1637 (also printed in Posthumus, 80) and NHA ONA 149/134v–135, not. Jacob Schoudt, February 3, 1638, incompletely/ inaccurately printed in Posthumus, 81–82. His attendance of the Amsterdam meeting is recorded in GAA NA 1269/28v, not. P. Barman, February 24, 1637 (the meeting took place on February 23, but the document about the agreement is dated February 24).

2. NHA ONA Haarlem 166/130–130v, not. Jacob van Bosvelt, April 14, 1637. Similar cases of contracts being transferred to others to give them the ability to collect debts for tulips include GAA NA 919/438v–439, not. Barent Jansen Verbeeck, December 22, 1637, when the Amsterdam embroiderer Dirck Glaude took over a debt by François Heldewier to Claes Harmensz for tulips, paying Harmensz so that Heldewier now owed the sum to him; GAA NA 1009/106, not. Gerrit Coren, April 6, 1638, in which Wilhelmus Tiberius passed on to Jan Hendricxsz Admirael the right to collect a debt he was owed by the notary Cornelis de Haes for a quarter bulb of Admirael van der Eyck; and, in a slightly different case, Willem van Dael and his wife, Anna van Dael, of Amsterdam were owed money for silk bought in November 1635 by Admirael, who told them that because Cornelis van Breugel owed *him* money for tulips, in May 1636 Van Breugel would pay them ƒ1,100 directly (GAA NA 695/73, not. Jan Warnaertsz, June 12, 1636; I am grateful to John Michael Montias for having brought this case to my attention).

3. NHA ONA Haarlem 166/130v–131, not. Jacob van Bosvelt, April 14, 1637.

4. NHA ONA Haarlem 166/245–245v, not. Jacob van Bosvelt, July 9, 1637. This document also includes an addition dated July 27 concerning the use of a superarbiter. A fuller document about the superarbiter, with a note at the end saying that the compromise was not called into play and that the question was subsequently solved, is NHA ONA Haarlem 166/265–265v, not. Jacob van Bosvelt, July 24, 1637.

5. Emmanuel Sweerts, *Florilegium* (Frankfurt am Main: Anthonius Kempner, 1612), advertisement on back of title page, Latin, Dutch, German, and French; UBL BPL 2724d, Christiaen Porret to Matteo Caccini, Leiden, August 22, 1610.

6. On Falquin Baltin, UBL Vulc. 101, Jean de Maes to Clusius, letter 8, Brussels, November 11, 1601. For Willem Willemsz, J. G. and P. J. Frederiks, eds., *Kohier van de Tweehonderdsten Penning voor Amsterdam en Onderhoorige Plaatsen over 1631* (Amsterdam: Koninklijk Oudheidkundig Genootschap, 1890), 72 (f. 318 in original, and f. 319 for de Goyer). The sale of bulbs owned by Pieter Pietersz Tuynman is GAA WK 5073/952, September 25, 1626. I am grateful to John Michael Montias for alerting me to its existence. Marcus Cornelisz Flora, the son of the sugar refiner Cornelis Marcusz, was himself a florist (thus his chosen name), and Jeronimo Victory ultimately became one, although at this time he was still involved in trade. But the other figures here, as we have noted, were not professionally involved with

horticulture. The transaction between Mahieu and Coninck is discussed in NHA ONA Haarlem 56/20, April 29, 1611 (also in Posthumus, 11–12); the confrontation between De Goyer and Elbertsz is GAA NA 341/155–156, not. Willem Cluyt, September 26, 1611; an *insinuatie* about this case, GAA NA 357B/203, July 19, 1611, is also incompletely printed in Posthumus, 12, although Posthumus, by leaving out part of the document, forgets to indicate who besides Coornhart was involved.

7. PRO SP 84/72/170, Dudley Carleton to John Chamberlain, The Hague, May 1, 1616, printed in Maurice Lee, Jr., ed., *Dudley Carleton to John Chamberlain 1603-1624: Jacobean Letters* (New Brunswick, NJ: Rutgers University Press, 1972), 199. Visscher's comments appear in Roemer Visscher, *Zinne-Poppen*, ed. Anna Roemers (Amsterdam: Johannes van Ravesteyn, 1669; orig. ed. Amsterdam: Willem Jansz, 1614), 5; Franeau's in Jean Franeau, *Iardin d'Hyver ou Cabinet des Fleurs* (Douai: Pierre Borremans, 1616), p. 132, note (x); the "Registre" is in *Traitté Compendieux et Abregé des Tulippes et de leurs diverses sortes et especes...* (Paris: Melchior Tavernier, 1617), 8.

8. David Beck, *Spiegel van Mijn Leven: Haags dagboek 1624*, ed. S. E. Veldhuizen (Hilversum: Verloren, 1993), 27, January 1, 1624; Nicolaes van Wassenaer, *Historisch verhael alder ghedenk-weerdichste geschiedenissen, die hier en daer in Europa ... voorgevallen syn* V (April 1623): 40.

9. Wassenaer, *Historisch verhael* V (April 1623): 40–41; VII (June 1624): 111–12; IX (April 1625): 10.

10. The Caers op de Candelaer prices and the four beds of tulips are all mentioned in NHA ONA Haarlem 108/235, not. Wouter Crousen de Oude, July 10, 1612, also printed incompletely in Posthumus, 13–14; the prices of the Saeyblom van Coningh and Latour come from a sale by the painter Joost Jansz van Haverbeeck, discussed in NHA ONA Haarlem 149/2v-3, not. Jacob Schoudt, December 18, 1635, also inaccurately and incompletely printed in Posthumus, 19–20; the low price for the Groot Gepluymaseerde from December 28, 1636 (2,000 *asen* for ƒ140) is in GAA NA 676/76v, not. Jan Warnaertsz, September 29, 1637, and the high price (2,000 *asen* for ƒ300, paid in barley) is recorded in GAA NA 919/20–21, not. Barent Jansen Verbeeck, January 12, 1637, very inaccurately and incompletely printed in Posthumus, 36. Many of the prices modern authors have cited for tulips, including several of the picturesque ones involving trading goods for tulips come from Abraham Munting's 1671 *Waare Oeffening*, which in turn copied them straight from the pamphlet *Samen-spraeck tusschen Waermondt ende Gaergoedt*; they are not to be trusted.

11. The low and high points of the Switser price series are GAA NA 918/554v, not. Barent Jansz Verbeeck, December 31, 1636, and GAA NA 676/146–147, not. Jan Warnaertsz, November 9, 1637, also very inaccurately and incompletely printed in Posthumus, 79. As mentioned in the notes to my introduction, one of the many inaccuracies of Posthumus' transcription of this document is in his rendering of a price, when he said that the price of the Maxen or Hagenaers sold in this transaction was ƒ4,000, rather than the actual ƒ400. If Posthumus had not insisted on changing the original written-out figures ["vierhondert guldens"] to numer-

als, this kind of error would not have happened. I should note that another set of price series has been done by Peter Garber in *Famous First Bubbles*. I have based my prices on my own manuscript research and am cautious about including some of the prices Garber uses, both because they rely on an apparently unchecked use of the error-ridden Posthumus and because Garber trusts the prices in the printed pamphlets about the Alkmaar auction of February 5, 1637, about which, lacking any real manuscript confirmation, I remain somewhat skeptical. It is true that one manuscript source, the lawsuit against Willem Lourisz, who bought an Anvers Festus bulb, confirms that this particular bulb was really sold at the price listed in the pamphlets about the auction (*f*510), so perhaps there is some reason to trust these prices. (For this case, see RAA ORA Alkmaar 87/3.) However, I have not included them in my series. On Schoudt's purchase of tulips, see the beginning of chapter 3. The statement by Olfert Roelofsz and Jan Schouten is AWG ONA Enkhuizen 973/act 142, not. Reyer Sampson, May 7, 1638.

12. The contract with Cock is GAA NA 918/554v–555v, not. Barent Jansen Verbeeck, December 31, 1636; that with Abraham van Meeckeren is GAA NA 919/20v, not. Barent Jansen Verbeeck, January 12, 1637 (printed in Posthumus, 36–37), and is called off at Van Meeckeren's request in GAA NA 919/61–61v, not. Barent Jansen Verbeeck, February 10, 1637 (also printed very incompletely and inaccurately in Posthumus, 45–46). That it was Van Meeckeren's idea to cancel the transaction is indicated by the fact that his agent, Pieter Ketelaer, was to pay Halmael *f*160 for calling off the deal (*rouwkoop*). Prices from the Alkmaar auction are printed in *Lijste van Eenige Tulpaen, verkocht aen de meest-biedende op den 5en Februarij 1637...*, which is reprinted in *Economisch-Historisch Jaarboek* 12 (1926): 96–99. On the one price we can confirm for this sale, see note 11 above. Documents about Winckel's estate include RAA Weeskamer 36/32, Register van Voogdijen, July 16, 1636, and August 6, 1636.

13. Cornelis de Bruyn's contract for sale of his bleachery is NHA ONA Haarlem 168/30–31, not. Jacob van Bosvelt, January 6, 1638. On a case of refusal to pay for a tulip bought at the Alkmaar auction, see chapter 5.

14. On Cock and Halmael, GAA NA 918/554v–555v, not. Barent Jansen Verbeeck, December 31, 1636. Alleman's visit to Schouten is recorded at NHA ONA Haarlem 158/211, not. Wouter Crousen de Jonge, September 31, 1636. On Groes' deal with Maes, AWG ONA Enkhuizen 972/act 69, not. Reijer Claesz Samson, November 15, 1636: my italics.

15. RAA ORA Alkmaar 87/4, stuk 2, January 15, 1637. Six coopcedullen are tied together here.

16. Schoft's report on his encounter with Casteleyn is AWG ONA Enkhuizen 970/act 154, not. J. J. Coppen, December 6, 1635. Van Gennep's experience is described in GAA NA 919/50–50v, not. Barent Jansen Verbeeck, January 28, 1637, also inaccurately and incompletely published in Posthumus, 40–41.

17. NHA ONA Haarlem 149/75–75v, not. Jacob Schoudt, February 2, 1637, also printed

inaccurately and incompletely in Posthumus, 42–43 (with outdated folio number).

18. NHA ONA Haarlem 162/173, not. Jacob Steyn, June 10, 1636, also printed inaccurately and incompletely in Posthumus, 23–24. Further argument about this issue and discussions about it at the Vergulden Kettingh inn are to be found in NHA ONA Haarlem 162/175–175v, not. Jacob Steyn, June 17, 1636, also printed inaccurately and incompletely in Posthumus, 24–25.

19. The only source we have that actually describes sales at inns is the pamphlet series by Adriaen Roman. The *borden* auctions are described in *Samen-spraeck tusschen Waermondt ende Gaergoedt Nopende de opkomste ende ondergangh van Flora* (Haarlem: Adriaen Roman, 1637), which is reprinted in *Economisch-Historisch Jaarboek* 12 (1926); in this edition the passage about the auction is on pp. 22–23. The details of the sales are not all entirely clear from Roman's account. An attempt to shed light on these details, not always successful, appears in Posthumus' introduction to the Roman pamphlets, in *Economisch-Historisch Jaarboek* 12 (1926): 12–17, and his "The Tulip Mania in Holland in the Years 1636 and 1637," *Journal of Economic and Business History* 1, no. 3 (May 1929): 440–41. Besides an understandable lack of clarity on some of the details, Posthumus makes some errors, such as suggesting in the Dutch introduction to the pamphlets that *wijnkoop* was half the purchase price in *borden* sales.

20. The *in 't ootgen* auctions feature in the second dialogue between Waermondt and Gaergoedt, a reprint of which is published in the *Economisch-Historisch Jaarboek* 12 (1926): 68: *Tweede T'Samen-spraeck tusschen Waermondt ende Gaergoedt, zijnde het vervolgh Van den op ende nedergangh van Flora* (Amsterdam: Cornelis Danckaertsz, 1643). The comment about *wijnkoop* appears in the first dialogue, in the modern edition, p. 23. The example of Jaques de Poer is GAA NA 866/26, not. Jacob van Swieten, February 11, 1637, incompletely and inaccurately printed in Posthumus 1934, 233–34. According to the late John Michael Montias, Jaques de Poer might be Jacques du Pours, a wool sorter turned wool merchant (private communication, October 7, 2002). Examples of *wijnkoop* being used as a sign that a tulip transaction had been concluded include GAA NA 866/27–28, not. Jacob van Swieten, February 11, 1637; NHA ONA Haarlem 149/71–71v, not. Jacob Schoudt, January 12, 1637; and NHA ONA Haarlem 56/20, not. Egbert van Bosvelt, April 29, 1611; a use of *wijnkoop* in a transaction not concerning tulips (here, a painting) is NHA ORA 116/20, KBJ, June 20, 1638.

21. Reymont de Smith's contract with François Heldewier is GAA NA 670/unfoliated, not. Jan Warnaertsz, March 21, 1635; Jan Minuit's with Nicolaes Block is GAA NA 866/19–20, not. Jacob van Swieten, January 3, 1637. Minuit was clearly wealthy, or became so: in 1668 his widow sold a series of grain mills and shares in grain mills totaling ƒ43,500 (GAA NA 2997/73–76, not. Jacob de Winter, November 30, 1668, summarized in J. G. van Dillen, *Bronnen tot de Geschiedenis van het Bedrijfsleven en het Gildewezen van Amsterdam* III [RPG Grote Serie 144, 1974], 793). The addition of

Rogge to the Amsterdam-Haarlem company is in NHA ONA Haarlem 134/270–270v, not. Jacob Schoudt, December 29, 1636, also printed inaccurately with old folio number in Posthumus (who does not note that Philips Jansz signed his name Rogge), 35–36. On the Huybertsz/Jansz company, see NHA ONA Haarlem 159/143, not. Wouter Crousen de Jonge, February 20, 1638, and NHA ONA Haarlem 150/143–143v, not. Jacob Schoudt, September 27, 1645.

22. NHA ONA Haarlem 134/261–261v, not. Jacob Schoudt, November 6, 1636, also printed inaccurately and incompletely in Posthumus, 24–25. Another copy of the document is at NHA ONA Haarlem 120/387, not. Jacob Schoudt, November 6, 1636. Unfortunately the initial contract referred to in this document, from September 9, 1635, seems no longer to exist.

23. Varwer's lease of a garden is AWG ONA Enkhuizen 931/act 18, not. Cornelis Antonisz Stant, January 2, 1636. The contract forming the tulip company is AWG ONA Enkhuizen 931/act 72, not. Cornelis Antonisz Stant, February 23, 1636. A note on names: both Jan Jansz Apotheecker and Cornelis Cornelisz Varwer had surnames denoting their actual professions (Varwer's was written correctly, Verwer, by the notaries, but as he always signed Varwer, that is the spelling I use), but the documents make it clear that they used these as names, whereas Anthony Jacobsz Apesteijn usually signed his name simply as Anthony Jacobsz.

24. AWG ONA Enkhuizen 931/act 72, not. Cornelis Antonisz Stant, February 23, 1636.

25. The loan of ƒ2,700 was made on July 25, 1636, but was recorded only in AWG ONA Enkhuizen 931/240 [folio number: no act number], not. Cornelis Antonisz Stant, August 17, 1636. The new contract is described by witnesses in AWG ONA Enkhuizen 932/act 193, not. Cornelis Antonisz Stant, December 31, 1636. The sale of three offsets is AWG ONA Enkhuizen 972/act 93, not. Reijer Claesz Samson, January 28, 1637.

26. The repayment of the debt is at AWG ONA Enkhuizen 965/act 354, not. Jacobus Vael, June 2, 1646, and is also referred to at the end of the document recording the loan, AWG ONA Enkhuizen 931/240, not. Cornelis Antonisz Stant, August 17, 1636.

27. On Pieter de Clercq's purchase, NHA ORA 116/19, unfoliated, KBJ, April 24, 1637.

28. Joseph de la Vega, *Confusion de Confusiones*, ed. and trans. Hermann Kellenbenz (Boston: Kress Library of Business and Economics, Harvard University, 1957, orig. publ. 1688), 5–6. On the future trading of commodities, see, among others, Jonathan Israel, *Dutch Primacy in World Trade, 1585-1740* (Oxford: Clarendon Press, 1989), 75; Violet Barbour, *Capitalism in Amsterdam in the Seventeenth Century* (Johns Hopkins University Studies in Historical and Political Science LXVII [1949], no. 1), 74–75; and Pit Dehing and Marjolein 't Hart, "Linking the Fortunes: Currency and Banking, 1550–1800," in Marjolein 't Hart, Joost Jonker, and Jan Luiten van Zanden, eds., *A Financial History of the Netherlands* (Cambridge: Cambridge University Press, 1997), 53. On futures in grain, see Milja van Tielhof, *De Hollandse Graanhandel, 1470-1570: Koren op de Amsterdamse Molen* (The Hague: Stichting Hollandse Historische Reeks, 1995), 195; on VOC *in blanco* shares, Dehing and 't Hart,

"Linking the Fortunes," 44–45, and J. G. van Dillen, "Isaac le Maire en de Handel in Actiën der Oost-Indische Compagnie," *Economisch-Historisch Jaarboek* XVI (1930): 1–165, especially 17; on futures selling of shares in general, see Neil De Marchi and Paul Harrison, "Trading 'in the Wind' and with Guile: The Troublesome Matter of the Short Selling of Shares in Seventeenth-Century Holland," in Neil De Marchi and Mary S. Morgan, eds., *Higgling: Transactors and Their Markets in the History of Economics* (Durham, NC: Duke University Press, 1994), 47–65. Among those suggesting that it was only money, not bulbs, that changed hands, is the much-copied Johann Beckmann, who was probably reflecting on the futures trade in his own time, the late eighteenth century: Beckmann, *History of Inventions* (4th ed., 1846), I, 27–28; he was followed in this error by, among others, Wilfrid Blunt, *Tulips and Tulipomania* (London: The Basilisk Press, 1977), 28. We are also told by Mackay that speculators made money by manipulating the markets: "The tulip-jobbers speculated in the rise and fall of the tulip stocks, and made large profits by buying when prices fell, and selling out when they rose" (Mackay, *Extraordinary Popular Delusions*, 97), but in fact no such manipulation is evident, nor did prices fall, except at the end of the craze in early February 1637.

29. Johannes Cloppenburgh, *Christelijcke Onderwijsinge van Woecker, Interessen, Coop van Renten ende allerleye winste van Gelt met Gelt* (Amsterdam: Theunis Jacobsz, 1637), 9 and *passim*. On disapproval of gambling, see Leendert F. Groenendijk, "Kansspelen in het ethische discours van gereformeerde theologen in de Noordelijke Nederlanden," *De zeventiende eeuw* 15, no. 1 (1999): 74–75, and Herman Roodenburg, *Onder Censuur: De kerkelijke tucht in de gereformeerde gemeente van Amsterdam, 1578–1700* (Hilversum: Verloren, 1990), 333–35. The English observer wrote in *The Politia of the United Provinces*, in Somers, *Tracts* III (c. 1625), 630–35, quoted in C. D. van Strien, *British Travellers in Holland during the Stuart Period* (Leiden: E. J. Brill, 1993), 197. On the decline of lottery culture after 1618, see Anneke Huisman and Johan Koppenol, *Daer compt de Lotery met trommels en trompetten! Loterijen in de Nederland tot 1726* (Hilversum: Verloren, 1991), 66–68. On the Haarlem lottery and lotteries in general, see Kitty Kilian, *De Loterij van Haarlem 1606–1607: Een onderzoek naar de mentaliteit van Hollanders en Zeeuwen in de vroege zeventiende eeuw* (doctoraalscriptie, Rijksuniversiteit Utrecht, 1988), and Kitty Kilian, "De Haarlemse loterij van 1606–1607: Loterijen en loterijrijmpjes," *Haerlem Jaarboek* (1989): 8–37; details given here appear in *De Loterij*, 29–30, and "De Haarlemse loterij," 24, 26.

30. The tontine in Leiden is referred to in Leiden GA NA 425/26, not. Caerl Outerman, March 24, 1631, and GAA NA 861/244v–245, not. Jacob van Swieten, July 26, 1632, printed in Walter J. Strauss and Marjon van der Meulen, eds., *The Rembrandt Documents* (New York: Abaris Books, 1979), 74–75, 87; for the kneading-trough bet, see A. Th. van Deursen, *Plain Lives in a Golden Age: Popular Culture, Religion and Society in Seventeenth-Century Holland*, trans. Maarten Ultee (Cambridge: Cambridge University Press, 1991), 105. The bet by Castels is NHA ONA Haarlem 184/115, not. Barent Jansz Deteringh, July 27, 1641; by De Jongh, NHA ONA Haarlem 133/123–123v, not. Jacob Schoudt, August 17, 1631; by Alleman, NHA ONA Haarlem 180/69,

not. Salomon Coesaert, March 19, 1648. Some examples of bets about paintings can be found in John Michael Montias, *Artists and Artisans in Delft* (Princeton, NJ: Princeton University Press, 1982), 201–2.

31. The Hazes bet is AWG ONA Hoorn 2089/3, not. J. Volkertsz Oli, November 12, 1636; this document was very kindly sent to me by Piet Boon. The Tjallis bet is AWG ONA Enkhuizen 911/act 233, not. Olbrant Smetius, February 7, 1637. On the siege of Schenckenschans, see Jonathan Israel, *The Dutch Republic: Its Rise, Greatness and Fall 1477–1806* (Oxford: Clarendon Press, 1995), 529–30. The bet by Coelembier and De Wet appears in Jacob de Wet, *Schetsboekje*, f. 62v, March 31, 1636, printed in Strauss, *Rembrandt Documents*, 138; despite the apparent hugeness of the bet, given the inclusion of a Dürer and two Rembrandts, if Coelembier had lost he would only have had to pay De Wet *f*3:10 for the prints. The bet between Jan Jansz and Tuenis Sijmonsz over an Oudenaerde is discussed in NHA ORA 116/18/225, 226, KBJ, September 19 and 22, 1636. A further bet involving life expectancy, tulips, and the war is NHA ONA Haarlem 166/208, not. Jacob van Bosvelt, August 6, 1637, in which we learn that in the summer of 1635 Andries de Preyer and Reyndert Huybertsz had bought from Lambert Reyniersz two Sayblommen on the condition that, if there was peace between the Netherlands and Spain before either Reyniersz or De Preyer died, then De Preyer and Huybertsz would pay *f*236 for the tulips, which presumably would otherwise be free. As it happened, Huybertsz, whose life was immaterial to the bet, died; we can see how important the bet was, as this document is a renegotiation of the terms of the bet between De Preyer and Huybertsz's heirs.

32. On risks to trade, see, among others, Violet Barbour, "Marine Risks and Insurance in the Seventeenth Century," *Journal of Economic and Business History* I, no. 4 (August 1929): 562–63; Peter Mathias, "Strategies for Reducing Risk by Entrepreneurs in the Early Modern Period," in Clé Lesger and Leo Noordegraaf, eds., *Entrepreneurs and Entrepreneurship in Early Modern Times: Merchants and Industrialists within the Orbit of the Dutch Staple Market* (The Hague: Stichting Hollandse Historische Reeks, 1995), 8. On the depredations of pirates, see Israel, *Dutch Primacy in World Trade*, 134, and Marjolein 't Hart, *The Making of a Bourgeois State: War, Politics and Finance during the Dutch Revolt* (Manchester: Manchester University Press, 1993), 56–57.

33. On Dutch trade during the period, see especially Israel, *Dutch Primacy in World Trade, 1585–1740*. On the directorate of the Levant trade, see P. W. Klein, "The Trip Family in the 17th Century: A Study of the Behaviour of the Entrepreneur on the Dutch Staple Market," *Acta Historiae Neerlandica* I (1966): 201–2; on shares in voyages, Barbour, "Marine Risks," 569–70, and Mathias, "Strategies for Reducing Risk," 22–23; on families and credit, Mathias, 5–6; on bottomry loans, Israel, *Dutch Primacy in World Trade*, 76–77.

34. On marine insurance, see Frank C. Spooner, *Risks at Sea: Amsterdam Insurance and Maritime Europe 1766–1780* (Cambridge: Cambridge University Press, 1983), 18, and Lorraine J. Daston, "The Domestication of Risk: Mathematical Probabil-

ity and Insurance 1650–1830," in Lorenz Krüger, Lorraine J. Daston, and Michael Heidelberger, *The Probabilistic Revolution* (Cambridge, MA: MIT Press, 1987), I, 239, 244; Daston writes on pp. 247–48 that life insurance at this time "remained a gamble, whose buyers and sellers emphasized and indeed reveled in the element of risk and uncertainty. . . ." Philip II's edict banning insurance was dated March 31, 1568, and his edict reordering the trade is printed as *Ordonnance, Statut et police faite par le Roy nostre Sire, sur le Fait des Contractz des Asseurances es Pays Bas* (Antwerp: Christoffel Plantijn, 1570).

35. Liebert van Axele's dealings in saltpetre are notable in GAA NA 621/58v, not. Sibrant Cornelisz, May 5, 1616, and GAA NA 364/7, not. Willem Cluyt, November 20, 1620; for his involvement with Venetian mirror glass, see GAA NA 371/21, not. Willem Cluyt, February 6, 1630, and GAA NA 695/105, not. Jan Warnaertsz, May 3, 1635; for insurance, see, for example, GAA NA 643/84, not. Sibrant Cornelisz, June 25, 1635.

36. The possibility of various new taxes, or of raising current taxes on luxuries, was discussed, among other places, in *Resolutiën, Staten van Holland 1636*, pp. 54–55, March 12, 1636, and p. 199, October 1, 1636. The tulip tax was singled out to go forward on p. 150, July 10, 1636, and the resolution sent to the towns was on p. 183, number XVIII of a series of proposals from the session of September 17–October 15, 1636. Comments on the tax occur in AWG OA Hoorn 112, resolutieboek van burgemeesteren, September 12, 1636; RAA Alkmaar, Oud-Stadsarchief 44/132, resoluties van de vroedschap, September 15, 1636; AWG OA Enkhuizen 33 (253)/577, vroedschapsregisters, September 5, 1636; GAA Arch. 5025/16/136, vroedschapsresoluties, October 8 1636; NHA Stadsarchief Haarlem, Rood 86/6v, vroedschapsresoluties, November 8, 1636. Amsterdam called the tax "niet practicabil"; Haarlem "inpracticabel." The abandonment of the tax occurs at *Resolutiën, Staten van Holland 1637*, p. 84, May 3, 1637.

37. Prices of commodities on the Amsterdam Beurs come from price courants for 1637, cited as yearly averages, in N. W. Posthumus, *Nederlandsche Prijsgeschiedenis* (Leiden: E. J. Brill, 1943) I, 100 (table 51), 106 (table 53), 109 (table 54), 147 (table 66), and 225 (table 96). I have recalculated Posthumus' prices to show what quantities one could buy for ƒ1,000. Prices of everyday commodities for 1637 come from a database of prices by the economic historian Jan Luiten van Zanden, "The Prices of the Most Important Consumer Goods, and Indices of Wages and the Cost of Living in the Western part of the Netherlands, 1450–1800," at the website of the Internationaal Instituut voor Sociale Geschiedenis in Amsterdam (www.iisg.nl). I have again recalculated to show the values for ƒ1,000. A contemporary pamphlet, *Clare ontdeckingh der dwaesheydt der ghener die haer tegenwoordigh laten noemen Floristen* (Hoorn: Zacharias Cornelisz, 1636), reprinted in KP 82, gives the famously astounding list of goods (four fat oxen, eight fat pigs, etc.) that one might have been able to buy for the price a bulb costing ƒ2,500 (which in any case was a very high price for a bulb). As noted earlier, it was not claimed in the pamphlet that these items were actually exchanged for a bulb. It is true that goods were some-

times exchanged for tulips, although the various "crazy" prices often cited, such as a horse and carriage, two silver beakers, and ƒ150, come ultimately not from documented sources but from the pamphlet literature via Munting (*Samen-Spraeck tusschen Waermondt ende Gaergoedt*, 79–80, and Munting, *Waare Oeffening der Planten* (1672 ed.), 632–34. Wage figures come from Leo Noordegraaf, *Daglonen in Alkmaar 1500–1850* (no place of publication: Historische Vereniging Holland, 1980), 77, 85. The translation of ƒ1,000 into the purchasing power of modern currency comes from a website calculator, "Value of the Guilder," constructed from the series of data about prices and wages mentioned above, also constructed by Jan Luiten van Zanden and also on the website of the Internationaal Instituut voor Sociale Geschiedenis in Amsterdam. The exchange rate calculation from euros to dollars was made on July 9, 2006.

38. Groes' transaction is AWG ONA Enkhuizen 972/act 69, not. Reijer Claesz Samson, November 15, 1636; Abrahamsz's is mentioned in NHA ONA Haarlem 149/71–71v, not. Jacob Schoudt, January 12, 1637; Huybertsz (a *vinder* for his guild) is discussed in NHA ONA Haarlem 149/126, not. Jacob Schoudt, November 29, 1638, also printed in Posthumus, 83.

39. GAA Arch. 5077, rekeningboek Wisselbank, vol. beginning February 1644. (The account book is not properly inventoried but can be found at Depot 63, Stelling 43, Kast 6, Plank 1). For Reymont de Smith's account from April 12–May 9, see f. 910. For purchasers of VOC shares, see J. G. van Dillen, *Het oudste aandeelhoudersregister van de Kamer Amsterdam der Oost-Indische Compagnie* (The Hague: Martinus Nijhoff, 1958). Halmael's deal with Onderborch is GAA NA 919/490v–491, not. Barent Jansen Verbeeck, November 22, 1636.

40. Peter Mundy, Relation XXXII, "A Passage from England over into Holland, with some Particularities of thatt Country," in *The Travels of Peter Mundy*, Hakluyt Society, series II, vol. LV (1925), 75. Economists have debated whether or not tulipmania was in fact irrational. Most economists support irrationality. One exception is Peter Garber, who in a series of articles and his 2000 book has suggested that the pattern of price changes for bulbs fits the pattern of new, fashionable commodities, in particular flowers; he uses eighteenth-century pricing patterns for tulips and hyacinths to suggest that it was normal for flowers to be valued highly at first, and then for their prices to decline. Although I agree that prices reflect fashion and the value buyers placed in them (as long as this value was commonly held, it seems to me not to be "irrational," but merely an expression of a market price), it seems to me that the suddenness of the price rise and of the tulip crash still needs explanation, despite Garber's other arguments. He states, correctly, that we do not know how far prices fell; but it must be assumed that at first the prices were no more than 10 percent of their previous value; otherwise this figure would not have appealed to the *bloemisten* meeting in Amsterdam on February 23, 1637. Even if in the long term prices remained reasonably high for tulips—a point on which my impressions agree with Garber's—I would argue that the behavior of sellers from 1637 through 1639 makes plain that a major fall in price afflicted the market.

See Peter Garber, "Tulipmania," in Robert P. Flood and Peter M. Garber, *Specula-tive Bubbles, Speculative Attacks, and Policy Switching* (Cambridge MA: MIT Press, 1994), 55–82, especially 55, 69–70, 72, and Garber, *Famous First Bubbles*, especially chap. 11. Opponents of Garber, supporting the idea of a bubble, include Charles P. Kindleberger, *Manias, Panics, and Crashes: A History of Financial Crises*, 3rd ed. (New York: John Wiley and Sons, 1996), 100–101, and Edward Chancellor, *Devil Take the Hindmost: A History of Financial Speculation* (London: Macmillan, 1999), 23–25.

41. *Meteranus Novus* (Amsterdam: Johannes Jansson, 1640), IV, 510 (this German text seems to have been written in 1638); Theodorus Schrevelius, *Harlemias, Ofte, om beter te seggen, De eerste stichtinghe der Stadt Haerlem* (Haarlem: Thomas Fonteyn, 1648), 214; Cornelis de Koning, *Tafereel der Stad Haarlem* (Haarlem: A. Lousjes Pz., 1808), 180; De Koning's (altered) source was Lieuwe van Aitzema, *Saken van Staet en Oorlogh, In, ende omtrent de Vereenigde Nederlanden* (The Hague: Johan Veely, Johan Tongerloo, and Jasper Doll, 1669) II, book 17, p. 503. The Coornhart chain sparked a number of suits: NHA ORA 116/19, unfoliated, KBJ, January 27, January 30, and Febuary 3, 1637. The Braem chain is NHA ORA 116/18/189v, KBJ, August 12, 1636, and f. 191v, August 15, 1636. The Francken chain is NHA ORA 116/18/217v, KBJ, September 12, 1636, and f. 219v, September 16, 1636.

42. Grimmaris' statement in court is at NHA ORA 116/19, unfoliated, KBJ, February 3, 1637. The (rather expensive) burial of Volckert Coornhart and Anneke Braems is GAA DTB 1045/85v, August 4, 1636; perhaps Grimmaris might have been able to collect the bulbs from their son Clement Coornhart, to whom Anneke Braems, who slightly outlived her husband, willed Coornhart's shop, spices, sugar, and other goods: GAA NA 1045/104, not. J. van de Ven, August 1, 1636. The case of De Wroo and Jansz is NHA ORA 116/18/[227v], KBJ, September 26, 1636.

43. [Adriaen Roman], *Samen-spraeck tusschen Waermondt ende Gaergoedt*, 35–36.

44. Quakel's quarrel with Jacob vander Meer and Jacob vander Gheest, the guardians of the children of Wouter Bartholomeusz Winckel in Alkmaar, is detailed in NHA ONA Haarlem 149/210, not. Jacob Schoudt, September 1, 1639. (I should note that the sale on February 5, 1637, is not explicitly mentioned in this document, but as Winckel's bulbs appear to have been sold all at once, with elaborate inventorying and preparations beforehand, it seems likely that Quakel bought his bulbs then. For the handling of the bulbs by the Weeskamer, see RAA, Weeskamer 36/32, Reg-ister van Voogdijen, July 16 and August 6, 1636, and Weeskamer 36/3, December 3, 1636, when the bulbs were ordered to be inventoried for sale.) Another indica-tion that the crash was not so thoroughly known in Haarlem on February 4 is an appearance before a notary by Jan Willemsz Cortoor, worried that Jan Smuyser would renege on a sale Smuyser had made to Cortoor on December 9, 1636: NHA ONA Haarlem 149/76–76v, not. Jacob Schoudt, February 4, 1637, also inaccurately printed in Posthumus, 43. The KBJ session for February 6 is NHA ORA 116/19, KBJ, February 6, 1637. Tjallis' bet is AWG ONA Enkhuizen 911/act 233, not. Olbrant Smetius, February 7, 1637. Documents about the De Busscher/Van Cuyck sale are GAA NA 866/27, not. Jacob van Swieten, [February 11, 1637], and NHA ONA Haar-

lem 166/65, not. Jacob van Bosvelt, February 11, 1637. (Posthumus prints the latter document inaccurately and incompletely in Posthumus, 46; one of his inaccuracies is to mistake the date of the transaction, February 6, for February 9. The fact that it is February 6 is clear not only from the document [vi^c] but also, in case there were any doubt, from the fact that the document states that the sale took place on a Friday; February 9 was a Monday.) I am not certain of Andries de Busscher's relationship to Alister van der Cruijs, but I suspect they were related by marriage, because De Busscher was brother-in-law of David van der Cruijs, as is evident from NHA ONA Haarlem 164/70, not. Jacob van Bosvelt, no date (April 1635). Again, we have an example of someone who on February 8 still seems unaware of the crash: Cornelis de Vogel of Amsterdam was still trying to buy bulbs on behalf of unknown buyers in Haarlem from Zacharias Lepij, from whom he wanted guarantee of delivery. Later he would refuse to receive them. See GAA NA 544A/1637/3-3v and 12–12v, not. Jacob Westfrisius, February 8 and May 19, 1637.

45. *Clare ontdeckingh*, printed in Krelage, *Pamfletten*, 67–87; Schrevelius, *Harlemias*, 213–14, 212; De Koning, *Tafereel*, 183; Blunt, *Tulips and Tulipomania*, 28. Among others adopting this explanation was W. P. Sautijn Kluit, "De Tulpen- en Hyacinten-Handel," *Handelingen der Maandelijksche Vergadering van de Maatschappij der Nederlandsche Letterkunde te Leiden*, October 1866, 29, where he cited "overproductie." The point about long-term increases in supply and short-term increases in demand (feeding on previous price increases) I owe to John Michael Montias (private communications, August–September 2003). In "Tulipmania: Fact or Artifact?," an article published on the internet, Earl A. Thompson and Jonathan Treussard argue that tulipmania "was an artifact created by an implicit conversion of ordinary futures contracts into option contracts in a movement led by several Dutch burgomasters to bail themselves out of previously incurred speculative losses in the impressively efficient, fundamentally driven, market for Dutch tulip futures." They base this view on a variety of incorrect or unsubstantiated claims about what happened in 1636–37, including the apparent deliberate selling of tulips in November by unnamed "burgomasters" and the flooding of the market by tulips dug up in Germany after a battle in the Thirty Years War. A correspondence with Professors Thompson and Treussard in February 2006 did not convince me of the validity of these claims. Professor Treussard renounced his connection with the article in an e-mail of February 22, 2006.

46. Beckmann, *History of Inventions* (4th ed. 1846) I, 27.

47. Roman, *Samen-spraeck tusschen Waermondt ende Gaergoedt*, 36. Peter Garber appears to suggest that the trade was not taken seriously anyway: "this was no more than a meaningless winter drinking game, played by a plague-ridden population that made use of the vibrant market." He assumes that the buyers thought the state would not enforce the contracts and that no one took the trade seriously. See Garber, *Famous First Bubbles*, 81. The documents associated with the trade, however, suggest a very serious intent to trade and to carry through deals to their conclusion; the scrambling for solutions after the crash makes that evident.

48. Halmael's contract with Van Meeckeren is GAA NA 919/20v, not. Barent Jansen Verbeeck, January 12, 1637, also printed in Posthumus, 36–37; it is canceled in GAA NA 919/61–61v, not. Barent Jansen Verbeeck, February 10, 1637, also printed, very inaccurately and incompletely (leaving out, e.g., Maria Vlaminghs), in Posthumus, 45–46.

49. GAA NA 1269/28–28v, not. Pieter Barman, February 24, 1637. The agreement was signed on February 24, but the meeting had taken place the previous day (the date of February 24 is usually cited, incorrectly). For some reason the solution proposed at this meeting is often taken in accounts of tulipmania to be the one actually implemented, which is not the case.

50. NHA Stadsarchief Haarlem, Rood 86/17v–18, Vroedschapsresoluties, March 4, 1637; NHA Stadsarchief Haarlem, Rood 217/154, Burgemeestersresoluties, March 7, 1637. Hoorn's letter is printed in Posthumus, 52, but Posthumus' citation for it is vague and so far I have not seen this letter in the original at AWG. Alkmaar's resolution is RAA Oud-Stadsarchief Alkmaar 44/145v, Resoluties van de Vroedschap, March 14, 1637. The influence of the burgemeester Johan de Wael and the oud-schepen (and future burgemeester) Cornelis Guldewagen on Haarlem's official policy on the tulips is evident. They stood to lose a great deal of money if the trade was not regulated in their favor. When the burgemeesters of Haarlem wrote to this effect on June 16, they specifically cited the actions of De Wael, Guldewagen, and Hendrick Lucasz before urging the Hof van Holland to withdraw their order of April 27, no doubt particularly its notional restrictions on lawsuits; see below.

51. Nat. Arch. 3.01.04.01, inv. 1388, f. 367v, States of Holland to the Hof van Holland, April 11, 1637, also printed in Posthumus, 53. The court responded in a letter of April 25, 1637, printed in Posthumus, 58. The April 27 plakkaat is printed in the Groot Placaet-Boeck II, cols. 2363–64. The postscript by the States is again cited by Posthumus, vaguely, as in "G. A. Hoorn" (i.e., AWG), but I have not found it. It is printed in Posthumus, 60. A local reaction to the request for information is AWG Oud-Archief Enkhuizen 33 (253)/591, vroedschapregisters, May 5, 1637, but the States took no further action on this subject.

52. Nat. Arch. 3.03.01.01, inv. 388, ff. 15v–16v, burgemeesters and council of Haarlem to Hof van Holland, April 15, 1637, also printed in Posthumus, 57–58. On satiric songs, see especially Louis Pieter Grijp, "Spotliederen in de Gouden Eeuw," in Annemieke Keunen and Herman Roodenburg, eds., Schimpen en Schelden: Eer en belediging in Nederland, ca. 1600–ca. 1850, themed issue of Volkskundig Bulletin 18, no. 3 (December 1992): 340–59, and Louis Pieter Grijp, Het Nederlandse lied in de Gouden Eeuw: Het mechanisme van de contrafactuur (Amsterdam: P.J. Meertens-Instituut, 1991), esp. 289ff. The songs are mainly reprinted in Krelage, Pamfletten. The resolution banning them is NHA Stadsarchief Haarlem, Rood 217/155v, burgemeestersresoluties, March 17, 1637; this order rather belies the suggestion that these were governmental propaganda (cf. Schama, Embarrassment of Riches, 361–62).

53. Baert's purchase of the garden is NHA ORA Tp. 76-56/126, February 19, 1636. Baert was called on as an expert in NHA ONA Haarlem 172/144v, not. Salomon Coesaert,

September 16, 1639, also inaccurately printed in Posthumus, 85. Among the cases when he was appointed arbiter by the KBJ are NHA ORA 116/18/159, KBJ, July 15, 1636; 116/18/192v, August 15, 1636; 116/19/18v and 19, November 14, 1636. He had a Wisselbank account whose balance on August 15, 1644, was ƒ31,203:15:8, and dealt with large transactions, receiving, for example, ƒ3,607:10 from Guilliam Momma on July 18, 1644 (GAA Arch. 5077, Rekeningboek Wisselbank 1644, f. 797). He was probably a Mennonite, as is evident from some of his contacts: see NHA ONA Haarlem 149/53v–54, not. Jacob Schoudt, August 27, 1636, which shows he has contacts with the De Clercqs and the Wynants, and NHA ONA Haarlem 169/240v–241, not. Jacob van Bosvelt, October 2, 1642, in which he takes part in discussions over the estate of Jacob van der Hulst. His insinuations of Coster, Kistgens, Neckevelt, and Schouten are GAA NA 675/87, June 25, 1637, and GAA NA 676/4v–6, June 24, 1637. The insinuation of Coster is also inaccurately and incompletely printed in Posthumus, 71–72, but note that Posthumus could not give the citation and also provides an incorrect price (ƒ125 for ƒ175).

54. Axele's response to De Goyer is GAA NA 919/191v, not. Barent Jansen Verbeeck, June 11, 1637; Cruidenier's to Schodt is GAA NA 675/86, not. Jan Warnaertsz, June 25, 1637; Swaech's to Poelenburch is AWG ONA Enkhuizen 933/act 116, not. Cornelis Antonisz Stant, July 1, 1637; Coster's to Schoneus is GAA NA 676/147, not. Jan Warnaertsz, November 9, 1637. Baert's second round of *insinuaties* is GAA NA 676/76–77, not. Jan Warnaertsz, September 29, 1637, to Coster, Schouten, and Hendrick van Bergom.

55. The statement by Clement and others is NHA ONA Haarlem 57/89–89v, not. Egbert van Bosvelt, June 20, 1637, also incorrectly printed in Posthumus, 70–71 (among other problems, Posthumus' printing of "sulcks" as "selffs" changes the sense); Cruidenier's statement is GAA NA 730B/78, not. P. Carelsz, February 23, 1638, also incompletely transcribed in Posthumus 1934, 240.

56. The prohibition on legal action is NHA Stadsarchief Haarlem, Rood 217/164, May 1, 1637. The comments on this are NHA ONA Haarlem 57/89–89v, not. Egbert van Bosvelt, June 20, 1637.

57. Seys' KBJ suit against the dead Haverbeeck's father is NHA ORA 116/19, unfoliated, KBJ, August 9, 1637; a case over a skirt, which the defendant, Giesbert Tiecert, claimed was bought via exchange for flowers, is NHA ORA 116/20/35, KBJ, December 18, 1637. The case of Jan Stoerm v. Joost Soene is NHA ORA 116/19, KBJ, May 12, 1637; Alleman v. Ryp is NHA ORA 116/19, unfoliated, KBJ, May 18, 1637. For another form of words on "order" in the trade, see NHA ORA 116/19, unfoliated, KBJ, May 26, 1637.

58. Burgemeesters of Holland to Hof van Holland, in Hof van Holland, letters 1636–1639, June 16, 1637, printed in Posthumus, 68–69; this is probably located at Nat. Arch. 3.03.01.01, inv. 4605 (folio unknown); I was not permitted to check the original documents because of their fragility. Baert's *insinuatie* of Van Bergom is GAA NA 676/76–77, not. Jan Warnaertsz, September 29, 1637; among his solutions was to go to a commission in Amsterdam set up to deal with tulips, although it does

not appear such a commission existed. In November 1638 he instructed a notary in Amsterdam, Jacob van Vliet, to pursue the cases of all those who owed him money for tulips: NHA ONA Haarlem 168/163, not. Jacob van Bosvelt, November 5, 1638. Wolphertsz' KBJ case is NHA ORA 116/19, unfoliated, KBJ, September 25, 1637.

59. The order setting up the CBS is NHA Stadsarchief Haarlem, Rood 217/203v–204, burgemeestersresoluties, January 30, 1638. We know of an Alkmaar commission from the documents surrounding Pieter Willemsz van Rosven's suit against Wouter Tullekens, which mentions three men, Adriaen Cornelisz Sevenhuijsen, oud-schepen, Valerius van Mulich, and Johan Coppier, who had been appointed by the burgemeesteren and schepenen "tot decise van sacken van flora omme partijen te hoiren en[de] vereenigen": RAA ORA Alkmaar 87/4, pieces C–G.

60. An extract from the "Blom rolle" of the CBS, dated February 13, 1638, appears in RAA ORA Alkmaar 87/4, piece I, part of the Rosven-Tullekens suit. Tullekens paid on January 22, 1639, although there may have been a further problem, since a document about this is dated June 7: RAA ORA Alkmaar 87/4, piece B, June 7, 1639. The first KBJ case to be sent to the CBS is NHA ORA 116/20/67v, KBJ, February 26, 1638. This will of course not have been the first case the CBS handled; others will have come directly to the commission, such as the Rosven case. Unfortunately any records kept by the CBS (a secretary was stipulated in the founding resolution of the burgemeesters) are no longer extant. The proposal to impose 3.5 percent *rouwkoop* is at NHA Stadsarchief Haarlem, Rood 217/221, burgemeestersresoluties, May 22, 1638. It was approved on May 28 (f. 222).

61. For references to the "bloem rolle," the records of the CBS, see NHA ORA 116/20, unfoliated, KBJ, September 21, 1638, and NHA ORA 116/20, unfoliated, KBJ, June 22, 1638. Seys v. Pietersz is NHA ORA 116/20, unfoliated, KBJ, June 14, 1638; Grimmaris v. Jeroensz is NHA ORA 116/20, unfoliated, KBJ, July 9 and 14, 1638; De Clercq v. Gerritsz is NHA ORA 116/20, unfoliated, KBJ, August 28, 1638; Preyer v. Van Gennep is NHA ORA 116/20, unfoliated, KBJ, September 7 and 10, 1638; Abrahamsz v. Coelembier is NHA ORA 116/20, unfoliated, KBJ, August 6, 1638 (the court ordered further investigation). The calculations of original prices are mine. Not all cases mention the CBS, but when the phrase "affmaken van bloemen" is used, it appears to denote cases that had previously been treated by the CBS.

62. NHA ONA Haarlem 149/126, not. Jacob Schoudt, November 29, 1638, also inaccurately/incompletely printed in Posthumus, 83.

63. GAA NA 676/75–75v, 76, and 76v–77, not. Jan Warnaertsz, September 29, 1637; *Groot Placaet-Boeck* II, col. 2364; letter from burgemeesters of Haarlem to Hof van Holland, June 16, 1637, printed in Posthumus, 68–69: as above, citation is probably Nat. Arch. 3.03.01.01, inv. 4605 (folio unknown), but because these documents are in poor condition I was not permitted by the Nationaal Archief to consult the original; Varwer's repayment is AWG ONA 965/act 354, not. Jacobus Vael, June 2, 1646; Schouten's claim of a settlement is GAA NA 676/147–147v, not. Jan Warnaertsz, November 9, 1637; Tullekens' transport of money to Rosven—ƒ2,823,

actually more than he owed, given that Rosven owed *him* ƒ352—is dated January 22, 1639, and is at RAA ORA Alkmaar 87/4, piece B, June 7, 1639; on Swaech and Van Resom, AWG ONA Enkhuizen 990/act 32, not. Remmet Jansz Keijser, April 28, 1637.

64. Mackay, *Extraordinary Popular Delusions,* 99; the settlement of Francisco Gomes da Costa's 1646 financial troubles is GAA Arch.2072/872/27, Desolate Boedelskamer, Accoorden, December 18, 1646; reference to his earlier bankruptcy can be found in GAA NA 942/312, not. Daniel Bredon, April 18, 1633 (I am grateful to Susanne Weide, curator of the Stedelijk Museum Vianen, for sending me this document). Alingh's bankruptcy sale is NHA ORA 87-1/19, Desolate Boedels Executieboek, April 4, 1640; his sale to Van de Broecke is discussed in NHA ONA Haarlem 149/136v–137, not. Jacob Schoudt, February 25, 1638. Van Limmen's application for *cessio bonorum* is Nat.Arch. 3.03.02, inv.41, Rekesten Hoge Raad, July 8, 1637; he is *borg* for Cornelis Dircksz in NHA ORA 87-1/23, Desolate Boedels Executieboek, November 12, 1642. Theunis Jansz's bankruptcy is mentioned in NHA Stadsarchief Haarlem loketkas 7-15-11-3, Memoriael . . . Schepenen, February 16, 1639.

65. Documents about the tulip transactions between Van Goyen and Ravesteijn and a section of Ravesteijn's inventory are reprinted in Abraham Bredius, "Jan Josephszoon van Goyen. Nieuwe bijdragen tot zijne biographie," *Oud-Holland* 14 (1896): 116–17. On his speculation in houses, see Bredius, 116–18; Christiaan Vogelaar, ed., *Jan van Goyen* (ex. cat. Leiden, De Lakenhal, 1996), 18; and especially Hans-Ulrich Beck, *Jan van Goyen 1596–1656* (Amsterdam: Van Gendt & Co., 1972), I, 19–20 and 30 ff.

66. The sales mentioned are NHA ORA 90–92, Desolate Boedels, pakje Grietgen Jans; and, in the Desolate Boedels Executieboeken, NHA ORA 87-1/34, August 26, 1648; NHA ORA 87-1/12, November 10, 1638; NHA ORA 87-1/12, November 16, 1638; NHA ORA 87-1/23, December 31, 1642; NHA ORA 87-1/21, March 27, 1641; NHA ORA 87-1/28, January 25, 1645. Among those either acting as *borgen* on such purchases or making unsuccessful bids are Jacob Theunisz Ram, Jan van Clarenbeeck, Hans Bartelsz, Cornelis de Coninck, Gillis de Milt, Michiel van Limmen, Bartholomeus van Rijn, Carel van Wansele, Jan Cornelisz Sael, Hendrick Wynants (one of two *borgen* for ƒ15,375 in 1651; it is not stated which Hendrick Wynants this is). See the Executieboeken: NHA ORA 87-1/14v, 19–21, 23, 25, 26, 29v, 37v, 44v. Bailly's purchase of a house is NHA ORA Tp. 76-57/119v–120, April 18, 1637; Van Welsen's is NHA ORA Tp. 76-57/68–68v, April 1, 1637; Baert's garden is NHA ORA 87-1/23, December 31, 1642; the Jan Basse sale is GAA WK 5073/962, March 9–30, 1637; De Goyer's inventory is GAA NA 968, unfoliated, not. Benedict Baddel, March 18, 1653; Mackelenberch's (on the occasion of the death of his first wife) is NHA ONA Haarlem 153/7v–13v, not. Jacob Schoudt, October 19, 1638. The potash company is set up in NHA ONA Haarlem 169/16–16v, not. Jacob van Bosvelt, November 20, 1640. It should be noted that the Amsterdam florist Jeronimus Victory appeared to be in financial difficulty at his death in 1647, but he had found the wherewithal

to buy more gardens on the Nieuwe Pad and the St. Jorispad in the early 1640s, and his tulips were his most valuable possession in 1647. See his inventory at GAA NA 1914/486–495, not. F. Uyttenbogaert, December 20, 1647.

67. Malkiel, *A Random Walk down Wall Street*, 33. A fundamental disagreement exists between economic historians such as Jan de Vries and Ad van der Woude, who believe that the Dutch economy continued to expand with few setbacks until 1650, at which point it went into decline, and Jonathan Israel, who posits a period of economic stagnation following the ending of the Twelve Years Truce in 1621 and lasting until 1647, when, he suggests, the economy begins to expand. Israel's views are based mainly on the fortunes of overseas trade, although he also suggests that certain industries, such as whale oil, ceramics, paper, tobacco, sail-cloth, and clay pipes, also succeeded, and that centers of economic success before 1647 tended to lose out to less prominent places later. I find the evidence provided by De Vries and Van der Woude more convincing, but whichever view one takes, there is little place for a depression after the tulip crash. For Israel's views, see Jonathan Israel, *Dutch Primacy in World Trade*, chap. 5 and p. 196, and Israel, *The Dutch Republic*, 610–12, 616–17, 619. For the opposing view, see Ad van der Woude, *Het Noorderkwartier* (Wageningen: A. A. G. Bijdragen, 1972) II, chap. 6, and Jan de Vries and Ad van der Woude, *The First Modern Economy: Success, Failure, and Perseverance of the Dutch Economy, 1500–1815* (Cambridge: Cambridge University Press, 1997), *passim*, but for a firm statement about economic growth until 1650, see p. 335. On periods of hardship, see Leo Noordegraaf, *Hollands welvaren? Levenstandaard in Holland 1450–1650* (Amsterdam: Octavo, 1985), 20, 40. Marjolein 't Hart characterizes tulipmania as mere conjuncture in 't Hart, *The Making of a Bourgeois State*, 178–79; De Vries and Van der Woude summarize what took place but make no claims that it had a serious effect on the economy: see *The First Modern Economy*, 150–51. Some similar points to mine are made by Peter M. Garber, *Famous First Bubbles*, 76–77. In Amsterdam, bankruptcies fell in the late 1630s from fifty-five in 1636 to twenty-nine in 1641, and although there was a leap to ninety in 1646, potentially a residual effect of the crash, this higher level of bankruptcy continued for many subsequent years, suggesting no link with events of 1637. See for these figures W. F. H. Oldeweit, "Twee eeuwen Amsterdamse faillissementen en het verloop van de conjonctuur (1636 tot 1838)," *Tijdschrift voor Geschiedenis* 75 (1962): 432.

68. De Preyer's case against Van Gennep is NHA ORA 116/20, unfoliated, KBJ, September 7 and 10, 1638.

69. The fact that the 3.5 percent was specifically *rouwkoop* is stated in the decision to set the fine at this level: "op drye en[de] een halve gulden vant hondert tot roucoop." See NHA Stadsarchief Haarlem, Rood 217/221, burgemeestersresoluties, May 22, 1638. Van Meeckeren's payment is mentioned in GAA NA 919/61–61v, not. Barent Jansen Verbeeck, February 10, 1637.

70. The phrase "seecker order" is used for the first time in NHA ORA 116/19, unfoli-

ated, KBJ, May 26, 1637. The statement of Clement, Gael, and others on conditions after the crash is NHA ONA Haarlem 57/89–89v, not. Egbert van Bosvelt, June 20, 1637.

71. NHA ONA Haarlem 166/130–131, not. Jacob van Bosvelt, April 14, 1637.

Chapter Five

1. *Tegen de Verachters der Floristen* (Hoorn: Zacharias Cornelisz, 1637), in *KP*, 113. "Hoe legh ick hier in dees ellende," here called "Een Klaegh-Liedeken," in *Haerlems Oudt Liedtboek* (Haarlem: Vincent Casteleyn, 1630?), 108–10. It was clearly known by its first line, which is given as the tune for a variety of tulip songs. For the tune of this song, see Louis Paul Grijp, *Het Nederlandse Lied in de Gouden Eeuw: Het mechanisme van de contrafactuur* (Amsterdam: P. J. Meertens-Instituut, 1991), 64.

2. Similar biblical messages, some of which are quoted or noted in tulip pamphlets, include Psalms 103:15–16, Isaiah 40:6–7, 1 Peter 1:24. On *vanitas* still lifes, see, among others, Liana De Girolami Cheney, "Dutch Vanitas Paintings: The Skull," in Cheney, ed., *The Symbolism of Vanitas in the Arts, Literature and Music* (Lewiston, NY: Edwin Mellen, 1992), 113–33. On attitudes to death, see Philippe Ariès, *The Hour of Our Death*, trans. Helen Weaver (New York: Alfred A. Knopf, 1981), chap. 7, esp. pp. 327–32. The song quoted is from *Nieuwen Jeucht-Spieghel*, c. 1620.

3. On Leiden, Laurens van Zanten, *Spiegel der Gedenkweerdighste Gheschiedenissen Onses Tijts* (Amsterdam: Joannes vanden Bergh, 1661). Population figures (for 1632) come from Jonathan Israel, *The Dutch Republic*, 113. On the death toll in Amsterdam in 1635, Jan Wagenaar, *Amsterdam, in zyne Opkomst, Aanwas, Geschiedenissen, Voorregten, Koophandel, Gebouwen, Kerckenstaat, Schoolen, Schutterye, Gilden, en Regeeringe* (Amsterdam: Isaak Tirion, 1760) I, 531. On Enkhuizen, Sebastiaan Centen, *Vervolg der Historie van de vermaarde Zee- en Koop-Stad Enkhuizen* (Hoorn: Jacob Duyn, 1747), 82. Haarlem's first reaction is NHA Stadsarchief Haarlem, Rood 217/50, September 10, 1635. On deaths in Haarlem, see Schrevelius, *Harlemias*, 204.

4. The regulations about the plague are reprinted in Schrevelius, *Harlemias*, 205–8, and are dated April 23, 1636; his comments on the mood in Haarlem are on p. 210. On appointment of officials, see NHA Stadsarchief Haarlem, Rood 217/51v, 56, 89, 91v, 93v, 104v, 105, 106,107–107v, 109, 110, 114v, 116v; on the cemetery, f. 98 (June 12, 1636). On the prayer day, NHA Kerkenraad van de Hervormde Gemeente no. 21, Register, July 12, 1636. Mortality figures from Van Zanten, *Spiegel*, 129–30.

5. Coopall's renewed contract with Cornelis Bol den Jongen is NHA ONA Haarlem 134/261, not. Jacob Schoudt, November 6, 1636, inaccurately printed (with old citation) in Posthumus 33–35. The Weeskamer accounts of Pieter de Jonckheer's child Joost are NHA WK 160/308a and 160/308b; information on sales of bulbs appears in NHA ONA Haarlem 63/402v, not. Egbert van Bosvelt, September 10, 1637. On De Bruyn's apparent cheating of Abigael Verschuyll, widow of Ysack Schot, NHA ONA Haarlem 159/3, not. Wouter Crousen den Jonge, January 13, 1637, also printed

in Posthumus, 37–38. On Coopall's family's deaths, NHA DTB 70/253, 254, 255, 257. Aeltgen Jansdr's plague is mentioned in her contract with Jan van der Linde, of which there are copies at both NHA ONA Haarlem 120/391 and 134/264–263v, not. Jacob Schoudt, November 22, 1636. The copy in ONA 134 is more complete, with an added clause referring to Van der Linde's salary.

6. Crousen's will is NHA ONA Haarlem 165/369, not. Jacob van Bosvelt, October 6, 1636. On will-writing during this plague, J. Buisman, *Duizend Jaar Weer, Wind en Water in de Lage Landen* IV (Franeker: Van Wijnen, 2000), 436. On England and the plague, Paul Slack, *The Impact of Plague in Tudor and Stuart England* (London: Routledge & Kegan Paul, 1985), 240; comments on the Dutch are from BL Sloane ms. 1293, ff. 29–30v, "On the customs of Holland" (c. 1677).

7. The point about the financial consequences of plague I owe to Marten Jan Bok (conversation, April 1, 2002); see also, on this point, Brian Pullan, "Plague and Perceptions of the Poor in Early Modern Italy," in Terence Ranger and Paul Slack, eds., *Epidemics and Ideas: Essays on the Historical Perception of Pestilence* (Cambridge: Cambridge University Press, 1992), 20. Geertruyt Schoudt's purchase is reported in NHA ONA Haarlem 149/78v–79, not. Jacob Schoudt, February 20, 1637, and for a discussion see chapter 3 above. The burgemeesters' suggestion of a "danck-dagh" is in NHA Stadsarchief Haarlem, Rood 217/144v, burgemeestersresoluties, January 28, 1637. On a sense of invulnerability at the end of plague epidemics, see Pullan, 118–19. On social divisiveness and plague, Slack, *The Impact of Plague*, 20.

8. The song is "Als my Flora heeft van doen," in C. P. van Wesbuch, *Haerlemsche Duyn-Vreucht* (Haarlem: Thomas Fonteyn, 1636), 57. Marcus Cornelisz Flora was identified simply as "Flora" at the flower auction of Pieter Pietersz Tuynman, GAA WK 5073/952, September 25, 1626; on his house, see Joh. C. Breen and A. W. Weissman, "Geschiedenis van het huis Keizersgracht 317," *Jaarboek Amstelodamum* 17 (1919): 52, n. 1, and E. W. Moes and N. W. J. Coorengel, "Alphabetische Lijst van Huisnamen," *Jaarboek Amstelodamum* 3 (1905): 149.

9. Jan Soet, *Floraas Swijmel-Snicken*, reprinted in *KP* 160–63; [Steven van der Lust], *Haerlems Buur-Praetjen, van Floraes Sieck-Bedde in 't poortal van 't gast-huijs*, printed in *KP* 149–51; *Een Nieu Rou-Mantels Liet voor de Floristen* (Hoorn: Zacharias Cornelisz, 1637), printed in *KP* 145–46; Jan Soet, *Dood-Rolle ende Groef-Maal van Floortie-Floraas*, printed in *KP* 174–79; [Steven van der Lust], *Troost voor de Ghescheurde Broederschap der Rouw-dragende Kap-Broertjes, ofte Floraes Staet-Ionckers*, printed in *KP* 184–86; [Johannes Marshoorn?], *Troost-Brief aen alle Bedroefde Bloemmisten, die treuren over 't sterven oft 't overlijden van Flora, Goddinne der Floristen* (Haarlem: Hans Passchiers van Wesbusch, 1637), reprinted in *KP* 288–302; Jan Soet, *Testaments Openinghe en Uytdeelinghe, Ghedaen by de Vrienden ende Erfghenamen Wijlen Floortje Floraas*, printed in *KP* 180–83. The piece of street theater is mentioned in Soet, *Floraas Swijmel-Snicken*, in *KP* 162. Van der Lust's membership of the Wijngaertrancken is mentioned in NHA, Archief Wijngaertrancken, members' list 1617, printed in F. C. van Boheemen and Th. C. J. van der Heijden, eds., *Retoricaal Memoriaal* (Delft: Eburon, 1999), 410; on Jan Soet, see G. Kalff, *Geschiedenis der Nederlandsche Letterkunde*

IV (Groningen: Wolters, 1909), 460–65, and Jan Zuidema, "Jan Zoet," *Oud-Holland* 23 (1905): 83–104, 175–88. Soet, who was living in Amsterdam, was probably no longer a member of the Wijngaertrancken in 1637.

10. For an overview of the plague in the Netherlands, see Leo Noordegraaf and Gerrit Valk, *De Gave Gods: De Pest in Holland vanaf de late Middeleeuwen* (Amsterdam: Bert Bakker, 1996). [Johan van Beverwijck], *Kort Bericht om de Pest voor te komen. Ten dienste van de Gemeente der Stadt Dordrecht* (Dordrecht: Francoys Boels, 1636), 6–7; P. van Godewijck, *Remedie voor de Pest. In Rijm gestelt . . .* (Dordrecht: Hendrick van Esch, 1636), unpaginated; Jacobus Viverius, *De Handt Godes; Of, Een Christelijck Verhael van de Peste, of Gaeve Godes* (Haarlem: Thomas Fonteyn, 1636), 14.

11. *Clare ontdeckingh der dwaesheydt der ghener die haer tegenwoordigh laten noemen Floristen* (Hoorn: Zacharias Cornelisz, 1636), printed in *KP* 75, 87 n. 2x); "Van de Floristen," in *Twee Nieuwe Liedekens van de Floristen met een Liedeken teghen de Verachters der Floristen* (Hoorn: Zacharias Cornelisz, 1637), printed in *KP* 107; the image of the Rose of Sharon also features in H. Hofman, *Korte aenwijsingh van de blomme te Saron, ende een rose in 't dal*, printed in *KP* 115–19, and Van der Lust, *Troost voor de Ghescheurde Broederschap*, in *KP* 186. On Verdiza, Steven van der Lust, *Nieu-Iaers Pest-Spiegel* (Hoorn: Zacharias Cornelisz, 1637), printed in *KP* 95; on the plague, Van der Lust, *Troost voor de Gescheurde Broederschap*, in *KP* 186. The non-saving tulip is in "Van de Floristen," in *KP* 107.

12. Schama, *The Embarrassment of Riches*, 130–37, 601; for the argument about reactions to prosperity, *passim*. See also, among many others treating this theme, Norman Bryson's chapter, "Abundance," in his *Looking at the Overlooked* (Cambridge, MA: Harvard University Press, 1990), 96–135, and the discussion of and notes on still life painting in chap. 2 above.

13. On the accidental consumption of tulip bulbs, see Carolus Clusius, *Rariorum aliquot Stirpium, per Pannoniam, Austriam, et vicinas quasdam Provincias observatum Historia* (Antwerp: Plantijn, 1583), 169; the quotation here is from John Evelyn, "De Vita Propria," in De Beer, ed., *Diary* I, 86–87. John Parkinson also refers to those who have had bulbs sent "from beyond Sea, and mistaking them to bee Onions, have used them as Onions in their pottage or broth" and "accounted them sweete Onions": Parkinson, *Paradisi in Sole Paradisus Terrestris*, 67.

14. On the 1611 exchange, see Johan Koppenol and Garrelt Verhoeven, "Krakeel in het bloemperk. Rederijkers, tulpen en vreemdelingenproblematiek in 1611," *Literatuur* 18, 5 (2001): 274–86; I am grateful to the authors for sharing their work with me before publication. On the jealousy of other flowers and the tulip's uselessness, *Clare Ontdeckingh* in *KP* 71, 73; *Ghesanck*, in *KP* 221; *Een Klaegh-Liedt weghen de Lelye Narcisse, ofte Tulipa*, in *KP* 126. Similar themes appear in pre-crash pamphlets such as *Mandament op ende jeghes de Heyden- ende Turcksche Tulp-Bollen* in *KP* 89, as well as the later *Geschockeerde Blom-Cap* in *KP* 134.

15. On the worthlessness of the tulips, *Van de Floristen* in *KP* 111; on the possibility of increases in price, *Clare Ontdeckingh*, in *KP* 84 note r). On gold and diamonds compared with tulips, *Clare Ontdeckingh* in *KP* 74.

16. On collectors of naturalia, *Apologia ofte Verantwoordinghe van Flora* in *KP* 268; on the value of paintings and other luxury objects, *Clare Ontdeckingh* in *KP* 86–7.

17. *Aenleydingh tot Opmerck van 't Misbruyck en rechte Ghebruyck der Bloemen* in *KP* 169; "Van de Floristen" (second song by this title) in *Twee Nieuwe Liedekens van de Floristen* in *KP* 111; "Ghesanck" in Pieter de Clopper, *Ghesanck-Boecxken* in *KP* 218–19.

18. UB Gent Meul. 2424, "Waerschouwinghe aen alle goede Inghesetenen van ons lieve Vaderlant, teghen de Betoverende Bedriegerie der genen die haer laten noemen Blomisten oft Floristen," published by E. H. Krelage as "Het Manuscript over den Tulpenwindhandel uit de Verzameling-Meulman," *Economisch-Historisch Jaarboek* XXII (1943): 40–41; *Samen-Spraeck tusschen Waermondt ende Gaergoedt*, 41; GAA Arch. 520/120/4, Particulier Archief Museum Amstelkring, Gerrit Jansz Kooch, "Op het Wonderlijck Jaer der bloemisten Anno 1637."

19. *Geschockeerde Blom-Cap* in *KP* 137; *Clare Ontdeckingh* in *KP* 86 note 2r; *Klachte van Joost van Kortrijcke over de Bedriegerije van Flora* in *KP* 165. I should note that my use of the word "artisan" here is in the traditional historian's sense of a craftworker, not to denote an artist, as Pamela Smith uses the word in *The Body of the Artisan: Art and Experience in the Scientific Revolution* (Chicago: University of Chicago Press, 2004).

20. On damage to the economy, see, for example, *Geschockeerde Blom-Cap* in *KP* 138; on horses and carriages, *Floraas Malle-Wagen, ofte Voor-Winds Uyttocht nae Kales en Reyn-Uyt, om in Lethis Vloet te Versuypen*, in *KP* 191; Jan Soet, "Transformatie," in *Floraas Swijmel-Snicken* in *KP* 163; *Samen-Spraeck tusschen Waermondt ende Gaergoedt*, 29, 30; *Een Klaegh-Liedt, weghen de Lelye Narcisse, ofte Tulipa* in *KP* 125; *Mandament op ende jeghens de Heyden- ende Turcksche Tulp-Bollen* in *KP* 89. On banquets, Steven van der Lust, *Troost voor de Ghescheurde Broederschap*, in *KP* 184, 187; *Floraas Malle-Wagen*, in *KP* 191; and *Memoriael-Liedt van de daet der Blommisten*, in *KP* 222.

21. For an analysis of the community of tulip traders, see chap. 3 above. *Tweede t'Samen-spraeck tusschen Waermondt ende Gaergoedt*, 47; *Waerschouwinghe* in Krelage, "Het Manuscript over den Tulpenwindhandel," 39; Pieter Jansz van Campen, *P.I.C. Biggel-Tranen, over de Schielijcke Veranderinge van de Vermeynde Groote Winst-Coopmanschap der Bloemisten* (printed by the author, 1637), printed in *KP* 205; Soet, *Floraas Swijmel-Snicken* in *KP* 163; Van Campen, *P.I.C. Biggel Tranen*, 202.

22. See, for example, N. W. Posthumus, *De Geschiedenis van de Leidsche Lakenindustrie* (The Hague: Martinus Nijhoff, 1939) III, 1176; on numbers of workers, see for saaidrapiers III, 556–57, and dyers, III, 686. De Vries and Van der Woude suggest that in fact the cloth trade was growing at this point; see Jan de Vries and Ad van der Woude, *The First Modern Economy*, 285.

23. On *rederijkers* in general, see especially F. C. van Boheemen and Th. C. J. van der Heijden, *Met Minnen Versaemt: De Hollandse Rederijkers vanaf de Middeleeuwen tot het begin van de Achttiende Eeuw* (Delft: Eburon, 1999) and A. C. van Dixhoorn, *Lustige Geesten: Rederijkers en hun Kamers in het Publieke Leven van de vijftiende, zestiende, en zeventiende eeuw* (Proefschrift Vrije Universiteit Amsterdam, 2004), which I regrettably was unable to consult for this study. On Haarlem specifically, see F. C.

van Boheemen and Th. C. J. van der Heijden, "De rederijkers en Haarlem," in E. K. Grootes, ed., *Haarlems Helicon: Literatuur en toneel te Haarlem vóór 1800* (Hilversum: Verloren, 1993), 49–60.

24. Van Boheemen and Van der Heijden, "De Rederijkers en Haarlem," 54–56; HNA, Archief Wijngaertrancken, members' list 1617, printed in Van Boheemen and Van der Heijden, *Retoricaal Memoriaal*, 410; *KP*, "Inleiding," 14; *Sparens Vreughden-Bron, Uytstortende Veel Nieuwe als Singens Waerdighe Deuntjens*, vol. 2 (Haarlem: Michiel Segerman, 1646), 6, 16–19, 42–44, 66–69, 87–90, 126–29, 158–59. Among Van der Lust's plays was the *Olyf-Kransen, Gevlochten om 't hooft van de Hemelsche Vrede. Op de Triumph-doot van de Bloedthondt den dullen Mars*, a celebration of the peace of 1648. See F. C. van Boheemen and Th. C. J. van der Heijden, *Met Minnen Versaemt: De Hollandse Rederijkers vanaf de middeleeuwen tot het begin van de achttiende eeuw: Bronnen en bronnenstudies* (Delft: Eburon, 1999), 81, 103; *Troost-Brief aen alle bedroefde bloemisten* in *KP* 293. The more elite members of the Haarlem chambers were often *beminders*, adjuncts or friends of the group, rather than the regular members, *kameristen*; on this see Dorren, *Eenheid en Verscheidenheid*, 176. I am very grateful to Arjan van Dixhoorn for sharing with me the results of his social study of the *rederijkers*. My comments here on their social standing are based chiefly on his correspondence with me in the spring of 2002.

25. Marcus Zuerius Boxhornius, *Toneel ofte Beschrijvinge der Steden van Hollandt* (Amsterdam: Jacob Keyns, 1634), 38; H. F. K. van Nierop, *The Nobility of Holland: From Knights to Regents 1500–1650*, trans. Maarten Ultee (Cambridge: Cambridge University Press, 1993), 212–15; Marten Jan Bok, "Art Lovers and their Paintings: Van Mander's Schilder-Boeck as a Source for the History of the Art Market in the Northern Netherlands," in Ger Luijten et al., *Dawn of the Golden Age: Northern Netherlandish Art 1580–1620* (ex. cat. Amsterdam, Rijksmuseum, 1993–1994), 150; Philips and Joan Vingboons, *Afbeelsels der voornaemste Gebouwen* (Amsterdam: Philips and Joan Vingboons, 1648), 3, concerning plates 30–32. On the invention of noble ancestors, see S. A. C. Dudok van Heel, "Amsterdamse burgemeesters zonder stamboom: De dichter Vondel en de schilder Colijns vervalsen geschiedenis," *De Zeventiende Eeuw* 6, no. 1 (1990): 144–51; S. A. C. Dudok van Heel, "Op zoek naar Romulus en Remus: Zeventiende-eeuws onderzoek naar de oudste magistraten van Amsterdam," *Jaarboek Amstelodamum* 87 (1995): 43–70, where Schaep is discussed on 56–57; and Marten Jan Bok, "Laying Claims to Nobility in the Dutch Republic: Epitaphs, True and False," *Simiolus* 24, nos. 2–3 (1996): 209–26. On aristocratization, see especially D. J. Roorda, *Partij en Factie* (Groningen: Wolters-Noordhoff, 1978); English summaries of the social arguments can be found in D. J. Roorda, "The Ruling Classes in Holland in the Seventeenth Century," in J. S. Bromley and E. H. Kossmann, eds., *Britain and the Netherlands* II (Groningen: Wolters, 1964), 109–32, and H. van Dijk and D. J. Roorda, "Social Mobility under the Regents of the Republic," *Acta Historiae Neerlandicae* IX (1976): 76–102. On living standards in general, see in particular Leo Noordegraaf, *Hollands welvaren?*

Levenstandaard in Holland 1450–1650, and Jan de Vries and Ad van der Woude, *The First Modern Economy*.

26. *Teghen de Verachters der Floristen* in *KP* 112; Jan Soet, "Transformatie," in *Floraas Swijmel-Snicken*, in *KP* 163; "Mary Smuls vreught," in *Tweede Deel van 't Haerlems Liedt-Boeck, Anders ghenaemt den Laurier-krans der Amoureusen*, 7th ed. (Haarlem: Vincent Casteleyn, 1643), 6.

27. These arguments about labor are made by Ilja M. Veldman, "Images of Labor and Diligence in Sixteenth-Century Netherlandish Prints: The New Work Ethic Rooted in Civic Morality or Protestantism?" *Simiolus* 21, no. 4 (1992): 227–64; on consistories, R. B. Evenhuis, *Ook was dat Amsterdam* (Amsterdam: W. ten Have, 1967), II, 46; Waermondt's story is in *Samen-Spraeck tusschen Waermondt ende Gaergoedt*, 27.

28. *Teghen de Verachters der Floristen* in *KP* 113; *Waerschouwinghe* in Krelage, "Het Manuscript over den Tulpenwindhandel," 37.

29. On honor and the maintenance of families, see Florike Egmond and Peter Mason, *The Mammoth and the Mouse: Microhistory and Morphology* (Baltimore and London: The Johns Hopkins University Press, 1997), 59; on Theunis Jansz, see NHA Stadsarchief Haarlem, Rood 219/217, burgemeestersresoluties, July 5, 1642; *Nieu-Iaers Pest-Spieghel* in *KP* 95; *Den Ondergang ofte Val van de groote Thuyn-Hoer, de Boeff-Goddin Flora*, in *KP* 187–88; *Klacht van Joost van Kortrijcke* in *KP* 166–67; *P.I.C. Biggel-Tranen* in *KP* 203; *Claech-Liedt op de Blom-Koopers* in *KP* 213; *Geschockeerde Blom-Cap* in *KP* 136; *Een Nieu Liedeken van Soeters Nae-Smaeck* in *KP* 194–95.

30. Pieter de Clopper, *Ghesanck Boecxken van de Blommisten, ende van de Liefhebbers van Flora* in *KP* 212 ("Voor-Reden").

31. *Samen-Spraeck tusschen Waermondt ende Gaergoedt*, 25, 38; Jan Soet, *Floraas Swijmel-Snicken* in *KP* 163; Pieter Jansz. van Campen, *P.I.C. Biggel-Tranen* in *KP* 210, 204.

32. Taverne, *In 't land van belofte*, 487, n. 24; Pieter Biesboer, "De Vlaamse immigranten in Haarlem 1578–1630 en hun nakomelingen," in Pieter Biesboer et al., *Vlamingen in Haarlem* (Haarlem: De Vrieseborch, 1996), 38–39; J. G. C. A. Briels, *De Zuidnederlandse Immigratie in Amsterdam en Haarlem omstreeks 1572–1630*, 26–27; Erika Kuijpers, *Migrantenstad, passim*; Oscar Gelderblom, "De Deelname van Zuid-Nederlandse Kooplieden," 237–58; Gabrielle Dorren, "De eerzamen: Zeventiende-eeuws burgerschap in Haarlem," in Remieg Aerts and Henk te Velde, eds., *De Stijl van de Burger: Over Nederlandse burgerlijke cultuur vanaf de middeleeuwen* (Kampen: Kok Agora, 1998), 66–67; Gabrielle Dorren, *Eenheid en verscheidenheid*, 119–21; Gerbrand Adriaensz Bredero, *Spaanschen Brabander* in E. K. Grootes, ed., *Moortje en Spaanschen Brabander* (Amsterdam: Athenaeum-Polak & Van Gennep, 1999), line 2223.

33. Pieter Jansz van Campen, *P.I.C. Biggel-Tranen* in *KP* 204; Jan Soet, "Hedensdaagsche Mantel-Eer, voor-stellende de groote Geld-zugt dezer bedorven Eeuwen," in *d'Uitsteekenste Digt-Kunstige Werken, door Jan Zoet, Amsterdammer* (Amsterdam: Jan Klaasz ten Hoorn, 1675), 5, 11, 13, 29.

34. "Van de Floristen," in *Twee Nieuwe Liedekens van de Floristen* in *KP* 110–11 and also

in *De Haestige Op-Komst ende de Schielijcke Nedergangh der Nieu-aen-gekome Floristen* in *KP* 197–98; *Floraas Malle-Wagen* in *KP* 191.

35. "Van de Floristen," second song of this title in *Twee Nieuwe Liedekens van de Floristen, met een Liedeken teghen de Verachters der Floristen*, in *KP* 108–11; *Clare Ontdeckingh* in *KP* 77.

36. On this theme, see Julius S. Held, "Flora, Goddess and Courtesan," in Millard Meiss, ed., *De Artibus Opuscula XL: Essays in Honor of Erwin Panofsky* (New York: New York University Press, 1961), I, 201–18 (plates: II, 69–74); *Een Nieu Rou-Mantels Liet voor de Floristen* in *KP* 145; *Een Nieuw Liedeken van de Floristen* in *KP* 148; *Een Klaegh-Liedt van Flora* in *KP* 158; Jan Soet, *Floraas Swijmel-Snicken* in *KP* 160; Steven van der Lust, *Den Ondergang ofte Val van de Groote Thuyn-Hoer* in *KP* 188; *De Haestige Op-Komst ende Schielijcke Neder-gangh* in *KP* 196. On prostitution and honor, see Lotte van de Pol, "Beeld en Werkelijkheid van de Prostitutie in de Zeventiende Eeuw," in Gert Hekma and Herman Roodenburg, eds., *Soete minne en helsche boosheit: Seksuele voorstellingen 1300–1850* (Nijmegen: SUN, 1988), 139; Lotte van de Pol, *Het Amsterdams Hoerdom: Prostitutie in de Zeventiende en Achttiende Eeuw* (Amsterdam: Wereldbibliotheek, 1996); on Flora's deceptions, *Een Klaegh-liedt van Flora* in *KP* 158 and *Buyre-Praetje tot Vertroostinge van Iantie Floraas* in *KP* 155.

37. The theme of marriage comes up in *Een Nieu Rou-Mantels Liet* in *KP* 145–46 and *Een Nieuw Liedeken van de Floristen* in *KP* 147–48. Krelage writes of this latter song that it was based on an earlier song criticizing marriage; see *KP* 32. On female sexual honor and male bankruptcy, see Laura Gowing, *Domestic Dangers: Women, Words, and Sex in Early Modern London* (Oxford: Clarendon Press, 1998; orig. ed. 1996), 118; Lotte van de Pol, *Het Amsterdams Hoerdom*, 72; Peter Mathias notes a similar tendency in eighteenth-century Britain: Peter Mathias, "Strategies for Reducing Risk," 14. On notions of financial responsibility and insults, see Herman Roodenburg, "Eer en oneer ten tijde van de Republiek: een tussenbalans," *Volkskundig Bulletin* 22, no. 2 (Oct. 1996): 134; David Garrioch, "Verbal Insults in eighteenth-century Paris," in Peter Burke and Roy Porter, eds., *The Social History of Language* (Cambridge: Cambridge University Press, 1987), 107–8; Florike Egmond and Peter Mason, *The Mammoth and the Mouse*, 64–65. On Van Beringen and the Wynants, NHA ONA Haarlem 150/102–102v, not. Jacob Schoudt, January 21, 1644. As they were all in the cloth trade, there is no particular reason to think this quarrel was about tulips. Pieter Wynants was already dead by this time; Hendrick Jacob Wynants was defending his own reputation and the posthumous reputation of his brother.

38. Pieter Jansz van Campen, *P.I.C. Biggel-Tranen* in *KP* 199; Jan Soet, *Dood-Rolle ende Groef-Maal van Floortie-Floraas* in *KP* 174–77; Jan Soet, *Testaments Openinghe* in *KP* 180–83; *Waerschouwinghe* in Krelage, "Het Manuscript over den Tulpenwindhandel," 41–42; *Floraas Malle-Wagen* in *KP* 193. My remarks on credit are inspired by Craig Muldrew, *The Economy of Obligation: The Culture of Credit and Social Relations in Early Modern England* (London: Macmillan, 1998), 4, 150–51.

39. GAA NA 919/193v–194, 194v, 194v–195, not. Barent Jansen Verbeeck, June 12, 1637; GAA NA 919/201–201v, not. Barent Jansen Verbeeck, June 17, 1637; GAA NA 951,

unfoliated, not. P. Venturin, May 14, 1637; RAA NA Alkmaar 113/71v–72, not. Baert Jansz Harenkarspel, July 23, 1637.

40. NHA ORA 116/19, unfoliated, KBJ, April 24, 1637; the experts' opinion on the problem of varying bulbs is NHA ONA Haarlem 172/144v, not. Salomon Coesaert, September 16, 1639, also inaccurately printed in Posthumus, 85. The suit against Francken is NHA ORA 116/18/165v, KBJ, July 22, 1636; Seys' suit against De Jongh is NHA ORA 116/18/206, KBJ, August 28, 1636.

41. Mahieu's comments are in NHA ONA Haarlem 56/20, not. Egbert van Bosvelt, April 29, 1611, also printed in Posthumus 11–12; Van Breugel's comments are in RAA ONA Alkmaar 107, unfoliated, not. Cornelis de Haes, November 20, 1637.

42. NHA ORA 116/18/153, KBJ, July 11, 1636; NHA ORA 116/18/192v, KBJ, August 15, 1636; NHA ORA 116/18/196v and 198v, August 18 and 22, 1636; NHA ORA 116/18/214v, KBJ, September 9, 1636. Van Gennep's *insinuatie* is GAA NA 919/50–50v, not. Barent Jansen Verbeeck, January 28, 1637, and see, for this story, chap. 3.

43. On De Vogel and security, GAA NA 544A/1637/3–3v, not. Jacob Westfrisius, February 8, 1637. On De Busscher and Van Cuijck, see GAA NA 866/27–28, not. Jacob van Swieten, [February 11, 1637]. The *insinuatie* of Wachtendonck is GAA NA 674/217v, not. Jan Warnaertsz, May 23, 1637.

44. AWG ONA Enkhuizen 946/act 99, not. Jan van Conincxvelt, September 20, 1636.

45. On the Tiberius quarrel, see GAA NA 918/228–29, not. Barent Jansz Verbeeck, July 16, 1636; GAA NA 995/534, not. Gerrit Coren, August 23, 1636; GAA NA 918/519v, not. Barent Jansen Verbeeck, December 8, 1636; RAA ONA Alkmaar 107, not. Cornelis de Haes, January 3, 1637; GAA NA 919/64–64v, not. Barent Jansen Verbeeck, February 13, 1637, also very incompletely (more than half the document is missing) and inaccurately transcribed in Posthumus 46–47; GAA NA 1009/106, not. Gerrit Coren, April 6, 1638. Tiberius had an unspecified counterclaim against Admirael, and at the end of August the matter was submitted to four arbiters, Wouter Hermansz, Gerrit Woutersz, Simon van Poelenburch, and the professional florist Willem Willemsz. The quarrel was still raging in the winter, in part because the principals could not get on with the arbiters. In December 1636 Admirael, unable to obtain copies of the papers Tiberius had submitted about the case, accused the arbiter Willem Willemsz, who was refusing to hand them over, of having a conflict of interest and said he would not hold to a compromise that had been reached. On February 13, 1637, Admirael insinuated another arbiter, Gerrit Woutersz, still angry about the same matters. Woutersz, not surprisingly, said that he no longer wished to be involved with the case and (rather more surprisingly) that "he had no understanding of flowers" ("dat . . . hij geen verstant van bloemen is hebbende"). They were still involved in settling the case more than a year later. On Tiberius, see Alewijn Visser, *Latijnse School en Gymnasium te Alkmaar* (Alkmaar: Het Curatorium, 1954), 49, although Visser's account of Tiberius' fate seems chronologically confused.

46. De Goyer had insinuated Abraham van Wachtendonck about his tulips in GAA NA 919/190v–191, not. Barent Jansen Verbeeck, June 10, 1637 (incompletely and in-

accurately printed in Posthumus 65–66), and Liebert van Axele about his in GAA 919/191-2, not. Barent Jansen Verbeeck, June 11, 1637.

47. Cesare Ripa, *Iconologia: Or, Moral Emblems*, ed. P. Tempest (London: Benjamin Motte, 1709), 21 ("Debt"); Mark Steele, "Bankruptcy and Insolvency: Bank Failure and its Control in Preindustrial Europe," in *Banchi pubblici, banchi privati e monti di pietà nell'Europa preindustriale: Amministrazione, techniche operative e ruoli economici*, Atti della Società Liure di Storia Patria n.s. 31, no. 15 (1991), vol. 1: 185; Lyndal Roper, "'Going to Church and Street': Weddings in Reformation Augsburg," *Past and Present* 106 (1985): 82; Evenhuis, *Ook was dat Amsterdam* II, 145–46, 152; Herman Roodenburg, *Onder Censuur: De kerkelijke tucht in de gereformeerde gemeente van Amsterdam, 1578-1700* (Hilversum: Verloren, 1990), 378; NHA Stadsarchief Haarlem, Rood 217/286, burgemeestersresoluties, February 19, 1639.

48. Nat.Arch. 3.03.02, inv. 41, Rekesten Hoge Raad van Holland en Zeeland, August 26, 1637. One of the *borgen*, Cornelis Adriaensz van Duyn, was the uncle of the buyer Jan Joosten Plavier twice over: his wife, Flora Abrahams van Neste, was sister of Plavier's father's first wife and also widow of his father's brother Hans Plavier. The Sprangers document is GAA NA 1158/144-144v, not. Joost van de Ven, December 27 and 29, 1636. Susanna Sprangers must have moved in circles where tulips were discussed; not only was her husband the son of Dirck Cluyt, but her brother was the major collector Gommer Spranger and her uncle the painter Bartholomeus Spranger. Outger Cluyt's pamphlet on the care of bulbs was Outger Cluyt, *Memorie der Vreemder Blom-bollen, Wortelen, Kruyden, Planten, Struycken, Zaden ende Vruchten: Hoe men Die sal wel gheconditioneert bewaren ende over seynden* (Amsterdam: Paulus Aertsz van Ravesteyn, 1631).

49. For example, GAA NA 676, 75-75v, not. Jan Warnaertsz, September 29, 1637; GAA NA 675/86, not. Jan Warnaertsz, June 25, 1637. On the Lourisz lawsuit, RAA ORA Alkmaar 87/3, document C, September 14, 1638; document D, 1638; document E [? undesignated], 1638.

50. Van Campen, *P.I.C. Biggel-Tranen* in KP 204; NHA ORA 116/18/168, KBJ, July 29, 1636; NHA ONA Haarlem 149/2v-3, not. Jacob Schoudt, December 18, 1635, also inaccurately/incompletely printed in Posthumus 19–20; *P.I.C. Biggel-Tranen* in KP 205; NHA ONA Haarlem 162/289, not. Jacob Steyn, June 12, 1638; NHA ORA 116/19, unfoliated, KBJ, September 25, 1637; *Apologia ofte Verantwoordinghe van Flora* in KP 267. One reference to "quaeder trouwen" (bad faith) can be found in NHA ORA 116/19, unfoliated, KBJ, September 25, 1637, suit of Jacob Theunisz against the widow of Harman Stoffelsz.

51. *Waerschouwinghe*, in Krelage, "Het Manuscript over den Tulpenwindhandel," 47; *Prophetye* in KP 132; Muldrew, *Economy of Obligation*, 199–200; Willem Frijhoff and Marijke Spies, *1650: Bevochten Eendracht* (The Hague: Sdu Uitgevers, 1999), 218–24; Dorren, *Eenheid en verscheidenheid*, 29.

52. Roman, *Tweede t'Samen-spraeck tusschen Waermondt ende Gaergoedt*, 47, 53; Apostille by the States of Holland, April 27, 1637, printed in Posthumus, 60.

53. *Een Nieu Rou-Mantels Liet voor de Floristen* in *KP* 146; *Aenleydingh tot Opmerck van 't Misbruyck en Rechte Gebruyck der Bloemen* in *KP* 169; *Ghesanck* in *KP* 219.

54. On Simon Stevin, see Schama, *Embarrassment of Riches*, 363, and D. Onno Wijnands, "Commercium Botanicum," 79. On carnival and boats with wheels, Saumuel L. Sumberg, *The Nuremberg Schembart Carnival* (New York: Columbia University Press, 1941), 134, 148, 149–50, 176–77; Maximilian J. Rudwin, *The Origin of the German Carnival Comedy* (New York: G. E. Stechert, 1920), 2–12; Herman Pleij, *Het gilde van de Blauwe Schuit: Literatuur, Volksveest en burgermoraal in de late Middeleeuwen* (Amsterdam: Meulenhoff, 1979), 187–196.

55. Cornelis van der Woude, *Toneel van Flora*, in *KP* 232, 237–39, 243, 244, 248–49, 257; *De Rechte Bloem-Prijs*, in *KP* 270.

56. Van der Woude, *Toneel van Flora*, in *KP* 239, 232.

57. "Clause," in Pieter de Clopper, *Ghesanck-Boecxken van de Blommisten*, in *KP* 227.

Epilogue

1. On the various schemes in 1720 see especially P. G. M. Dickson, *The Financial Revolution in England: A Study in the Development of Public Credit 1688–1756* (London: Macmillan, 1967), 90–156; John Carswell, *The South Sea Bubble*, revised edition (London: Alan Sutton Publishing Ltd., 1993; 1st ed. 1960); Frans De Bruyn, "*Het groote tafereel der dwaasheid* and the Speculative Bubble of 1720: A Bibliographical Enigma and an Economic Force," *Eighteenth-Century Life* 24, no. 1 (February 2000): 62–87; Julian Hoppit, "The Myths of the South Sea Bubble," *Transactions of the Royal Historical Society* 12 (2002): 141–65. In our concurrent research, Julian Hoppit and I discovered independently very similar types of myths about the bubble in his case and tulipmania in mine, as we discussed when I attended a paper he presented on the bubble at the seminar on British History in the Long Eighteenth Century at the Institute of Historical Research in London in 2001. It would be interesting to consider why many of the same myths grew up about these two events, as at least in the case of tulipmania most of these were present in early accounts.

2. Dickson, *Financial Revolution*, 140–41, 152; De Bruyn, "*Het groote tafereel*," 69–70; Carswell, *The South Sea Bubble*, 136, 165–66.

3. *Het Groote Tafereel der dwaasheid* is a strange collection in that different copies of it contain different selections of items. The copy I consulted was BL 789.g.3: *Het Groote Tafereel der Dwaasheid, vertoonende de opkomst, voortgang en ondergang der Actie, Bubbel en Windnegotie in Vrankryk, Engeland, en de Nederlanden, gepleegt in den Jaare MDCCXX.* (No publisher, 1720). The play and song mentioned here appear in this copy. On the bibliographic background of the *Tafereel*, see De Bruyn, "*Het Groote Tafereel*"; Arthur H. Cole, *The Great Mirror of Folly (Het Groote Tafereel der Dwaasheid): An Economic-Bibliographic Study* (Boston: Baker Library, Harvard University, 1949); and Kuniko Forrer, "De wereld is vol gekken: de onstaans-

geschiedenis van *Het Groote Tafereel der Dwaasheid,*" *De Boekenwereld* 14, no. 3 (March 1998): 106–24. On playing cards with scenes from the *Tafereel*, see *In de kaart gekeken: Europese speelkaarten van de 15de eeuw tot heden* (ex. cat. Amsterdam, Museum Willet-Holthuysen, 14 May–5 July 1976), 72–74.

4. The print showing monkeys and cabbage is "De Lachende Ezopus op het kool-maal, gehouden ter Arscheyd van de Actieapen," in *Het Groote Tafereeel der Dwaas-heid* (copy in BL 789.g.3), 1720. The accompanying verse to this print ends with "Koop je geen Kool!" The scene with the satyr is on the title page of *Merkurius onder de Actionisten. Of Quinquenpoix in Allarm, over 't daalen van de Zuidzee Acties,* in the same copy of the *Tafereel.* The Company of Cabbage was in the play *De Wind-handel of Bubbels Compagnien,* II.iv, and the carrot shares and cabbage selling in *De Bedreigelyke Actionist, of de Nagthandelaars* (possibly by Pieter Langendijk), II.i., also in the same copy of the *Tafereel.* I am grateful to Frans De Bruyn for advising me about the meanings of these symbols. Besides his article cited above on these events, see also his "Reading *Het groote tafereel der dwaasheid:* An Emblem Book of the Folly of Speculation in the Bubble Year 1720," *Eighteenth-Century Life* 24, no. 2 (2000): 1–42; I would also like to thank him for sending me his two essays before their publication.

5. For comments on *Floraes Gecks-kap* in this context, see Frans De Bruyn, "Read-ing *Het groote tafereel,*" 7. The print with a wind car is "Afbeeldinge van 't zeer vermerde Eiland Geks-Kop," printed in the BL *Het Groote Tafereel der Dwaasheid;* on the seventeenth-century version, see chap. 5 above. Comparison with tulip-mania occurs in the verses accompanying the print "Het uitgeteerde en stervende Actie boomtje" in the same copy of the *Tafereel.* The surpassing of tulipmania is mentioned in the play *Quincampoix, of de Windhandelaars,* and the same views are expressed in the poem *Klagt en Raadsvergadering der Goden,* also both in the BL *Tafereel.*

6. BL copy of *Het Groote Tafereel;* Munting, *Waare Oeffening der Planten* (1671), 636.

7. Jacob van Lennep, *De Voornaamste Geschiedenissen van Noord-Nederland* (Am-sterdam: Gebroeders Kraay, 1856), II, 336–37; P. J. Blok, *Geschiedenis van het Ned-erlandsche Volk,* 2nd ed. (Leiden: A. W. Sijthoff, 1913), II, 602–3; J. C. H. de Pater, *Geschiedenis van Nederland* (Amsterdam: Uitgevermaatschappij "Joost van den Vondel," 1936), IV, 431.

8. The virtues of the hyacinth were extolled in George Voorhelm, *Traité sur la Jacinte,* 3rd ed. (Haarlem: N. Beets, 1773; 1st ed. 1752), 9–14; remarks on the price of Voor-helm's tulips are in BL Add.Ms. 32,096, f. 108, Robert Hale to (?) Dr. Harbin, May 19, 1713; E Musis Aeternitas [club], *Flora's Bloem-Warande in Holland, Alwaar haare Heerlykheid weêr ten troon werd verhéven, geviert en aangehéden van Flora's Lievelingen* (Amsterdam: Dirk Swart, 1734–1736) I, 9–10; Justus van Effen, *Hollandsche Specta-tor* (2nd ed. Amsterdam: K. van Tongerlo and F. Houttuin, 1756; 1st ed. 1733), IV, 93; [E. H. Krelage], "Windhandel," *De Tuinbouw* I, no. 1 (January 4, 1913): 9–10.

9. Johann Beckmann, *Beyträge zur Geschichte der Erfindungen* (Leipzig: Paul Gotthelf Kummer, 1782) I, 227; Cornelis de Koning, *Tafereel der Stad Haarlem* (Haarlem:

A. Lousjes Pz., 1808), II, 182; [H. Graf zu Solms-Laubach], *Tulpen und Staatspapiere: Ein Beitrag zur Geschichte des Handels des 17ten und 19ten Jahrhunderts* (Hamburg: Hoffman und Campe, 1830), iii–iv; Beckmann, *History of Inventions*, 4th ed. (1846), p. 30, n. 1.

10. N. W. Posthumus, "De Speculatie in Tulpen in de Jaren 1636 en 1637," *Economisch-Historisch Jaarboek* 12 (1926): 3–99; 13 (1927): 3–85; and 18 (1934): 229–40; Burton G. Malkiel, *A Random Walk down Wall Street* (New York: W. W. Norton, 1973), 31 (this is hardly the only error in Malkiel's account, which is one of the most extreme cases of simple invention of facts to suit a desire for drama); John Kenneth Galbraith, *A Short History of Financial Euphoria* (New York: Whittle Books, 1990), 13, 26–34, 108. On the other side, according to Edward Chancellor, Peter Garber's articles (beginning in the late 1980s) arguing for the rationality of tulipmania were published in order to block attempts by the U.S. government to regulate futures trading on the stock market: see Edward Chancellor, *Devil Take the Hindmost: A History of Financial Speculation* (London: Macmillan, 1999), 24, footnote. There are many contemporary references to tulipmania in the newspapers and on the internet; one website, already on the Internet in 1999, which felt it necessary to warn against repetitions of tulipmania, is http://itulip.com.

11. Thus, for example, AnnaPavord remarks that "it was inevitable that tulipomania would be followed by an equally intense hatred of the flower" and states that *vanitas* still lifes (which actually dated from the later sixteenth century) were a result of the "chastening experience" of the tulip crash (*The Tulip,* 175, 178). Paul Taylor is perhaps less guilty of this cliché than some, but he still remarks that Jacob Gerritsz Cuyp's unusual picture of a bed of tulips from 1638 "must have been so many hot needles in the flesh of someone bankrupted in the previous year." Paul Taylor, *Dutch Flower Painting,* 14.

12. GAA NA 989/1924–5, not. Jan Bosch, June 30, 1652, will of Abraham de Goyer.

13. Honig, "Making Sense of Things," 170.

14. On the Nonpareille case, see NHA ONA Haarlem 177/351, not. Salomon Coesaert, June 17 and 18, 1645; NHA ONA Haarlem 173/531, not. Salomon Coesaert, June 19, 1645; NHA ONA 161/133, not. Jacob Steyn, no date, but in ledger in 1645 (this is also incompletely and incorrectly printed in Posthumus, 20, but Posthumus incorrectly dates it 1635); NHA ONA Haarlem 177/372, not. Salomon Coesaert, July 26, 1645; NHA ONA 177/414, not. Salomon Coesaert, September 20, 1645.

15. On Van Meeckeren's and Baert's tulip deals, see chap. 4 above. For Heda's quarrel over a tulip with Jan Domijs, see NHA ORA 116-33, KBJ, May 19, 1654. Van Adrichem's remarks are in NHA ONA 173/513, not. Salomon Coesaert, June 19, 1645, where he is identified, however, as "Abraham Huygen Suyckerbacker."

INDEX